The Genesis of East Asia

221 B.C.–A.D. 907

D1016007

ASIAN INTERACTIONS AND COMPARISONS
General Editor Joshua A. Fogel

Sovereign Rights and Territorial Space in Sino-Japanese Relations:
Irredentism and the Diaoyu/Senkaku Islands
Unryu Suganuma

The I-Ching *in Tokugawa Thought and Culture*
Wai-ming Ng

The Genesis of East Asia, 221 B.C.–A.D. 907
Charles Holcombe

Charles Holcombe

The Genesis of East Asia
221 B.C.–A.D. 907

ASSOCIATION FOR ASIAN STUDIES

and

UNIVERSITY OF HAWAI'I PRESS

Honolulu

Asian Interactions and Comparisons, published jointly by the
University of Hawai'i Press and the Association for Asian Studies,
seeks to encourage research across regions and cultures within
Asia. The series focuses on works (monographs, edited volumes,
and translations) that concern the interaction between or among
Asian societies, cultures, or countries or that deal with a comparative analysis of such. Series volumes concentrate on any time
period and come from any academic discipline.

Printed in the United States of America

11 10 09 08 07 06 6 5 4 3 2

LIBRARY OF CONGRESS CATALOGING-IN-PUBLICATION DATA
Holcombe, Charles.
    The Genesis of East Asia, 221 B.C.–A.D. 907 / Charles Holcombe.
    p. cm.—(Asian interactions and comparisons)
    Includes bibliographical references and index.
    ISBN 0-8248-2415-6 (cloth : alk. paper)

    ISBN-13: 978-0-8248-2465-5 (pbk. : alk. paper)
    ISBN-10: 0-8248-2465-2 (pbk. : alk. paper)
    1. East Asia—History. I. Title. II. Series.
    DS514 .H65 2001
    950—dc21

                                               00-066664

University of Hawai'i Press books are printed on acid-free paper
and meet the guidelines for permanence and durability of the
Council on Library Resources.

DESIGNED BY TERESA W. WINGFIELD FOR G&S TYPESETTERS, INC.
PRINTED BY THE MAPLE-VAIL BOOK MANUFACTURING GROUP

CONTENTS

We are extremely pleased to present Charles Holcombe's work, *The Genesis of East Asia, 221 B.C.–A.D. 907,* the third volume in our series, Asian Interactions and Comparisons. Holcombe's is neither an original monograph nor a textbook in the traditional sense of the term but more like a synoptic history of the first millennium of East Asian history, corresponding to the first millennium of imperial Chinese history. East Asia here consists of what we today dub China, Japan, Korea, and Vietnam—all toponyms of considerably later vintage. It is a Sinocentric history, but only in the sense that the great Chinese empire formed the core around which the elites of Japan, Korea, and Vietnam forged their identities.

This sort of work has long been needed—and we still need a sequel for the second millennium—now that the old standard, *East Asia: Tradition and Transformation* by John K. Fairbank, Edwin O. Reischauer, and Albert M. Craig, has become outdated in the face of the enormous volume of scholarship produced around the world since its publication. While not a textbook in the mold of *East Asia: Tradition and Transformation,* Holcombe's book may be used in that capacity.

More important, though, Holcombe shows us that there is much that can be learned at all levels by adopting a comparative approach to East Asian history. Whether we agree, for example, that early Japanese history resembles Chinese history is beside the point; what is incontestable is the fact that we learn much about both histories through such a comparison.

While sensitive to the plaints and underlying causes of modern nationalism, Holcombe has not allowed this to determine his explanations of premodern history. Thus, many readers may not be entirely prepared, for example, for his description of the emergence of the first Vietnamese state in 939. While his view accords with recent scholarship on the subject, it flies in the face of the nationalist Vietnamese narrative of 1,000 years of Chinese oppression. We leave it to readers to make up their own minds on this particularly contentious topic as well as others presented in this volume.

JOSHUA A. FOGEL, SERIES EDITOR

ACKNOWLEDGMENTS

Special thanks (in alphabetical order) to Arano Yasunori, Andy Burstein, C. S. Chang, Patricia Crosby, Bob Dise, Judy Dohlman, Lou Fenech, Joanne Goldman, Vickie Hanson, He Qinggu, Reinier Hesselink, Rich Newell, Chawne Paige, Peng Wei, Victor Xiong, and the ever-reliable staff of the interlibrary loan office at Rod Memorial Library. And, above all, thanks to Jen and Andrea.

Any mistakes or misunderstandings are entirely my own.

Research in East Asia in 1994 and 1996 was facilitated by two University of Northern Iowa Summer Research Fellowships. A most satisfying culmination to this project came with the opportunity to spend the autumn of 1999 teaching and refining some of this material at the University of Michigan.

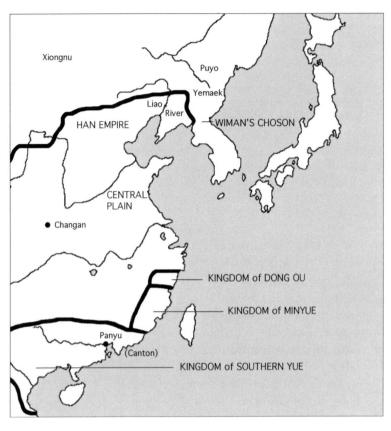

EAST ASIA IN THE EARLY HAN DYNASTY

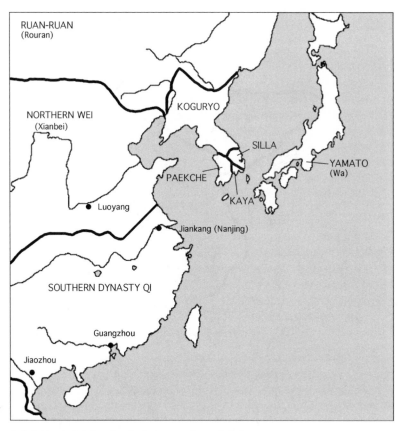

E A S T   A S I A   C I R C A   A . D .   5 0 0

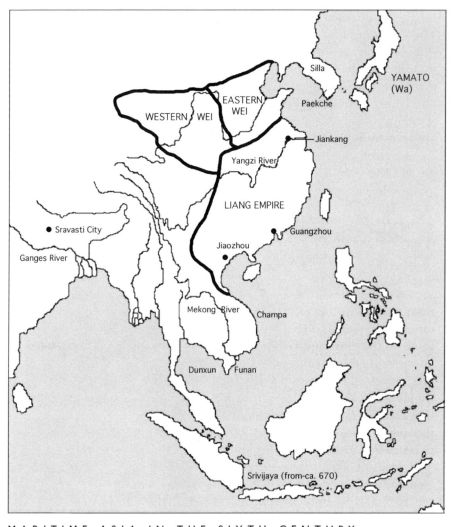

MARITIME ASIA IN THE SIXTH CENTURY

Introduction

Few people today seem to know very precisely where East Asia is, what exactly makes it "East Asian," or why any such broad regional iden- tification should matter anyway as more than only some empty geo- graphic abstraction. Surely it is the nation-state instead (if not the multinational corporation) that is everywhere the essential unit of in- ternational affairs. In East Asia, this means specifically China, Japan, Korea, and Vietnam. If, as of 1942, a majority of Americans notori- ously "could not locate either China or India on an outline map of the world," most Americans today surely have a sharper mental image of China and India, as presumed nation-states, than they do of either East or South Asia as regions.[1]

One leading authority on Asian-American history insists, cor- rectly, that "there are no Asians in Asia, only people with national identities, such as Chinese, Japanese, Korean, Indian, Vietnamese, and Filipino." Asia, a label that conventionally includes both an enor- mous continent and far-flung island chains such as Japan, Indonesia, and the Philippines, is much too large and heterogeneous an area for the label "Asian" to signify much more than "not European." "There is no cultural or historical entity that can rationally be subsumed un- der this single term," concludes one modern geographer.[2] From a purely geographic perspective, physically contiguous Europe would seem to be a more logical component of Asia (part of the same conti- nent) than the widely scattered island archipelagoes. As a final absur- dity, East Asia—the subregion that includes quintessentially "Asian" China and Japan—actually falls outside of the scope of what was orig- inally designated Asia altogether.

According to the so-called father of history, Herodotus (ca. 484–428 B.C.), Asia began at the Nile and extended only as far as India. "East of India it is empty," he reported. For Herodotus, Asia was effectively coterminous with the Persian empire. By his own definition, Herodotus himself was born in Asia (modern Turkey), and he observed with more than a touch of irony that even the woman who supposedly gave her name to Europe, Europa, also "came from Asia." As for the name Asia, Herodotus confessed that he was uncertain about its origin but repeated the opinion of "most Greek authorities . . . that Asia is named after the wife of Prometheus."[3] In modern East Asian languages, this all too obviously foreign term, "Asia," is merely reproduced phonetically, as in the Chinese "Yaxiya," Japanese "Ajia," or Korean "Asia." There is no native East Asian word for Asia—or, by extension, for an East Asia that is clearly only a subcategory of the whole.

Premodern East Asians had never heard of East Asia—by any name. However, if, in Herodotus' day, Asia was an unknown alien concept in East Asia, "Japan," "Korea," and "Vietnam" did not exist at all yet, either as native or as foreign ideas. These names had not yet been coined, there were no independent states or countries in the places now designated by those labels, and the Stone Age populations who inhabited these regions had not yet coalesced into recognizable "nations." China, it is true, had a lengthy head start and was in some important senses already in familiarly identifiable existence in Herodotus' lifetime (Confucius died in China at about the same time that Herodotus was born into the Hellenic world), but only as a cluster of contending principalities rather than a single nation-state called "China."

China was first unified into one empire (and even then it was a classic multiethnic conquest empire rather than an ethnically homogeneous nation-state, as modern imagination would have it) by the series of conquests completed by the kingdom of Qin in 221 B.C. These Qin conquests, in turn, set off political, military, and economic repercussions that impacted what we think of today as Vietnam and Korea directly and indirectly reverberated as far as the Japanese islands. The various peoples inhabiting what we now think of as Japan, Korea, and Vietnam were each subsequently transformed over the course of the next roughly 1,000 years from obscure prehistoric societies into members of a broadly (though far from completely) uniform East Asian civilization under the looming shadow of this enormous Chinese empire.

By the tenth century, when the fall of the Tang dynasty in China in A.D. 907 and the rise of a new Song dynasty in 960 marks a major watershed (between what might be styled the early imperial and later imperial epochs), Japan, Korea, and Vietnam had each generated independent native states and begun to evolve along their own, sometimes quite divergent, historical trajectories. By then, our familiar modern East Asian framework of Chinese, Japanese, Korean, and Vietnamese "nations" was already in place (although I will argue strenuously in what follows that ethnic nationalism is a misleading and generally pernicious concept that should be applied to the history of early East Asia only with extreme caution). Our study will focus on this critically formative period that falls between the third century B.C. and the tenth century A.D., when a distinctive East Asian region first took shape.

For, if there is no meaningful "Asia," there is a reasonably coherent East Asia (however arbitrary and exotic the English label "East Asia" itself may be). This East Asia could even be said to be older than the nation-states it subsumes and in some ways more fundamental. As Jared Diamond points out in a recent Pulitzer Prize–winning book, *Guns, Germs, and Steel,* "The world's two earliest centers of food production, the Fertile Crescent and China, still dominate the modern world, either through their immediate successor states (modern China), or through states situated in neighboring regions influenced early by these two centers (Japan, Korea, Malaysia, and Europe), or through states repopulated or ruled by their overseas emigrants (the United States, Australia, Brazil)."[4] East Asia—the modern countries that can trace some degree of evolutionary continuity back to the earliest Neolithic and Bronze Age developments in what is now China—may even be said to represent the single most important major alternative historical evolutionary track to Western civilization on the face of this planet, with a continuing history of success that can rival what we call the West.

This implies neither the inevitability of some future conflict, East versus West, nor that "never the twain shall meet." None of these differences are primordial or fixed, and difference, anyway, need not breed antagonism. However, it does mean that East Asian history should be considered roughly comparable in scope and importance to the history of the West. We need to take East Asia seriously. For centuries, the Chinese empire—the self-styled "Middle Kingdom" and the largest individual state in East Asia—was also the single most economically developed state on earth. As recently as 1800, China was still "probably the richest country in the world."[5]

This traditional material wealth was paralleled by cultural sophistication. Tsien Tsuen-Hsuin estimates, for example, that until 1500 (if not later) China produced more books than all the rest of the world combined.[6] Furthermore, this profusion of written documents is only one measure of premodern China's overall level of achievement, crude when compared to the exquisite subtleties of a Tao Qian poem or a Guo Xi painting but relatively easy to quantify. The rise of the industrialized modern West in the nineteenth and twentieth centuries, it is true, did profoundly shatter this old Sinocentric global balance, but in recent years East Asia has once again become rather conspicuously successful. There is every reason to believe that East Asia may now be recovering some of its former economic importance.[7]

It bears emphasizing, moreover, that despite the preceding emphasis on China, East Asia is, internally, a tremendously diverse region, as richly complicated as the West. No two places in East Asia are altogether similar. Even China, by itself, is a realm of many realms, and in this book we will be especially concerned with the emergence of the quite different places we call Japan, Korea, and Vietnam.

We also need to avoid the error of what might be called reverse segregation. East Asia has never, not even in the Stone Age, existed in total isolation from other parts of the Old World. East Asians are not fundamentally different from other human beings. We are all, everywhere, one people. To say otherwise would be poor science, un-Christian, un-Confucian, un-Buddhist—and dangerously racist. There have always been important movements and exchanges linking the disparate parts of the world together, starting with the initial dispersion from Africa that presumably originally populated every corner of this planet (although a respectable body of scholarship does still question the "out of Africa" origins of *Homo sapiens*). The common origins of humanity, at some more or less distant point, can hardly be doubted.[8]

However, it is also true that, especially in high antiquity, when long-distance transportation and communication really were slow and awkward, East Asia was largely left to its own devices, free to blaze its own evolutionary trail without much reference to other models. This book is an attempt to explain how—and to what extent—early East Asia became a coherent world-within-a-world.

It has been observed that the absorption of what we think of now as southern China into a Chinese empire that had previously been concentrated only in the north parallels the Roman expansion of Hellenistic civilization into Western Europe.[9] The spread of East Asian "civilization" to Japan, Korea, and Vietnam might be viewed as merely a further, weaker extension of the same process by means of which East Asian civilization had already (and was still continuing to) spread, also incompletely and imperfectly, within what we now think of as China itself.

No tool was more critical to the spread of this common East Asian civilization than the extension, throughout the entire region, of the Chinese script and classical written language. East Asia may, in fact, be defined precisely as that part of the world that once used Chinese writing. In addition, although some experimentation with writing in local vernacular languages had already begun during the early period under consideration here, classical Chinese remained the most prestigious written language throughout the East Asian region until as late as the nineteenth century—the visible insignia of a common literate standard of civilization.

The shogunal library in Edo (Tokyo) Japan, for example, according to its last catalog compiled in 1864–1866, still contained 65 percent "Sinological" (i.e., Chinese) material. In Korea, classical Chinese remained both the official and the most prestigious written language until China's shocking defeat in the Sino-Japanese war of 1895, which shifted dominance over the Korean peninsula from China to Japan and sparked novel sentiments of modern nationalism in Korea. In Vietnam, the prestige of Chinese letters was only undermined by French colonial policy and colonial force, beginning in the 1860s, and even then encountered some resistance. Within China itself, the final abandonment of the classical written language and move to a modern Chinese vernacular was associated with the radical westernization of the May Fourth movement in the early twentieth century.[10]

The consequences for premodern East Asia of this shared literary language, and the common textual canon composed in it, were profound. In Japan, for example, it is said that seventeenth- and eighteenth-century scholars "thought of [classical] Chinese civilization as their own."[11] Yet, on the other hand, even in China itself the society described in those classical texts had long since evaporated into history (to the extent that it was ever more than an imaginary projection). The world of the Confucian classics was remembered and cherished by Chinese (as well as Japanese, Korean, and Vietnamese) scholars, whose idea of reform invariably seemed to mean a return to idealized antiquity, but for many illiterate Chinese villagers and practical-minded shopkeepers, the literary golden age of the textual past must have often seemed remote.

Everywhere in premodern East Asia, including internally within China, we find shared "universal" East Asian core elements overlapping local cultural peculiarities—at multiple levels. The broad "national" distinctions among China, Japan, Korea, and Vietnam that seem so glaring today are only one level of local variation—tremendously important, to be sure, but also to some extent deliberately exaggerated for political purposes. It is no great overstatement to say that the nations of East Asia, like all other nations everywhere, were semiconscious political creations.

Vietnam is an interesting case in point. Until the very end of the period covered in this book, there literally was no Vietnam, and the territory that is today northern (since Vietnam's own southward expansion is yet another, later story) Vietnam was merely a remote southern salient of the Chinese empire. The people who lived there were no less "Chinese" than many of the people who lived elsewhere within the empire, albeit (as was also true of many if not all other parts of the empire) with an undertow of local popular subcultures and languages.

Even within that southernmost part of the Chinese empire that would eventually become exclusively Vietnamese, there existed simultaneously a considerable range of ethnocultural variation, stretching from the educated local Chinese imperial elite at one extreme to residual tribal minorities at the other. Nor should it be supposed that these tribal minorities preserved the essence of some eternally distinctive Vietnamese national identity, since they were themselves internally diverse and scarcely distinguishable from the tribes on what is today the Chinese side of the border. In 939, however, local strongmen achieved what turned out to be permanent political independence, and what would eventually (in the nineteenth and twentieth centuries) come to be known as Vietnam was born.

The dynamic process of ethnogenesis in East Asia, of which the foregoing is an interesting example, will be a major recurring theme throughout this book. In general, primordial ethnonational distinctions are all chimera—that is, imaginary monsters. This is to say not that nations do not exist and are totally a figment of our imagination but only that they are created and evolve through both deliberate and unintended human action. Nothing has simply "always been that way." Too easily do we take China, Japan, Korea, and Vietnam as permanent fixtures of our mental landscape. In fact, they are each the product of a lengthy evolutionary process, whose final shape was, to a surprising extent, clarified only in the twentieth century.

Moreover, although I spoke of a "final shape," this too is illusory. There can be no final shape prior to extinction. The historical process does not end. Today, the forces of modernization have seemingly obliterated many of the old local differences, yet most of the "nations" in the world today did not exist 100 years ago and are new creations. Everywhere, the pace of change, interaction, and innovation has accelerated enormously. History continues to unfold. East Asia—China, Japan, Korea, and Vietnam—will be remade again in the twenty-first century. Yet the past is not thereby rendered irrelevant. What East Asia has been in the past will continue to play a role in shaping what it may become in the future. The Buddhists call this "karma."

E Pluribus Sericum

Before there was an East Asia, there was China, but what is "China"? The answer is not as obvious as it may seem. Elements of a remarkably sophisticated higher civilization first emerged in quite remote antiquity, clustering around the core Central Plain region of what is today the northern People's Republic of China. By as early as 4000 B.C., the distinguished archaeologist K. C. Chang already feels comfortable calling the distinctive "megacivilization," which had resulted from the fusing together of the various regional Stone Age cultures in that area, "China."[1]

Chinese language inscriptions, and therefore Chinese history in the truest sense, first appear on the Central Plain around 1200 B.C. This was a development whose significance cannot be overstated. The continuous use for over 3,000 years of this same language and this same script (with some modifications) lies at the very heart of the Chinese cultural tradition, and literature written in the classical Chinese language also forms the most critical link binding China to the other, non-Chinese parts of East Asia, very visibly demarcating them from the rest of the world. The East Asian (Chinese-based) scripts have been called the only writing systems on earth still in normal use today that did not derive ultimately from Egyptian.[2]

"China," however, is an English word that arguably had no precise premodern Chinese counterpart at all. It is true that the roughly equivalent modern Chinese term *zhongguo*, which literally means "middle kingdom(s)" or "central state(s)," does have an extremely ancient pedigree, appearing in some of the very earliest known Chinese texts and inscriptions. However, the expression only really became equivalent to the English word "China" in the twentieth century as China struggled to redefine itself as a nation-state in conformity with distinctly modern expectations. In premodern times, the label *zhongguo* was always more of a simple geographic description and claim to centrality than it was the proper name of a country. The exact same term—written with identical Chinese characters, that is, although it was naturally pronounced differently in the different spoken languages (J: *chūgoku;* V: *trung-quoc*)—was sometimes used by both premodern Japanese and Vietnamese authorities to depict themselves as (Chinese style, but presumably not therefore in any recognizable modern sense "Chinese") middle kingdoms.[3]

Even to speak of "China" is, therefore, already to impose a modern and primarily Western-derived frame of reference. There is an obvious sense in which China truly is one of the oldest countries extant in the world today, but this China has been repackaged (repeatedly) in the twentieth century. China the nation-state is new. Premodern China was something else (and it, too, underwent repeated reinvention): an enormous empire, embracing much internal cultural diversity (it saw no reason to exclude anyone) but also imposing certain universal expectations on all its subjects, especially those who aspired to elite status. The early Chinese empire was no more an ethnically defined "nation" than its European contemporary, the Roman empire.

It follows that being Chinese—not unlike being Roman, although Roman citizenship was more precisely and more exclusively at first defined—was a matter of political submission (with political participation, through service in the government, an option that was theoretically at least potentially available to all members of the elite or upwardly mobile subjects) and adherence to certain outward symbols of belonging. Initially, there were multiple Chinese states or countries, each known by different names. None, by itself, was "China," but each might fairly have been called Chinese. Even after the various Chinese (as well as some that were arguably originally not Chinese at all) kingdoms were unified into a single, supposedly universal empire, there continued to be chronologically distinct successive Chinese dynasties. From one traditional perspective, we can view all these consecutive dynasties as minor discontinuities in a single grand narrative history of "China," but from the perspective of the people who served at each of the different courts, these changes of dynasty were all-important. In a sense, each dynasty was also a different country.

Central to what we think of as China was an ancient and glorious cultural core that may legitimately be called Chinese civilization. However, in traditional times, the people who participated in this core civilization did not think of it as "Chinese" civilization—in contrast to other alternative, non-Chinese civilizations—so much as simply the universal standard of civilization. Anyone could, potentially, learn to be civilized, especially through the study of certain classical texts and through the practice of certain ritual procedures. In combination with political loyalty to one or another Chinese state or dynasty, this effectively made a person Chinese.

The first Chinese countries were probably only tiny walled city-states, or central places. The key term *zhongguo,* in particular, may have initially referred only to the royal capital city.[4] However, with the conquest of the Central Plain by the royal house of Zhou (traditionally dated to 1122 or 1027 B.C.), the idea of a single universal world order, legitimated by Heaven itself and assembling all of the various peoples "under Heaven" *(tianxia)* together under the rule of a relatively homogeneous and tightly intermarried—but now, as a result of the far-flung Zhou conquests, widely distributed—elite Zhou nobility, was born.[5] We may certainly call this Zhou universe "China," but it was less a single unified *zhongguo* than a sprawling pluralistic "All-under-Heaven."

From the beginning, the core kingdoms of the Central Plain area interacted with neighboring local cultures in a never-ending process of mutual stimulation and exchange in which the Central Plain may have tended to be culturally dominant but peripheral states were sometimes militarily more powerful. It was, in fact, one of these at best semiperipheral states, the Qin, that eventually conquered all the others, forging in 221 B.C. the first Chinese empire, whose modern progeny is the Chinese nation. This enormous Chinese empire should be understood to have been initially a quite purposeful and somewhat artificial political and military creation, in many ways comparable to the Roman empire in the West, rather than some simple fact of nature.

Beyond the borders of this Chinese empire, in what are today Japan, Korea, and Vietnam (each of which had, almost equally purposefully and artificially, already formed independent states by the end of the period covered in this book—or, in the case of Vietnam, shortly after the end of our period), a more nebulous Central Plain cultural ascendance left as its high-water mark an East Asia region notable both for its broad overarching traditional elite community of culture and its rich local popular diversity. This East Asia may be considered roughly parallel in terms of overall complexity, significance, and tradition of success to Europe and "the West."

CHINA, PLURAL

The story of East Asia begins in China, but China itself had many beginnings. The once popular image of Chinese civilization expanding outward from a single point of origin on the Central Plain has been forced to yield now to a more nuanced realization that what we commonly think of as Chinese civilization actually represents the gradual melding together of what had previously been several distinctive regional prehistoric cultures. The great German-American Sinologist Wolfram Eberhard (1909–1989), for example, discerned ten significantly different ancient local cultures that, he believed, each contributed to the ultimate formation of "China."[6]

Broadly speaking, however, during the formative period of Chinese civilization, all these various local cultures can be reduced to three major geographic cultural zones: the northern and western, marginal lands abutting on the desert and the steppe; the lush, exotic south; and the northern Yellow River valley Central Plain—with the latter, in fact, forming a kind of nucleus for the emerging Chinese identity.[7] In other words, our revised new understanding is not so radically different from the old expanding Central Plain core hypothesis, but with a greater sensitivity to the various contributions to the emerging cultural whole made by all the regions that were eventually engulfed by it.

Even this Central Plain core itself also had multiple origins, however. It has been speculated that what we may call the ancestral Chinese language was originally spoken only toward the western end of the Central Plain, where writing and the earliest East Asian uses of metal also first appeared, and that people speaking radically different, possibly Austroasiatic languages originally inhabited the eastern coastal region of the Central Plain. These non-Chinese speakers were, furthermore, "initially more advanced in many ways," and they contributed significantly—except in the matter of language—to the eventual emergence of a recognizably Chinese civilization. Even the

Chinese-speaking, western Xia cultural core itself seems to have begun to coalesce only in the third millennium B.C. as population groups from still farther west moved into what is now Henan Province, merged together with previous inhabitants, and absorbed multiple waves of influence from the eastern coast.[8]

During the later Neolithic there remained a range of separate peoples in northern China who were evocatively referred to in traditional writings as the "ten-thousand kingdoms." These were ultimately succeeded by the legend-haunted Three Dynasties (Xia, Shang, and Zhou) of familiar Chinese tradition, and even these various proto-Chinese peoples still lived, moreover, in close proximity to other peoples who were not proto-Chinese at all, even in the Central Plain area, even well into historical times.[9]

During the final millennium B.C., a degree of universality in what is now northern China was achieved under the aegis of the Zhou dynasty (ca. 1027–256 B.C.). It was during this formative Zhou era, as Cho-yun Hsu remarks, that "the Chinese defined for themselves a culture as well as a world." However, the universal sovereign power of the central Zhou kings tended toward the purely nominal. Within the Zhou *tianxia* there remained multiple *guo* (states, countries, or kingdoms), ruled more immediately, and increasingly autonomously, by their own hereditary nobles.[10]

These states or principalities were without exception quite small to begin with, but they were gradually consolidated into a reduced number of larger, increasingly well organized territorial kingdoms. Despite the early uniformity of the conquering Zhou elite, each of these separate kingdoms in time evolved its own practices, laws, standards of weights and measures, and even languages—their "speech had different sounds, their scripts had different forms," reports a first-century lexicon. During the aptly named Warring States subperiod (403–221 B.C.), toward the end of the lengthy Zhou dynasty, the Central Plain was split into an array of different Chinese kingdoms, "each having different customs."[11]

These various Chinese kingdoms had distinctive burial practices, manners of dress, calendrical systems, religious beliefs, and even scripts. Tombs from the state of Qin, in the far northwest, for example, reveal distinctive bent lower-limb burials and bronze implements. The state of Yan, in the far northeast, allegedly engaged in marital practices that would have been quite shocking to later Confucian sensibilities: "in exchanges of guests, they had their wives attend them overnight." A book known as *Guan zi*, traditionally attributed to a seventh-century B.C. author, caricatured Yan people as "simple-minded but fond of integrity, rash and prone to death," and offered similarly crude stereotypes of the Qi, Chu, Yue, Qin, Song, and Qi-Jin peoples based on a kind of simplistic geographic determinism. These stereotypes are not to be taken very seriously but are nonetheless indicative of perceived regional differences.[12]

Particularly distinctive was the southern state of Chu, even though a certain amount of both textual and archaeological evidence supports the claim that Chu did not really represent any genuinely indigenous southern cultural tradition, separate from the Central Plain. Tradition has it that Chu was founded, instead, by a noble house closely associated with the Zhou court, which was dispatched from the Central Plain to colonize the south and which only later diverged somewhat from the northern cultural mainstream.[13]

According to Chinese historical records, the ruling house of Chu was enfeoffed among the barbarians in what is now Hubei Province near the beginning of the Zhou dynasty and specifically charged in 671 B.C. with garrisoning the southern frontier to guard against barbarian raids on the middle kingdoms *(zhongguo)*.[14] While extremely dubious claims to descent from ancient Chinese nobility would later become almost de rigueur among East Asian ruling families, in this case the claim to Central Plain origin may have some plausibility. On the other hand, however, even the best recent archaeological evidence still leaves one modern expert uncertain whether Chu should be regarded as a colonial enclave originating from the north or an indigenous southern development.[15]

Unless we are willing to presume some kind of mass migration from the north, physical Central Plain origin must in any case have been limited to at most a thin stratum of the Chu ruling elite. Perhaps the continuing ambiguity of Chu's status is best resolved by viewing it simply as the Sinification (that is, Chinese-ization) of a portion of the southern lands and peoples through the leavening influence of northern cultural contacts, migration, and conquest. The Chu state, prior to its own absorption into the larger Chinese empire, has been pointedly described by modern scholarship as a kind of multiethnic conquest "empire," one that "eventually absorbed over sixty states and a number of tribal peoples." In the process, the Chu conquerors were themselves transformed, and the resulting Chu empire generated its own distinctive cultural synthesis—one that, furthermore, itself still subsumed much local internal variation.[16]

Chu's proximity to indigenous southern populations, especially the so-called Hundred Yue, encouraged intermingling. "Originally Wu, Yue, and Chu were adjacent, and often annexed each other. Therefore their popular customs are roughly the same," reported the first-century *Han shu*. At the same time, archaeologically recovered Chu artifacts remained distinct—though not necessarily separate—from the more indisputably indigenous southern Yue assemblages and retained their distinctive Chu flavor until as late as after the Qin imperial unification of all China.[17]

The emerging new and increasingly distinctively Chu culture received its classic distillation in the fourth- to third-century B.C. "Songs of the South," contained in the book called *Chu ci*. These poems are conventionally said to represent a southern literary tradition sharply distinct from the Central Plain *Odes*. Yet the obvious but crucial point that they are, after all, written in the same Chinese language should not be overlooked. In a broader sense, both the *Odes* and the *Chu ci* belong to "one main stream of Chinese literary evolution."[18]

The philosopher Xun Zi (313–238 B.C.) famously distinguished the Chu people from those of both Yue and Xia, the latter of which was the Central Plain Chinese core dynasty par excellence. Significantly, however, Xun Zi's main point was that what might be termed the "national" differences among these Chu, Yue, and Xia kingdoms were not essential and immutable truths ordained by Heaven but merely the result of "accumulated practice."[19] The modern descendents of all three of these peoples are unquestionably now equally all Chinese, and all three states today fall squarely within the borders of what is sometimes called "China proper." Indeed, the once peripheral lands of ancient Chu and Yue today form the very demographic and economic heart of modern China.

An ability to overlook local ethnic differences, without necessarily either denying or obliterating them, may be regarded as one of the strengths and one of the more attractive features of ancient Chinese civilization. The *Intrigues of the Warring States*, a pseudohistorical text whose compilation is attributed to the last century B.C., observed, for example, that although the completely non-Chinese Hu people of the northwestern frontier and the (then still) non-Chinese Yue people of the south spoke entirely different languages and could not communicate with each other, if you placed some of them together in jeopardy, "riding the waves in the same boat," they would quickly enough find a way to overcome their mutual cultural barriers in order to survive.[20]

The constant belligerence of the various warring states of late Zhou China was, moreover, viewed with horror by some observers and provided the incentive for an argument that the reason why the numerous and the strong were able to intimidate the few and weak was because of the absence of any common authority—a "Son of Heaven" like the hapless Zhou kings, but with real coercive power— who could forcibly impose peace and justice. "That all under Heaven are tormented by warfare without cease is because there are [independent] nobles and kings," explained the ultimately successful pacifying unifier Qin Shi Huangdi (the First Emperor of Qin and therefore of China). As recently as 1914, the famous nationalist author Zhang Binglin (also known as Zhang Taiyan [1869–1936]) could still praise the First Emperor for the just and equitable government that his absolute autocratic authority, which suppressed all special private interests equally, finally made possible.[21]

If the embers of an ideal of universal order under Heaven still smoldered amid the contending kingdoms of the late Zhou era, the climate of intense interstate competition they fostered also stimulated the elaboration of ever more efficient methods of political control. New techniques for centralized bureaucratic administration, codified law, and effective systems for taxation and military conscription forged the political machinery for conquest and direct centralized rule over huge territories that had simply been lacking to the early Zhou monarchs.[22] These new political technologies, which go under the general rubric of Legalism, made possible, for the first time, the unification of All-under-Heaven into a genuinely centralized imperial state, the Qin (221–207 B.C.) in 221 B.C.

Coincidentally, far away in the subcontinent of India, a parallel regime, the Magadhan, was almost simultaneously pulling together a vast empire based on the similarly ruthless doctrines of the *Arthaśāstra*.[23] Still farther west, Rome was waging its epic struggle with rival Carthage across the waters of the "Sea at the Middle of the Earth" (the Mediterranean) in the very years that Qin Shi Huangdi was wresting the Chinese middle kingdoms into the first Chinese empire.

Much as Rome was originally peripheral to Hellenistic civilization, Qin once was marginal to the middle kingdom. The *Shi ji* (Records of the Grand Historian), composed in the last century B.C., records, "At first Qin was a small and remote state, and all the Chinese treated it like a guest, comparable to the Rong and Di" barbarians. However, this originally obscure northwestern frontier country of Qin was open to innovation and outside talent and experimented with the novel administrative procedures of the Legalists that had been pioneered somewhat earlier in the Central Plain kingdom of Wei just to its east.[24]

Although it has been argued that these warring states' legal codes never escaped entirely from "the religious and ritual practices of the society from which they emerged," it would be a mistake to underestimate the genuine originality and practical effectiveness of these new administrative procedures. In particular, it was Qin's dedication to the methodic Legalistic buildup of state wealth and military power—*fuguo qiangbing,* a slogan (J: *fukoku kyōhei*) that was, incidentally, quite consciously resurrected 2,000 years later by Meiji era Japanese leaders to motivate their drive toward industrial modernization in the late nineteenth century—that enabled Qin to ultimately conquer the entire known world.[25]

"Those who desire a rich state must extend their territory; those who desire a strong army must enrich their people," observed the *Intrigues of the Warring States* of Qin strategy. Despite the benevolent implications of "enriching the people," Qin objectives were resolutely statist. Wealth and power were to serve state goals; by Qin law, citizens who did not devote themselves to agricultural production would be conscripted into the army.[26]

Milestones in the Qin military buildup include the collection of the first systematic tax in kind on agriculture in 408 B.C.; the opening of commercial markets in 378 B.C., followed by the imposition of mandatory household registration in 375 B.C.; the reorganization of the existing rural communities into centrally administered districts; and the erection of a standardized grid layout for farmland in 350 B.C., followed immediately by the first collection of another new form of tax in 348 B.C. Particularly critical to the accumulation of state power was the system of household registration, which provided a direct mechanism for universal adult conscription and taxation. Qin was thus able to effectively mobilize its entire population for state projects.[27]

Qin achieved a degree of administrative organization that some modern governments might envy. Such discipline may seem wildly improbable for an ancient state, but it was not in fact incompatible with the existing level of technology. Indeed, prior to the industrial and scientific revolutions, the mobilization of human labor was the prime form of technology that was available to the state. There can, furthermore, no longer be any doubt that these Qin measures actually were implemented. In 1975, a cache of third-century B.C. Qin documents was uncovered from a grave at Yunmeng, in modern Hubei Province, which prove conclusively that Qin central directives did penetrate to all levels of the empire.[28]

What is particularly astonishing is that these documents now make it clear that Qin officials attempted to micromanage almost every detail of the local economy. Recent archaeological discoveries thus strikingly confirm the impression of bureaucratic sophistication (and intrusiveness) for the Qin machinery of state that had been suggested all along by the more traditional historical sources.[29]

The Qin conquests filled in the contours, very roughly, of the modern map of China. Despite claims to universality, Qin obviously did not conquer the entire planet, and even contemporary Chinese themselves were aware of lands extending far beyond the effective borders of the Qin *tianxia*. The First Emperor's grandiose boast that "wherever there are traces of men, there are none who are not my subjects" should therefore be understood as intentional hyperbole.[30] However, the claim to have forged a universal sociopolitical order was nonetheless a serious and not entirely unfounded one: it was possible to imagine this new empire as corresponding at least to the entire civilized world, beyond whose borders lived only a scattering of insignificant savages.

Having conquered the civilized world, Qin still needed to unify it. The First Emperor ordered stone inscriptions carved in the various newly conquered kingdoms to proclaim the legitimacy of his rule. One of the earliest measures adopted by this new universal empire was to impose a dramatic standardization of weights and measures and the writing system. The whole world was now to be a single empire, and the First Emperor took steps to reduce the different regional cultures to conformity with the new imperial norms.[31]

To obliterate the memory of the older kingdoms, with their potentially divisive separate, protonational identities, he ordered that the histories of kingdoms other than Qin be burned. "In destroying other people's countries, you must first extinguish other people's histories," comments one modern scholar. Yet, as the Yunmeng documents also attest, even after half a century of Qin rule in one particular region, a representative of the central government there still complained that "the illicit fondness for local customs has not changed."[32]

Qin discipline was harsh. In the construction of the First Emperor's enormous tomb alone, one modern authority estimates that every able-bodied male in the entire empire must have labored an average of 120 days, some of them apparently literally in chains. Such heavy burdens did not endear the Qin state to its subjects. Within a year after the First Emperor's death, the whole world was, it seemed, in active rebellion. The great Qin empire was overthrown after only fifteen years, and its most obvious legacy was one of revulsion. "Since antiquity there has never been another who . . . greatly injured the people under Heaven like Qin," castigated Dong Zhongshu (ca. 195–105 B.C.).[33]

Yet, despite Qin's ephemeral rise and fall, the Qin unification in 221 B.C. is still quite properly regarded as "by far the most important single date in Chinese history before the revolutionary changes of the present [twentieth] century." Qin's excesses were undeniable, admitted the Tang dynasty author Liu Zongyuan (773–819), but the basic centralized imperial system was not to blame. In its broad outlines, if in more moderate form, the imperial state that had been pioneered by Qin survived for 2,000 years, and the continuity of this grand centralized imperial project was essential to the formation of what we think of today as "China."[34]

THE SINIFICATION OF CHINA
(HOW CHINA BECAME CHINESE)

As scholars in the People's Republic of China increasingly now recognize, the early Chinese empire was a multiethnic state that brought the metropolitan capital, a wide array of unevenly developed and settled imperial provinces, distant transitional frontier zones, and often extensive bulges of imperial influence projecting far out beyond the official borders into a single grand interactive structure. In a gesture symbolizing both the universality of his dominion and the diversity of his conquests, the First Emperor of Qin caused replicas of palaces from all the conquered kingdoms to be reconstructed at his capital, near the modern city of Xi'an.[35]

Some of the old warring states that were thus reassembled under Qin rule may have really been only minimally different from each other in terms of culture—prime examples of what the Chinese so eloquently call *da tong xiao yi* (minor variation amid broad uniformity)—but this vast new empire also incorporated large areas that were still rather radically different. After "Qin unified the Six Kingdoms," the ancient Yi peoples who had formerly inhabited what is now the east-central Shandong, Jiangsu, Anhui area of China "were all dispersed as subject households." One of the major themes of subsequent imperial history would be the gradual assimilation of the so-called Yue peoples of the south.[36]

Yue, the name of one of the southernmost of the late Zhou era warring states, became a generic Chinese label for nearly all the various prehistoric native populations inhabiting the southeastern portion of what is now the People's Republic of China. From approximately the line of the Yangzi River south, these early indigenous peoples seem to have been speakers of languages significantly different from, and unintelligible to, the Chinese languages of the Central Plain. It is possible that these ancient southeastern languages were ancestral to the modern Austroasiatic and Austronesian language clusters, which today include Vietnamese, Mon-Khmer, Thai, and the native languages of (aboriginal) Taiwan, Indonesia, and the Philippines.[37]

While linguistic difference was a significant cultural marker distinguishing the Yue from the Chinese of the Central Plain, these Yue languages were themselves internally quite diverse—multiple translation being necessary for internal communication in the far south, even long after it had fallen under direct Chinese imperial administration. In other words, while a broad archaeologically discernable Neolithic "southern culture complex" can be identified that we may label Yue in opposition to the more mainstream Chinese cultural nucleus in the north, the Yue were by no means a single homogeneous foreign "people."[38] In addition, while not originally "Chinese" in any sense (apart from residence in the geographic area that we now call China), many of their descendants would eventually become Chinese in every conceivable sense.

The prehistoric Yue, in particular, were said to occupy the region of modern Zhejiang, Fujian, Guangdong, and Guangxi Provinces, as well as northern and central Vietnam. To their west, in modern Sichuan, Guizhou, and Yunnan, lay a tier of slightly different cultures, notable for dressing their hair in topknots, while still farther west was to be found yet another range of peoples who plaited their hair and lived a nomadic pastoral existence. The Yue peoples of the coastal southeast had a pronounced maritime inclination, chewed betel nuts, and stereotypically tattooed their bodies—a custom that apparently spread from prehistoric southern China throughout Southeast Asia and Japan. They are also notable for initiating the cultivation of rice some 10,000 years ago in the lower Yangzi valley, a practice that also spread widely south and east and, from there, northeast to Korea and Japan.[39]

Despite residence in territories that were incorporated into the Chinese empire almost from its inception in the third century B.C., the Yue of prehistoric times were culturally more closely affiliated to what is now Southeast Asia than they were to the Chinese Central Plain. In fact, this geographic region of what is now southern China has even been called the cultural "heartland" of Southeast Asian civilization. In a burst of expansion that was "perhaps the most rapid, successful, and widespread in the history of humanity prior to the recent dispersals from Europe," beginning around 3000 B.C., first Taiwan, then the Philippines, Borneo (Kalimantan), Java, Sumatra, Indochina, Thailand, the Malay peninsula, and beyond, were all settled by migrating peoples who apparently had their cultural and linguistic roots in the Yue zone of what is now southern China.[40]

Not long after this great age of Yue expansionism, however, Zhou interests from the Central Plain may have begun to push south into the Yue regions, perhaps in search of tin and copper for bronze manufacture.[41] As we have seen, Zhou supposedly ensconced the Chu ruling house there to defend the Central Plain from Yue incursions and perhaps also as a forward projection of Central Plain civilization. Within a single generation in the third century B.C., then, Qin imperial conquests not only unified the Central Plain but also extended its political power across all of the Yue regions in the south, reaching deep into what is today Vietnam. Yet the north long remained unmistakably the focus of this Chinese empire.

The Yangzi River drainage basin would eventually become the very demographic heart, and center, of China. Its gradual incorporation into what we think of today as China began very early, and from the fourth century A.D. it already formed the nucleus for a series of so-called Southern dynasties that could lay plausible (though far from uncontested) claim to being the only truly legitimate Chinese empires. However, as late as A.D. 754, the officially registered population of the (reunified) empire still remained heavily concentrated on the Central Plain. The slowness of China's southward crawl owed something to the very foreignness of the south and, no doubt, also something to the forbiddingly "steep disease gradient" created by the malaria, dengue fever, and other unfamiliar tropical infections lurking there. Jiangnan—the region south of the Yangzi River—long presented a somewhat exotic alien landscape, "low-lying and damp, [where] gentlemen often die young."[42]

To pacify the newly conquered south, the government of the Qin empire placed garrisons along the middle reaches of the Yangzi River. A number of the administrative regions in what are now southern Hunan, northern Guangdong, and Jiangxi Provinces actually began as such bases for military operations.[43] More than a century after the original Qin conquest of the south, troops from the Central Plain stationed in the Yue regions still found themselves amid quite alien surroundings:

> Today, the horses and soldiers from East of the Mountains who are guarding frontier Commanderies are isolated and remote. Their bodies are among the Hu [peoples of the north and west] and Yue, but their hearts cherish their old mothers. Their old mothers shed tears and their wives grieve, imagining their hunger and thirst and thinking of their bitter cold.[44]

In A.D. 35, Han dynasty (202 B.C.–A.D. 220) troops were camped amid still identifiably Lạc-Yue (an extreme southern Yue group) native auxiliaries in what is now Hubei Province. However, by the first century A.D., Wang Chong (27–ca. 100) could observe that the Yue people now wore Chinese clothing.[45]

During the second half of the Han dynasty (the Later Han, A.D. 25–220), regional differences within the empire became less pronounced. The Han imperial administration in what is now northern Korea, to take a possibly somewhat extreme example, is said to have been archaeologically "indistinguishable from any other part of the

Han Empire." Over the course of the following several centuries, many of the different ethnic groups that had once figured so prominently in ancient history were absorbed into the general "Chinese" population. China was slowly becoming "Chinese."[46]

This was partially the accomplishment of administrators appointed from the Central Plain core who took their civilizing mission seriously, such as Diwu Lun, who, as governor of a commandery in what is now northern Zhejiang after A.D. 53, worked vigorously to stamp out uncanonical sacrifices. The almost total monopoly of literacy enjoyed by the classical Chinese language tended also to subordinate local spoken languages to the level of "dialects," if not suppress them altogether.[47] In addition, widespread emigration from the northern Central Plain accelerated the Chinese transformation of the south incalculably.

Early imperial policy was to intentionally dislocate preexisting Yue populations from their homelands in the south and encourage in-migration from the Central Plain. As a haven for refugees from the continually troubled north, Jiangnan became the only region of the Han empire whose population witnessed consistent increases, although the jostling of different cultures there also made it particularly prone to civil disturbances during the final century of the dynasty. An estimated three-quarters of a million settlers moved to Lingnan—the southeastern-most section of the empire—during the century following the end of the Han dynasty, representing a 60 percent increase in population there.[48]

Southward migration began in earnest in the mid-Han and reached a crescendo during the fourth century, when the Central Plain itself was overrun by semi-alien nomadic conquerors at the start of what are called the Northern dynasties. Following this massive fourth-century southward exodus, the very spot in modern Hubei Province where Lạc-Yue native auxiliaries had been camped in A.D. 35 became an urban center, increasingly steeped in Confucian high culture, where people "gathered from all directions." By the time the empire was finally reunified at the end of the sixth century, it could be said of the former Southern dynasty capital city that "shops were lined up in its market just like in the two [northern] capitals, and the people were a mixture from all directions, so that their customs were all rather similar."[49]

From the time of the Han dynasty, it had been imperial policy to treat ethnic non-Chinese within the frontiers as much as possible like ordinary imperial citizens—in particular with regard to their payment of taxes and fulfillment of service obligations. Despite such heavy civic burdens, it was not uncommon for non-Chinese to willingly become "naturalized," perhaps because of the increased stature conferred on their leaders by imperial titles. In A.D. 36, for example, a tribal leader from beyond the Han southern frontier, in what is now central Vietnam, led his people to submit and was enfeoffed as "the village lord restored to Han." Only four years later, however, a devastating native rebellion led by the Trung sisters (A.D. 40–42) broke out along the border between what is now China and Vietnam, indicating the somewhat precarious loyalty of many such naturalized tribal chieftains.[50]

Despite continuing friction, significant numbers of non-Chinese were successfully assimilated into the empire. Around 230, for example, a loyal Man tribesman (a native population that was concentrated especially in the area of modern Hubei, Hunan, Jiangxi, and Anhui Provinces) named Tian Yizong was appointed imperial inspector of a region in modern Henan Province in the Central Plain area. A famous fourth-century Buddhist monk, Kang Sengyuan (ca. 300–350), although in physical appearance obviously of central Asian descent, was born in Chang'an as a native speaker of Chinese. Other newly "Chinese" people who were of broadly Mongolic genetic stock would have been visibly less obvious but may have been large in number.[51]

With the Sui (581–618) and Tang (618–907) imperial reunification, after 589, the process of assimilation was intensified. For the year 629 alone, it is recorded that an incredible 1.2 million expatriates and tribesmen were returned to or incorporated into the Tang empire. In 632, another 300,000 of the western Qiang people are reported to have submitted to Tang. One modern scholar estimates that in a little over a century following the founding of the Tang dynasty, 1.7 million foreigners became Tang subjects.[52]

The remarkable, and justly renowned, cosmopolitanism of the early Tang dynasty is exemplified by the boast of Emperor Taizong (r. 626–649), in 647, that "since antiquity everyone has honored the Chinese and looked down upon barbarians; I alone love them as one. Therefore their tribes follow me like a father or mother." Members of minorities and foreigners not only were accepted into Tang society but also sometimes rose to the highest positions in government. By one count, no fewer than forty-three ethnic non-Chinese served as grand councillors during Tang.[53]

Between 742 and 755, a central Asian merchant served as Tang protector-general of Annan ("the Peaceful South") in the Red River valley area of what is now Vietnam. Another eighth-century protector-general of Annan was the Japanese-born Abe no Nakamaro (d. 770), who spent fifty-three years in Tang and became intimate with leading Chinese literary figures, often acting as mediator between the Tang court and Japanese embassies. Koreans were especially numerous and well integrated into Tang society. It was a Korean general who led the Tang armies to their historic defeat by the forces of Islam at the battle of Talas in central Asia in 751.[54]

Tang rule extended deep into what we sometimes now call Turkestan. At its peak in the seventh century, Tang authority may have extended as far west as the Oxus River (Amu Darya), although the region west of the Pamir Mountains appears to have never been regularly garrisoned. Sogdians and other central Asians became registered Tang citizens, and, even as the Tang imperial frontier reached out to embrace much of central Asia, a Uighur petition in 771 for imperial patronage of Manichaean religious institutions in what are now Hubei, Jiangsu, Jiangxi, and Zhejiang Provinces indicates a strong central Asian presence in the eastern Yangzi valley Chinese heartland during the Tang period, possibly reflecting Uighur "commercial interests" in that region.[55]

However, direct imperial rule over incorporated tribal groups was often quite tenuous, and native chieftains were frequently permitted a high degree of autonomy. Despite early Tang political and military ascendance in Turkestan and the elaboration of a formal imperial administrative structure there, official appointments normally went to indigenous tribal leaders, and "tribute, taxes, and household registers often did not reach the Ministry of Revenue."[56]

These were the so-called loose rein prefectures (*jimi zhou*)—administrative units whose submission to central imperial authority was often purely nominal. Nor were they limited to the distant central Asian frontier. Internal tribal reservations, with native chieftains, were created along much the same lines deep within the heart of the empire. In Tang Sichuan, there were 168 prefectures of Qiang and ninety-two of Man people, the latter of whom "all were without cities,

dressed their hair in buns, and wore skins. Only those who congregated in the Area Command [cities] dressed like Chinese people."
In Tang Jiangnan, the region just south of the Yangzi River, there
were fifty-one such internal reservations of Man people; in what
is now Guangdong, Guangxi, and northern Vietnam, there were
ninety-two.[57]

In other words, despite imperial China's undeniable success at
assimilating "whole populations, on the order of European states"
over two millennia and despite the notable cultural homogeneity of
the modern Chinese people and small percentage of acknowledged
minorities (8 percent) within the People's Republic today, not only did
regional cultural variations long persist, but considerable numbers of
unassimilated tribespeople clearly continued to inhabit extensive regions deep within the interior of the empire at least through the end
of the Tang dynasty.[58]

It is estimated that ethnic non-Chinese people constituted more
than half—a majority, in other words—of the total population of the
Chinese Southern dynasties. Modern Fujian Province was not made
"an integral part of the Chinese Empire" by Chinese settlers until
about the seventh century. Some of the Man people of Hunan Province were not brought under direct central government control until after the end of Tang, and the Pearl River valley area near Guangzhou city (Canton) had not even begun to have a mainly "Chinese"
population by that date—the end of the period under consideration
in this book.[59]

"THE MORE THINGS CHANGE . . .":
THE TENACITY OF DIVERSITY

Throughout history, China's borders have expanded and contracted
in periodic cycles. The ultimate limits of even a self-proclaimed "world
empire" were perhaps somewhat mechanically determined by the
forces of what Paul Kennedy calls "imperial overstretch": "If a state
overextends itself strategically—by, say, the conquest of extensive territories or the waging of costly wars—it runs the risk that the potential benefits from external expansion may be outweighed by the great
expense of it all."[60] The Chinese imperial "All-under-Heaven" never
did include the entire world and gradually consolidated instead into
what we think of today as China.

Even within China, even at the peak of centralized imperial unity under the legendary Han dynasty, lay the reality of what was often a great deal of local autonomy. This tendency became all too obvious as the Han dynasty weakened. In 193, for example, Tian Chou (169–214) grew disaffected from his local warlord and withdrew with "several hundred of his clan" to a remote spot in the mountains along the Great Wall in modern Hebei Province. His community grew to number 5,000 households, for which he established customs and laws as well as diplomatic relations with neighboring tribes. Tian founded, in other words, a quite independent little Chinese community that was, however, in this case also quite ephemeral: in 207, he eagerly accepted appointment, and imperial reintegration, under the centralizing regime of the rising northern strongman Cao Cao (155–220), whose heir would establish the Three Kingdoms Wei dynasty in 220.[61]

For 400 years after the fall of the Han dynasty at the end of the second century, imperial governments remained weak and typically fragmented. Contemporaries spoke of "mountain-dwelling recluses, and valley-hidden, unbridled, subjects" who disclosed themselves to central government only when they felt it worthy of them. Zhuge Ke (203–253) complained of evidently large numbers of people near modern Nanjing (Nanking) in the third century, living in the deep mountains, who had never entered a city and who relied on force of arms to evade imperial officials. In addition, throughout this period, quite thoroughly Chinese local magnates often dominated their communities with little reference to any faraway emperor. The dramatic decline of registered population in China after the Han dynasty probably reflects, more than anything else, a progressive reorientation of the rural population away from the central imperial government toward dependence on private local "great families." Groups of "retainers" surrounded some of these strongmen, working their fields and providing them with independent military force.[62]

Not only was imperial unity shaken, but local differences also remained pronounced—or even resurfaced—in this era. "The most striking feature of sixth-century China was its cultural diversity," observes Arthur Wright. The seventh-century *Sui shu* described the local customs of Jiangnan in almost the same words as the first-century *Han shu*. The *Han shu*, in turn, echoed phrases drawn from the *Shi ji*, of two centuries yet earlier.[63]

To be sure, this apparent continuity may be more a reflection of

Chinese scholarly conservatism and a preference for quoting vener-able masterpieces over providing updated information than it is proof of the persistence of a distinctive Jiangnan regional culture. When the *Sui shu* says of a region in modern Jiangxi Province, for example, that "gentlemen often have several wives, who expose their faces in the market, haggling over small change for their husbands," the com-pilers may well be doing nothing more than repeating an already anachronistic and overly simplistic stereotype. Yet as late as the twelfth century, it was still felt necessary to regulate against the practice of women immodestly venturing out of the house, without covering their faces, in adjacent Fujian Province. Even into modern times, the practice of uxorilocal marriage, which involves the groom moving in with his wife's family—the exact opposite of the normal Central Plain custom—was still exceptionally common in Jiangnan, suggesting some tenacious survival from ancient Yue.[64]

The peculiar dialects of the southeast also remain unmistakable even today. In 805, in Tang times, Liu Zongyuan was banished to what is now southern Hunan for a decade. His comments testify both to the persistence of linguistic difference and to the relative speed of accli-matization that was possible across a generation or two:

> Voices are especially different in Chu and Yue. Shrike tongued clamor—I listen to it pleasurably now without finding it odd. I am already of a kind with them. Small children born into my family all naturally jabber [in the local dialect]. Day and night it fills my ears. When they hear a northerner speak, they, twitter-ing, go and hide. Even a sickly fellow—they still marvel at him with alarm.[65]

The persistence of regional stereotypes cannot be doubted. The fifth Chan (Zen) patriarch Hongren's casually sweeping dismissal of all people from Lingnan (modern Guangdong and Guangxi Prov-inces and northern Vietnam) as lacking a "Buddha nature"—that is, not being fully human—is sufficient testimony that such prejudices were still current in the late seventh century, even if he was being de-liberately perverse in the well-known Zen manner.[66]

Aside from differences among regional Chinese cultures, there remained the problem of the native (still unassimilated, non-Chinese) tribes. Throughout the period under consideration in this book, although the Man people who lived among large concentrations of Chinese reportedly became almost indistinguishable from ordinary citizens, those who lived in remote mountainous areas maintained their own separate languages, tastes, and styles of dwellings. Even the Man who formally submitted to imperial jurisdiction paid so few taxes that impoverished Chinese allegedly took refuge among them to evade taxation. The Man tribespeople "fill up the imperial domain and associate with Chinese rascals, easily giving rise to mischief," lamented Shen Yue (441–513). Since the time of the Han dynasty, they had repeatedly rebelled.[67]

The so-called Liao (or Lao) people first pushed north from Guizhou and Yunnan into modern Sichuan Province only in the mid-fourth century. There they reportedly settled into over 100,000 locations in the mountain valleys. Those who lived mixed together with "people" (i.e., the Chinese) paid some taxes, but those who occupied the deep mountains existed as "bandits."[68]

Chinese interaction with tribal peoples took various forms. Sometimes local Chinese people "went native." Sometimes the natives became Chinese. Sometimes the two populations coexisted peacefully. However, intrusive imperial authority often generated friction. In A.D. 33, for example, it was reported that

> the *Qiang* barbarians have hair hanging disheveled down their backs and fasten their garments on the left [unlike the Chinese], but live mixed together with the Han [Chinese] people. Because their customs are different and their language unintelligible, they are often seized by petty officials and unscrupulous people. They are thoroughly enraged, but helpless, therefore driving them into rebellion.[69]

A candidate for imperial office complained in 271 that regional officials sometimes defrauded or massacred border tribes for their own gain. In 322, when an official from Sichuan sent his son to court accompanied by several hundred tribesmen from the region, wild rumors of their cannibalism circulated in the capital. In the early sixth century, officials in Sichuan staged allegedly annual raids on the Liao tribes and altered population registers for their own profit. There is also the (possibly apocryphal but fascinating) story of an evil official in what is now Guangdong Province (Canton) around the year 800 who was fond of polo *(cuju)* but lacked suitable mounts, so he commanded teams of subject natives to rush about bearing sedan chairs carrying the players. When they grew sluggish, he struck them with his riding crop.[70]

Not surprisingly, the tribes often took up arms against what was sometimes felt to be an oppressive imperial power. To offer a few fairly random examples, in 672, during the Tang dynasty, Man tribes staged border raids in Yunnan; in 676, the Liao rebelled in Sichuan; in 694, the Liao struck in the Guangdong-Vietnam area; in 707, the Man joined with the neighboring Tibetan empire to raid Yunnan; in 713, the Man attacked again in Yunnan; and in 715, the Man raided Sichuan. In 724, a Tang eunuch-general reportedly beheaded 30,000 rebel tribesmen in northwestern Hunan and shortly thereafter buried 60,000 Man rebels in Guangdong (Canton). Between 756 and 771, Liao and Man tribesmen seized control over much of Guangxi, established several petty principalities, and severed all land communication between the important Tang cities of Guangzhou (Canton) and Jiaozhi (near modern Hanoi).[71]

During the first 1,000 years of empire, in other words, the assimilation of native peoples within what we now think of as the borders of China did not proceed smoothly. Although there can be no doubt about the ultimate Sinification of most of China, officials sometimes even legislated against it: in 779, for example, Uighurs and other foreigners in the capital were ordered to wear their native costumes and not mix with the Chinese. In addition, a certain military commissioner of Lingnan between 837 and 841 dealt with a situation in which Liao and Chinese people lived mixed together and intermarried and, when treated unjustly by petty officials, incited each other to rebel by issuing a ban on cross-cultural marriage.[72]

THREE

Civilizing Mission

CONCEIVING EAST ASIA

Beyond the borders of China's All-under-Heaven, countless numbers of foreign peoples lived out their lives in blissful ignorance of their exclusion from the one true universal civilization. The Chinese people who gave the matter a moment's thought must have always been aware of the existence of at least some of these foreigners. However, the conceit that the Chinese empire was synonymous with All-under-Heaven was, nonetheless, not really so fantastic. Not only is some not too dissimilar degree of ethnocentricity an almost universal human trait of which nearly everyone is guilty, but the truth was that, in its early centuries, the Chinese empire really did not confront any comparably organized governments or literate and economically productive cultures anywhere nearby.

The northern portions of what are now both Korea and Vietnam fell within the perimeters of the Qin empire. Beyond lay only prehistoric tribal societies. In the Japanese islands, the transition from hunting (or fishing) and gathering to agriculture was scarcely complete, and the first traces of literacy remained in the distant future. Rome and India were far away. There simply were no immediate external rivals to the early Chinese empire. To the north, it is true, the mighty steppe confederation of the Xiongnu did mount a serious military challenge to the early empire, beginning around 209 B.C. In 200 B.C., the Xiongnu even defeated and nearly captured a Han emperor. However, in terms of literacy and overall productive capacity, the seminomadic Xiongnu offered no comparison at all to Han China. From the Chinese perspective, these steppe nomads were simply barbarism incarnate and the obvious exception that exactly proved the rule that China corresponded to the entire civilized world.

For the gradually emerging independent states and civilizations in Japan, Korea, and Vietnam, therefore, China offered essentially the only available inspiration and model. However, from the final century B.C., the most conspicuous Chinese political and cultural program was no longer the Legalism of the Warring States and Qin but the new Confucian orthodoxy of the Han and subsequent dynasties. The emerging East Asian world came to coincide, accordingly, with what became the world of Confucianism.

Previously, Qin had constructed the very epitome of a Chinese government based on effective organization and codified written law. Qin law was a harsh tool, wielded in the service almost exclusively of state interests, but it indisputably was rule by law. Even the modern, Western-sounding ideal that legal constraints should be binding on rulers as well as on subjects had been articulated already in early imperial China.[1] In addition, although Legalism was progressively submerged by encroaching waves of Confucian influence from the time of the Han dynasty on, it never entirely vanished from the imperial agenda. Certainly, the idea of rule by law remained an indispensable component of the Chinese administrative model at least until the end of Tang—that is, throughout the entire formative stage of East Asian history.

As late as the end of the seventh century, to take one Tang dynasty example, when a certain attendant censor impeached a court official for malfeasance, the accused official was able to appeal privately to the emperor. However, when the emperor tried to personally override the censor's judgment, the censor protested against such arbitrary royal intervention, arguing that "the law is hung in balance for all under Heaven, and is shared by all people. If Your Majesty sets that aside for emotional reasons, of what use is the law?" The censor ultimately prevailed, even against imperial wishes, although at the cost to himself of imperial disfavor and a demotion.[2]

It should come as no surprise to learn that ideal standards were frequently violated in practice and elaborate theoretical systems often haphazardly implemented. However, the established principle was that "by law, all-under-Heaven are equal."[3] Without unduly exaggerating the systematic efficiency of premodern China's bureaucratic institutions, early imperial government was far from being simply a matter of autocratic caprice.[4] The Chinese empire really was a remarkable administrative achievement by any premodern standard.

At the other end of the political spectrum, however, Confucian

critics of Legalism, from the beginning, advocated leadership by virtuous example instead. This confronts us, immediately, with the surprisingly difficult task of defining what we mean by "Confucianism."
The word itself is Latin rather than Chinese. It has even been argued,
in one revisionist critique, that "Confucianism is largely a Western
invention." Although the Confucianism of Western imagination certainly does have a rough native equivalent in the Chinese tradition
known as *ru*, the two terms really do not correspond exactly, and both
are multifaceted, elusive concepts: "Ambiguity is the most prominent
characteristic of both Confucianism and *ru*."[5]

There is, in other words, nothing very indisputably concrete on
which we can confidently hang our Western label "Confucianism."
However, if language is not to be reduced to utter incoherence, there
must be certain propositions that we may still cautiously call Confucian—some discernable shape to the Confucian nebula. Of these central Confucian concepts, Mencius' assertion in the fourth century B.C.
that the true gentleman has only to "cultivate his own person, and All-
under-Heaven will be pacified" is surely one of the most fundamental.[6]

This Confucian vision of rule by moral example applied to foreign as well as domestic relations. "If distant people do not submit,"
recommends the *Analects* of Confucius, "then cultivating the refining
influence of literature will bring them." The attractiveness, or cha-
risma, of the king is the surest weapon in the arsenal of diplomacy.
"Having virtue insufficient to endear neighbors and culture insufficient to attract the distant, and therefore making warfare decisive:
this is certainly what the *Spring and Autumn* [*Annals,* a book of history
traditionally attributed to Confucius] deeply detested," concluded the
Han dynasty Confucian Dong Zhongshu.[7]

This was precisely, the Confucian critics insisted, where Qin had
gone wrong:

> What destroyed Qin was external preparation for the Hu and
> Yue [barbarians] but internal neglect of its own government.
> For the deployment of troops outside [the borders] is the ruin
> of government within. . . . [But] if the Lord of Men grasps the
> Tao, then [people from] far and near will surreptitiously revert
> to him.[8]

If only "the King has clearly virtuous conduct in the world, the
four quarters will all respond to it." Through the power of his ex-

ample, the just monarch could "pacify external regions without troubling a single soldier, without losing a single spear." As a trusted adviser instructed one emperor after the loss of the Central Plain to semiforeign conquerors in 317, "If ritual and right conduct are adhered to firmly . . . the Man and Yi [barbarians] will submit even as you politely yield to them."[9]

The Confucian approach to empire building was, in effect, to declare victory and retire and graciously allow neighboring peoples to eagerly subordinate themselves of their own volition.[10] Instead of empire building in "fit of absentmindedness" or Qin- and Roman-style military subjugation, Confucians would rule the world through benevolent nonintervention, purely by the presumed attractiveness of their example. "As a military treatise has it: 'Those who devote their attention to the expansion of virtue prosper; those who devote their attention to the expansion of territory perish.'"[11] Curiously, this seemingly ridiculously impractical Confucian approach effectively succeeded in dominating East Asia for 2,000 years, albeit with a military backing that might be inconspicuous at times but rarely was entirely absent.

In part, the Confucian idea was based on a prescientific, and certainly no longer tenable, understanding of physics in which it was naively seriously presumed that like attracts like, so that "beautiful deeds cause things that are beautiful, and evil deeds cause things that are evil." Dong Zhongshu in particular is credited with promoting the notion that Heaven and man interact in such a way that the ruler's moral posture is decisive in maintaining the very balance of nature. Without diminishing our respect for the early Confucians, therefore, it must be acknowledged that theirs was an essentially magical faith in the efficacy of ritual and gesture to exert a tangible effect on the physical world. Thus, for example, the solution that was proposed for a famine in early fourth-century China was to "establish a day in Spring for the Son of Heaven to pray for grain on high."[12]

This Confucian vision of a natural moral order spread throughout East Asia. In Japan, it was summarized as follows in 1135:

> Changes in the weather and abnormalities in the earth are what are used to caution rulers. . . . For instance, the occurrence of epidemics is brought about by governmental disregard for the seasons. . . . In my humble opinion, between Japan and China, whenever there has been a portent [wise rulers] have either pro-

moted the good and the virtuous, favored the aged and aided poor citizens, or remitted the tax grains, reduced the commodity taxes, and diminished service obligations.[13]

Aside from any welcome restraint that the threat of cosmic repercussions might have placed on the arbitrary behavior of otherwise theoretically absolute monarchs, there is also a less mystical explanation for the Confucian advocacy of rule by means of benevolent posture. The key Confucian instrument for exercising control over society has been called "model emulation,"[14] that is, setting the right example. Dong Zhongshu explains, "The Son of Heaven and Great Officials are what the people below observe and imitate, and distant regions gaze in on from all sides. Those who are nearby observe and accord with them; those who are distant watch and imitate them."[15] All eyes were on the monarch, and the best way for him to rule others was by setting a good personal example.

"Those who are good at rewarding reward one good, and everything good under Heaven is encouraged. Those who are good at punishment punish one evil, and everything evil under Heaven is eliminated."[16] Better yet, royal humanity and virtue alone would be enough to transform All-under-Heaven and effectively "encourage the people without rewards, and govern the people without punishments."[17]

Ceremony and ritual might not have any appreciable effect on the weather or the planetary orbits, but they certainly had an impact on the people who observed them. By imitating these ceremonies, the common people could then be made to restrain themselves and behave in an orderly fashion without any need for their superiors to apply coercion. "When desires have no limits, disaster is born. The sages feared this harmful laxity, and therefore created music to harmonize their natures, and ordered the rites to restrict their feelings," explained the treatise on ceremonies in the *Old Dynastic History of the Tang*.[18] Civilization, in this view, is precisely the inhibition that induces people to practice self-restraint, which may be conditioned into anyone through the performance of ritual propriety.

Confucians thus developed a quite consciously minimalist vision of government, one that blended Confucian ethical ideals with the Taoist prescription of taking no purposeful action *(wu wei)* but that was sharply at odds with the more activist and coercive Legalists. The wise ruler, Dong Zhongshu informs us, should model himself on the movements of Heaven, "not trouble himself with affairs," and "take non-action as his Way."[19] "'How do you govern the country?' The answer is: 'By not governing do I govern it.'" "Those who wish to effect the transformation of the four Yi [barbarians] must use non-action. With non-action the uncivilized will come by themselves."[20]

Specifically, the Confucian recipe for governing the empire well was to keep taxes and labor service requirements to a minimum, promote virtue, and express concern for those in distress.[21] Such a formulation would induce domestic satisfaction and attract strangers from afar. The demonstration of imperial concern for the unfortunate was even more important than any systematic program for materially relieving their misfortune since such concern by itself was proof of that imperial virtue which was the crucial Confucian consideration, while intrusive (even when they were effective) Legalist-style administrative measures were viewed by Confucians with some suspicion.

Following the destruction of the Legalist Qin dynasty, Confucian criteria increasingly became the recognized standards for imperial government in China. Penal sanctions were relegated to a subordinate position, as inducements of last resort for a rectitude that more ideally should be spontaneous and voluntary.

The codification and enforcement of law remained, it should be emphasized, essential government functions at least through Tang times. During the Han dynasty, no less a Confucian paragon than Confucius himself was revealingly portrayed as a stern, uncompromising enforcer of the law.[22] However, Dong Zhongshu, in his quest to break away from the despised Legalist traditions of Qin, actively judged lawsuits with reference to the Confucian *Spring and Autumn Annals,* which he believed to contain expressions of Heaven's moral order that were binding even on an emperor. "I carefully follow the precedents in the text of the *Spring and Autumn* to seek clues to the Kingly *Tao*." "The law of the *Spring and Autumn* is for the people to follow their lord, and their lord to follow Heaven."[23] It was Heaven's intention, in Dong's interpretation, that kings rule by the example of their virtue rather than by the coercive force of law. "To employ punishments in government is called going against Heaven."[24]

Even Dong Zhongshu acknowledged that penal law was an indispensable tool of government, but the Confucian ritual standards known as *li* came to be regarded as a kind of higher "natural law," for which criminal law should be invoked only as a secondary human support.[25] Although the Han emperor Wu's (r. 140–86 B.C.) innovative policy of honoring Confucian scholars probably was initially mostly a public relations ploy, it set the stage for the more sincere rise of Confucian ideology soon thereafter. Even before the end of the Former Han dynasty (in A.D. 9), it had already become common to seriously apply legal sanctions as enforcement to the ritual standards of behavior prescribed by the Confucian classics.[26]

Toward the end of the Former Han, for example, persons with aged parents or who were in mourning for the death of their parents were exempted from compulsory labor service, and in A.D. 116, during the Later Han dynasty, high officials were required to observe the Confucian three years of mourning for their fathers. This tendency only became more pronounced in the centuries after the fall of Han. A third-century criminal law code, for example, was explicitly intended to be "stern in the defense of the teachings of ritual, and to regulate the five degrees of mourning with fixed punishments." What would come to be known as the "ten abominations" (shi e)—particularly heinous crimes, defined in terms of Confucian values, such as unfilial behavior or disrupting the proper order of human relations—were introduced into Chinese law under the Northern Qi dynasty (550–577). This fusion of the once rather sharply distinct and even contradictory attitudes of Confucianism and Legalism with Confucianism in the ascendant position culminated in the Tang dynasty and reached a kind of reductio ad absurdum in a text called the Six Statutes of Tang, completed in 738, which placed Tang administrative law into the framework provided by the idealized Confucian classic The Rites of Zhou.[27]

As Linghu Defen (583–666) instructed one mid-seventh-century Tang monarch, "Kings employ virtue, tyrants employ punishment." Although a mixture of the two techniques might prove useful, as under the Han dynasty, the virtuous style of proper kings should be given priority. In the most successful governments of antiquity, Linghu Defen claimed, the sage kings had taken "purifying their hearts and simplifying affairs as fundamental."[28] The long-term result of this sequence of developments was a curious but effective blend of Legalist-style coercive machinery and Confucian moralism under the Tang dynasty.

Even as early as the end of the Former Han dynasty, the Confucian ideal of government by moral example was already clearly ascendant. By Tang, another 600 years later, it was simply expected that emperors would rule, Confucian style, by means of "mild punishments and light taxation." Even a vigorously martial emperor such as Tang Taizong (r. 627–649), who devoted much of his leisure time to hunting, notoriously murdered two of his own brothers, and personally expressed some skepticism about the significance of Confucian portents, nonetheless carefully represented his administration in those same ideal Confucian terms.[29]

The beginning of Taizong's reign was marred by a summer drought in Shandong, which Taizong turned to his advantage as an opportunity to demonstrate his virtue by remitting the year's taxes for the region; later that same year, he ostentatiously reduced his own consumption of delicacies to exhibit his sympathy for the general famine. In 628, the emperor dispatched messengers to investigate conditions in the vicinity of the capital, putting up his own personal valuables to redeem children whose parents had been forced by starvation into selling them. Blaming himself for the drought and a plague of locusts, Taizong issued a mass pardon of criminals in an impressive display of imperial generosity. In 629, the emperor distributed grain as a reward to households of the filial and just, the aged, and the mothers of newborn children. A decade later, in 639, in response to another drought, Taizong again reduced his own consumption of delicacies, lifted labor service requirements, regulated imprisonment, aided the needy—"and then it rained."[30]

Early imperial government was a hybrid mixture of seemingly rational Legalist bureaucratic procedures, apparently empty Confucian ceremonial, and presumed supernatural sanctions. By modern standards, it could be appallingly ineffective. Tax relief for disaster areas and welfare provisions for the needy were often simply grand gestures, unrealized through any effective administrative programs. To critical (if not entirely uncomprehending) modern observers, such a Confucian empire can easily appear to be "a system that involves a certain amount of make-believe on the top" and a government that "ruled but did not administer the affairs of society at-large."[31]

In Japan, although conventional wisdom holds that Confucianism did not really have much impact until as late as the seventeenth century (and conventional wisdom is correct to the extent that few books of lofty Confucian philosophy were being written in the early period and popular behavior may not have been very much altered by Confucian moral strictures), the entire initial approach to state building was profoundly colored by contemporary Chinese Confucian ideas. This explains much about the early Japanese empire that may seem peculiar from the perspective of the modern West (or, for that matter, from that of Qin-style Legalism as well), such as the allegedly "almost pathetic reliance upon government by exhortation" of a Heian period (794–1185) imperial court whose institutions, we are told, seemed to be "concerned more and more with ceremony and form, rather than with the practical aspects of administration."[32] Rather than being some sort of nativistic Japanese degeneration away from, or failure to ever effectively implement, Chinese-style bureaucratic institutions, this can be interpreted as simply being a profoundly Confucian approach to government.

To be sure, during the Han dynasty in China, "Despite metaphysical and political theories . . . the crucial factor in government had been the military power of the emperor." In China, the importance of maintaining a strong army was rarely entirely lost sight of even by the most idealistic of Confucians. In 637, for example, the Tang emperor Taizong was reportedly advised to "devote your attention to peace within the realm, and do not seek to expand your lands" but also to "fill your quivers with bows and arrows, and do not forget military preparations." Chinese statesmen were not fools, yet, ideally at least, Confucian governments sought not to conquer their enemies but to civilize them.[33]

MISSION CIVILISATRICE[34]

A truly universal empire, by definition, would not have any foreign enemies or any need for a military establishment beyond a modest domestic police force. Since the Chinese empire was not literally universal, however, there was no escaping a continuing need to maintain an army for defense against border raids. However, it is also true that premodern China, after the Qin unification, seldom had to confront potential enemy states wielding even approximately equivalent overall war-making, productive, and organizational capacities (except when China itself was redivided into opposing kingdoms or dynasties).

The other East Asian states rarely posed particularly alarming military threats to Chinese security in premodern times. Their very existence could even be magnanimously explained (and generously tolerated) in imperial minds as derivative, subordinate vassals of the Chinese Son of Heaven. They, therefore, did not have to be conquered (at most, they had to be "chastised" periodically). They usually did not even require extensive guarding against.

At various times throughout imperial Chinese history, allegedly "non-Chinese" peoples did erupt onto the Central Plain, to conquer part or all of China. However, this was a China that had always been very much a multiethnic empire. Many of these conquering "foreigners" actually started their careers of conquest from "homelands" that were already inside the frontiers or at least the borderlands of the Chinese empire—a point that I will examine at greater length in chapter 5. Although they may, indeed, in some ways have been culturally distinct from what we might think of as mainstream Chinese civilization, they triumphed precisely by becoming rulers of China. They can hardly be considered, therefore, external rivals of the empire, at least not for long.

The nomadic cavalry of the northern steppe clearly did constitute a significant external military threat. However, the nomadic lifestyle was so fundamentally different from sedentary Chinese culture and this lifestyle was so geographically determined by conditions on the steppe that even the greatest steppe empires tended to function normally (with the obvious exception of the enormous Mongol world empire in the thirteenth and fourteenth centuries) not so much as competitive challenges to the Chinese *tianxia* as almost symbiotic (harsher critics might say parasitic) counterbalances to it: a kind of nomadic yang to complement the Chinese yin.

Military superiority always remained ultimately decisive in imperial politics, but its importance was chiefly for establishing and maintaining control within the empire. The most vital strategic consideration tended to be not defense against foreign enemies but rather the prevention of any concentration of internal forces that might challenge the established rulers.

Nomad raids, in particular, did have to be constantly defended against. The Chinese *tianxia* was not literally everything under Heaven. However, the territories beyond the effective borders of the empire could at least be imagined as marginal and, in every sense of the word, peripheral. It was not merely the ideological ascendance of Confucianism, therefore, but the very logic of the final triumph of imperial arms and the unification of All-under-Heaven that demanded subsequent demilitarization. After the Qin unification, there did not seem to be much left to conquer and little reason for militarism.

The great Han dynasty that was rebuilt on the ruins of the abruptly shattered Qin conquest empire, therefore, witnessed "the progressive dismantling of the society organized for war through universal military service [exemplified by the Warring States and Qin], and its replacement by a state defined through the propagation of cultural and literary models."[35] The so-called Confucianization of Han dynasty China coincided, therefore, with a reorientation of imperial priorities away from military conquest and colonization and toward the more subtle, but perhaps therefore more insidious, idea of a civilizing mission—the peaceful transformation of strangers (or internal deviants), and the winning over of enemies, through cultural assimilation.

Because the criteria for selecting government officials under the empire (which gradually evolved into the justly renowned Confucian Civil Service Examination System of late imperial times) emphasized Confucian scholarly and literary qualifications almost from the beginning, the dominant sociopolitical imperial elite consisted increasingly of demilitarized literati and scholars. "Why not study [*The Book of*] Poetry?," Confucius had long before asked. Confucian China, to an extraordinary degree, became a place where "an intimacy between art and politics" was assumed to be normal. Cultural and political leadership were commingled. The result was a stereotypically (and not unattractively) refined and delicate, humanistic Confucian (East Asian) civilization.[36]

This Confucian civilization was supposed to be exportable and not confined only to China. Its basic principles were asserted to be universal truths. As the Buddhist Seng You (435–518) explained, even for the secular truths of Confucianism, to say nothing of the boundless cosmic doctrines of the Buddha,

> The presence of the Tao takes precedence over the [particular] place. . . . The Yi and Luo [river area, in modern Henan Province] was originally Xia [the Chinese core dynasty par excellence], but has been reduced to a barbarian waste [under the, at best, semi-Chinese Northern dynasties]; Wu and Chu [in what is today central China, south of the Yangzi River] were originally barbarian [kingdoms], but have been turned into

Hua [Chinese] regions. The Tao circulates, and lands have no constant influences.[37]

Wherever the Confucian Tao was realized, there too was civilization. This civilization, when combined with the political rule of a legitimate Son of Heaven, effectively defined "China." It was not necessarily tied to any particular piece of real estate. When the imperial court was forced to abandon the Central Plain and flee into refuge south of the Yangzi River early in the fourth century, for example, the emperor expressed mortification at having to "sojourn in other county's lands" but was reassured that the true "King takes All-under-Heaven as his home." Moving the capital to a distant frontier region or even into exile in what were once foreign lands did nothing to change his universal sovereignty.[38]

The Central Plain heartland of Chinese civilization could be lost to "barbarian" invaders in the fourth century, and China could still survive and flourish because "China" was not a place so much as it was a civilization, and not only "a" civilization but the essence of civilization itself. The crucial distinguishing feature of this universal civilization was something called *li*. To be without *li* was to be less than fully human: "A man without *li* is an ape—only the semblance of a man, but the substance of an insect," in one third-century opinion.[39]

By departing from the ceremonial standards of *li*, even people who had formerly been considered Chinese would be reduced to the status of "new" barbarians. On the other hand, though, it was also theoretically possible for anyone to acquire mastery of the *li* and, on acknowledging the overlordship of the imperial Son of Heaven, become Chinese. This goes far toward explaining the powerful assimilative capacity of Chinese civilization—and why a modern Western-style ethnonational image of premodern China is so misleading. Within the Chinese mental universe, there could be only a binary choice: Chinese or barbarian. Thus, as late as 1841, one emissary to Qing China from Vietnam took offense at being labeled a "Vietnamese barbarian" *(Yue yi)*, quite literally insisting instead that we "are Chinese, not barbarians." He did not mean by that to renounce the political autonomy of Vietnam—which was by then a self-styled Middle Kingdom with an emperor of its own—but only that the Qing dynasty in the north and Vietnam in the south were equally parts of the same, indivisible, true civilization.[40]

It is difficult, however, to explain in English exactly what was meant by *li*. "*Li* is a term that baffles translation." Conventional attempts to come up with an English equivalent range from courtesy to propriety, decorum, politeness, ceremony, and ritual or rites. Originally, the term seems to have referred to religious sacrifice. Gradually, over the course of the Bronze Age, the *li* evolved from religious ceremonies intended to mediate with the spirit world into sociopolitical instruments for dealing with people. Eventually, *li* became (it often seems) little more than an imprecise synonym for proper civilized behavior.[41] In each of the modern Chinese, Japanese, and Korean languages, to "forget *li*" is today simply a standard expression for discourtesy (C: *shi li;* J: *shitsurei;* K: *shil lye*).

However, the *li* were never entirely drained of all religious significance, and quasi-religious ritual always remained an inescapable integrating feature of state and society in premodern China. Tang dynasty institutions, for example, were overwhelmingly ritual institutions.[42] Therein, in fact, lay their most glaring departure from modern Western expectations. Xun Zi had said, "By proceeding in accordance with ritual, kings gain possession of the world." As the *Book of Rites* claimed, "Of all the methods for the good ordering of men, there is none more urgent than the use of ceremonies."[43]

The *Book of Rites* supposedly reflected the perfect institutions of antiquity, but in its final form it was very much an idealized Han dynasty production. It was only during the Han dynasty that Confucianism first achieved the status of formal orthodoxy in China. After the Han dynasty, during the subsequent period of division and Sui-Tang dynasties, Confucianism as a strictly intellectual activity is often, not unfairly, said to have been eclipsed by the rise of Buddhism and Taoism—but the study of *li* flourished as never before. During the great period of division in China especially, the *li* became a vehicle for political action and an index of qualification for elite status.[44]

These *li*, which included ancestral sacrifices, funeral, diplomatic, and military ritual, and congratulatory ceremonies for happy occasions such as weddings, were regulated according to family status and formed the core of the ethical system on which Confucian statecraft was balanced. During the Southern dynasties, such things as mourning apparel, court ritual, and music were all regarded as indices of civilization, and the *Classic of Filial Piety* was regarded with favor as an especially important text. Filial piety was, in many ways, the central

Confucian virtue. According to the *Book of Rites*, filial piety was "the source of all *li*."[45]

The book known as the *Classic of Filial Piety* was compiled in the early Han dynasty as a synthesis of traditional family values and imperial statecraft intended to reconcile filial piety with political loyalty—private and public virtue—through a graded hierarchy of relations. The resolution to the often-contradictory claims of loyalty to state and family came with the determination that the parallel vertical relationships between father and son and between ruler and subject can be mutually reinforcing. This convergence of private and public morality, filial piety and political loyalty, operating within a universal field of particular hierarchical relationships, contributed immensely to the astonishing stability of the Confucian *tianxia* over thousands of years.[46]

Among all the living creatures on this planet, human beings are notably physically weak and vulnerable. What made it possible for humanity to dominate the earth, according to one early Chinese theory, was our ability to form mutually beneficial groups based on the Tao of the true sovereign, which in turn assumed the proper observance of hierarchical distinctions based on seniority, gender, and the varying degrees and kinds of social-political relationships.[47]

Hierarchical relations were as central to the traditional Confucian social ideal as they are anathema, today, to the equally universalistic modern American ideals of individual rights and equality. According to Han Yu (768–824), the sage kings of the past had devised the "*li* to order the sequence of first and last." "Administrative codes," explained the Treatise on Criminal Law in the *New Dynastic History of the Tang*, "are the ranking and numbering of noble and base—the institutions of the state." As one Japanese emperor put it in 797, "When male and female are separated, the rule of *li* is deeply respected; if there is no distinction between superiors and inferiors, Confucian etiquette is already lacking."[48]

Those who deviated from this ideal hierarchy were presumed to be savages, like the Tibetan contemporaries of the Tang dynasty who were said, shockingly, to esteem youthful virility over seniority and whose "sons treated their fathers haughtily, in coming or going putting the young ahead of the aged." Such behavior represented, in traditional Chinese eyes, not the acceptable standards of some alternative culture but the absence of culture altogether. It has only been recently, under the devastating impact of the modern West, that Chinese civilization has been forced to confront the possibility that there might be multiple, roughly equivalent competing "cultures" in the world, among which Chinese culture might be only one particular "national" example.[49]

However, if civilization, rooted in the *li*, was assumed to be uniform and universal, the traditional Chinese also simultaneously expected that there would naturally be much local variation in terms of customs and language and other minor matters.[50] Three polarities were notably anticipated: between the universal ideal and variant local practices, between the center and the periphery (i.e., civilization was, somewhat contradictorily, supposed to be both universal and, at the same time, defined by the standards of the center), and between educated gentlemen and uneducated commoners.

Not all Chinese were considered equally civilized.[51] In classical antiquity the literally so-called little people had been almost totally excluded from the *li*-based higher culture.[52] While the ancient Bronze Age aristocracy had long since been discarded and imperial Chinese society was, by almost any global premodern standard, remarkably egalitarian with regard to matters of hereditary status, an illiterate Chinese peasant villager still might not have been regarded as being as thoroughly civilized as some courtier-poet from Japan or Vietnam. In addition, a gentleman from the imperial court (who might, however, not be Chinese at all in the modern ethnoracial sense) might well suppose himself to be a finer embodiment of the universal standards of civilization than any provincial scholar.

The disjunction frequently commented on in non-Chinese East Asia between the prescribed elite official Chinese-style standards of the court and the actual behavior of ordinary people should not be taken automatically (as it so often is) simply as proof of the alien-ness and unsuitability of those adopted Chinese norms—of a Chinese versus native duality. In nineteenth-century Vietnam, for example, it was observed that the mandarins "looked Chinese" while the peasants "looked Southeast Asian."[53] However, while Vietnam does present an especially complicated situation, straddling as it does the cultural fault line between East and Southeast Asia, a not altogether dissimilar discrepancy between central elite and local commoner could also be found in many parts of China as well, albeit perhaps to a less extreme extent. Chinese and Vietnamese mandarins participated in a shared elite universal culture that was expected to vary somewhat from local popular culture everywhere. This was not even a contradiction. In part, the disjunction between elite civilization and local common practice merely gave added validation to the social hierarchy that was so much prized by the Confucian elite.

The *Tale of Genji* is an eleventh-century Japanese masterpiece, written in the Japanese language (unlike the bulk of documents in Japan at that time that were still being written in classical Chinese) and supposedly representing uniquely "Japanese" sensibilities. As David Pollack notes, however, when one of its characters says of a group of local (Japanese) villagers that "their speech was as incomprehensible [to him] as the chirping of birds, but no doubt their feelings were like his own," *Genji*'s Japanese author was consciously and deliberately echoing the words of the ninth-century Chinese poet Bo Juyi (Po Chü-i, 772–846) regarding a group of Chinese aborigines.[54] The effect is to suggest a common literate universe inhabited by both Heian aristocrats and Tang literati in which neither Japanese nor Chinese commoners necessarily could partake.

The elite at both courts may have, in some ways, had as much in common with each other as either did with their own less refined subject populations in remote corners of their respective empires. However natively "Japanese" the *Tale of Genji* may be, moreover, only a tiny handful of native Japanese people at the time could or did read it. At the risk of some exaggeration, it may be said that there was both one universal elite East Asian high culture and as many different local popular cultures as there were local communities.

The grand moral principles of Confucianism applied uniformly to All-under-Heaven, but in more trivial matters everyone was released to follow their own local practices. "Cultivate their instruction, do not change their customs; make equal their administration, do not change what is suitable for them," recommends the *Book of Rites*. As Ch'oe Sŭng-no (927–989) observed from tenth-century Koryŏ (Korea), "The institutions of China must be observed, but the customs of the four directions each follow their local nature and seem difficult to entirely convert." Nor was this merely an apology for the incompleteness of Sinification in Korea: the same formula applied in China as well. Within the Chinese empire, variant local customs and universal truths were fully expected to cohabit, both in theory and in practice. "The genius of the Chinese approach to cultural integration" was that it permitted "a high degree of variation within an overarching structure of unity."[55]

This diversity in local customs was only expected to increase with distance. That is because, in addition to the polarity between universal and local (which was applicable everywhere), there was also an anticipated polarity between the center and the periphery, deriving from an operative assumption that the universal standards should be set by the imperial court. It was, we might say, the specific function of the Confucian monarch to set the leading tone for civilization. As Fujiwara Atsumitsu (1063–1145) explained in twelfth-century Japan, "The local customs of native places are each different. . . . [But] the Court distinguishes ceremonial standards which trickle down to those on the Eastern Sea."[56]

Beyond a certain point, moreover, the courtly model was not even supposed to trickle down to the periphery in any great detail. One Sui dynasty emperor flatly refused a nomad request in 607 to be allowed to adopt Chinese-style clothing, explaining that "a gentleman instructs the people without asking them to change their customs." In newly Confucianized Japan, when a Sillan (Korean) "tribute embassy" reportedly arrived in 651 wearing Tang-style (Chinese) clothing, the Japanese court was appalled by this "unrestrained change of custom" and scathingly dismissed it.[57]

A celebration of the peculiarities of one's own Old Home was always at least as dear to East Asian sensibilities as admiration for some distant courtly center. Part of the universal Confucian truth was supposed to be respect and appreciation for particular relations. Perhaps for this reason, the Tang regulation was that disputes between foreigners who were from the same place of origin should be settled according to their own customary procedures and that only altercations between foreigners who were each from different places should be judged according to Tang law.[58]

The prevailing Chinese balance between universalism and pluralism is nicely summarized in the "Treatise on Geography" from the dynastic history of the Former Han:

> All people have natures that contain the Five Constants [humanity, justice, propriety, knowledge, and trustworthiness], but their firmness or gentleness, slowness or haste, and differences in their voices are connected to the atmosphere in their environment—therefore we call them habits [literally, "breezes"].

Their likes and dislikes, choices, conduct, and failure or continuity follow their ruler's desires—therefore we call them customs. . . . When there is a Sage King above to regulate human
relations. . . . this merges All-under-Heaven into a single harmony, after which the teaching of the kings is complete.[59]

This fascinating passage—so difficult to translate into English—
reveals several important Chinese assumptions. All human beings,
everywhere, are basically alike. Local customs differ, but these differences are not in any way fundamental. Rather, they are merely ac-
cidents of habit or circumstance. The state, personified by its ruler,
through its powerful levers of control, must play a role in sculpting
this protean national culture—and the good king has a heavy obligation to do this according to universal moral principles. Then, in all
that really matters (but not the trivial details), All-under-Heaven will
become one, and education—"the teaching of the kings"—is the
mechanism by means of which this is all to be accomplished. To teach
the people the universal truths of Confucianism was the supreme art
of governing them. Rulers, above all else, were supposed to be examples—teachers—to their people.

"For the ancient kings, in establishing their countries and ruling
their people, education came first," comments the *Book of Rites*. Education was the primary tool in promoting the spread of civilization
throughout China and East Asia more generally. The word for this
civilizing process is, in fact, *jiaohua*—the transformation caused by
teaching—and, as Dong Zhongshu noted, the "ultimate source for
jiaohua" was the imperial university.[60]

An imperial university was first established in China in 124 B.C.,
and over the next century and a quarter, a network of official schools
was created stretching down to the local community level. From the
Han dynasty through the Tang, official schools were an integral part
of the system of government by administrative law. The pervasiveness
of educational establishments in Tang China was sufficient to impress
the visiting Japanese monk Kūkai (774–835), who was inspired by
their example to convert a Fujiwara mansion in Heian Japan into a
school in 828. Although the official Chinese imperial schools were
largely supplanted by private education during the Tang dynasty, this
privatization only had the effect of magnifying the pervasiveness of
the indoctrination.[61]

Already, during the late Han period, independent scholars had established private academies throughout the countryside. Through intercommunication among themselves, and because of the deliberate regional balance that was maintained by the Han official recommendation and appointment systems, these Confucians generated an empire-wide community of elite values. The integrative role of the imperial government in circulating "the different styles of the various gentlemen and the peculiar customs of the four quarters" by means of a conscious balance of regional appointments was noted by Lu Ji (261–303), who for that reason protested against the absence of southerners at the (briefly reunified) imperial court in the third century. To spread the "transformation caused by teaching" to All-under-Heaven became the ideal of Confucians from the Later Han on. During the late Han dynasty, for example, the homes of exemplary scholars and virtuous citizens were marked with tablets "so that good conduct might flourish."[62]

This civilizing mission was aided by the increasing availability of books. The contrast here is with Rome, where a relative decline in literacy after the fourth century helped break the continuity of the old civilization. China, too, faced "barbarian invasions" in the fourth century, but in China the barbarians learned to read the Chinese classics and legitimated their governments by appealing to them. The barbarians became Chinese, and themselves furthered the Confucian civilizing mission.

It may be unfair and inaccurate to dismiss early medieval European history as the "Dark Ages." Christopher Beckwith points out that the Franks were becoming more, not less, literate during this period. However, the literary orientation of contemporary East Asian civilization was much deeper and far more profound. No more startling contrast could be found to medieval Europe, with its knightly and often illiterate aristocracy of the sword, than the claim that "medieval Chinese society" first dates from the time "when book-learned and cultured men began to emerge as the real ruling class" in the third century.[63]

Until the end of the empire—indeed, until today—education and schools have served as powerful agents for the assimilation, or at least pacification, of minorities in China. In the mid-second century B.C., the governor of the frontier commandery of Shu, in modern Sichuan Province, established a school in Chengdu city to promote local cultural development and sent ten promising youths to the imperial capital for advanced study. In what is now Anhui Province, south of the Yangzi River, the governor built a school in A.D. 30 and instructed the local Yue people in the rites. Around the same time, similar educational efforts were being made by officials in what is now northern Vietnam.[64]

An indication of the seemingly interminable, Sisyphean nature of this process, however, is the fact that the educational and examination systems were still only just incipient in Lingnan (modern Guangdong and Guangxi Provinces and northern Vietnam) in the seventh century. A millennium after the establishment of the previously mentioned school in Chengdu, the military governor of the Tang salient in Sichuan that stood between the Tibetan empire to the west and the kingdom of Nanzhao in the south still found it expedient, beginning around 785, to gather some of the local Man (barbarian) children in Chengdu and instruct them in writing and calculations. The impact of 1,000 years of schooling in the area had obviously been rather limited. After some fifty more years, and over 1,000 students later, the local government began to find this program something of a burden. The civilizing mission never seems to end.[65]

Ethnonational identities are, as we know, "imagined communities," based more on the consciousness of difference than on any inalterable reality.[66] This does not mean that ethnicity is exactly a lie (although self-deception and mythology are common features of more extreme nationalism). Humanity really does divide up into many different groups, for many different reasons. These groups all have their own distinctive characteristics. All groups are, in a strict sense, artificial human creations, but some coalesce "naturally" enough in their own way, and even artificiality does not automatically make such groups illusory or unimportant. What these ethnonational identities are not, however, is primordial, eternal, or essential in any mystical way.

The traditional Chinese have at times been as ethnocentric ("Sinocentric") as any other people. Some scholars claim to detect a certain protonationalistic ethnic consciousness among the Chinese from a very early date.[67] China might even appear to be the biggest and most obvious exception to the supposed rule that nations and nationalism are modern phenomena. Ethnocentric Chinese prejudice against "barbarians" would be evident in the very use of the word— except that "barbarian" is really an English word (of Greek derivation) for which the traditional Chinese did not have an exact equivalent, invariably referring instead directly to the specific Chinese names for the various regional tribal groups (Rong, Di, Yue, Yi, Man, Liao and so on). Still, even this terminology is indicative of a clear consciousness of difference, and the instinctive Chinese assumption of their own superiority is usually unmistakable.

Some sort of awareness of a "Chinese" identity, in opposition to the Rong, Di, Man, Yi, and others, obviously did emerge in antiquity. Not uncommonly, these assorted barbarians were even scorned as bestial or subhuman. However, from about the time of Confucius, there also arose an apparent conviction on the part of at least some of the more thoughtful Chinese people that these barbarians could be assimilated and become civilized. Antiforeign prejudice was certainly still prevalent even in cosmopolitan early Tang China, but it was counterbalanced by a sometimes astonishing degree of self-confident toleration and an open-minded (if also arrogant) universalistic conviction that the foreigners, too, can and should become Chinese.[68]

The locus classicus for expressions of Chinese ethnoracial exclusivity is sometimes said to be the passage in the *Zuo zhuan* where the duke of Lu was dissuaded from allying with Chu against Jin, in 586 B.C., by a quotation from an even older text: "The minds of those who are not our kind must be different."[69] "Our kind," here, translates the Chinese *zulei,* which in modern usage conventionally means clan, race, tribe, or class and approximates quite closely the Latin *natio*—tribe, race, breed, or class—which forms the root of the modern English word "nation." To be precise, however, the duke of Lu was advised against allying with one distant Chinese principality against another, closer one because its ruling family had a different surname (and, hence, was quite literally "not our clan"). This certainly represents a quite meticulous calculus of difference but was not exactly either nationalism or racism.

This same *Zuo zhuan* passage could be cited later in different contexts to refer to the supposedly immutable difference between Chinese and barbarians, as Jiang Tong used it around the year 300 to emphasize the immediacy of the danger posed by large numbers of sullen Rong and Di tribesmen in residence near the capital. In general, however, the Confucian tradition was inclined to believe that civilization was something that could be either learned or unlearned and was not biologically innate. "When Confucius composed the *Spring and Autumn Annals,* he treated the various lords who used Yi [barbarian] ritual as Yi, and those who approached the Middle Kingdom as Middle Kingdoms." Nor was this attitude exclusively Confucian. As the eclectic early Han-period text *Huai nan zi* observed, "If a three month old baby is born and then moves to another country, he will be unable to know his [own] native customs" but will instead acquire the practices of his new home.[70] For Confucians, there was a recognized universal standard of higher civilization, adherence to which was partly a matter of conscious choice and commitment.

A particularly excellent example of this line of thinking is provided by an essay, "The Chinese Mind," written by Chen An in the late Tang. A certain Arab was recommended to court around the year 850, given an examination, and awarded the prestigious Jinshi degree. This provoked some grumbling that a Chinese person should have been recommended instead, prompting Chen to write his essay, in which he reminded his readers of famous examples of ethnic (native-born) Chinese who had nonetheless defected to enemy states and of loyal foreigners who had faithfully served the empire. "Someone who was born in the central lands [China]," wrote Chen, "but whose behavior does violence to the *li* and *yi* [justice], is Chinese in appearance but barbarian in his mind; someone who was born in barbarian regions, but whose behavior conforms to the *li* and *yi*, is barbarian in appearance but Chinese in his mind."[71] Being Chinese was a civilized state of mind.

In Samuel Huntington's dictum, "Imperialism is the necessary logical consequence of universalism." The inverse side of the liberally open-minded early imperial Chinese confidence that anyone could become Chinese was a rather expansive cultural imperialism. Everyone should become Chinese. An early third-century (ca. 226–230) Chinese exploratory mission to Funan (in what is now Cambodia and southern Vietnam), for example, found the native men still going about naked in public. This was incompatible with the presumed universal standards of civilization. The Chinese therefore taught the natives to be ashamed of their "indecency," thus supposedly initiating the South Sea custom of wearing sarongs.[72] The resemblance to the nineteenth-century European sense of a *mission civilisatrice*, exhibited in some of precisely the same places, is striking.

The post-Qin Chinese empire largely discontinued its quest for military expansion, although a newly reunified Sui dynasty did greedily invade Champa (in modern central Vietnam) in 605 to acquire its rumored treasures, and both Sui and early Tang launched a series of massive "punitive" invasions of Korea. Nevertheless, the Confucian empire staked its claim to universal sovereignty over *tianxia* not on conquest but on a looser paternalistic framework of international tribute relations that obliged the empire to treat its neighbors with active benevolence in exchange for sometimes little more than pro forma allegiance. In ideal Confucian hierarchies the heaviest obligations are supposed to fall on those at the top.[73]

In 631, Tang constructed 1,200 new dormitory rooms in the capital, luring in a reported "over 8,000" foreign students—especially from Korea but also from Tibet, Parhae and Malgal (both in the northeast), Japan, and elsewhere—with the temptations of Tang high culture and Tang state financial assistance. By this means, instead of having to subdue the barbarians, they could simply be converted, and, queried a Tang emperor in 715, for inducing barbarians to "admire our Chinese style, what takes precedence over the Confucian *li?*" His command was that, henceforth, all foreign guests be ushered into the Directorate of Education and exposed to instruction in the *li*.[74]

In 732, when a Tibetan embassy formally requested a number of Chinese books for a Tang royal bride of the Tibetan king, one Tang official objected that divulging the secrets of good government contained in these classics would strengthen the Tibetan position and threaten the Tang, but others replied that an introduction to Confucian literature was just what would be necessary to teach the barbarians "honesty and integrity" and bring them into the civilized world.[75]

It is not clear whether the books were sent at this time. Tibet remained effectively beyond the gravitational pull of Tang culture in those centuries when the East Asian region began to acquire recognizable shape and, indeed, became Tang China's most formidably aggressive foreign enemy. However, in this period, Korea slipped firmly within the East Asian cultural fold at the same time that it was first becoming politically independent; Japan was sweepingly transformed along Tang lines, even though it configured itself as a rival Chinese-style *tianxia* with an independent orbit of its own; and the Tang Chinese administration in Vietnam headed unknowingly toward independence—but one within East Asian norms. The borders of the empire did not expand much after Qin, and sometimes even contracted, but the extension of Central Plain civilization reached its peak in this period.

THE DIPLOMATIC ORDER

The theoretical resolution to the glaring contradiction between Chinese imperial claims to universal sovereignty over all *tianxia* and the obvious counterreality of the existence of multiple independent foreign states was found in the ancient Zhou concept of vassalage. During the lengthy Zhou era, increasingly independent hereditary local lords (eventually, self-styled "kings") had nonetheless been expected to at least formally acknowledge the universal, if largely nominal and ceremonial, sovereignty of the Zhou Son of Heaven.[76] As Chinese mental horizons expanded, the king's (now emperor's) core personal demesne expanded to become the entire empire proper, and the surrounding fringe of semiautonomous vassals expanded, in theory, to fill the entire earth.

Modern Japanese scholars in particular have been inclined to describe the early East Asian world in terms of an international political framework structured around China's self-proclaimed authority to appoint (or, in practice, at least confirm the selection of) the rulers of neighboring states. In Japanese, this is called the *sakuhō* system, which is approximately what English-speaking scholars refer to as "the tribute system" but more precisely means a system of "investiture" or enfeoffment. The claim, in other words, was not only that foreign countries should offer tribute to the Chinese emperor but also that their rulers, properly, owed their positions to the emperor, should assist him in punitive military operations, and should observe the Chinese calendar and ceremonial norms.[77]

The result was an unmistakably Sinocentric vision of the ideal world order. During the peak years of Tang glory in the early eighth century, the view from the center was exultantly triumphal. It appeared, from the Tang capital at least, to be an age when there was international harmony under the Chinese lead, and "Chinese and barbarians followed a common course." The local chieftains of the north and west left their felt tents behind and traversed rope bridges across yawning chasms to present themselves before the Tang court. Tributary trinkets from Guangdong (Canton), Sichuan, Korea, and even more exotic provenance "clogged the Translation Bureau." Distant tributaries paid obeisance and sang barbarian songs beneath the palace walls. The Son of Heaven "civilized the hundred *Man* [barbarians] and made uniform ten-thousand *li*."[78]

This was not entirely a delusion of the Tang court, but it did require some exaggeration. In practice, not every foreign government (or independent chieftain) with which the empire interacted participated in the "investiture system," and Tang China did not have contact at all with much of the planet. Early Tang, which perhaps coincides with the peak elaboration of this system, enjoyed relations with over seventy foreign countries, but only the East Asian kingdoms fell within the realm of investiture relations proper, while the Tibetans, for example, remained defiantly recusant.[79] Active participation in the system was confined to China's immediate satellites. Even within East Asia, Japan soon withdrew from full participation, preferring instead to replicate the Tang tributary model with itself as the new sovereign center.

The central conceit of this system was the global sovereignty of the imperial Son of Heaven, and the descending hierarchy of subordinate kingdoms was officially ranked more in terms of the priority of their relations with the imperial court than according to their intrinsic size and power. For example, the early Southern dynasties (fourth through fifth centuries) formally graded their relations with Koguryŏ first, Paekche second, and Japan third. The Northern Wei dynasty, in 484, placed the residence of the Koguryŏ ambassador second only to that of the ambassador from the Southern Chinese imperial dynasty, Qi.[80]

The imperial claim to universal sovereignty was obviously something of a fiction. In 472, for example, one Northern Wei monarch informed the king of Paekche, "We look down upon the Four Seas as Lord, and govern all living things." Yet the emperors of Northern Wei were themselves at best semi-Chinese rulers of at most half the old Qin-Han realm, which itself had never really spanned the world. Their pose as Sons-of-Heaven could therefore even be described as a kind of double imposture: alien conquerors pretending to be emperors of China pretending to be rulers of the whole world. The early Tang dynasty boasted that it had converted all of the "sixteen kingdoms" that stretched from Khotan west to Persia into imperial prefectures and districts. However, the view east toward China from Persia no doubt looked somewhat different. In practice, Turfan, after its conquest by Tang in 640, was probably really "the most remote northwest area governed by a Chinese administration."[81]

Imperial China, it has been said, "tended to cover over with the rhetoric of universalism" its encounters with alternative worldviews. At bottom, this universalism was really a form of Sinocentrism that could conceive of foreigners only in terms of their relationship to the Middle Kingdom—relationships that were often comfortably understood as being literally familial. In keeping with the early Chinese proclivity for thinking not in modern Western-style ethnonational terms but rather in terms of actual family relations, the Xianbei rulers of the Northern Wei dynasty claimed, for example, to be descendants of the mythical Yellow Emperor (to be Chinese, that is, and not barbarian "Hu"), who had been enfeoffed in the far north (near Xianbei Mountain), in remote antiquity. This story seems to have been a late fabrication, deliberately concocted to win Chinese acceptance for Xianbei rule.[82]

In southern China, the story that the local Yue people were descendants of the ruling house of the first Chinese dynasty, Xia, was widespread already by the Spring and Autumn era of Zhou. Although the particular Warring States kingdom called Yue was located in what is now almost central China, the broader Yue cultural zone extended from there south into what is now Vietnam, and in Vietnam, traditional native Vietnamese histories also proclaimed their own descent from mythical Chinese sage kings. Even today, some modern Chinese scholars still seriously (if somewhat ludicrously) claim, for example, that the Lạc-Yue inhabitants of prehistoric Vietnam can be literally traced to origins in the upper Yellow River valley of northern China.[83]

While it is conceivable that some Central Plain noblemen did venture south at quite early dates to assume positions of leadership over local populations, it was probably more common for indigenous chieftains to acquire some of the trappings of Chinese higher civilization for its prestige, if not for its greater practical effectiveness, and in this way become Sinified. After only a few generations, physical Central Plain ancestry could easily be imagined. Certainly, we know from surviving stone inscriptions that by the Sui-Tang period, many so-called barbarian chieftains in Lingnan (the far southeast of modern China and northern Vietnam) were already claiming to be from families of Central Plain origin. In addition, in the southwest during this period, the "claim to prestigious Chinese roots" by local families was "rather pervasive." Into quite recent times, indigenous persons in Guangdong Province (Canton) were still fabricating claims to Central Plain ancestry to enhance their status and "become Han

[Chinese] as they actively acquired the cultural symbols of the larger polity."[84]

Not unlike traditional Vietnamese claims to descent from ancient Chinese sage kings, early Chinese sources also report an alleged Japanese claim to descent from the royal house of Wu (in modern Jiangsu), which in turn itself claimed descent from the Zhou founders. There are, in fact, enough tantalizing links between early "native" prehistoric Japanese culture and the Yue culture of the lower Yangzi delta to make some kind of prehistoric Jiangsu connection not implausible, but any claim to generic Japanese descent from Zhou royalty is absurd. Individual Japanese claims to Chinese ancestry, however, often with quite obviously inflated pedigrees, continued to be made well into the historical period. The renowned monk Saichō (767–822), for example, was reputedly of Chinese descent.[85]

Similarly, there was a venerable Korean tradition that the royal house of Koguryŏ was founded by a scion of the Chinese Shang dynasty. This is unsupported by any archaeological discoveries, at least from sites within the Korean peninsula proper. The idea has also understandably become rather unpalatable to certain modern Korean nationalists.[86] As objectionable as claims to Chinese descent might be to modern nationalists, however, in premodern times they provided a measure of status within the East Asian world. Such relationships situated alien peoples within the Chinese mental landscape, in Chinese terminology, helping to make both foreigners and Chinese comprehensible to each other in the global lingua franca of premodern East Asia.

However fantastically conceited this tribute system may appear to modern eyes, it in fact provided the structure for international relations in early East Asia and served to transmit common values and perspectives throughout the region. Independent states in East Asia really were founded, in part, through this investiture process, contradictory as that may sound. In A.D. 32, for example, the ruler of Koguryŏ supposedly sent tribute to the Han emperor and for the first time styled himself "king," using the borrowed Chinese title *wang*. The first recorded contact between Paekche and the Chinese empire (in this case the Eastern Jin dynasty) was in 372, and by 386 the Paekche ruler had been invested as a Chinese imperial general and deputy "king" of Paekche.[87]

In 581, the newly proclaimed Sui dynasty in China recognized the local ruler of northern Korea as "king of Ko[gu]ryŏ" and that of southwestern Korea as "king of Paekche." A few years later, in 594, the more remote monarch of the southeastern corner of the peninsula was dubbed "king of Silla." Interestingly enough, these three kings were also simultaneously appointed as the dukes of Liaodong, Daifang, and Lelang commanderies, respectively, thus perpetuating at least a shadow of the old imperial Chinese colonial administrative organization over Korea.[88]

Such interaction between the initially rather minor local chieftains of Korea and the established authority structure provided by a succession of imperial dynasties in China helped legitimize, in terminology recognized and understandable throughout East Asia, what we might think of as the first independent kingdoms in Korea. The original conferral of the Chinese royal title *wang* on Sillan rulers early in the sixth century, for example, preceded the promulgation of Chinese-style law codes there and the rapid and ultimately triumphant expansion of that realm.[89]

In Japan, too, as early as the third century, one priestess-chieftain also actively sought Chinese imperial investiture as an aid in consolidating her authority over the fractious Japanese tribes. Over the course of the fifth century, no less than thirteen tributary missions are known to have been dispatched from the would-be Japanese court to garner Chinese imperial recognition and support for its claim to be the legitimate rulers of Japan and of southern Korea as well.[90]

State formation in early East Asia was accomplished using Chinese forms and titles and was surprisingly dependent on formal recognition from the Chinese empire. In the case of Japan, however, Chinese imperial investiture ended with the sixth century, and Japan thereafter maintained a more autonomous distance though still, for a time, continuing to offer "tribute" to the empire.[91]

A new era of more direct Japanese contact with China, and consciously methodical emulation of it, began with tribute embassies to Sui in 600 and 607. However, by this time, Japan no longer sought or accepted Chinese imperial titles, and, perhaps making a virtue out of necessity, in 631 the Tang emperor absolved the Japanese of their presumed requirement to offer annual tribute, ostensibly out of compassion for the vast distances involved.[92]

On the Korean peninsula, Chinese attempts at direct colonial imperial rule had failed utterly by the fourth century, but, as we have seen, the independent native kingdoms that emerged to take its place long continued to accept Chinese investiture as at least nominal vassals. Relations between the Korean kingdoms and China continued to be close. Koguryŏ, for example, is known to have dispatched no fewer than eighty-six missions to the Northern Wei dynasty, including forty-one during the single reign of the emperor Xiaowen (471–497) alone. In the sixth century, however, the number of embassies Koguryŏ sent to the Northern dynasties in China dwindled, and tribute missions to the rival Southern empires became more frequent. Koguryŏ was obviously not averse to playing multiple would-be All-under-Heavens off against each other.[93]

Nor was Koguryŏ always a very obedient tributary. A Koguryŏ raid on Sui China in 598, penetrating south of the Great Wall near the coast, provoked the Sui emperor to revoke Koguryŏ's Chinese imperial titles and send an expeditionary force to chastise his unruly vassal. The discovery in 607 that Koguryŏ was violating protocol by making secret unilateral diplomatic overtures to the Türks provoked an imperial threat to "make a tour of inspection" through Koguryŏ territory in retribution. Invasion followed in 612. Before this conflict was resolved, there would ultimately be four massive Sui invasions and some thirteen serious Tang military campaigns against the Korean peninsula in the early seventh century. A comparable situation also developed on the western flank of the empire when the Tang vassal kingdom at Turfan cultivated an alliance with the Türks, prompting the Tang invasion and conquest of Turfan in 640.[94]

In the meantime, Koguryŏ acquired a tributary of its own— Silla—around 421, while Japanese sources at least represented themselves as receiving tribute from Paekche in the fifth century.[95] Clearly, the investiture system did not function in a neatly Sinocentric fashion, creating obedient rings of vassals for the imperial Son of Heaven. Instead, this so-called tribute system was simply the shell or framework within which diplomatic relations took place, which every state, quite rationally, juggled to advance its own interests.

This realization has led some modern Korean and Japanese scholars to theorize that diplomatic relations were only formulaically represented in Chinese texts in tributary terms but actually were conducted under conditions of diplomatic "equality." Indeed, the truth was that the various states did enjoy de facto independent sovereign power and imperial foreign relations had to operate within the constraints of that reality. Often, claims to imperial suzerainty were the thinnest of diplomatic niceties, perhaps recognized only at the Chinese end. However, diplomatic equality is a modern Western concept. It was not part of the vocabulary of early East Asian social and political relations, which invariably were understood at the time as being unequal and hierarchical, both internally and externally. Inequality was the ideal, and independent East Asian regimes aspired not toward equal relations but instead toward becoming centers of their own diplomatic universes.[96]

Korean tributary traditions of *sadae,* or "serving the great" (meaning the Chinese empire), are inseparable from the very establishment of a unified, independent Korea.[97] In the wars among the three Korean kingdoms during the mid-seventh century, Silla allied itself with Tang. In 651, a member of the Sillan royal family named Kim In-mun was sent to the Tang court to serve in the imperial bodyguard. After his return home, he was selected again as an emissary to request Tang military assistance against Paekche. Tang duly dispatched 130,000 soldiers, over whom Kim was made assistant commander and for whom he served as a guide. The ensuing joint Tang-Sillan campaign in 660 successfully captured the Paekche capital and royal family. Kim then resumed his former position in the Tang imperial bodyguard, and when Tang subsequently accused Koguryŏ of violating the principle of *sadae,* Kim became a mediator for further joint Tang-Sillan action against Koguryŏ.

In the meantime, the new Sillan king Munmu (r. 661–681) had himself also attended the Tang court in his youth. After participating with merit in the combined Tang-Sillan assault on Paekche in 660, he ascended the Sillan throne in 661. In 663, he was invested with Tang official titles. The epic final Sillan conquest of Koguryŏ and unification of the Korean peninsula in 668, then, came under the aegis of overall Tang claims to sovereignty. When the Sillan king began taking independent military action against his erstwhile Tang superiors in 674, the Tang court wanted to depose the truculent Sillan king and replace him with his own brother, who was none other than Kim In-mun. Kim In-mun earnestly declined this Tang offer of his brother's throne, however, and helped mollify Tang anger at his brother's impudence. Kim finally died at the Tang capital in 694.[98]

From about 676, the Korean peninsula was both unified and independent, but it remained at least a nominal tributary of the Chinese empire until as late as the end of the nineteenth century. In the case of Korea, we therefore have perhaps the best example of an independent, non-Chinese East Asian state fitting fairly comfortably within the loose framework of the so-called *sakuhō* system.

BACK FROM BABEL: THE *KANJI* SPHERE

The East Asian diplomatic community that was arranged around this *sakuhō* ideal, as it happens, stood atop a deep linguistic fault line, straddling the extremes of two very different language stocks: the Sino-Tibetan languages of China and the Eurasiatic (or perhaps more narrowly Altaic) languages of Korea and Japan. This was no mere matter of linguistic diversity, of which there is a considerable amount within the borders of China alone, but of fundamentally different linguistic affiliations. The so-called Eurasiatic languages, which all enjoy certain points of (sometimes distant) resemblance to one another and share a presumed common ancestry, range across much of the northern half of the world, from the Indo-European languages of the west to Eskimo-Aleut in the east, and include Japanese and Korean. Altaic speakers occupy a relatively smaller (but still very broad) belt of northern Asia. Neither includes the languages of China.[99]

To the south, in much of what is now southern China and Vietnam, still another set of non-Sino-Tibetan languages, possibly ancestral to modern Austroasiatic and Austronesian, were also apparently spoken in prehistory. Most of these prehistoric southern languages, however, were eventually either displaced or absorbed by Chinese languages and reduced to the level of what are now conventionally called the "dialects" of Chinese.

Vietnamese remains distinct, a presumed legacy of the formerly widely spoken Austroasiatic languages of the south. However, even Vietnamese was once seriously considered (by some late nineteenth-century French colonial officials) to be "a mere dialect of Chinese"—"a Chinese patois" and not "a language" at all in its own right.[100] Such a categorization would surely be intolerable today, although Vietnamese as a "national language" is (like Chinese) to some extent an artificial creation of modern nation building. In any case, the linguistic border to China's south seems less starkly drawn than the one separating it from Korea and Japan, if only because there is such a large fuzzy transitional area—stretching from the Yangzi River to the Pearl

River—in between. The major division falls to the northeast, where East Asia is linguistically split into two unequal parts, roughly at the line formed by the Yalu River.

This allows us to make the striking observation that East Asia does not coincide, even roughly, with any major linguistic frontiers. East Asia includes both Eurasiatic- (or Altaic-) speaking Korea and Japan, Sino-Tibetan–speaking China, and Austroasiatic-speaking Vietnam, but it excludes a huge number of other Eurasiatic-speaking areas, a somewhat more limited range of other Sino-Tibetan–speaking regions to the west and south, and the vast Austroasiatic- and Austronesian-speaking arc of modern Southeast Asia. Therefore, language, at least spoken language, was clearly not a determining factor in giving shape to the East Asian region.

Written language, on the other hand, was decisive. East Asia exists, despite enormous internal linguistic diversity, in large part because of the universal application throughout the region—and only this region—of the Chinese writing system. The effectiveness of this Chinese writing system and the depth of its impact on East Asia, in turn, depended in large part on certain peculiarities of the Chinese script, which it is therefore essential to examine here.

Nothing was more decisive in giving coherence to the East Asian region than the writing system. Nothing is more fundamental to Chinese cultural identity. However, from the Chinese perspective, this was simply "writing." The full significance of this peculiar script may be more easily grasped if we approach it from partly outside, from the perspective of the fringes of the traditional East Asian world, using the Japanese term for it, *kanji*, which literally means the "writing of the Han" dynasty and, by extension, of China. (Since there was not really any traditional Chinese word for "China," one way to specify the "Chinese" language was to designate it as the language of a particular Chinese dynasty. The name of the archetypical early imperial Han dynasty was often, though not always in premodern times, chosen for that purpose. Similarly, when it became necessary in modern times to imagine an ethnic label for the Chinese "race," the old dynastic title was resorted to again, and we began to hear of the Chinese as the "Han people.")

The Japanese speak of *kanji* to distinguish Chinese characters from the two native Japanese *kana* syllabaries, derived from simplified *kanji* but having exclusively phonetic properties, and from Western alphabetic systems. This Japanese perspective provides sufficient distance for us to discuss the Chinese writing system as a distinct phenomenon. It is not simply writing but, rather, a very particular kind of writing.

The peculiarity of these *kanji,* by comparison with conventional Western expectations, is illustrated by the fact that the corresponding Korean term, *hanja,* and the modern Chinese label *hanzi* (which is relatively rarely used, however, simply because in China the Chinese writing system is taken for granted and does not ordinarily need to be specified as "Chinese writing"), are identical to the Japanese word *kanji,* when written in *kanji.* That is, the written forms of the Chinese, Japanese, and Korean words for "Chinese characters" are completely indistinguishable from one another, even though their pronunciations vary at least slightly.

The explanation for this strange congruence is, in part, the obvious one that these are all loan words originating with the same two Chinese graphs—Han, the name of a Chinese dynasty, and *zi,* meaning "logograph," or Chinese-style written word—but the curious fact remains that when spoken or when written using a phonetic script like our alphabet, they cease to be interchangeable, even though they are exactly the same when written in *kanji.* This trick would be impossible to perform with an alphabet.

In western Eurasia, the sea voyages of the Phoenicians, in the period between about 1100 and 800 B.C., promoted the spread of alphabetic writing systems, which became the nearly universal instrument of writing in the West. At the opposite end of Eurasia, in China, the ancient writing system of the Bronze Age Shang dynasty became the ancestor of all written Chinese.[101] The use of *kanji* then expanded together with the imperial frontier to encompass all of what we think of today as China, that splinter fragment of the empire now known as Vietnam (since Vietnam remained directly a part of the Chinese empire throughout the period covered in this book, *kanji* use in Vietnam at this time was as unremarkable as its use, for example, in Canton [Guangzhou]), and beyond to Korea and Japan. Both the *kanji* script and the classical Chinese written language became the dominant form of writing in use throughout East Asia until as recently as the nineteenth century.

The elaboration of schools and formal higher education in each of China, Japan, Korea, and Vietnam around a shared canon of especially revered texts, all written in *kanji* in the classical Chinese language, resulted in a surprisingly universal standard of literate higher civilization throughout traditional East Asia.[102] The manifestly cacophonous differences in pronunciation between the various spoken languages of East Asia should not blind us to the important point that in each of the Chinese, Japanese, Korean, and Vietnamese languages, the written word for "civilization" is the same: literally, the "transformation caused by writing" (C: *wenhua;* J: *bunka;* K: *munhwa;* V: *văn-hóa*). To a great extent, it was the same writing and the same civilization.

Although *kanji* use has largely been rejected in twentieth-century Korea and Vietnam, in Japan *kanji* are still normally combined with *kana* for most writing purposes. A typical sentence in a modern Japanese-language book or newspaper will be written using a mixture of the two systems. To a rather peculiar degree, *kanji* manage in Japanese eyes to be simultaneously both alien "Chinese characters" and a cherished part of the "native" Japanese tradition.[103]

The profound significance of the parallel development of alphabetic writing in the west and of *kanji* in East Asia (*kanji* are not really all that much older, chronologically, than early alphabets) is that alphabets are ideologically neutral but *kanji* are not. An alphabet is a conventional system for recording sound, which in itself conveys almost nothing by way of meaning. Alphabets are empty of meaning. *Kanji,* however, are not ideologically neutral but inherently laden with culture-bound significance. The use of *kanji* is therefore a potent unifying force—almost beyond the capability of alphabet users to even imagine.

It has long been conventional to describe *kanji* as "ideographs"—that is, as graphic representations of ideas. One influential recent Western school of thought vehemently objects to this depiction, however. "Chinese characters are a phonetic, not an ideographic, system of writing." More than that, "there never has been, and never can be, such a thing as an ideographic system of writing," insists one much respected modern authority. "No character ever stood for an 'idea' independently of a word. Chinese characters stood . . . for words, and only via that phonetic medium for the ideas that those words convey," writes another. *Kanji,* it is argued, represent not "an 'alternative' form of writing" to the alphabet but only "the arrested development of a universal process" toward the generation of simple phonetic writing systems like our alphabet.[104]

Yet to dismiss *kanji* as merely a crudely underdeveloped phonetic writing system may be stretching too far to counter conventional wisdom. *Kanji* certainly do have phonetic properties and applications, and phonetic principles were involved in the very creation of the vast majority of them, but generations of users have also seen something more in these *kanji*. Any suggestion that *kanji* are only a primitive protoalphabet—one that has, unfortunately, failed to be improved on over the centuries—requires much faith in the kind of unilinear model for universal progress that once was fashionable but is no longer scientifically tenable.[105]

This last assertion, furthermore, comes perilously close to implying that the West, with its more advanced alphabetic systems, has been at a higher evolutionary stage than East Asia, at least with regard to writing systems, since the Bronze Age. While such an idea (put in those terms) was surely never intended, an inference of Western superiority is latent in any assumption that an evolution from something like *kanji* to an alphabet is the universally inevitable line of progression. Once again, the familiar stereotype of an unchanging Asia, stranded outside of history by the forces of its own obscurantism and the march of Western progress, floats before our eyes; but, however relatively inconvenient *kanji* may indeed be as a writing system, the use of *kanji* at least did not prevent China from becoming the most economically developed and technologically advanced place on earth for many intervening centuries.

It is possible that the alphabet really is a better, more efficient writing system than *kanji*. An alphabet is unquestionably easier to learn, and *kanji* may well be doomed to eventual future extinction in the global computer age. It is, furthermore, theoretically conceivable, had history unfolded differently in China, that *kanji* might have evolved into or been replaced by some kind of phonetic system—as, in fact, actually happened with the Japanese *kana* (although in practice *kana* have not replaced *kanji* so much as merely supplemented them) and as Western alphabets actually derived from Egyptian hieroglyphics. However, there is nothing inevitable about this line of development, as is demonstrated by the fact that it did not happen.

Any hypothetical future alphabetization of Chinese could surely be explained as the result of overwhelming Western influence rather than as the natural direction of spontaneous evolution. How confident can we really be that such a development would "spell" progress? Much might be gained in terms of utility, but what would be lost?

One thing that would be drained away with the advent of a phonetic writing system is meaning. *Kanji* do, it is true, have phonetic properties, but, unlike an alphabet, *kanji* have a semantic dimension as well. Any given *kanji* quite normally has a variety of different pronunciations across a range of different languages or dialects. Even within the single modern standard "national language" of Japan, *kanji* typically have multiple oral readings, but the same *kanji* usually conveys approximately—or even precisely—the same meaning everywhere, regardless of how it is pronounced.

To be sure, *kanji* do always have at least one pronunciation. They do represent the words (more precisely, the morphemes, or smallest meaningful units) of all the various languages they are used to transcribe. If *kanji* manage to break the sound barrier and exceed the physical limitations of speech, so too, to some extent, do all other forms of writing. In part, that is the whole point of literacy: to escape the bounds of oral culture. The question is simply, Do *kanji* go too far, past the point of diminishing returns, in detaching themselves from the spoken language? [106] *Kanji* go farther in this direction than any phonetically based writing system possibly could.

It might be argued that *kanji* originally designated only the morphemes of the spoken Chinese language, which were later clumsily adapted to suit the needs of various other spoken East Asian languages. *Kanji*, in that sense, were only a vehicle for writing Chinese. However, writing is a whole new dimension for any language, something more than mere recorded speech. This was especially true in a China where it is doubtful that anyone ever normally spoke the classical written language aloud in ordinary conversation. In traditional China, the written language—"the only real language in the minds of many"—"had not the slightest thing to do with the modern vernacular." [107]

Much of the confusion over whether *kanji* should be described as ideographs revolves around an implicit Western assumption that when we say that *kanji* "represent ideas," this means universal (Platonic) ideals. However, *kanji* do not and cannot magically or intuitively convey transcendent, universal "ideas." Such Platonic ideals are themselves only ideas, which can have no independent existence outside of people's minds. Ideas do not simply exist but must be framed within a specific person's brain as specific (if sometimes vague or even vacuous) concepts. Such ideas may then, indeed, represent universal truths about nature that nearly everyone else can appreciate—the universe, after all, really is universal—but ideas about the universe can exist only in individual people's heads. *Kanji* cannot therefore be disembodied universally intelligible truths but instead must be somewhat arbitrarily chosen symbolic representations of specific ideas, as encoded in the specific medium of the Chinese language and culture.[108] One may therefore reasonably object to calling them ideographs, but the fact that *kanji* represent meaning as much as or more than sound is incontrovertible.

Kanji stand for words, but words do not necessarily have to be spoken. The visual may be more precise than the oral. Even some of the sharpest modern Western critics of *kanji* acknowledge that in East Asian languages, the written graph "almost always does a better job identifying the meaning than does the sound to which the meaning is joined." An individual *kanji* not only commonly means approximately the same thing when used to write different East Asian languages, but even within a single language system the written morpheme tends to be more unmistakably precise than the spoken morpheme. This remarkable property of *kanji* facilitates communication in writing even where multiple and mutually unintelligible spoken languages are in use. East Asians who cannot talk to each other can and do communicate—though perhaps only haltingly—through *kanji*. This facility should be neither denied nor exaggerated. Claims to universal intelligibility for *kanji* are clearly "fanciful fabrications.[109] They do have to be learned first, since *kanji* do not represent transcendent universal Platonic ideals but rather the ideas of a specific language and culture.

Unlike the letters of an alphabet, which can be impartially adapted to represent the sounds of any spoken language, precisely to the extent that ideas (or words or morphemes) are their essential burden, *kanji* are tied inextricably to a particular set of ideas—to a specific vocabulary, or "ideology." After their importation, *kanji* can later be domesticated and put to a variety of applications, and new *kanji* can be coined that are utterly unknown in China itself (such as Japan's *kokuji* and Vietnam's *nom*). However, the imported *kanji* initially and fundamentally bring with them the vocabulary of Chinese higher civilization. The use of *kanji* throughout East Asia therefore creates an "empire of ideas," which simultaneously circulates and reinforces Chinese concepts and excludes other ideas or at least makes their expression difficult. For this reason, they are the most powerful glue that could possibly bind together East Asia: a shared and exclusive universe of written thought.

In early East Asia, it was not only Chinese graphs but also the classical Chinese written language itself that served as the nearly universal medium of written communication. However, this written Chinese language also often remained quite remote from everyday life, almost everywhere. In nineteenth-century Vietnam, "even in Hue palaces," classical Chinese "was the written language of government documents but it was not always much else."[110] Much the same could be said of the role of classical written Chinese in Korea and Japan as well. In fact, to only a relatively lesser extent, the same thing was true even in China itself, where the spoken and written forms of the language were often quite far from identical.

In the early Han dynasty in China, it has been calculated that there were fourteen distinct spoken language systems in use throughout the empire, descending from the various languages of the old warring states. In the sixth century, Yan Zhitui (531–591) observed that people in different parts of China had always spoken different languages.[111] The differences between these regional "dialects" ("dialects" is the conventional English translation, but the Chinese themselves more forthrightly call them simply *fangyan,* or "local speech") were bridged, albeit somewhat artificially and awkwardly, by the imposition of a single standard written language. Still, for ordinary daily purposes everywhere, including China, the spoken language is more convenient, more immediate, and far more pervasive than writing. Nearly everyone speaks more than they read or write.

Literacy in premodern East Asia was very much the prerogative only of the elite. However, the elite especially had to travel or communicate with distant regions. Much of this could be done in writing, but it was convenient also to be able to talk to people who were not from one's own narrow locality. To meet this need, a kind of standard spoken lingua franca, based on Central Plain norms, seems to have already existed in China from the late Zhou era.[112]

During the Southern dynasties in China, native southerners imitated the accents of the northern émigrés who set the high cultural tone of the exilic Southern dynasty court, and everywhere during this period, "correct pronunciation" became an expected attribute of membership in the elite. The rhyming dictionary *Qieyun,* which was completed in 601, "represented a standard of correct speech common to the educated classes of north and south China in the sixth century."[113] It may safely be concluded that, while the formal written language may have been somewhat distinct from ordinary speech and accorded somewhat higher formal status, the traditional Chinese were scarcely any less concerned with oral communication than westerners have been with our alphabetic writing systems. When the Japanese began to study the Chinese language, they initially valued learning to speak Chinese properly in addition to reading and writing in *kanji*.

Like the ancient Greeks, the ancient Chinese "remained proudly monolingual." Few Chinese, local merchants aside, deigned to study the languages of foreigners. If the Japanese, for example, wished to communicate with the Chinese Son of Heaven, it would be helpful to cultivate a few Japanese people who could speak Chinese since Chinese officials certainly would not learn Japanese. As a Japanese edict acknowledged in 730, because customs are different in other lands, without interpreters it is difficult to conduct diplomacy. The Japanese court accordingly assigned several persons to study *kango*—that is, not *kanji*, or written Chinese, but specifically the spoken language of the Han dynasty (i.e., "Chinese").[114]

Somewhat earlier, in 691, the Japanese court had bestowed twenty taels of silver on two erudites of pronunciation from "Great Tang" and two erudites of writing from Paekche. Their benefits were sweetened by a grant of paddy land the next year. While Korean instructors might make superb intermediaries for teaching reading and writing in classical Chinese, for conversation only native Chinese speakers could pretend to convey the Tang court standard. By the eighth century, the Japanese system of administrative law contained detailed provisions for a Chinese-style court university, at which two erudites of pronunciation were to be appointed to supervise instruction in the correct oral readings of the Chinese classics. In 778, a Chinese official who had escorted the Japanese ambassador on his return to Japan was awarded a new Japanese name, employed as an erudite of pronunciation, and eventually ascended to the position of president of the university. From 794, within the Buddhist *sangha* in Japan, it became obligatory by imperial decree for yearly ordinands to recite the sutras in correct Chinese pronunciation.[115]

However, the extreme importance that was obviously attached to correct Chinese pronunciation may have been due as much to the conventional East Asian practice of reading aloud as it was to any desire to be able to communicate orally. The *Qieyun* in China, for example, represented a somewhat consciously artificial standard of pronunciation chiefly intended "as a guide to the recitation of literary texts."[116]

The early Japanese authorities were certainly interested in training at least a small number of Chinese speakers who could communicate face to face with representatives of "Great Tang." However, opportunities to practice speaking Chinese in ancient Japan were sharply limited, and linguistic contact was most commonly in writing. Literacy in Nara-Heian Japan may not have been very widespread, but it was undoubtedly far more common than fluency in spoken Chinese. In Heian Japan, "Chinese was not taught as a spoken language," and "by the end of the period for a Japanese to be able to speak in Chinese at all was cause for amazement." In general, early Japanese knowledge of continental civilization derived far more from the reading of classic texts than from personal firsthand exposure to contemporary Tang society.[117]

Premodern East Asia was, simultaneously, solidified as a region by its reliance on a single universal writing system and internally fractured by the persistence of many different spoken languages. This is another illustration of the pervasiveness of universal-local and elite-commoner polarities in traditional East Asia. Everywhere, literacy was a mark of elite status: "Literature," claimed a seventh-century Chinese historian, is what makes "the gentleman different from the common crowd." In the Chinese empire, mastery of writing characterized a "ruling elite whose members were separated from the common people . . . through the very words in which they expressed their thoughts or conversed with their fellows." Everywhere in traditional East Asia, a single universal writing system for the elite was opposed by a multiplicity of humble spoken tongues.[118]

By the seventh century, Joan Piggot argues that "book and writing brush" had displaced sword and armor "as insignia of royal rule" in the Japanese islands. This interpretation may give too much credence to an idealized, civilian and literary, imperial Japanese ideal, but perhaps the most striking point is that not very long before this time there had been no writing in Japan at all. The earliest evidence of purposeful writing in Japan that has been discovered to date is found on inscriptions, such as the 115 *kanji* on the famous fifth- or sixth-century Inariyama sword that was discovered in 1968 in Saitama Prefecture.[119]

The traditional claim that the *Analects* of Confucius was introduced from Paekche in 285 remains unproven and doubtful, at least as to the date. By the mid-fifth century, however, the Japanese court was reportedly very active in establishing offices relating to the keeping of written records, and occupational groups of scribes appear amid the immigrant Korean communities living in the Japanese islands. Indeed, such advanced continental technologies as writing were long associated with distinctly immigrant communities in Japan. Patriotic modern Korean scholars even claim to be able to detect evidence of the old Paekche language in the Japanese Inariyama sword inscription. Whether this is the case or not, literacy in Japan certainly long remained the specialized preserve of continental immigrants.[120]

The codes of administrative law that were drafted beginning in the late seventh and eighth centuries contained detailed provisions for the establishment of an educational system in Japan, and, although qualified instructors remained scarce outside the capital, a Chinese-style curriculum was planted in the archipelago. Texts in classical Chinese began to accumulate, and by the end of the ninth century, a good proportion of the entire existing Chinese oeuvre was available at least somewhere in Japan.[121] Since few people could read, however, this served only to further elevate elite participants in the universal East Asian high civilization above the humble representatives of local popular culture.

Yet every literate member of the elite also had roots in some particular local culture. In Japan, the introduction of *kanji* and Chinese texts involved "the imposition as well of an alien mode of thought, at once powerfully acculturating and uncongenial, upon native Japanese patterns of thought and expression." It has been argued that although the outward trappings of continental civilization found ready acceptance in early Japan, the deeper meaning of the Chinese scriptural heritage was poorly grasped; the Japanese school system, with its Chinese texts and examinations, "remained fundamentally alien," and despite their extensive use of *kanji,* the early Japanese "showed little sign of thinking in Chinese at all."[122]

Or, so concludes David Pollack, although the specific example he adduces of not "thinking in Chinese"—the notorious seventh-century letter to the emperor of China addressed "from the Son of Heaven in the land where the sun rises"—on closer examination appears more ambiguous. While, on the one hand, it may indeed suggest a fundamental failure to grasp the basic Chinese conceit that there can be only one legitimate Son of Heaven on earth at any given time, on the other hand it also represents an ambitious attempt to apply the Chinese conceptual model to Japan and portray Japan in thoroughly Chinese terms.

In any case, as inconvenient as it undoubtedly was for the premodern Japanese to learn the classical Chinese language, it was presumably no more awkward or alien for them than being expected to learn English today. The trouble with any international language is that, for many people, it must also be a foreign language.

Most early "native" Japanese texts were recorded in the classical Chinese language, but the *Shoku Nihongi,* an official history of the Japanese court for the years 697 to 791, also contains the texts of sixty-two imperial oral proclamations, known as *semmyō,* that are recorded in somewhat cumbersomely transcribed Japanese. These illustrate the multiple personalities of a still largely oral Japanese culture, "where the spoken word was believed to have magic properties," that we must unfortunately now try to recover today almost solely from classical Chinese language texts.[123]

Far sooner, or at least more extensively, than either the Koreans or the Vietnamese, however, as far as we can determine from surviving texts, the Japanese began adapting *kanji* to the needs of writing their own distinctive spoken language. Because spoken Chinese and Japanese are not only different languages but "almost exactly antithetical in their phonological, morphological, and syntactic systems," *kanji* were not easily suited to the task of transcribing Japanese; one consequence of the tortuousness of this hybridization between Chinese *kanji* and the spoken Japanese language is that, in the opinion of many, "written Japanese still has the dubious distinction of being the most complicated system of writing in use in the modern world."[124]

The fifth- or sixth-century Inariyama sword inscription already employed *kanji* both semantically, reflecting their original Chinese meanings, and phonetically, to transcribe domestic Japanese words. Another early inscription, the Yamanoue monument in Takasaki, Gumma Prefecture, dated 681, reversed the natural Chinese grammatical word order *wei mu* ("for mother") to represent the native Japanese *haha no tame ni* ("mother for"). Ironically enough, as we have seen, immigrant Korean scribes were deeply involved in creating these early "native" Japanese-style readings of *kanji.*[125]

Hybrid forms of writing combining various balances of Chinese and Japanese elements had begun to appear as early as the late sixth century, and by the ninth century the *kana* syllabaries had been devised, finally making it theoretically possible to transcribe the Japanese spoken language entirely phonetically, without the necessary mediation of either the classical Chinese language or *kanji*, although the first true book written in Japanese *kana* probably did not appear until the *Kokinshū* of 905, and even this still had a preface in Chinese.

Thereafter, especially in the tenth and eleventh centuries, the Heian court produced a burst of marvelous diaries and novels written exclusively in Japanese—the so-called woman's hand—that surely rank among the finest literary glories of the world. Even amid the greatest of these masterpieces of early Japanese literature, however, the Chinese influence was still not so far removed. The remarkable, and quite distinctively "Japanese," novel *The Tale of Genji* quotes Chinese texts, directly or indirectly, in 185 places. In "Japan the fall of [written classical] Chinese, which was the language of both Buddhism and Confucianism, and the disintegration of the communities it bound together, did not take place until the end of the nineteenth century." Until modern times at least, it was possible to imagine that China and Japan were still "countries that share a common literature."[126]

Everywhere in East Asia, ironically, the most ancient "native" records were mostly written in Chinese—making the primary sources for early Japanese, Korean, and Vietnamese history, paradoxically, relatively inaccessible to modern natives of those countries but transparent to scholars trained in classical Chinese. (As a further irony, most Chinese people today cannot read classical Chinese, either.) Because so many of the early Japanese documents were written in classical Chinese or at least in *kanji*, it becomes sometimes very difficult to retrospectively disentangle "native Japanese" from "imported Chinese" cultural elements. To some extent, the truth is that there never really was any one purely "native Japanese" tradition. "Japan" (like "China") was a mixture of various influences from the start. Perhaps the most arresting example of this is the standard modern Japanese name for Japan itself: Nihon.

The available evidence suggests that the Japanese court selected this name and began to consciously promote it sometime in the second half of the seventh century. Amino Yoshihiko even associates the invention of the new name with what he calls "the birth of 'Japan.'" However, this was a specifically written name, chosen for the meaning of its *kanji* ("origin of the Sun") rather than a name in the indigenous spoken Japanese language. In speech at home, the Japanese may have long continued to say Yamato rather than Nihon. The new *kanji* were selected because the older written term, Wa, was deemed insufficiently elegant. Whether the old name Wa had originated as the transcription of a word in the spoken Japanese language or had itself also been a Chinese *kanji* graft, the new name—the one that stuck and is still in use today—was not a "native" Japanese name at all but a *kanji* compound chosen for its intelligibility and agreeable meaning everywhere throughout the East Asian *kanji* sphere. The Japanese pronunciation Nihon is merely incidental.[127]

Kanji arrived in Japan from Korea, where they had already been in use for some time. Like Japanese, the Korean spoken language is radically different from the languages spoken in China. Indeed, Korean grammatically resembles Japanese rather more than it does Chinese. Originally, moreover, there does not seem to have been any single, uniform "Korean." The modern Korean language, which is spoken today with a reasonable degree of uniformity throughout the entire peninsula, derives in particular from the language of the early southeastern kingdom known as Silla.[128] Other early communities on the peninsula seem to have once spoken at least slightly different languages—different, that is, not only from "Chinese" and "Japanese" but from each other as well.

The *Samguk sagi,* for example, felt it necessary to translate for its twelfth-century Korean audience the word for "gate" used in the "Kaya language," which was presumably spoken among the six city-states of the old "Kaya League" that had once been located in the area of the lower Naktong River. A third-century Chinese account remarks explicitly that the language spoken in Chinhan, in the southeastern corner of the Korean peninsula, was "not the same" as the language spoken in Mahan, in the southwest.[129]

Once written records began to be kept, however, which in Paekche supposedly started in the mid-fourth century, there was no available alternative but for them to be recorded in *kanji*. Moreover, early Korean documents were written mainly not only in *kanji* but in the classical Chinese language as well. The surviving early Korean histories, for example, were written in Chinese, although one, the *Samguk yusa,* does include fourteen short poems that were laboriously transcribed, using *kanji,* in an archaic form of Korean vernacular.[130]

In A.D. 32, according to *Samguk sagi,* the six clans of what would eventually become the Sillan kingdom were each granted Chinese-style surnames. We may presume that this date is unreliable, but the event is noteworthy nonetheless. Although the use of patrilineal surnames (family names descending in the male line) in Korea remained inconsistent, even among royalty, throughout the Sillan era, which ended only in 935, it is striking that the Korean people have eventually come to be known by names that are not merely in the Chinese style but also, at least in writing, often almost indistinguishable from specifically Chinese names.[131]

The assumption of a name in the host language is an important first step in the process of assimilation. The Tuoba rulers of the Xianbei Northern Wei dynasty in northern China, for example, as part of their sometimes quite conscious Sinification program, adopted for themselves the Chinese-language surname Yuan. With Chinese-style names, it sometimes becomes possible for "foreigners" to submerge themselves and even entirely disappear into the Chinese-language historical record—to cease to obviously be "foreigners" altogether and become Chinese.

While it is not to be suggested that Koreans or Vietnamese ever became "Chinese" (quite the opposite, they became Koreans and Vietnamese—a process of "becoming" that remains endlessly ongoing), it is nonetheless an important contribution to the regional coherence of East Asia that, whether because of the spread of some original usage or because of conversion from some other alternative nomenclature, in the historical period most East Asians have been known by approximately similar Chinese-style names, written in *kanji*. The partial exception to this rule is Japan. Although they are to this day still invariably written in *kanji*, Japanese names are immediately distinct from all other East Asian names in both written and spoken form, as perhaps befits a culture on the margins of the traditional Chinese imperial *tianxia*.

In Korea, early leaders of what would eventually coalesce into the Sillan state had once been known by such indigenous Korean titles as *kŏsŏgan*, or "chief." After a reported twenty-two generations of use, however, in 503 all such native titles were discarded in favor of the imported Chinese title *wang*, or "king." At the same time, the *kanji* transcription of the name "Silla" was also permanently settled. "Because of successive changes over time," the *Samguk sagi* reports that the official titles of the mature Sillan state eventually became "a mixture of Tang [Chinese] and native."[132]

"These Sinifications were not merely terminological changes but

reflected Silla's readiness to accept China's advanced political institutions."[133] Korea's subsequent historical development was to be extensively informed by the imported Chinese repertoire of ideas.

As in Japan, an attempt was made in Korea to adapt *kanji* to the
purpose of writing the native Korean language, in a style of writing
that came to be known as *idu,* beginning as early as the fifth century.
By the fifteenth century, the unique and eminently practical *hangŭl*
alphabet had also been devised. Thereafter, it was entirely possible to
write Korean without recourse to either the Chinese language or *kanji.*
However, the prestige of *kanji* remained high, and, unlike in Japan,
where the native and imported Sino-Japanese languages were able to
coexist in *kanji* representation relatively separately and distinctly, "in
Korea, borrowed Chinese vocabulary simply drove the indigenous
words out, impoverishing the language's native component." When
written in *kanji,* the distinction between Chinese and Korean tended
to blur altogether. Even when they are not written in *kanji* (and in the
twentieth century both the Koreans and the Vietnamese have almost
completely abandoned the everyday use of *kanji*), the ghosts of those
imported Chinese words still haunt the modern native languages, not
unlike the verbal legacy of Greek and Latin in the West. An estimated
30 to 60 percent of each of the modern Japanese, Korean, and Vietnamese lexicons consists of "borrowed Chinese vocabulary."[134]

The permeation of Chinese vocabulary throughout East Asia
can alternatively be interpreted as either blighting or enriching "native" culture. Nationalistic purists may be discomfited, but the spread
of Chinese words and ideas unmistakably played a role in the original
creation of the various modern "national" cultures that now exist in
East Asia, and more than any other single factor it is this common vocabulary pool—a shared universe of expression—that gives coherence to the region. The remarkable longevity of East Asian and Chinese civilization was rooted in the universal elite study of a common
body of classical literature, written in *kanji.* If the Chinese empire "became an empire of writing," which "vanished only when the texts that
defined it ceased to command the hearts of men," this empire of the
written word extended also to wherever the Chinese classics were
deeply revered, that is, to all of East Asia.[135]

Literacy in elegant classical Chinese was indispensable to the successful conduct of diplomacy in premodern East Asia. Rulers of marginal states found it necessary in order to find their place under the

East Asian sun, to reach some accommodation with *kanji* literature. Shi Le (274–333), for example, was a warlike Xiongnu ruler who conquered much of northern China in the early fourth century under the so-called Later Zhao dynasty (319–351). Although he was personally illiterate, he established a system of examinations over the Confucian classics and reportedly commanded to be read aloud to while on campaign. Helian Bobo (d. 425) was a northwestern Xiongnu emperor who "stressed steppe traditions" and whose government "was self-consciously tribal and rejected Chinese forms of administration." Yet even he tried to impress a Southern dynasty Chinese ruler with his feigned literary skill, commanding an assistant to the imperial secretary to draft a document, secretly memorizing it, and then publicly dictating it as though it were an impromptu reply.[136]

However, while China's East Asian neighbors were incorporated into the *kanji* sphere because no alternative writing system was known to them, the empire's western neighbors were exposed to other kinds of literature, in other writing systems. In sixth-century Turfan, for example, it was reported that both *kanji* and the "Western barbarian script" were simultaneously in circulation and that, although the inhabitants studied the Chinese classics, they invariably read them in the "Western barbarian language." At Dunhuang, in what is now China's Gansu Province, ancient documents have been uncovered written in "Sanskrit, Khotanese, Sogdian, Uighur, and the earliest known examples of Tibetan" as well as in Chinese.[137] A plethora of languages thrived to the west of China, and, from the beginning, these people had alternative scripts to chose from. It was only in East Asia—in China, Japan, Korea, and Vietnam—that *kanji* and the classical Chinese language became the dominant form of writing.

Within premodern East Asia there was a transparency of literary discourse, in *kanji*. Words and ideas were shared and relatively easily intelligible. Beyond China's western frontier, however, communication was occluded. The ideas of Indian Buddhism, for example, were digested only with very great difficulty in East Asia, in part because of the immense linguistic barrier.

Kanji do not readily lend themselves to the expression of foreign words and ideas, partly because they themselves already are Chinese words and ideas. However, even an alphabet can only indicate the sound of a foreign word. How do you communicate foreign ideas? The Chinese Buddhist Seng You (435–518) had an almost Platonic faith that the barriers presented by different scripts and languages could be overcome. They were, in his optimistic view, merely inter-changeable devices for transmitting universal principles—"the strokes of the writing are truly different, but the principles that are passed on are the same."[138] However, it is not really so evident that principles and ideas have any existence independent of the language in which they are expressed.

Even the supremely gifted translator Kumārajīva (344–413)—who was born in Kuchā in modern Xinjiang Province to an Indian fa-ther and a local mother and who spent some years in Kashmir as a child becoming "conversant with the local speeches of both east and west" and who could furthermore rely on the services of an almost equally brilliant Chinese disciple to do the actual writing and settle the Chinese terminology—still complained that too much was lost in translating Indian texts into Chinese, "although we may get the main idea." Serious errors (or changes) often crept into the translation of Buddhist texts from the Indian languages into Chinese.[139]

Once Buddhism became popular in China, the Chinese ex-pended truly stupendous efforts, both publicly and privately, in trans-lating and studying the ideas of Indian Buddhism. Yet, in translating this Buddhist material into *kanji,* they could not avoid imbuing it with Chinese ideas.[140] Buddhism in China was accordingly Sinified by the constraints of the Chinese language itself—transformed by the very process of translation. Buddhism then spread to the rest of East Asia in the Chinese-language version, further cementing the solidarity of the region. *Kanji,* in traditional East Asia, thus illuminated the entire region, made it conceptually rather uniform at elite levels, and facili-tated internal communication but cast the world beyond the civilized *kanji* circle into nearly impenetrable darkness.

FOUR

Beyond East Asia

GLOBAL CONNECTIONS

FOREIGN TRADE

East Asia took shape around the multidimensional theme and variations of the ancient Central Plain prototype civilization as it played off against a variety of local cultures both within and beyond the present-day borders of the People's Republic of China. Other forces also contributed to this regional integration while at the same time threatening to upset the ponderous harmony of *tianxia* by introducing new external influences. East Asia did not and could not exist in isolation, even in this early period.

Buddhism, for example, was an Indian religion that swept through East Asia and contributed significantly to its early formation. East Asia would have been unrecognizably different without this Buddhist leavening. However, Buddhism was also an intrusion from beyond. In nearby Southeast Asia, during this same time period, Buddhism figured in the vanguard of a remarkable wave of so-called Indianization. In East Asia, the degree of Indianization that accompanied the spread of Buddhism was much more attenuated, but the introduction of Indian motifs certainly does complicate any simplistic picture of the genesis of East Asia based on the model of Sinification (to say nothing of pristine nativism).

If Indian Buddhism became the characteristic higher religion of East Asia, international trade was essential to the circulation of both material commodities and ideas, including those of Buddhism. Commercial contacts aided the spread of Buddhism and promoted other features of a shared East Asian community. Though largely beneath the notice of the traditional East Asian elite and openly disdained by

both Legalist and Confucian value systems, commerce in early imperial China was already surprisingly exuberant and vital to imperial
prosperity. This much-neglected business community underwrote the
dynamism of a region whose economy was already in the process of becoming the most developed on earth. Yet the mobility of these anonymous merchants, across political and cultural frontiers, was also always at least potentially subversive to the closed and stable East Asian
world order.

The early empire in China, from the Qin and Han dynasties until the late Tang, always anticipated a quite active role for government
in managing the economy. Not only was it viewed as the government's
particular responsibility to regulate the market and stabilize prices,
but merchants were consciously assigned a place at the bottom in the
Confucian social order and often burdened with intentionally heavy
taxes and sumptuary restrictions. The Tang ban of 667 on artisans
and merchants riding horses is a typical example. It essentially reiter-
ates previous ordinances dating from as early as 199 B.C.[1]

This restrictive approach to commerce was rooted in a fear that
the greater ease and profitability of trade would lure farmers out of agriculture, unless they were artificially restrained, and in a simplistic cal-
culation that "for each person who did not cultivate someone would
go hungry." The fundamental vision was of a bureaucratically guided
agrarian empire, consisting of vast numbers of self-sufficient, roughly
equal farm families, in which commerce was a peripheral if not wholly
unwelcome activity.[2] As one Sillan (Korean) king expressed the elite
aversion to commerce in 834, trade encouraged "the people to com-
pete in extravagance, and only esteem the rarity of foreign things,
disdaining the rusticity of local products. The *li* frequently are lost
amid pretension, and customs decay."[3] In the traditional East Asian
ideal, agriculture was valued over trade, and frugality—even noble
poverty—was considered a virtue.

The Tang government established rigorous border-control restrictions. Although systems of border passes had been in use from
early Han times and had clear pre-Qin antecedents, they reached a
new peak of rigor under the Tang dynasty (and served as a model for
contemporary Japanese imperial practice). Commerce was strictly
regulated by Tang officials. In 851, for example, an officer was required to be assigned to supervise the markets of all districts having
3,000 or more households. By one estimate, in the mid-eighth century

there was an official for every twenty-one or twenty-two households in the entire Tang empire. In what may be a kind of ultimate display of imperial ambition to intervene in private affairs, an edict of 627 commanded local officials to facilitate the marriage of all men between the ages of twenty and sixty to all unmarried women of fifteen to fifty years of age and compel wealthy neighbors or relatives to fund those who were too poor to conduct the marriages by themselves.[4]

This same basic imperial vision was replicated everywhere in East Asia. In 144, in the little Korean statelet that would later come to be known as Silla (recall that the name "Silla" was not finally settled on until 503), a directive was handed down affirming that "farming is the foundation of government" and urging local officials to complete embankments and open new fields. The use of gold, silver, and other valuables among the people was specifically forbidden. In 489, the Sillan court attempted to force its vagrant subjects "back to farming." Since some limited trade was obviously potentially beneficial, Silla attempted to duplicate the Chinese imperial model for regulating commercial exchange, opening a market in 490 in the capital for the first time "to circulate the commodities of the four quarters." In 505, the Sillan court established regulations for shipping (and also first commanded officials to store away winter ice for use in summer), and in 509, Silla established another, eastern market at the capital.[5]

The same types of policies were also adopted by the other Korean statelets. In 510, for example, in response to incessant fighting with Koguryŏ and the nearby Malgal, the king of Paekche issued orders to drive the internal and external vagrant population "back to farming."[6]

In Japan as well, the imported vision of a bureaucratic agrarian empire of self-sufficient farm villages became deeply rooted. In Japan, however, the problem initially was not so much to restrain commerce as to promote just a little bit of it. Coins, supposedly having magical efficacy, are known to have been minted in Japan from the late seventh century, but the issue of 708 remains something of a true beginning for a money-based economy in Japan.[7] Even then, the court still had to explain and encourage the use of these coins:

> Now, the usefulness of money is to circulate wealth, and exchange what you have for what you do not have. At the present time the common people are still confused in their practices, and do not yet understand this principle.[8]

Outside the capital area, rice sheaves rather than money continued to be extensively employed in barter, and in the ninth century there was even something of a reversion to commodity exchange because of inflation and other problems. In 958, the Japanese government minted its final issue of coins, after which time the needs of Japanese business had to be met chiefly by copper cash imported from China.[9]

A major difference between early historical Japan and contemporary China or even Korea was Japan's relative "economic backwardness." This is, perhaps, somewhat exaggerated by the "agricultural fundamentalism" of the Chinese-style official record, which obscures much of the petty commerce and occupational diversity that really did exist. A rare opportunity to peek behind the facade presented by the official, Chinese-style court histories is afforded us by "the earliest collection of Buddhist legends in Japan," the *Nihon ryōiki*, compiled around the year 800, which suggestively depicts rather more small-scale business activity than one might expect from the dawn of Japanese history. Still, early Japan could not begin to match continental levels of commercial development. "In a period when the wealthiest consumers were officials, when most trade goods were tax items, and when markets and transport were mainly government-sponsored, the most prominent merchants . . . were subordinate officials."[10]

As relatively underdeveloped as Japan's early economy certainly was, however, it is of particular interest that early Japan was at the same time much more of a maritime society than the Central Plain Chinese core civilization had ever been. This was an obvious consequence of Japan's insular geography and may also be related to prehistoric cultural influences from the Yue regions of what is now southern China. One of the most persistent Chinese stereotypes of the Yue peoples was that they were aquatic in orientation and "at ease in boats." The memory of these ancient Japanese maritime traditions has to some extent been buried under the weight of the imported Chinese model of an agrarian village empire, but it may be significant that the oldest collection of Japanese-language poetry, the eighth-century *Manyōshū*, contains "hosts of sea poets, such as are encountered nowhere else in Japanese literature."[11]

The earliest surviving written Chinese account of prehistoric Japan, recorded in the third century, observed that residents of the small islands in the straits between the Korean peninsula and the Japanese archipelago "ride boats north and south to trade for grain." Farther south, archaeological evidence now attests to a maritime trade in tropical shells with the Ryūkyū Islands, which flourished well before the third century. Illustrations in late prehistoric Japanese tombs depict vessels capable of oceanic travel and of carrying as many as fifty people. As Gari Ledyard suggests, the cultures of the Japanese islands in the third century were probably closely linked to, and little different from, those on the southern coast of what is now Korea. This "was essentially an area connected by water, not by land, and one of the most common scenes must have been people going back and forth in their boats."[12]

Contact between the mainland and the Japanese seaboard was surely achieved by local initiative long before the Japanese islands were consolidated into anything resembling a single Yamato state. Indeed, the rise of centralized political authority in Japan, in the period from the late fifth through the early seventh century, owed much to the court's ability to bring under its control and regulate this longstanding contact with the continent and to monopolize the distribution of foreign prestige goods. In 553, for example, the court supposedly appointed an official, of evidently Korean extraction, "to count and record the shipping taxes."[13]

From the imperial-bureaucratic perspective, regulating foreign trade was a greater priority than promoting it. Political control was all-important. However, even at the height of Chinese-style imperial regulatory effectiveness in Japan in the eighth century, it is evident that there was still a fair amount of economic activity outside the officially sanctioned parameters. These official controls became increasingly difficult to enforce. "The official market system was already in trouble by 835." Its eventual collapse, rather than resulting in a disintegration of business activity, was instead "accompanied by an expansion of commerce."[14]

This included an expansion of private trade with the continent after the eighth century. An official Japanese report, dated 842, observed that since the time of Emperor Shōmu (r. 724–749), Sillans had been slipping privately into Japan as traders without following the established procedure for tribute missions. The mid-eighth century seems to have been a turning point in the rise of unregulated private foreign trade with Japan. One indication of an evolving reorientation away from enforced official tribute embassies toward more private commercial exchange may be found in the court's award to top officials in 768 of half a million bolts of cloth for the purpose of individually purchasing Sillan trade goods. Although the full extent of private trade cannot possibly be measured now, one scholar has counted over thirty known private commercial ventures to Japan in the late Tang period alone.[15]

Early Japan's attempted official monopolization of all foreign contact, in other words, broke down. However, evasion of official regulation had been a constant since the beginning of the imperial system in China, perhaps even more so than in Japan. Adversarial relations between official state interests and those of at least some of its citizens were the norm everywhere.

In the early Han dynasty, for example, it was reported that people in the Ba-shu region of modern Sichuan Province slipped out past the borders to trade illegally with Yunnan tribesmen for horses, servants, and cattle—causing the region of Sichuan to become "wealthy" even as they subverted the official program. A millennium later, in the tenth century, an attempt to impose a government monopoly on fine silk in approximately this same region provoked "a large-scale rebellion." During the Tang dynasty there were three official salt-distilling stations in one section of coastal Guangdong, but locals nonetheless reportedly could not be prevented from illegally distilling their own salt. Even an imperfect application of the imperial regulatory apparatus required constant vigilance and the expenditure of considerable effort. It was always easier to simply let things slide.[16]

The strength of the Chinese imperial government had been based, in the first place, on the Warring States model of the mobilization of the entire population through the device of household registration. During the early Tang dynasty, the central government actively intervened in village life to the remarkable extent of actively allocating farmland to individuals. Yet, even as conceived, this Tang land system allowed for a great deal of elasticity in response to varying local conditions, and the program was at best imperfectly implemented. From the beginning of the dynasty, large numbers of persons seem to have successfully evaded household registration altogether, and an "unbelievably high proportion" of those who were registered turned out to be women, who were conveniently largely tax exempt. It is estimated that of the total registered population as of 754, an incredible 86 percent had managed to achieve some degree of tax-exempt status. Following a disastrous rebellion that began the next year, in 755, the system disintegrated almost entirely.[17]

There is an eternal contradiction between the official goal of government supervision and private frustration with and a desire to evade those regulations. However, some such tension between official and private interests is probably in everyone's higher interest. Too much government restriction of trade can dampen economic vitality; too little regulation may invite abuse. The proper balance is difficult to discern and even harder to achieve. The abrogation of imperial monopolies on the production of salt and iron, relaxation of restrictions on land use, and insistence that taxes be paid in cash, for example, arguably spurred the growth of private trade during the early Han dynasty.[18] On the other hand, it has also been argued that the power of the early Han state, especially under Emperor Wu (r. 140–86 B.C.), strangled and inhibited the development of a private commercial economy in China.[19]

It is important not to allow our evaluation of the early imperial Chinese economy to be too greatly overshadowed by our present-day knowledge that China never spontaneously generated a modern mechanized industrial revolution. Elite disdain for business may have contributed to this more recent negative outcome, but, except perhaps in extreme cases, the Chinese imperial intention was not so much to completely suppress trade as it was simply to subordinate it to "public" interests and maintain the proper social hierarchy. We are concerned here with a period that was still quite remote from the modern era in Europe as well as in East Asia. For its time, the early imperial Chinese economy was highly commercialized—perhaps less so than the Roman empire at its peak but certainly more so than Europe during the Middle Ages.[20]

In the early Han dynasty, Sima Qian (145–86 B.C.) had already argued that "the highest type of ruler accepts the nature of the people . . . and the very worst kind enters into competition with them." If only, Sima wrote, each person was simply allowed "to utilize his own abilities and exert his strength to obtain what he wishes," the economy would naturally prosper without any need for "government directives."[21] Sima Qian thus consciously anticipated what might even be described as a kind of laissez-faire approach toward the imperial economy.

Over the 2,000 years of the empire in China, in general, commerce thrived beneath the level of (much) official notice. Confucian moral admonitions against "selfish profit" were directly more toward the elite official class and its aspirants than toward commoner merchants, who were fully expected to be driven by their base commercial instincts.[22] To be sure, these commoner merchants were not supposed to become so rich and powerful that they could become political forces in their own right, destabilizing the sociopolitical structure, but this danger was perhaps most likely to be realized when officials joined the petty scramble for profit and exploited their political power for personal financial gain.

This scenario was played out at times and always spelled corruption. Civil and military officials of the Southern dynasties, for example, were exempt from pass and market taxes in the years prior to 583, giving them a decided commercial advantage over ordinary private merchants. Although the rescission of these privileges is portrayed in the traditional sources as an act of imperial greed intended to increase state tax revenue and as having been met with popular outrage, in all likelihood it was mainly those with official status, whose lucrative commercial sidelines were thus infringed on, who were particularly enraged.[23] In addition to its general efforts at economic management, the empire was particularly concerned to issue prohibitions, such as that of 779, against officials engaging in trade and "competing for profit with the people."[24] The struggle for business wealth was the proper business only of lowly commoners, not members of the elite.

There is no question that imperial prejudice favored agriculture over trade. Commerce was sometimes blatantly shackled by imperial regulations. Yet it is also clear that even in Qin times, there was already a reasonably flourishing petty commercial economy. This commercial base grew, if not steadily at least cumulatively, across successive dynasties, culminating shortly after the period covered in this book with the famous Song dynasty (960–1279) economic "revolution." These business activities were entirely premodern in form and no doubt mostly small-scale local transactions—although Sima Qian, in the early Han dynasty, did speak of great merchants who acquired so much wealth that they became almost the equivalent of an untitled nobility.[25]

Of particular interest here is not only the development of commerce in early East Asia but also trade that crosses political or cultural frontiers, linking together the various countries of East Asia and connecting them with even wider worlds. The late Zhou-era Warring States had all traded with one another, which undoubtedly facilitated their eventual integration into a single imperial *tianxia*. From still farther away, glass beads of evidently Mediterranean provenance have been found in east-central China dating from as early as the late Spring and Autumn era and indicating at least some level of long-distance exchange.[26]

Transcontinental trade must have traveled mostly overland initially, along what became the renowned "Silk Roads" of central Asia. Silk, literally, was an important early Chinese export. Although domestic production of silk had already begun in India, Sassanid Persia, and Byzantium by the fourth and fifth centuries, the volume of Chinese silk transported to India remained large and may even have increased in subsequent centuries.[27]

Maritime trade probably remained subordinate in volume and importance to overland trade throughout the lengthy period of the Han dynasty. Early contact between China and India and the initial transmission of Buddhism to China were undoubtedly achieved principally by Silk Road camel caravans. However, overland trade gradually came to be rivaled by seaborne commerce. The *Dynastic History of the Former Han* already tells of a certain chief of interpreters, in the early Han dynasty, who raised a crew and ventured out to sea to market precious goods, transshipped in barbarian merchantmen, and traded profitably (and killed and plundered) for several years before the survivors of his expedition finally returned to Han. Coming the other way, the sea-lanes between Egypt and India had been opened by approximately 120 B.C. By the second century A.D., "one more or less continuous commercial network" stretched from the coasts of Africa to southern China.[28]

The collapse of the Han dynasty and the protracted period of imperial weakness and division that followed from the third century until the sixth are then commonly assumed to have been accompanied by a retreat to a more subsistence-level agricultural economy. In fact, however, interstate rivalry and the monopolization of the central Asian caravan trade routes by dynasties situated in the north stimulated Southern dynasty Chinese to pursue the development of alternative maritime routes instead. "When the Jin [imperial] family [whose surname was Sima] moved south [in 317], they were separated from the Yellow River and the northwest, Rong and Yi [barbarians] blocked the road, and the outer regions were cut off by Heaven . . . . But the supply of commercial goods sometimes came from Jiao

[Chinese-administered Vietnam], floating over the sea and crossing the waves, following the wind to arrive from far away."[29]

These new maritime routes had, moreover, the potential to carry much greater volumes of trade more economically than the old overland Silk Roads. One third-century Chinese text speaks already of large ships, over 200 feet in length, capable of carrying 600 or 700 persons and 5,000 bushels of cargo. Especially after environmental changes in the fourth century caused the prolonged disappearance of the Lop Nor oasis, making caravan trade across the Tarim basin substantially more arduous than previously, South Sea maritime traffic must have increasingly rivaled that along the Silk Roads.[30]

It is true that there was a noticeable decline in the number of official tribute embassies coming by sea during the period of imperial division. This is only to be expected given the political and military weakness of the Southern dynasties. Since traditional East Asian historians rarely condescended to notice private commerce, tribute missions are often the only form of nautical traffic for which we have any documentation. It would be a mistake, however, to leap from this to an assumption that the recorded number of tribute missions can necessarily be taken as reliable indicator of the total volume of shipping. There is, instead, reason to suspect that private overseas trade through southern ports grew fairly steadily during the period of imperial division.[31]

One indirect measure of a fairly substantial maritime traffic during this period is provided by the quite large number of foreign Buddhist monks who are known to have come to China by sea, often specifically on merchantmen, from western regions during the period of division. By the early third century, "more Buddhist activity" has been observed in the southern, maritime-oriented Chinese kingdom of Wu than in northern, Silk Road–oriented Wei.[32] It is often only in passing, in such tangentially related Buddhist religious contexts, that these humble merchant ships are mentioned at all in traditional Chinese textual sources. However, they nonetheless may have collectively been of great significance to Chinese society.

Another indication of a flourishing, if seldom mentioned, maritime commercial economy is the extent to which officials were notoriously often tempted by the opportunities for illicit gain provided by service in the great port cities of Jiaozhou (approximately the site of modern Hanoi) and Guangzhou (Canton), even during times when recorded tribute embassies were especially scarce. An "old saying," recorded in the fifth century, explained that in Guangzhou there was a "spring of avarice," drinking from which caused gentlemen to lose their incorruptibility.[33]

Periods of internal disruption within the empire, paradoxically enough, often coincided with bursts of especially active development of coastal and frontier regions, perhaps because of the arrival of many displaced persons in those regions. The very breakdown of official market regulations during the Southern dynasties may be in part a reflection of their unbridled commercial exuberance. Despite our easy tendency to view the interregnum between the great, unified imperial dynasties of Han and Sui-Tang simply as a time of collapse, it has long been recognized that commerce flourished in the south during the period of division. By the early sixth century, the population of the Southern dynasty capital, at modern Nanjing (Nanking), has been estimated to have reached 1.4 million. Such a huge urban population entailed considerable economic vigor.[34]

The commercial success of the Southern dynasties is yet another example of the adversarial relationship we have already noted between public administration and private profit seeking. A strong state may be able to successfully impose unwelcome restrictions on the activities of merchants, and, conversely, a haplessly ineffective imperial court may coincide with private commercial prosperity. The distinguished Japanese historian Kawakatsu Yoshio has even gone so far as to speculate that the money-based private commercial prosperity of the late Southern dynasties may actually have exceeded that of the subsequent unified Sui and early Tang dynasties, despite the insistent modern Chinese tendency to believe that only Sui-Tang unity could be glorious.[35]

In 610, the Sui dynasty sent a military expedition to an island, tentatively identified as the one we now call Taiwan. When the local islanders "first saw the warships they took them for travelling merchants, often going amidst the army to trade."[36] This is testimony to the extent that merchantmen must have been familiar sights in the waters off the coast of China. It was invasion fleets that were a Sui novelty.

The restoration of imperial unity under the Sui and Tang dynasties represented a dramatic reassertion of Chinese imperial military and political power and effective bureaucratic surveillance of the economy. To the extent that government regulation is inimical to commerce, this may have put a damper on business activity. However, the Tang dynasty is also well known to have been a period of prosperity.

In 626, the Tang emperor Taizong made the grand gesture of lifting many of the barrier taxes and prohibitions so that "public and private," "Chinese and foreigner," could come and go without obstruction on the roads. Another one of our incidental mentions of trade in an unrelated Buddhist context describes the harbor at Guangzhou in the mid-eighth century as being filled with "unknown numbers of Indian, Persian, South Sea and other boats, laden with incense, drugs and precious things piled up like mountains." In 879, toward the end of the Tang dynasty, a certain vice director of the Department of State Affairs acknowledged that "profits from the South Sea trade" were vital to dynastic survival. Although documentation is admittedly scanty, all the available evidence suggests fairly unmistakably that the empire's maritime trade began to accelerate (unevenly) from about the fourth century to the end of the period covered in this book.[37]

At the same time, the Tang dynasty did reassert government controls. Anyone traveling beyond his or her place of registration, whether on business or for any other purpose, was required to carry an official travel permit. Systems of passports and travel documents, as well as barrier passes intended both as checkpoints and for the collection of tariffs, were erected both at the borders of states and internally, beginning as early as the Warring States period in China. No doubt their effectiveness fluctuated in accordance with the strength of the various political regimes. The enormous difficulty that the Japanese pilgrim Ennin (794–864) experienced in attempting to travel in China without official permission in 838–839 demonstrates, however, that these regulations were enforced reasonably efficiently under the Tang, even toward the end of the dynasty during a period of relative imperial weakness.[38]

Early Tang efforts to seal the border were directed primarily at the strategically vulnerable northwestern land frontier. There, the export of sensitive commodities was banned and the border strictly monitored "to separate Chinese and barbarian." In 743, it was even determined that, although cross-border trade had been tacitly permitted for a long time, it was "really not safe and convenient. From now on it is entirely prohibited."[39] Total interdiction of private trade across the northwestern frontier was thus prescribed. Internal trade, however, and maritime trade along the eastern coast posed less of a perceived threat to the dynasty and was interfered with less. Even in the northwest, a degree of almost willful self-deception about who were Tang citizens and what constituted an official tribute embassy may have ensured that some level of foreign trade was usually maintained despite the sometimes draconian legal restrictions.

This type of interference with international trade for political reasons was hardly unprecedented, however, or unique to China. The Roman empire, for example, also closely monitored strategically sensitive transactions with its neighbors: "The Romans defended their frontiers not only with legions and fortresses but also with trade bans and the prohibition of exports of goods of military value."[40] Some such conflict of interests between governments and private merchants is simply normal.

The Chinese empire had a long history of deliberately limiting foreign trade in order to advance its political agendas—of putting politics ahead of profits. During the period of her regency between 188 and 180 B.C., for example, the Han dowager empress Lü had forbidden the export of metal farm implements and of female livestock for breeding purposes to the southeastern barbarians. The policy backfired this time, however, because it induced the king of Southern Yue, based at Guangzhou (Canton), to form allegiances with the other Yue principalities of the southeast, arrogate to himself the prerogatives of a Chinese-style empire ("like the Middle Kingdom"), and attack Changsha (in modern Hunan Province). A Han imperial punitive expedition had to be aborted because of the insalubrious tropical southern climate, and Empress Lü's successor was forced to appease the king of Southern Yue by sponsoring sacrifices at his family tomb (located in the north in modern Hebei Province, near Beijing) and by lavishing honors on the king's relatives who had remained there in the north.[41]

The policy of manipulating foreign trade for diplomatic purposes failed that time, but on another occasion it reportedly worked splendidly. Toward the end of the third century, the southernmost Chinese administration, in what is now northern Vietnam, was troubled by so-called southern bandits (possibly Chams). The regional inspector proposed that since "the southern coast depends upon our salt and iron, if you cut them off and do not trade with them, it will ruin all of their agricultural implements. If you continue this for two years, you can destroy them with one battle." According to the Chinese historical record at least, this plan worked perfectly.[42]

The Chinese imperial lack of enthusiasm for foreign trade and its tendency to view commerce as a concession benefiting foreigners more than it did the Middle Kingdom was to some extent a self-fulfilling prophecy. It meant that, in practice, the conduct of early imperial China's foreign trade tended to be very much in the hands of foreigners. This, in turn, limited the empire's ability to project its influence abroad and simultaneously made the empire vulnerable to whatever outside influences might be introduced by these foreign merchants.

Overland trade, for example, seems to have been dominated by central Asians, and the late Tang court was troubled by the indebtedness of some of its leading families to Uighur moneylenders. Ironically, however, when it was proposed to alleviate a fiscal shortfall in 880 by confiscating half the property of "wealthy households and Hu [northwestern barbarian] merchants," Gao Pian (d. 887) successfully dissuaded the court from doing so by pointing out that the empire was already swarming with bandits who had been driven to that extreme by adverse economic conditions and that only the wealthy households and Hu merchants were still dependably loyal. A person of central Asian ancestry who profited from trade in Tang China might well feel a deeper commitment to Tang dynastic survival than a starving "Chinese" peasant.[43]

By the end of the fourth century, China's maritime trade with the South Seas and India was already well established, but the sailors who plied these waters were mostly so-called Kunluns rather than Chinese subjects. Kunlun was a generic term used in Chinese-language texts of this period to refer to the inhabitants of what is now called Southeast Asia. The Chinese viewed the Kunluns with some disdain—one report had them "living by plunder and fond of cannibalism"—but they must have reaped many of the benefits of China's lucrative South Sea trade.[44]

Kunlun merchants were joined by an indeterminable number of Indians. One Buddhist text specifically mentions five large Indian merchant vessels penetrating well up the Yangzi River, above Lake Dongting, in the early fifth century. By mid-Tang times, Persians and Arabs had also become prominent in the China trade—direct maritime contact with the Abbasid caliphate dates from the late eighth century—and Sillan (Korean) ships in particular came to dominant northeastern Asian waters. The great Sillan merchant prince Chang Po-go (d. 846) is an example of the latter, but Chang also symbolizes, as a less-than-entirely loyal servant of both Tang and Sillan states alternately and a potent meddler in Korean royal politics, the uncontrollable matrix of piracy and mobile independent power that maritime trade permitted, illustrating why the open seas often seemed to pose more threat than opportunity to traditional East Asian governments.[45]

A number of Indians came to China both as merchants and as Buddhist missionaries. The two incentives were often commingled. The spread of the Buddhist religion to East Asia was facilitated by the arrival of Indian and central Asian monks, who often came in merchant vessels and whose proselytizing, in turn, created a need for certain ritual commodities, such as the so-called seven treasures (saptaratna), which could be obtained only from India or other distant places. The result was a religiously motivated trade in "holy things" across the South Seas during the fifth and sixth centuries, which probably exceeded the older secular elite demand for luxury products in volume.[46]

The intermingling of the two themes of Buddhism and business is exemplified in the career of Kang Senghui ("the Kang, or central Asian, monk Hui," d. 280). His family was originally from Samarkand but reportedly had lived for generations in India proper. Kang Senghui's parents eventually moved to the great southern imperial port near what is now Hanoi "on business." Both his parents soon died, and the orphaned child became a monk, moving north to the capital of Three Kingdoms Wu (modern Nanjing) in 247.[47] There, he seems to have played a pioneering role in the conversion of southern China to Buddhism.

Many modern scholars prefer to emphasize the northern overland transmission of Buddhism to China, and some have been dismissive of the Kang Senghui story. The distinguished Chinese specialist Tang Yongtong, for example, emphasized the precedence in Three Kingdoms Wu of another monk coming from northern China (Zhi Qian) and raised some reasonable doubts about the credibility of Kang Senghui's hagiography. However, tradition portrays Kang Senghui as a pathbreaking figure not only in the south but in the history of Chinese Buddhism as a whole. A monk from what is now Henan Province in northern China was quoted (in an early Korean source) as claiming in 576 that, although Buddhism had been known in China since the Later Han dynasty, "when Kang Senghui arrived in Wu, then the teachings of the dharma spread."[48]

Today, Southeast Asia is closely associated with a Theravāda Buddhism (based on the Pali-language scriptures), which differs notably from the Mahāyāna Buddhism that is characteristic of China and East Asia. However, this should not be taken as proof that Southeast Asian waters played little role in the transmission of Buddhism to China. The forms of Buddhism that spread by sea from the south in this early period would not necessarily have been any different from those that spread overland from the north. Early Buddhist artistic influences in what are now Southeast Asian Malaysia and Indonesia have been traced mostly to northeastern Indian sources and are characterized as Mahāyāna. Theravāda Buddhism may not have been fully established in Southeast Asian Thailand and Burma until as late as the eleventh century. Hīnayāna (which is often somewhat mistakenly equated with Theravāda), on the other hand, still prevailed in such far northern centers of Buddhism dissemination as Khotan until the third or fourth century and was introduced into China from the north. The Chinese themselves seem to have remained blissfully unaware of any rivalry between Hīnayāna and Mahāyāna until the fifth century.[49]

The importance of the southern maritime trade routes in circulating Buddhist ideas to China may have been greater than is sometimes realized. Another example of the reciprocal stimulation between seaborne commerce and Indian Buddhism is provided by the case of the central Indian monk Guṇavṛiddhi (d. 502), who arrived in what is now Nanjing around 479 and who was the recipient there of generous donations from the "South Sea traders" to whom he apparently specialized in ministering.[50]

Both trade and Buddhism played critical roles in the process of forging a common culture for traditional East Asia, but both also transcended purely regional perspectives. By penetrating the barriers of East Asian civilization and linking it to a much wider world, these two related outside forces conspired to generate "new cultural configurations" and draw "new cultural boundary lines" in East Asia.[51]

The East Asian region that emerged as a result was shaped not merely by local forces but also in part by interactions that spanned the entire Eurasian world. Marylin Martin Rhie emphasizes, for example, that the stylistic influences on the late second-century Chinese "Flame Shouldered Buddha," now in the possession of the Arthur M. Sackler Museum at Harvard University and regarded as one of the finest examples of early Chinese Buddhist art, derive from northern Bactria or even Parthia in the remote west. A third-century fresco discovered southwest of Dunhuang, in modern Xinjiang Province, China, may have been executed by "an itinerant painter from the late Roman Empire" and is certainly in the Roman style. By the eighth century, artistic motifs from distant Sassanid Persia had successfully hurdled virtually the entire Eurasian land mass to find a home at the court of faraway Japan. In addition, a reddish dye, referred to in the earliest (eighth century) collection of Japanese-style poetry as "South China Indigo" *(kurenawi)*, may have really originated not in China but in what is now Afghanistan or possibly even farther west. As a more catastrophic example of early Eurasian interdependence, Denis Twitchett has traced the spread of an epidemic disease that may have originated in the Near East along Tang dynasty trade routes in the seventh through ninth centuries and from Tang China to both Korea and Japan. Both for better and for worse, East Asia was already part of a much larger planet.[52]

It is difficult to measure precisely, however, the extent to which these commercial contacts really transformed the societies situated at opposing edges of the Old World. Liu Xinru suspects, for example, that the striking similarity between the sumptuary laws and royal monopolies on fine silks, extending even to small matters of detail in color and design, between the contemporary Byzantine and Tang empires could hardly have been "purely coincidental," but she is nonetheless forced to admit that "evidence of direct exchange" between Tang and Byzantium is "meagre." Buddhism was probably the most pervasive external influence on East Asia during this period, but even Buddhism was quite thoroughly East Asian-ized. The "international" standard set for Buddhist art in China, Japan, and Korea, for example, was the "Tang" style. Buddhism, it might even be said, in practice served less as an agent for the promotion of Indian influences on East Asia and more as a lubricant for further Sinification.[53]

BUDDHIST INTERNATIONALIZATION

In China, Buddhism initially held little appeal for the cultural arbiters among the educated elite. Its attraction was felt far sooner by commoners (and certain members of the imperial family). From the commanding vantage of the elite heights, Buddhism may have long appeared to be simply another of the motley array of heterodox popular religious beliefs that percolated everywhere just beneath the surface of Chinese high culture, subject to official proscription at times but ultimately ineradicable. However, by the time of the establishment of the Sui dynasty in 581, and with the Sui repeal of the previous dynasty's ban on Buddhism and open allocation of state tax support for the circulation of the sutras, the Buddhist scriptures allegedly became more numerous among the common people of China than even the Confucian classics.[54] From about the fourth century to the end of the period covered in this book, China and East Asia became a thoroughly Buddhist region.

The Southern dynasty Liang emperor Wu (r. 502–549) famously donated his person to the *sangha*, to be redeemed by huge contributions from the imperial coffers. A devout Sillan king, Chinhŭng (r. 540–576), "served Buddha with all his heart" from youth and eventually shaved his head, donned a monk's garb, took a religious name, and had his consort become a nun and enter a temple. In early Japan, the taking of the tonsure by retired emperors even became something of a routine. Imperial monastic retirement in Japan may not have always really been driven by unquenchable religious piety, but it is testimony to the deep commingling of secular and sacred authority in early Japan. In the mid-eighth century, the Construction Agency for the Great Eastern Temple in Nara, responsible for casting the giant sixty-four-foot bronze great buddha statue, became the single largest Japanese imperial bureau even though it had no place at all in the formal administrative structure.[55]

East Asians became Buddhists, and Buddhism then transformed East Asian culture in significant ways. The Bodhisattva Vows (*Bodhisattva śīla;* C: *Pusa jie*) imposed ten major prohibitions on believers: not to kill, steal, commit adultery, speak falsely, sell wine, discuss the transgressions of other Buddhists, glorify the self and revile others, be greedy, be angry, or slander the Triratna (the Three Jewels: Buddha, *dharma,* and *sangha*). In China, even lay Buddhists were expected to live up to these vows, and, although abstention from alcohol was widely flouted, they put a particularly heavy burden on those who earned a living through the death of other living creatures, such as butchers and fish mongers.[56]

The animal sacrifices that had long been an essential part of native Chinese religious practice and that, by extension, were therefore crucial to the heavily ritualized Confucian polity were abhorrent in the eyes of Buddha. In 472, therefore, the father of a Northern Wei emperor ordered an end to them: "From today, in sacrificing to Heaven and Earth and at ancestral temples and altars to the spirits of the land, you may no longer use livestock. You can only make offerings of wine and dried meat." This command reportedly saved the lives of 75,000 beasts annually, although it still permitted the consumption of both meat and alcohol.[57]

In 517, the devout Buddhist emperor Wu of Southern dynasty Liang ordered the substitution of flour, vegetables, and fruit for animal sacrifices at the imperial suburban and ancestral temples. In 692, during her short-lived usurpation of the Tang dynasty, Empress Wu went so far as to prohibit all butchering and fishing "Under Heaven."[58] Buddhist ideals, in this way, had a profound impact not only on ritual practice but also on the imperial economy and the lifestyles of its subjects (although, as with other imperial decrees, these edicts were presumably chiefly grand gestures that were not even expected to be systematically enforced in practice).

Buddhist-inspired Chinese proscriptions on killing, like the rest of the imperial package, were echoed elsewhere in East Asia. In Korea, for example, the Sillan court issued a ban on the killing of living creatures in 529. In 599, a new king was enthroned in Paekche who proclaimed an end to killing, "released the birds of prey that were being raised [for hunting] by subject families, burned the equipment for fishing and hunting, and prohibited all of it."[59]

Among the other effects of these Indian influences, a mature form of "native" popular Taoist religion crystallized in imperial China amid fertile cross-pollination with the ideas of Indian Buddhism. The technology of block printing was developed in East Asia during the Tang period, and its economy and potential scale of reproduction were quickly and especially adopted for the mass dissemination of Buddhist and other popular religious materials. Buddhism's role in the development of print technology was only tangential, and there was nothing particularly Indian about it. However, among the Buddhist texts whose circulation was enhanced by the new technology were Indian folk songs, fables, legends, parables, epic poems, and hymns, which then enriched and permanently altered the range of Chinese-language literature. Buddhist monastic precedents also seem to have encouraged the introduction of striking parallels among the Confucian academies of later imperial times.[60]

Formal analysis of the tones of spoken Chinese and the elaboration of intricate rules for the tonal composition of verse—what came to be known as "recent style poetry"—began in the fifth and sixth centuries as an attempt to duplicate the metrical capabilities of Sanskrit. Although the Chinese tones had no counterpart in the Japanese (or Korean) language, the prestige of the Chinese literary model was so overwhelming that, by the early ninth century, Japanese court poetry in the Chinese style strove, with some success, to reproduce the tonal patterns of "recent style" verse. Chinese fashions in early Japan thus unwittingly also served as agents of Indianization. Victor Mair and Tsu-lin Mei, for example, argue energetically for the "Sanskrit origins" of much, including even the title, of Kūkai's famous Japanese treatise of 819, the *Bunkyō hifuron* (A Mirror for Literature and an Archive [of Verse]).[61]

The direction of cultural flow was almost entirely one way, from west to east. Chinese people went to India, but only to gain a better comprehension of the Indian Buddhist paradigm. The names of 169 Chinese monks who traveled to India in quest of the *dharma* between the fourth and eighth centuries are known today.[62] It is not known that they contributed much to the Sinification of India. The many Indians and other Indianized persons who ventured to China, on the other hand, left a profound and lasting impression there.

The precise date when Buddhism was introduced to China is a matter of much scholarly disagreement, but the first *śramana* to arrive in China, around A.D. 67, is sometimes said to have been Kāśyapa-Mātaṅga. He was a wandering missionary from central India who had vowed to spread the Buddhist message and, "fearing neither fatigue or hardship, dared to cross the flowing sands," coming overland to the Han capital.[63] Others like him followed.

Among the distinguished Buddhists who assembled on Mount Lu (in Jiangxi Province) in the early fifth century was a man from Kashmir, Buddhayaśas, who was called the "red-moustached Abhidharma master" because of the exotic color of his hair. Another Kashmiri monk, Guṇavarman (367–431), first voyaged by sea to Java, where he was "delighted" to receive an official invitation from the emperor of Southern dynasty Song China and, traveling by ship through the port of Guangzhou, arrived at the Song capital in 431.[64]

Numerous Indian and central Asian monks were active in early Tang China, and their exotic foreign faces haunted even the dreams and visions of the Tang faithful. Around the turn of the eighth century, one western monk reportedly used his reputation for occult skills to win unprecedented access to the inner chambers of the imperial court. The northern Indian monk Amoghavajra (705–774) came by the South Sea route to Tang in 720 and was welcomed at court, becoming preceptor of state for three Tang emperors. The Esoteric Buddhism that he espoused was then transmitted through a disciple to Kūkai, who brought it to Japan, becoming perhaps the most illustrious of all early Japanese monks. Tenuous as it may have been, a karmic chain had thus been laid down that stretched directly from India across China to Japan.[65]

On the Korean peninsula, Buddhism was introduced to the southwestern kingdom of Paekche by a Hu monk, Mālānanda, coming across from the Southern dynasty Jin in 384. "Taking advantage of dangers and riding over hazards, bearing successive difficulties, following every link of fate—there was no distance he would not travel." Although Korean Buddhism was mostly a transplant from China, a small amount of more direct exchange between Korea and the Buddhist wellsprings in India apparently did occur.[66]

Some Indic travelers even reached the distant shores of Japan. The *Nihon shoki* records that in 654 four persons from Tokhara (Afghanistan) and a woman from Śrāvastī (northeastern India) were blown off course by a storm to Hyuga, in southeastern Kyūshū, Japan. While the *Nihon shoki*'s great nineteenth-century English translator William Aston (1841–1911) was skeptical of this story, dismissing it as "absurd to speak of natives of India being cast ashore" in Japan at this early date, in truth this account is not really so implausible. The ceremonial "opening" of the eyes of the great buddha statue at Nara in 752 is known to have been performed by a Brahmin from southern India named Bodhisena, who had come to Japan in 736. In the early centuries of the Christian era (according to a Western Christian calendar that was unknown at the time in either India or China), Indians or Indianized persons were voyaging far afield as both missionaries and merchants. This was, after all, the age of the remarkable "Indianization" of Southeast Asia.[67]

From as early as the last centuries B.C., merchants from the Indian subcontinent began to explore maritime trade routes stretching out into what is now Southeast Asia. Although the impetus was commercial, the merchant community tended to be adherents of Buddhism, and Buddhist beliefs spread with them as they traveled. This was partly coincidence, but Buddhism also contributed to the movement by breaking down regional and caste barriers with its new cosmopolitan, universalistic message, and the Buddhist cult of Avalokiteśvara (who became the female deity Guanyin in China and is known as Kannon to the Japanese), as the patron Bodhisattva of mariners, also gave the faithful courage to confront the very real terrors of distant voyages.[68]

In the South Seas, Indian merchants brought more than just Buddhism. As a result of their travels, a vast "Sanskrit cosmopolis" gradually emerged, connecting what are now Burma, Thailand, Cambodia, Laos, (central and southern) Vietnam, Malaysia, and Indonesia with the Indian subcontinent (which was itself not yet a single unified "country" but a range of various local communities) through the universal application of Sanskrit in "royal celebratory inscriptions." This Indianized community in Southeast Asia lasted from the early years of the Christian era until as late as the thirteenth century.[69]

The "Indianization" of Southeast Asia strikingly paralleled the "Sinification" of East Asia. At approximately the same time that China, Japan, Korea, and Vietnam were coming together as an identifiable East Asian region, nearly all of South and Southeast Asia were swept into an enormous Indic *oikoumene*. Even on the remote, uncharted South Sea island known (in Chinese) as Piqian, where, according to Southern dynasty Chinese accounts, merchants were unwelcome and were killed and eaten if they dared to put ashore, the local ruler was still supposedly competent in the Indian script and in written communication with the mainland.[70]

In many ways, this Indianization of Southeast Asia was merely an extension of a process that was also occurring simultaneously on the Indian subcontinent as well: "Much of India itself was being Indianized at the very same period as Java or Khmer country—and in a hardly different way." Everywhere, a common elite style was superimposed on an enormous variety of local communities, overlaying but not replacing them. "Translocal" Indic standards were established across the region "that transcended the immediate community, and against which a wide range of vernacular cultures defined themselves."[71]

Sanskrit became the international language of public political expression in Southeast Asia but probably was not employed much for everyday use, even in India itself. It enjoyed instead a limited, if privileged, place amid a huge profusion of tongues. Unlike the large number of Chinese loanwords surviving among the modern Japanese, Korean, and Vietnamese lexicons, Indian vocabulary left a relatively limited linguistic residue in Southeast Asia.[72]

Precisely because Sanskrit was written with a phonetic script *(Devanāgarī)*, easily adaptable to writing any language, Indian terminology was vulnerable to competition, even in formal literary situations, from local vernaculars. This was much less the case with the ideologically loaded, semi- or even nonphonetic *kanji* script of East Asia. Although Sanskrit was reserved for certain kinds of important public inscriptions, throughout Southeast Asia inscriptions in the local vernacular languages soon began to appear in tandem with those in Sanskrit.[73] The result was, in some ways, a more superficial and transient Indianization of Southeast Asia than the Sinification that took place in East Asia.

Early Chinese descriptions of Southeast Asia make repeated references to "Brahmins," but many of these may have only been Indian-style holy men rather than actual persons from the subcontinent. Nonetheless, the physical presence of at least a few Indians on the South Seas was probably indispensable to the spread of elements of Indic civilization. Along the eastern shores of the Gulf of Thailand, in the region of what is now Cambodia and southern Vietnam, Chinese records state that an Indian Brahmin named Kauṇḍinya became king in the late fourth century and transformed local institutions along the Indian model. Other Indians are supposed to have already ruled in the area beginning as early as the first century, and archaeologically recovered Indian and even Roman artifacts and inscriptions from almost that early support the idea of visitors from the subcontinent.[74]

The arrival of Indian traders on the coast may have touched off a "ripple effect" in the form of material and cultural exchanges with preexisting inland native communities, and the interaction between these Indians and the "natives" resulted in the rise, between the first and sixth centuries, of "Southeast Asia's first state," Funan. Funan is the modern Mandarin Chinese pronunciation of the *kanji* designation that is preserved in our Chinese-language textual sources; George Coedès speculates that the name may have originated as an ancient form of the modern Cambodian word *phnom,* or "mountain." The state that emerged at this time in Funan is, perhaps, better understood to have been a loose network of chieftainships rather than a Chinese-style centralized government. In general, the political development of early Southeast Asia may have been greatly inhibited by the unhealthy tropical climate. In any case, Funan is especially interesting to us here because it provides a bridge between classical Indic civilization and East Asia.[75]

Tang dynasty Chinese believed that Funan "adjoined" eastern India and was "only separated from it by a small sea." From as early as the third century, merchants from India and still more distant lands "frequently" traded with Funan, which in turn communicated with the Chinese-administered ports in what is now northern Vietnam. In addition, although the known East Asian terminus of the South Sea trade route was located in the extreme south of China, a more general East Asian distribution of at least some of these products is revealed by the record that Paekche (in Korea) sent a royal offering of Funan goods and two slaves to Japan in 542.[76]

South of Funan and subject to it, straddling the narrow neck of the Malay peninsula, was a bustling entrepôt called (in Chinese) Dunxun, which communicated with the Chinese empire to the east and India and Persia to the west. "In its markets over ten-thousand persons from east and west converged each day. There was no treasure or precious commodity they did not have."[77]

Funan disintegrated toward the end of the sixth century (before the establishment of the Tang dynasty in China) and was replaced by one of its vassals, Zhenla (sometimes spelled Chenla). Funan's former commercial preeminence, however, was supplanted by yet another polity, the heavily Indianized Buddhist trading community known as Śrīvijaya. Śrīvijaya was located on or around the island of Sumatra, and it came to dominate South Sea trade for several centuries, beginning about 670. Śrīvijaya's trading prowess may have eventually helped make the Malay language become a kind of lingua franca in the region.[78]

In the meantime, more immediately on the Chinese border, and of much greater political and military consequence to the Chinese empire, a group of Austronesian-speaking people known as Chams established a heavily Indianized kingdom called Champa (C: Linyi, ca. 192–1720), in what is now central Vietnam, toward the end of the second century. The Chams do not appear to have suddenly arrived on the Vietnamese coast at this time but rather only to have finally organized themselves then into an independent political entity of some significance. According to Chinese accounts, these Chams practiced

Buddhism and wrote in an Indian script on the leaves of trees. They dressed in sarongs, frequently went barefoot, and accorded women with unusual respect—at least by Chinese standards. Some of their great families are referred to as "Brahmins." The early Cham kings dressed after the fashion of Buddhist images and went out in procession astride elephants, shaded by parasols, to the sound of the blowing of conches and the beating of drums.[79]

These Chams frequently clashed with the southernmost outposts of the Chinese empire. In the early fifth century, in particular, there were almost annual Cham raids, greatly weakening the local Chinese administration in what is now northern Vietnam. Chinese territory was overrun, and one sixth-century source reports that some southern Chinese people were absorbed by Champa and culturally "barbarized." It would not be until 1720 that the last remnants of Champa would finally be fully incorporated into the, by then, long-since-independent Vietnamese state.[80]

Indian cultural influences thus pervaded Southeast Asia during the first millennium A.D. and abutted on and even penetrated the Chinese empire. Indic civilization, it could be said, was actively expanding at Chinese expense. Going the other direction, however, Chinese influence on Southeast Asia (beyond the borders of the empire proper, which, it must be remembered, still stretched into what is now Vietnam) at this time was negligible. This was partly a consequence of the "passive" Chinese role in the thriving regional maritime trade.[81] It was also the result of a more uncompromising Chinese approach toward incorporation within *tianxia*.

The Indians did not pretend to universal rule in Southeast Asia but were content instead to merely provide (and may not have actively promoted even that) a prestigious model that various natives could adapt to their own purposes.[82] The resulting degree of "Indianization" in the South Seas was therefore rather mild and optional. Sinification, by contrast, did not usually allow so much leeway. The Chinese Sons of Heaven presumed to universal rule. While incorporation into the East Asian world did not necessarily really mean direct Chinese administration, the Chinese empire did expect at least nominal political subordination (though rivalries over who should be the true Son of Heaven were common), and the extension of *kanji*, to say nothing of the classical Chinese written language, throughout East Asia had profound ideological homogenizing consequences.

In India and Southeast Asia, the Buddhist commitment to pros-
elytization by whatever means was expedient—including the use of
local spoken languages, combined with the use of a phonetic script,
and in general a greater Indian respect for local vernacular speech
(deśa-bhāṣā) than in China—ensured that alongside the elite Sanskrit
literature a profusion of local literary traditions would also arise and
flourish. Indian Buddhists, we are told, consciously rejected the kind
of "linguistic imperialism" inherent in trying to maintain a privileged
sacred language.[83] The contrasting traditional Chinese obsession with
a fixed orthodox canon of standardized written texts may be less attractive to postmodern minds, but one consequence of these relative
postures was a much more thorough unification of traditional China
than of traditional India and a Sinification of East Asia that was more
complete and permanent than the so-called Indianization of Southeast Asia.

If Buddhists helped blaze the trail for the Indianization of the
South Seas, the rulers of these Indianized native principalities subsequently turned to Brahmanical ritual for further legitimization. Beginning as early as the fourth century, Southeast Asian royalty identified themselves increasingly with Siva and Vishnu.[84] However, this next
stage of "Indianization" never penetrated beyond the South Seas to
China and East Asia, where Indian influences remained largely confined to Buddhism and its penumbrae.

A good many central Asians, and even a few Indians, journeyed
to East Asia during these centuries as both merchants and missionaries. However, with a few prominent exceptions such as Amoghavajra
(who came at a young enough age to presumably absorb and become
fluent in the Chinese language), most played only an indirect role
in disseminating even the Buddhist message there, to say nothing
of other aspects of Indian culture. Their chief function was as bearers
of texts and translators. Even the principal translators tended to be
not Indians but central Asians, who occupied a kind of transitional
space, exposed to and comfortable with both Indic and Sinitic influences, and who were therefore relatively well poised to act as cultural
intermediaries.[85]

In large part, this is explained by the cultural "great wall" of language. Although travelers in central Asia had, of necessity, to become
conversant with multiple languages, foreign-language acquisition is
never easy. Many of the western Buddhist missionaries to China spoke

little Chinese. Śrīmitra (fl. ca. 310–340), in the fourth century, did not even try to study Chinese, relying instead on the services of translators. Although a future Chinese emperor supposedly quipped that this was "to save himself the trouble of answering questions," hagiographic hyperbole aside, it clearly must have limited his ability to interact with his Chinese audience.[86]

Japanese monks who traveled to Tang China in search of a more pristine font of Buddhist wisdom, such as Kūkai and Ennin in the ninth century, despite their declared interest in learning Sanskrit from western sources, were to some extent frustrated by the their inability to communicate and received most of their initiation from Chinese monks instead.[87] The Japanese could, at least, communicate with Chinese monks readily enough in writing, even if they could not easily talk to each other.

It is true that Kūkai did manage to study some with a monk from Kashmir and another from India and prided himself on his accomplishments in Sanskrit, but it is doubtful how much Sanskrit Kūkai could have really absorbed during a mere fourteen months at the Tang capital. In addition, Japanese contact with Buddhist emissaries from the west took place, physically, mostly in China; extremely few Japanese (or Koreans) personally penetrated into the western regions.[88]

Despite the obviously foreign origins of Buddhism in China, once Buddhism began to acquire a certain positive cultural cachet in Chinese society, ambitious and socially distinguished Chinese monks, such as Zhi Dun (314–366), seem to have cultivated relationships in circles that did not include many foreigners. Although a few resolute Chinese pilgrims, like Yijing (635–713), who spent twenty-five years in India and Southeast Asia, did apparently become fluent in certain Indian languages, most Chinese Buddhists remained scarcely familiar at all with any western tongue. Although it is an enormous subject, far beyond our ability to even begin to broach here, it is well known that despite repeated Chinese efforts to obtain a "correct" transmission of the Indian Buddhist truth, even Buddhism in China gradually became quite thoroughly Chinese.[89]

The Japanese monk Saichō once even argued for the outright superiority of the Chinese distillation of Buddhism over the Indian original:

> The Chinese *Tripitaka* harmonizes the contending doctrines of India; Chinese masters mix the multitude of interpretations in

the Sanskrit originals. In that wise omission, the divine land [China] is also good. In this generous flavor, Great Tang is also wonderful.[90]

Some of the most magnificent examples of western Buddhist cultural and artistic influence in early China are provided by the more than 120 stone grottoes that were carved at sites scattered across northern China beginning in the fourth and fifth centuries. Such grottoes have been found, however, no further east than Silla in Korea and no further south than approximately the line of the Yangzi River in China.[91] They are notably lacking in both Japan and southern China. This geographic distribution is testimony to the northern, Silk Road origin of this particular style, but it is also one more example of the limits of Indic influence on East Asia.

In East Asia, Buddhist missionaries from the western regions initially presented a literally quite outlandish spectacle, with their uncovered right shoulders, saffron robes, shorn heads, and bare feet. Some East Asians, like the hermit Gu Huan (420–483) and the emperor Wu of Northern Zhou (r. 561–578), found these and other alien practices objectionable, but the Buddhists were quick to reply that "in the extremity of the *Tao* there is no . . . near or far" and that all such differences are simultaneously both relative and irrelevant: at one level, the Chinese empire itself had incorporated a number of what had once been foreign states and cultures, while at yet another level both China and India were similarly just subregions in the vast realm of the great Buddhist Jambu Cakravartin king.[92]

Such an argument was persuasive because it resonated with preexisting Chinese Taoist ideals concerning the relativity of all things and because the imperial *tianxia* itself really was just such an international assemblage. If Buddhism ultimately did little to Indianize East Asia, it did contribute a language of universalism to an East Asia that was already increasingly cosmopolitan. Not unlike the multiethnic Christian monasteries of early medieval Europe, the early Buddhist Church in East Asia had a resolutely international flavor.[93]

One monk from Koguryŏ (in Korea) studied the Mādhyamika at Dunhuang, in the far northwest of what is now China, in the late fifth century. In the early sixth century, he transplanted himself to a scenic mountain in Jiangsu, near the east coast of what is now central China, where the devout Emperor Wu of Southern dynasty Liang deputed a mission of ten experts to consult with him on the doctrine in

512. In Japan, the first official head of the Japanese Buddhist Church, in 623, was a monk from Paekche (in Korea), and shortly thereafter another monk from Koguryŏ, who had studied in Sui dynasty China, was elevated to the top of the Japanese Buddhist hierarchy.[94]

When a decision was made to invite an ordination master to Japan in 733 to establish the proper monastic discipline, the Japanese approached Ganjin (C: Jianzhen, 687–763) in Tang China. He proved amenable to the idea, approvingly noting the universalistic devotion of Prince Nagaya of Japan (684–729), who had supposedly ordered 1,000 monks' robes to be embroidered with the following passage: "The mountains and streams of different lands share the wind and the moon of the same heaven. It is up to all the children of Buddha to bind their destinies together." After five abortive attempts at making the crossing to Japan, Ganjin set sail on his sixth, successful voyage to Japan in 753 with, in addition to his Chinese party, a Malay, a Cham, and another person vaguely described as Hu (northwestern foreigner).[95]

The early East Asian Buddhist Church was truly multinational. One modern scholar lists twenty-six of the "more famous" Chinese monks who went to Japan during the Tang dynasty. The Japanese monk Saichō studied in Tang China from 802 to 805. As he prepared for departure on his return trip, a Chinese governor observed, in his dedication to Saichō's catalog of manuscripts, that, while "in appearance the Priest Saichō is from a foreign land, his nature truly springs from the same origin." Buddhism promoted the notion that all people were alike and all regional differences ultimately irrelevant. The specifically Indian cultural elements that were transmitted to East Asia with the Buddhist religion were somewhat limited in range, though undeniable. However, Buddhist internationalism, like Confucian universalism, served as an excellent lubricant for cultural exchange and assisted in the further Sinification of East Asia.[96]

In the early sixth century, Paekche, in Korea, had close relations with the fervently Buddhist Southern dynasty Liang, which introduced Southern dynasty–style Chinese Buddhist motifs to the Korean peninsula. This transmission of Chinese-style Buddhist culture was accompanied by other elements of more specifically Chinese secular culture. In 541, for example, a Paekche embassy to Liang requested and received not only copies of the sutras but also physicians, craftsmen, painters, and specialists in the Chinese classic *Book of Odes*. Elsewhere on the peninsula, in Silla, the adoption of Tang-style court dress in 649 came at the recommendation of a Buddhist monk who had studied in China.[97]

Ganjin not only brought the orthodox forms of the Buddhist *Vinaya* to Japan in the eighth century but also taught Chinese-style pharmacology. Indeed, Buddhist monasteries became virtual islands of continental civilization in early Japan, playing an incalculably important role in the importation of Chinese influences. In the seventh century, for example, the Buddhist monk Min (d. 654) was arguably the foremost "China expert" of his day; in addition to his religious accomplishments, he also lectured on the Chinese classic *Book of Changes* and allegedly helped determine the structure of the reformed Japanese government following the Taika coup d'état of 645.[98]

At any rate, it is clear that in addition to being agents of religious Indianization, East Asian Buddhist monks were also carriers of Central Plain civilization; and, unlike the "great wall" of language that stood between China and western Buddhism, which required massive translation efforts to bridge, there was no need for translating the sutras into Japanese and Korean because such (admittedly extremely limited) literacy as existed in contemporary Japan and Korea was already in the Chinese language. The Buddhist scriptures were disseminated throughout East Asia in Chinese-language editions. In Japan during the eighth century, the Buddhist material in circulation seems furthermore to have been about equally divided between Chinese-language translations of originally Indian texts and new Chinese compositions.[99]

Indeed, so-called Chinese apocryphal texts constitute a large and important segment of the entire East Asian Buddhist canon. Not only did these Chinese compositions deeply color the forms of Buddhism that developed and spread throughout East Asia, but what might be termed the "return flow" from this Sinified East Asian Buddhism also extended back into central Asia, where "almost all the Sogdian Buddhist texts still extant are translations from Chinese, to the extent that even words of Indian origin appear in them in their Chinese garb." In Buddhist painting, the Chinese "very quickly absorbed the Central Asian and Indian elements and reworked them into a native idiom that was then exported back to Central Asia."[100]

The cultural gravity of the Middle Kingdom was so compelling that even religions of western origin were projected back on China's western frontier from Chinese centers. The initial conversion of the Uighur ruler to Persian Manichaeism, for example, took place in the ancient Chinese capital of Luoyang in 762–763. Even Tibet, which eventually generated a uniquely local version of Buddhism of its own under strong South Asian impetus, during the early period of its conversion, in the seventh and eighth centuries, drew almost equally on Buddhist missionary resources from South and East Asia. Tang emperors even regarded the dispatch of Buddhist teachers to Tibet as part of their transformation-through-education (*jiaohua*) civilizing mission.[101]

Culturally sophisticated models in ancient East Asia tended to radiate out from certain geographically limited focal points, such as the Chinese imperial capital, the city of Nara (and later Heian) in the Japanese islands, and the various Korean courts. Beyond these centers of refinement lay satellite rings of subordinate provincial cultural and economic vitality. Outside East Asia entirely, there were also other major centers of high civilization to the south and west. In between these great core Old World civilizations stretched vast expanses of often sparsely populated land. However, these seemingly desolate intervening spaces were never really totally uninhabited, and, if they sometimes served as barriers or buffers between the great civilizations of Eurasia, they also sometimes served as open doors, inviting movement and exchange.

Nuclear Implosion

East Asia connected with the great centers of South Asian (Indic) civilization through trade and missionary activity across the waters of the South Seas, but the front line of East Asian cultural confrontation with outsiders unquestionably lay elsewhere: to the north, across the very concrete line drawn by the Great Wall. Here, on its northern frontier, East Asia faced three different ecological zones, each with its own distinctive cultural rhythm. To the northeast were the forests of Manchuria, a transitional region connecting East Asian China with East Asian Korea but also leading northward to exotic Siberia and opening westward onto the steppe. To the northwest were the harsh deserts of Chinese Turkestan (in modern Xinjiang Province), centering around the Tarim basin and the Taklimakan Desert, with its fringe of oasis trading communities. Due north were the Mongolian steppes, home to seminomadic peoples who "were in almost every respect the opposite of the Chinese."[1]

The whole of central Asia was to some extent peripheral to the great ancient civilizations that congregated at the extremes of both eastern and western Eurasia, but it was also at the same time the "ultimate nodal center" of the entire Eurasian Old World. The fragile oases of the Tarim basin sustained a "slender dual thread," arcing both north and south around the desert's uninhabitable heart, that "was strong enough nevertheless to ensure that our planet should consist of a single world and not of two separate ones." These were the fabled "Silk Roads" linking China to the west. "North of this narrow trail of civilization, however, the steppes provided the nomads with a route of a very different order: a boundless route of numberless tracks, the route of barbarism." The northwestern frontier thus presented the Chinese empire with two quite different aspects: a desert caravan trade route maintaining tenuous commercial contact with the great civilizations of the west and a sea of grass, stretching from the Mongolian plateau, around the Altai Mountains, and through the Zungharian basin westward to the Danube River, that was inhabited by fiercely inassimilable barbarians—barbarians of a different kind from those on all the other frontiers.[2]

The "pre-Islamic ethnohistory" of central Asia is "a matter of great controversy." "The multiplicity of languages used along the Silk Road was extraordinary." The peoples of the region have called themselves by many names. Even today, within the boundaries of the single modern northwestern Chinese province of Gansu, alongside Mandarin-speaking Han Chinese (like those in my own father-in-law's home village there), can be found "Turkic-speaking Muslims, Mongolic-speaking Muslims, Chinese-speaking Tibetans, Tibetan-speaking Muslims, Monguor-speaking Muslims and non-Muslims, and more." The modern People's Republic "carefully but inconsistently" compresses these into a framework of officially recognized ethnic nationalities.[3]

In premodern times, the Chinese tended to generalize shamelessly, however, and a certain unaffected kind of honesty is conveyed by the very imprecision of their terminology. The nomadic pastoralists to the north and west were called Rong and Di in antiquity and during the imperial era often simply Hu, a generic label for northwestern frontier peoples that could sometimes also be applied to Indians, Persians, and almost any foreigner.[4]

As Yijing characterized the various native costumes of the world, in Southeast Asia people wear untailored sarongs wrapped and tucked around their waists (and, in some Indian Ocean islands, they go naked, wearing nothing at all), the Persians and Arabs wear shirts and pants, and the Hu wear felts and furs. A third-century source described the so-called Wuwan people and the nearly identical Xianbei as adroit mounted archers, having no permanent homes and living in tents, "following the water and grass" necessary for their livestock. They also, reportedly, had no fixed surnames, going instead merely by the names of their current strongmen. According to Ying Xiao (d. ca. 204), the Xianbei were a constant threat to the imperial border. "They come like birds in flight, and depart like snapped strings. They are a deep concern for the country."[5]

In fact, the peoples of the steppe tended to be semi- rather than fully nomadic, alternating regularly between summer high pastures and more sheltered areas in winter. However, their lifestyle made them highly mobile, and the steppe was an ocean of grass across which they could pass easily from shore to distant shore. In the ancient Mediterranean world, "Roman imperialist ethnogeography" fostered a conviction that the extreme climatic conditions at the edges of Greco-Roman civilization produced, through a kind of geographic determinism, successive waves of roughly interchangeable barbarians. "Even though these barbarians bore a different name, they were essentially the same." In a much more decisive fashion, the unique environment of the steppe really did impose broadly uniform cultural traits on a long succession of seminomadic peoples, known by many names, who for centuries roamed from Manchuria to the Black Sea.[6]

Fundamental to the evolution of this steppe culture was what has been called the "cavalry revolution," based on mastery of the difficult technique of mounted archery, which seems to have begun around the ninth century B.C. toward the western edges of the steppe. Following this pivotal breakthrough, the entire steppe, from the Danube to China, became an increasingly "uniform territory," where "warlike mounted groups appear everywhere." Undoubtedly, there was a substantial amount of physical movement and mixing of population, encouraged by the new mobility of horse riders, but this transformation of steppe culture was not so much the result of the triumph of any specific "people," displacing previous inhabitants, as it was simply the result of the spreading technology of mounted archery and economic specialization in the raising of livestock, which promoted a relatively uniform lifestyle.[7]

The modern mind looks instinctively for clearly demarcated ethnic groups ("nations" or "peoples") among the nomads, but the various central Asian ethnic names recorded in our sources for antiquity reveal themselves on closer inspection to be not so much ethnoracial markers as "political nomenclature"—organizational labels. There were few enduring identities larger than the tribe. As the seventh-century *Dynastic History of the Jin* succinctly puts it, "The northern barbarians use tribes for their classifications." There were larger political organizations, but they tended to be rather ephemeral and interchangeable. A string of empires succeeded each other on the steppe, "one after another, made of the same materials, though appearing to us to be very different in composition because we only hear about the ruling clans, which did change." Even the presumption that these empires spoke particular different languages (e.g., "Xiongnu") is misleading since "many of these ephemeral confederations were multi-lingual."[8]

The most significant cultural boundaries in central Asia coincided, unsurprisingly, with the difference between the steppe and oasis environments already remarked on. The urban, oasis-based society of the Tarim basin—a "crossroad of different peoples"—was home to broadly Indo-Iranian cultures in early antiquity but already often subject to nomadic military-political domination by early imperial times in China and eventually submerged under the northern Altaic-speaking steppe cultures by late in the first millennium A.D.[9]

The steppe cultures themselves were all broadly similar, and, although they undoubtedly spoke many different languages, most of these linguistic differences can be broadly subdivided into Turkic, Mongolic, and Tungusic groups, all of which, in turn, display sufficient similarities that they have often—though somewhat controversially—been classified together as genetically related offshoots of a single hypothetical "Proto-Altaic" language. All these Altaic-speaking steppe nomads, "leading the same life in the same climate, had an ethnical resemblance which has struck all travelers in those parts."[10]

Our ethnic labels for the various different central Asian populations, in other words, may at times provide a usefully abbreviated descriptive shorthand but should not be presumed to indicate fundamental, inalterable differences. The history of the early steppe is a history not of "peoples" but of rulers and their retinues. Even more so on the steppe than in permanently settled agriculturally based communities, premodern "nations" or "peoples" were fleeting fabrications, not primordial verities—shifting sands rather than the benchmarks of history.

Many small local population groups, often speaking languages and practicing customs peculiar to themselves, did live scattered throughout the Eurasian world in those days (indeed, still today). During the period beginning in the fourth century, something seems to have set some of these marginal groups in unaccustomed motion—across the frontiers of both the ancient Chinese and the Roman empires. However, it is a mistake to imagine these groups as homogeneous nations or assume much continuity across the centuries, especially among the seminomads of the steppe. Even in the case of relatively sedentary prehistoric populations, the emergence of firmly recognized large-group identities, based on clearly defined territories and having established leadership structures, tends to occur only on the peripheries of more politically developed empires and through interaction with them.[11] Since the population of the steppe was among the most fluid and mobile in the entire prehistoric world, these nomads were especially protean as "peoples."

An instructive recent parallel may be found in the creation of the "Manchu" ethnic identity at the time of the establishment of the Qing dynasty in China in the seventeenth century. "There was, in fact, no traditional 'Manchu' culture or identity." There had been no previous Manchu "nation." Instead, there had been only a scattering of relatively small Tungusic-speaking bands.[12] These were purposefully aligned, together with various other population groups, by the early leaders of the Qing dynasty into the conquering armies of Bannermen who overran the empire and came to be known as the Manchus. As the example of the Qing dynasty demonstrates, under the right leadership, an unlikely assortment of small population groups can sometimes be organized quickly into very large empires that often do then acquire distinctive identities of their own. There is a natural but fallacious human inclination to wish to project these new identities back into the remote past and to assume that they are eternal. They are not.

Thus, our quest for a history of the nations of the steppe turns out to be elusive. There was only a broadly uniform steppe culture within which many smaller groups formed shifting patterns of political allegiances and called themselves or were called by a variety of different names. Yet some of the larger political organizations were of great significance for the history of East Asia. Along the caravan trade routes of the Silk Road, the magnificent empire of Kushāna ruled from about the second century B.C. to the fifth century A.D., over regions stretching at their peak from modern Afghanistan and northern India as far east as Lop Nor in modern China's Xinjiang Province, just west of Dunhuang. A Kushān ambassador is traditionally credited with introducing Buddhism to East Asia in 2 B.C.[13]

On the steppe proper, the famous Xiongnu confederation confronted the Han dynasty for most of that great empire's duration. After the dissolution of both the Han and the Xiongnu empires, during the fourth century northern China itself was "barbarized" under the political domination of what Chinese sources call the "five Hu" peoples, who may be broadly understood as divided between western precursors of the Tibetans and northern steppe nomads who had formerly been affiliated with the Xiongnu. In the fifth and early sixth centuries, much of the steppe region was dominated by the so-called Ruan-ruan (also known as the Rouran), whom the Chinese considered to be a branch of the old Xiongnu.[14]

The Ruan-ruan story, as explained in the *Dynastic History of the Northern Wei,* is that toward the end of the third century a certain captive, obtained by nomadic raiding, was dubbed Mugulü ("baldy") by his new master. In slightly altered form, this became his new clan name. Condemned to execution in the early fourth century, Mugulü escaped to the desert, where he assembled a small following of other assorted absconders. His son and successor later gathered a more significant horde and named them the Rouran. Their alternate name, Ruan-ruan, which means "wriggly" in Chinese, was applied to them by the fifth-century (Tuoba Xianbei) Northern Wei dynasty as an indication of contempt for their allegedly wormlike nature.[15] As usual, it is difficult to know how seriously to take the details of this story, but the picture of a vast steppe empire originating with a small and quite motley warrior band is very credible, as is the extremely haphazard origin of the names that would later be proudly considered "ethnic" labels.

These Ruan-ruan, in turn, were conquered by the Tujue, or Türks, around 550. Although these "Türks are the earliest Inner Asian people whose language is well known and precisely datable" and their identity would seem to be relatively unproblematic, in fact the early Tujue population was rather heterogeneous, and many of the names of even the Türk rulers, including the two founders of their empire, are not even "Turkic." Chinese sources describe the Tujue nomads as originating among "mixed barbarians" and resembling the old Xiongnu.[16] This great Tujue, or Türk, empire was supplanted by a Uighur empire during the second half of the Tang dynasty. The Uighurs, who were themselves divided into ten different subgroups, came from one of nine so-called Tiele bands that had formerly been vassals of the Tujue.[17]

Although the political history of the steppe is extremely complicated, from the time of the breakup of the early Xiongnu confederation until the end of the period covered in this book, the seminomads of the steppe did not really form any great imperial rivals for China. The obvious exception would seem to be the period of "barbarian invasions" beginning in the fourth century. However, the nomadic empires that took shape on the steppe tended to be economically dependent on their ability to tap, through raiding and other means, into the tremendous resources of a unified and prosperous China. After the collapse of Chinese imperial unity, "there could be no unity on the steppe until north China was again stable." Somewhat surprisingly, therefore, it turns out that the semiforeign rulers who conquered northern China in the fourth century were not truly nomads from the steppe but rather hybrid regimes that managed to combine elements of nomadic military striking power with Chinese-style forms of administration over settled agrarian populations.[18]

After the restoration of a unified Chinese empire under Sui and Tang, the Tujue were to some extent claimed as Tang subjects, and the Uighurs remained at least nominal Tang allies throughout the period of their imperial ascendance (744–840).[19] Except during the early Han dynasty, in other words, the steppe and the Chinese worlds tended to maintain a precarious equilibrium, amid sometimes fertile cross-cultural pollination.

The situation on the western flank of East Asia was somewhat different, however. There, the various river valleys draining southward along the eastern scarp of the Tibetan plateau favored the north-south transmission of goods and ideas, from the north in central Asia, south to Yunnan, and from there on to the Red River and Mekong in what is now Vietnam. This created a vertical cultural fault line against which East Asia pushed and was pushed. There, as early as 111 B.C., even as the Han empire was busily subduing Chosŏn Korea in the northeast and Southern Yue in the far southeast, over 100,000 Qiang people "rebelled" and, coordinating their maneuvers with the Xiongnu empire, attacked Chinese imperial outposts in Gansu.[20]

In the mid-seventh century, from among the numerous different population groups along this western frontier that the Chinese generically labeled Qiang, emerged an extremely formidable Tibetan empire based at Lhasa (from 629 and before that in the Yarlung area immediately southeast of Lhasa). "The Chinese were frankly baffled by its quick rise to major power status."[21] Culturally connected to India and central Asia as well as China and possessing a larger agricultural economic base than the nomadic steppe empires, Tibet became the Tang dynasty's most consistently serious military and political ri-val. By 670, the Tibetans had overrun Kashgar, Khotan, and Kuchā in the Tarim basin and the Tang garrisons at the Chinese end of the Silk Roads. Dunhuang, in Gansu, was occupied by Tibet from 787 to 848. Then, toward the end of the ninth century, the Tibetan empire dis-integrated as suddenly as it had first appeared some three centuries previously.[22]

One other western state menaced the fringes of the East Asian world. Nanzhao, in what is now Yunnan Province, appeared as a con-solidated kingdom in the eighth century and became a substantial threat to Tang territory, especially in the vicinity of modern Hanoi, by the mid-ninth century. Nanzhao highlights the danger of trying to conceptualize premodern states in ethnonational terms. Both Nan-zhao and early Tibet were political and military constructs: empires and not "peoples." Within the framework of the Nanzhao organiza-tion were assembled a range of population groups, speaking a variety of—perhaps related—languages and having somewhat diverse cus-toms. While commoners reportedly rolled their rice into balls that they ate with their hands, the elite were apparently somewhat Sinified and used chopsticks East Asian style.[23]

Both Yunnan and Tibet are now officially part of the People's Republic of China, although Tibet's status, in particular, remains controversial even today.[24] During the Tang dynasty, these were en-emy states or, at best, peaceful neighbors. Although there was some cultural exchange between these western empires and Tang China, they remained outside East Asia and firmly demarcated China's west-ern frontier. Tibet and Nanzhao formed the often-hostile western edge of the East Asian world.

THE FOURTH-CENTURY "BARBARIZATION" OF NORTHERN CHINA

The two great empires at either end of the Old World, China and Rome, were afflicted roughly simultaneous with parallel bouts of eth-nic conflict, conventionally described as "barbarian invasions." Both episodes form important milestones in the overall course of their re-spective histories (for Rome it was more like a tombstone). To un-derstand what was happening in China at this time, it may be helpful, in view of these noteworthy parallels, to digress for a moment and consider the case of Rome in some detail.

The so-called Germanic invasions that afflicted the late Roman empire are further illustrations of the somewhat illusory quality of even our most familiar ethnic terminology. The scattering of northern barbarians sweepingly labeled "Germani" by the Romans were not, at the time, themselves very conscious of any common identity. In the fifth century, their languages were mutually unintelligible, and they did not even begin to label themselves *Deutsch* (German) until the ninth century.[25] The Germanic chieftain Odoacer (ca. 434–493), whose coronation at Pavia in 476 is sometimes said to mark the end of the western Roman empire, "was King of an army, not of a Germanic people," and a would-be "Roman patrician" who eventually took a Roman name and attempted to rule approximately in the Roman manner.[26]

Theoderic the Great (ca. 454–526), who led the Ostrogothic invasion of Italy in 489, had spent nine years of his youth in the capital of the eastern Roman empire, Constantinople. The Ostrogothic "people" he led, on closer inspection, prove to have been a mixed group whose only clear identifying characteristic was service in Theoderic's army. They all seem to have been able to speak Latin, and the "Gothic" language that a very small number of them are actually attested in the primary sources to have also spoken may have been nothing more than a "soldier's koiné" rather than some clear ethnic marker. Latin, at any rate, survived, while Gothic disappeared almost utterly.[27]

Following Theoderic's invasion of Italy, it is natural to imagine the "hostility of Goth and Italian" as two peoples who "differed in language, religion, tradition, in customs, and even in law." Theoderic's army, certainly, was composed of remote provincials who would have been predictably unfamiliar with local practices in Italy. However, Theoderic styled himself, on one Appian Way inscription, "King Theoderic, . . . protector of the freedom and enlarger of the Roman name." Similarly, the declared ambition of the fifth-century Visigothic leader Athaulf was to become "the author of the Roman restoration," and his successors struggled to rework their tribal society within the framework of the Roman state.[28] In general, Henri Pirenne remarked with astonishment on how "little Germanism" was apparent in these new barbarian kingdoms:

> The Ostrogoths, Visigoths, Vandals and Burgundi were governed in the Roman manner. There was hardly a trace, or none

at all, of "Germanic principles." Under the new kings the old system of government survived, though doubtless in an imperfect
form . . . everything that survived and functioned was Roman.[29]

There really were barbarian invasions crossing the *limes* during
the final centuries of the Roman empire, but the "modest" marauding barbarian armies that did penetrate deeply into the interior of the
Roman empire in the fourth through sixth centuries turn out, on
closer inspection, to be "altogether a disappointment" in terms of
numbers and coherence in comparison to the vast *volk* migrations of
Romantic imagination. In the end, the Germanic linguistic frontier
moved west only about sixty miles. The very considerable medieval
transfiguration of the map of Europe was as much a matter simply of
the collapse of the overarching "artificial political unity" formerly
provided by Rome, which permitted the reemergence of "a mosaic"
of "long-silent local cultures," as it was the result of external invasions.[30] Certainly, the previously Roman population was not sweepingly replaced by incoming Germans.

To be sure, a self-conscious division between *Romani* and *barbari*
remained evident in Gaul until as late as the eighth century. However,
in Merovingian Europe, barbarian military strongmen eager to seize
control of the established Roman administrative structure collabo-
rated surprisingly easily with members of the old local Roman elite,
who were themselves often as anxious to defend their own local autonomy from central imperial intervention as they were proud of
their Roman cultural heritage.[31]

Henri Pirenne once blamed the rise of Islam for finally terminating the ancient unity of Mediterranean civilization and obliterating Rome. However, this famed "Pirenne thesis" has been subject to
much revisionist criticism. New archaeological evidence suggests, for
example, viewing "the Arab advance after 630 as the consequence
rather than the cause" of Rome's dissolution. By almost any measure,
Rome was certainly already in considerable disarray long before 630.
However, whether or not Rome had already "fallen," the subsequent
expansion of Islam did help ensure that the damage was irreparable.
Rome would never rise again. After the mid-seventh century, "the Roman foundations crumbled away to nothing," and the great Mediterranean empire vanished from our maps forever.[32]

The Chinese empire, too, was in acute disrepair during these centuries. Following the collapse of the Han dynasty in the third and fourth centuries, China experienced an equally devastating parallel process of political fragmentation and barbarian invasion. Unlike the case of Rome, however, the grand continuity of the ancient civilization in China was not permanently broken. However, on the Central Plain, in the north, it did falter for a moment.

The "Treatise on Ceremonial" in the *Dynastic History of the Northern Wei* pronounced that "from the time of the *Yongjia* [307–313] disturbances, weeds luxuriated in the deserted fields of China, the *li* were out of order, music collapsed, and the human spirit was exterminated." At the beginning of the fourth century, vicious internal power struggles ripped the imperial family apart, resulting in the effective collapse of imperial government throughout much of northern China. Perhaps a million refugees were forced onto the roads, and the entire economy on the Central Plain collapsed to the extent that no new coins were issued from the early 300s until 495.[33] As a newly appointed inspector of what is now Shanxi Province described the situation, as he saw it, in 307,

> From as soon as I crossed the border of the region I witnessed hardship with my own eyes. People had fled in all directions, not two out of ten remaining, leading the elderly and supporting the weak without interruption on the road. As for those who remained, they sold their wives and children, giving themselves up for death. White bones lie across the countryside, and the sound of cries of mourning disturbs the peaceful air. Tens of thousands of Hu [barbarians] surround us on the mountains. If you move a foot you encounter robbery; open your eyes and you see bandits. Only in Huguan [a strategic pass in southeastern Shanxi] can you hear reports of buying grain.[34]

During the fourth century, much of northern China came under the domination of the so-called five Hu peoples. In the language of modern ethnonationalism, Li Zefen described these five Hu peoples, in a book published in 1987, as "foreign races," or "races." Even more so than in the case of the Germanic invaders of imperial Rome, however, these particular Hu people had nearly all long lived within the borders of the Chinese empire, sometimes for centuries. Li Zefen recognizes this, assigning ultimate blame for the fourth-century disaster to a false sense of security in the much earlier Han dynasty, which was lulled into tolerating the migration of these alien "races" into northern China beginning no later than A.D. 44.[35] One must wonder, however, how these foreigners managed to live in China for some 300 years or more without ceasing to be foreigners.

In fact, they were Han subjects. In important senses, many of these people already really were more or less Chinese. It is necessary to realize that the Han dynasty Chinese population was far from being ethnically homogeneous or even aspiring toward that ever-elusive goal. Moreover, the empire's internal diversity was, if anything, more the result of imperial expansion than of foreign immigration. While some northern peoples undoubtedly did migrate south into China in a seminomadic fashion during the four centuries of the Han dynasty, effective Han administration at the same time also reached outward into whole new regions, bringing with it Han officials, troops, and settlers and creating newly mixed populations along the frontiers. The northwestern region beyond the bend of the Yellow River, in particular, was extensively resettled by the Han government beginning in the second century B.C., and these new Han arrivals inevitably mingled there were a preexisting Hu population.[36]

The *Shi ji* reports that following the surrender of the Xiongnu prince Hunye in 121 B.C., the entire Gansu corridor west to Lop Nor was "devoid of Xiongnu." To the extent that this is not merely exaggeration, however, it obviously does not mean that the preexisting population had been completely exterminated or driven away but merely that the entire region had submitted to Han rule and thus ceased to be Xiongnu and became Han Chinese instead.[37]

Especially to the extent that the Han empire claimed universal authority over all *tianxia* anyway, these people were all equally subjects of the same emperor. However, at the same time, local populations in every corner of the empire surely did differ culturally somewhat from each other and from the metropolitan officials of the imperial court. Many people may have preserved some faint memories of pre-Han life. As one recent archaeological study puts it, "multi-culturalism was part of the life of the empire."[38]

The "five Hu" who resurfaced in fourth-century northern China were therefore not "foreign races." The very idea is an unfortunate anachronism. They were—most of them—Han subjects. However, they also, undoubtedly, did preserve some distinctive local customs, and in an age of political chaos and war, familiarity with the practice of mounted archery, in particular, could prove militarily decisive.

China's northern frontier had never been absolute or sharply cut despite the powerful image (and reality) of the Great Wall. There was, instead, usually a murky transitional middle ground, occupied by "partly sinicized nomads and semibarbarized Chinese." The tides of military supremacy and political control washed back and forth across wide disputed areas. There were zones where seminomadic economic activity was quite normally practiced, even well within the borders of the Chinese empire. Conversely, from antiquity, some regions commonly thought of as steppe land were also "far from being only inhabited by horse-riding pastoral nomads."[39]

Despite stern imperial regulations, the border could be quite porous. It is recorded that the Han general Ma Yuan (14 B.C.–A.D. 49), better known as the suppressor of the Trung sisters' revolt in the far southeastern region of modern Vietnam, earlier in his career had taken refuge in the "northern lands" after releasing a prisoner in his custody without authorization, becoming a seminomadic pastoralist with his own herd of several thousand head of cattle, horses, and sheep. A second-century complaint alleged that Chinese people were fleeing the Han empire to seek refuge among the Xianbei and assisting them with their strategies.[40]

People also passed the other direction, into China proper. In the mid-Han dynasty, infighting among the Xiongnu leaders caused one branch to submit to the Han and settle within imperial borders in the Ordos region, at the top of the great upward loop formed by the Yellow River. As these Xiongnu proliferated and the Han polity was shaken by various disturbances, they became a source of concern to the court. In 216, the Xiongnu population in what is now Shanxi was reorganized into five divisions who were allowed to continue following their own native leaders but over whom Han commanders were also appointed as supervisors.

Shortly after 265, natural disasters on the steppe induced some 20,000 nomadic camps (perhaps 100,000 persons) to enter the empire and settle among the "Jin" (Chinese) people. In 284, another group of 29,300 Xiongnu were admitted. In 286, 100,000 Xiongnu subordinated themselves to a certain member of the Chinese imperial family near modern Xi'an, and a year later 11,500 additional Xiongnu surrendered, bringing with them a reported 22,000 head of cattle and 105,000 sheep. Between 265 and 287, it is estimated that over 250,000 non-Chinese persons were deliberately resettled deep within the interior of northern China to provide economic and military manpower.[41]

To some extent, furthermore, these new arrivals resisted easy assimilation. By the end of the third century, nineteen "kinds" of northern people had reportedly settled within the borders of the empire, in separate tribes, "without mixing." By the year 300, it was complained, perhaps with considerable exaggeration, that Rong and Di tribespeople constituted half the total population in the area of the old Han capital at Chang'an (modern Xi'an). These tribespeople were often reduced to economic subordination as "guest" farmers or incorporated into the military, much as toward the end of the Roman empire *barbarus* became almost synonymous with "soldier." Some may have felt an understandably bitter sense of grievance against the imperial elite.[42]

The late Han empire was not really overwhelmed by hordes of alien immigrants or invaders, but the empire had been forged in the first place from and over a wide variety of local identities, and its population was still far from homogeneous. These groups did not rise up and overthrow the empire, but when the empire's rulers themselves ruptured the thin fabric of imperial unity, local identities floated naturally back to the surface.

Di tribespeople, for example, in what are now northern Sichuan, eastern Gansu, and western Shaanxi Provinces, had been driven up into the mountains by the establishment of a Han imperial administrative presence. Through living among the Han population under imperial jurisdiction, they gradually became familiar with the Chinese language but continued to speak a quite different language among themselves and retained shadowy native organizations.[43] Some of these Di people subsequently reemerged to play a conspicuous role as conquerors in the ethnic turmoil of the fourth century.

As the Han imperial administration disintegrated, beginning with the Yellow Turban rebellion of 184 and the warlord devastation of the capital in 190, military strongmen arose in every corner of the empire to construct local power bases for themselves, often at considerable disregard for the official Han administrative boundaries. The Han imperial conscript army ceased to function, and local commanders assembled their own independently armed companies in a markedly "ramshackle pattern." Some warlords sprang from relatively obscure backgrounds, while others had been closely associated with the old imperial court, but nearly all found mounted archers from the northern frontier zone to be useful auxiliaries.[44]

A semblance of imperial government was still preserved for another 100 years. For much of the third century, an uneasy balance of power was maintained between the so-called Three Kingdoms of Wei, Shu, and Wu. For a generation at the end of the third century, imperial unity was even restored under the Western Jin dynasty (265–317; unified ca. 280–304). Then dissension within the imperial court, beginning around 290, escalated into bitter civil war that, when combined with natural disasters, pushed many of the inhabitants of the Yellow River valley area into aimless motion.[45] The resulting chaos provided an opening for "barbarian conquest," but these barbarians were not, for the most part, really invaders coming from beyond the imperial frontiers.

Significantly, the initial Xiongnu rebellion that sparked the famous "barbarian conquest" of northern China in 304 erupted among already heavily Sinified Xiongnu, long resident in the empire, who simultaneously sought to restore not only long-lost Xiongnu glory but also the Han empire explicitly by name. The rebel leader claimed descent from both the Xiongnu and the Han imperial lines; was known by the old Han imperial surname, Liu; and was a native of what is now Shanxi Province who had personally long been resident in the Chinese capital city. Conversely, imperial forces sent to resist this self-proclaimed Xiongnu "king of Han" were themselves reliant on the support of Tuoba Xianbei tribal auxiliaries.[46]

Although the dynastic history of the Jin, the *Jin shu*, records that 80 to 90 percent of the Western Jin government officials either were killed or fled during this period of warfare at the start of the fourth century, and it is possible that a million people or more may have escaped to the relatively placid south during the fourth century, some modern scholars doubt that these events were as traumatic for the overall population figures as is traditionally supposed. Undoubtedly, however, imperial tranquility in northern China was disrupted by 136 years of "ethnic" strife, lasting from about 304 to 439. The population may or may not have greatly decreased, but it was driven to seek refuge behind fortified enclosures as the fabric of society was torn apart by a mixture of contending forces. One pirate camp on the Yellow River in Henan in the early fourth century, for example, "used fishing boats to seize travelers returning to the east, over the years subsequently becoming very wealthy." In the late fourth century, there were reportedly over 3,000 fortified sites in the region "within the passes" (around Chang'an) alone.[47]

However, this warfare was not between cleanly demarcated ethnic groups, such as invading barbarians and defending Chinese. During the civil war of the "eight princes" at the beginning of the fourth century, nomadic cavalry was recruited by each of the various rival factions. After the mutual destruction of these imperial princes, the residual military camps became centers of independent, often nomadic, power. However, even then the sometimes confusing alignments of opposing forces long maintained their old imperial factional affiliations, often pitting Hu (barbarian) against Hu and Han (Chinese) against Han as well as Hu against Han.[48]

In the mid-fourth century, one general, Zhang Ping, held over 300 fortresses in modern Shanxi Province, with a population of more than 100,000 households of mixed "Hu and Jin [Chinese]." Early in the same century, Liu Chou (d. 311) once took shelter in a defensive work together with "several hundred Hu merchants," who, it is true, did supposedly threaten his life until he charmed them with a tune.[49] This was a period of general chaos. It is not clear, however, that foreigners really invaded Chinese territory from outside during the fourth century, nor was "Chinese" as obvious an ethnic identity then as we tend to assume that it is now.

One of the numerous petty "barbarian kingdoms" that were established in fourth-century northern China was the so-called Cheng-Han state, which lasted from 304 to 347, with its capital at Chengdu in modern Sichuan Province. Li Zefen classifies Cheng-Han explicitly as a kingdom of the Ba-di barbarian "race." More specifically, however, the ancestors of the ruling house of Cheng-Han were Sichuan tribesmen who had been loosely incorporated into the Chinese empire since the time of the Qin conquest of the region in the fourth century B.C. They had, therefore, already been living inside "China" for some 600 or 700 years by this time, long enough to be considered Chinese themselves.[50]

A small group of these people were moved northward to a point just east of modern Tianshui city in Gansu toward the beginning of the third century, where they came to be known by the hyphenated label Ba-di—that is, a cross between the Ba tribespeople of Sichuan and the Di of Gansu. At the close of the third century, one of these men, Li Te, whose father had been a local leader of the hunt, became noted for his own skill as a mounted archer and began to serve the local imperial government in minor capacities. His skill with horse and bow was presumably not part of his tribal heritage from mountainous Sichuan but something acquired in recent generations on the northwestern Gansu frontier. Beginning around 296, local rebellions created famine conditions in the area, and in 298, Li Te joined thousands of other refugees in fleeing to the relative safety of Sichuan.

The imperial inspector in Sichuan, amid these conditions of chaos, allegedly developed ambitions to establish an independent kingdom of his own and cultivated the skilled mounted archers among these refugees as his personal "teeth and claws." With such encouragement from the local representative of the central imperial government, Li Te's armed band, by now consisting of some 4,000 horsemen, became marauding "specialists in plundering." They soon became a perceived threat to everyone, including the imperial inspector himself, and, as government forces turned on their armed camp, Li Te was killed in the resulting series of battles. At one point, even their own Di and Qiang tribal auxiliaries rose in rebellion against Li family leadership. However, by the end of 303, Li family forces had successfully gained military control of the entire region—although amid conditions of such general desolation that even the victors were able to survive only by digging up and eating wild roots. In the winter of 304, Te's third son assumed the title king of Chengdu, issued a general pardon, and proclaimed new law codes and a new reign period. In 306, his title was elevated to emperor.

These Li family conquerors of fourth-century Sichuan were hardly foreign "invaders." Sichuan was supposedly their ancestral homeland, and they had lived within the Chinese empire since even before its initial unification in 221 B.C. Skill as mounted archers was crucial to their military success, but this was a skill acquired as northwestern frontiersmen rather than as part of any particular ancient ethnic heritage. Above all, they were refugees who were able to use their military skills to advantage in a time of general chaos. They were rough warriors of little sophistication, but the empire they established was still as thoroughly "Chinese" as they could make it. The founding emperor reportedly even once tried to justify his rule by allusion to the *Spring and Autumn Annals*.[51]

The fourth-century Xiongnu rebels in Shanxi did have a more

clearly alternate non-Chinese identity, although, as we have already seen, they simultaneously also claimed to be the legitimate successors to the Han dynasty. When the first Xiongnu rebel leader died in 310, his fourth son, Liu Cong (d. 318), murdered the heir apparent and proclaimed himself emperor, dispatching armies that managed to successively capture the Western Jin capital at Luoyang in 311 and its fallback location, Chang'an, in 316. This effectively put an end to Jin imperial government in the north. Liu Cong made his new capital in Shanxi and established a kind of dual government, with directors of convict labor *(sili)* to superintend the conquered Han population and assistants to the Shanyu to govern the "six barbarians."[52]

One of Liu Cong's generals was a man named Shi Le, whom we have encountered already as an example of an illiterate conqueror who nonetheless affected an interest in Chinese-language literature. Shi proclaimed himself ruler of Later Zhao (319–350) following Liu Cong's death. He had been born into a minor tribal leader's family of the Jie branch of the Xiongnu, in what is now central Shanxi Province. That is, he was a native of Shanxi. As a youth, Shi Le was fond of mounted archery but also apparently worked at farming, mixing stereotypically Chinese and nomadic pursuits. At age fourteen, he went with a neighbor to the Western Jin imperial capital, Luoyang, on trade. When an imperial regional inspector seized several local tribesmen, selling them as slaves farther east toward the coast, Shi Le was among them. There, he struck up an acquaintance with the head of a nearby horse pasture, and together they assembled a gang of mounted bandits. In 306, in a group of several hundred horsemen, they rallied to the standard of a Chinese imperial general. Later, welcoming refugees and escaped prisoners into his band, Shi Le embarked on a career of pillage that took him to the throne.[53]

Shi Le quickly rose through the ranks of warrior commanders and in 319 proclaimed himself king of Zhao, which briefly became one of the more important states of fourth-century northern China. Shi Le seems to have remained quite sensitive to his embarrassingly uncultured Hu origins, and as ruler he openly privileged fellow Hu. He "designated the Hu to be his [fellow] countrymen," invoked the old Xiongnu title Shanyu, made various special provisions for Hu persons at his court (including arranging for the instruction of their sons in combat skills), ordered the compilation of a history of his Shanxi homeland (*Shangdang guoji* [The Annals of the Kingdom of Shangdang]), and placed a stern taboo on any use of the derogatory word "Hu" (barbarian) in his palace.

This last must have been a Chinese-language taboo, however. Shi Le presumably spoke reasonably fluent Chinese of some variety, and Chinese certainly remained the only available written language. In many other ways, Shi Le posed as a typically Chinese monarch. On his coronation, he issued a general pardon; equalized the land taxes; presented gifts of silk and grain to those who were filial, fraternal, orphaned, or widowed; and proclaimed a new Chinese-style reign period. He established altars to the soil and grain and an ancestral temple; made a show of at least formally promoting study of the Confucian classics, law, and history at the imperial university; prohibited insulting members of the Chinese elite; encouraged agriculture, sericulture, and local education; mandated Hu conformity with Confucian marriage practice; and ultimately designated Luoyang as his southern capital precisely because of its historical associations with the Chinese Zhou, Han, and Jin dynasties.[54]

The policies of separately administering Hu and Han populations pursued by these early fourth-century Xiongnu kingdoms, with their unmistakable bias in favor of the Hu, created ethnic tensions that erupted into gruesome violence by 350. "All China was convulsed, and no one returned to farming." Later rulers generally adopted more tolerant, inclusive policies that in the long run proved to be more successful.[55] Although there may not have really been any "barbarian invasions" in fourth-century China, there clearly still long continued to be perceived and often sharply felt differences.

The Former Yan dynasty (285–370), established by the Murong Xianbei in the far northeast, tried to make itself "a model Chinese court," "as Chinese as the Chinese emperors themselves." By this time, the Murong had already "lived inside the boundaries of China for several generations" and could not exactly be considered invaders.[56] Much of their subject population seems, moreover, to have felt little compunction about living under Murong Xianbei rule. Yet at least one lofty Chinese gentleman in the early fourth century still adamantly refused to join the Murong court despite the Murong ruler's earnest plea:

> Today, the Son of Heaven has moved to Yue, and the four seas collapse in division. . . . Why hold reservations because of the dif-

ference between Chinese and barbarian? . . . How can you refuse
to surrender your heart because of a difference in customs?[57]

Clearly, there was still a profoundly felt difference between civilization and barbarism in the fourth century. However, the most
deeply held prejudices were not necessarily conceived in what we
might call ethnic or racial terms. The intense concern with blood-
lines that was so prominent in this era revolved around literal family
trees, not nations. Proud literati from good families felt themselves
indiscriminately superior to Chinese soldiers, Chinese peasants, and
foreigners. The (Chinese-language) poetry of one fifth-century Hu,
for example, was contemptuously disregarded by lofty Chinese literati,
without regard for its intrinsic merit, simply because of his humble
background. However, the poetic efforts of other, indisputably Chinese people from undistinguished families or even members of great
Chinese families who had not yet established their own literary repu-
tations were sometimes accorded virtually identical treatment.[58]

"China," in this era, was a very complicated stew. Barbarians became Chinese, and Chinese became barbarians. Kingdoms and empires rose and fell. Each tried to approximate the ideal Chinese imperial model. The mixture of sometimes contradictory elements we
saw illustrated in the career of Shi Le may have been in some ways typical of this period. In the long run, the unified Chinese empire was
restored, but only because the empire was able to rise above these
many differences and embrace them, giving rise to a gloriously cosmopolitan new Sui-Tang world.

RE-GENESIS: URBAN NOMADS, SUI AND TANG

The nomads of central Asia were proud people, as apt to scorn the
fineries of Chinese civilization as to envy them. It is true that the nomads did sometimes covet Chinese luxury goods, but their own arts
and technologies conversely also sometimes inspired Chinese imitation and evident admiration. In antiquity, wheeled vehicles, saddles
and bridles, bronze mirrors, ornamental belt fittings, and various techniques for metalworking were all introduced to China from the north
and west. During the period of intense ethnic intermingling following the collapse of the Han dynasty, "ethnic" items, such as cooking
styles, utensils, and chairs (literally "nomad beds," *hu chuang*), became
rather fashionable among wealthy imperial citizens.[59]

When imperial unity was finally restored by the strong Sui and Tang dynasties, after the late sixth century, this was achieved by a decidedly mixed "Sino-barbarian" elite. Even as Tang China was exuding powerful examples for Korea and Japan to imitate, the direction of cultural influences on Tang China itself came primarily from the west. Among the central Asian Hu, fashions that were in vogue in Sui-Tang China were ceremonial music, apparel, and oven-baked flour pastries called "nomad biscuits" *(hu bing)*.[60]

At the same time, these western influences were limited in extent, and there truly was much continuity amidst the striking changes that convulsed the Chinese world throughout this period. The disintegration of Han imperial unity after the third century had made it possible for a number of independent regimes to establish themselves amid the ruins of the Han empire, but even those that were demonstrably "foreign" were also inextricably "Chinese" in significant ways. Some were as thoroughly "Chinese" as the Han dynasty itself.

Members of the Chinese elite sometimes eagerly seized on periods of imperial weakness to carve independent kingdoms for themselves. During the third century, for example, both Liaodong, in the far northeast, and the region of present-day northern Vietnam, in the southeast, became centers of effectively independent "Chinese" authority.[61]

In the case of Liaodong (we will examine the case of Vietnam in a separate chapter), the weakening of Han power beginning around A.D. 107 encouraged border raids in the vicinity of modern Beijing by Koguryŏ and the Yemaek coming from the east and the Xianbei and Wuhuan coming from the west. In 190, the general who had just then seized control of the Han imperial capital appointed a man named Gongsun Du (d. 204) to serve as governor of Liaodong. Striking both east and west at Koguryŏ and the Wuhuan, Gongsun proclaimed himself marquis of Liaodong and consolidated what amounted to independent Gongsun family rule, lasting for a half century from 190 to 238, over a region that at its peak stretched over much of southern Manchuria, northern Korea, and the northern coast of Shandong peninsula.[62]

Because Koguryŏ and the Xianbei were both strong, Gongsun Du cultivated marriage alliances with the Puyŏ, who were located between them, as a buffer. Gongsun march lords even arrogated to themselves the prerogative of conferring imperial titles, in competition with other Chinese strongmen from the Central Plain, as an enticement to prospective Wuhuan tribal allies. In addition to the Chinese population under their direct jurisdiction, the Gongsuns seem to have also won the submission of a fringe of un-Sinified "barbarian" groups.[63]

During the final decade of their rule, however, the Gongsun family in Liaodong was threatened by the reemergence of centralized power under Three Kingdoms Wei and Wu. For a time, they were able to play these rival Chinese Wei and Wu empires off against each other, posing as tributaries of both, but in 238 a Wei army killed the last Gongsun warlord and "pacified" Liaodong. This Three Kingdoms (Cao-) Wei victory may have temporarily reestablished Chinese imperial power in the region of Manchuria and northern Korea, but the most notable immediate result was the creation of a power vacuum in the region, which was filled by Xianbei tribesmen.[64]

The people known as Xianbei are said to have originated in the Khingan Mountains of northern Manchuria. At least in 443, the then-reigning Tuoba Xianbei emperor gave credence to a report that his original ancestral temple had been rediscovered in a grotto on the eastern slopes of the northernmost reaches of the greater Khingan range, in what is now the Inner Mongolian autonomous region of the People's Republic of China, and dispatched an official to perform sacrifices there. Whether this represents a fifth-century fabrication or a genuine rediscovery must remain uncertain. In any case, the distant precursors of the people who would become known as the Xianbei eventually became affiliated with the great Xiongnu imperial confederation, and when the Xiongnu turned on them and defeated them around the beginning of the second century B.C., the story continues that they took refuge in remote Liaodong at a place called Xianbei Mountain, from which they purportedly derived their name.[65]

When the various branches of the Xiongnu began fighting among themselves in the late Han dynasty, the Xianbei presided over an enormous new tribal alliance that overspread and briefly replaced the entire former Xiongnu empire. This soon dissolved, however. In the third century, the Murong branch of the Xianbei settled in the region of northeastern China just west of the Liao River (Liaoxi). For their assistance to Three Kingdoms Wei in exterminating Gongsun warlord power east of the river, in Liaodong, the Murong leader was promoted to "king," and the Murong Xianbei began to build a state of their own at the northern end of the Gulf of Bohai.[66]

The Murong Xianbei kingdoms in the region of modern southern Manchuria and northeastern China were known as Former (285–370), Later (384–407), Western (384–394), and Southern (398–410) Yan. Apart from the Murong royal family itself, however, the population consisted extensively of people whose ancestors had once been Han imperial subjects, and these Yan kingdoms were heavily influenced by the standards of Chinese civilization.[67] Even the name Yan itself is a reference to the Warring States kingdom that had formerly flourished in this area. By the end of the fourth century, these various Murong Xianbei states were being squeezed out by the rising power of their own cousins, the Tuoba (Toba or Tabgatch) Xianbei.

In the meantime, however, an older brother, by a concubine, of the Murong founder of Former Yan, named Tuyuhun, escaped the danger of fraternal conflict by migrating westward with his own band of followers early in the fourth century. They eventually made a new homeland for themselves in the Qinghai (Koko Nor) region, and their western nomadic empire, known by the name of its founder, Tuyuhun, remained potent for centuries, well into Tang times.[68] This episode is illustrative both of the broad reach of Xianbei nomadic power, stretching from Manchuria to inner Tibet, and of the ephemeral nature of many such ethnonational labels, which in this case signified nothing more than the personal name of a revered leader.

The Xianbei political entity of greatest consequence for the history of East Asia was that of the Tuoba. Originating as part of the great second-century Xianbei confederation that had briefly replaced the Xiongnu empire, by the end of the third century the Tuoba Xianbei had established themselves along the eastern bank of the extensive northward loop of the Yellow River, in present-day Shanxi Province. Serving as auxiliaries to the Western Jin dynasty during the crisis of the early fourth century, their leaders were rewarded by imperial investiture with the Chinese titles of duke and then king in 310 and 314, respectively.

Taking advantage of the subsequent political vacuum resulting from the rapid disintegration of Jin imperial authority everywhere north of the Yangzi, by 318 the Tuoba Xianbei had seized control of a vast region extending from Manchuria to the Ili valley, and they began to build an agricultural base for their expanding empire through forced mobilization of conquered peoples. In 386, they proclaimed the establishment of a Chinese-style (Northern) Wei dynasty (386–534), and by 439 they had unified nearly all of northern China under their control. Conquering the Murong Xianbei kingdom, the Tuoba Xianbei attempted to absorb the Murong royal family by taking a Murong daughter as empress for the new dynastic founder.[69]

This Northern Wei dynasty proved to be the most stable and potent of all the Northern dynasties during China's extended era of north-south division, not finally breaking up until 534. The ambiguity of its position is that Northern Wei is simultaneously one of the more successful dynasties of imperial Chinese history—one early seventh-century Chinese history in fact claimed that Northern Wei had "obtained the Middle Kingdom" (zhongguo) and was squarely in the legitimate line of imperial succession—and an Altaic-speaking alien nomadic conquest state.[70]

The Tuoba Xianbei had originated in the far north, and their customs had once been "simple." Whatever that means, we may safely say that they originated outside the gravitational pull of Chinese civilization. By the third century, the Tuoba had begun interacting extensively with the states in northern China: Three Kingdoms Wei, and its successor, Western Jin. Chinese influences were initially rather unwelcome, however, and even after their conquest of the Central Plain they continued to speak a "barbarian language."[71]

Exactly what this language was is a matter of speculation. In the opinion of Peter Boodberg, the Tuoba vocabulary was "essentially Turkish, with a certain admixture of Mongol elements." Edwin Pulleyblank, to the contrary, concluded that it was Mongolian. Liu Xueyao, more cautiously, suggests that the Xianbei may have had "their own" language, which, apart from a broad classification as Ural-Altaic, should not be assumed to be identical with any other known language.[72] In truth, it probably presumes too much to suppose that the Xianbei population coincided with speakers of any one particular language.

Designations such as Xianbei mark open-ended political or tribal confederations, not "nations." According to early Chinese reports, the Xianbei were a branch of the Eastern Hu barbarians (a broad generic label if ever there was one), who had taken the name of a mountain fastness for their self-designation (as opposed to, for example, the name of an individual strongman such as Tuyuhun) but who were otherwise identical to the nearby Wuhuan group in terms of language and custom. When the northern Xiongnu—themselves a political confederation rather than a "race"—were militarily crushed beginning around A.D. 89, the Xianbei took possession of their steppe homeland. "There were still over ten-thousand camps of remaining Xiongnu descendants, and they all proclaimed themselves Xianbei. After this the Xianbei gradually flourished."[73] It was thus apparently a relatively simple matter to switch from one identity to another. The rising Xianbei empire brought together a variety of older groups under one new name, including some which were undoubtedly somewhat different from one another in terms of language or culture, while probably leaving out certain other groups that might have appeared, from a cultural perspective, virtually indistinguishable.

In any case, this was clearly a non-Chinese and non-Chinese-speaking steppe confederation. However, in 398 the Tuoba headman reportedly was inspired to build a permanent Chinese-style capital, for what would then become a more Chinese-style Tuoba state, while inspecting the palaces and pavilions of a captured city. He reportedly transported 360,000 people from the far northeast and Koguryŏ and 100,000 other skilled artisans to construct and populate his new metropolis (near modern Datong in Shanxi) and promoted imperial Chinese-style official titles, music, ceremonies, legal codes, and the construction of an ancestral temple. Conquered peoples were extensively resettled onto the war-ravaged and depopulated fields of northern China in order to secure an economic base for the regime. Between 398 and 469, by one estimate, the Tuoba transplanted no fewer than 1,205,500 people—Chinese, Koguryŏ, Xiongnu, Yemaek, and other branches of the Xianbei—into their home area.[74]

Because much of the population still remained concealed by local strongmen from central government registration and taxation, in 485–486 the Northern Wei court reorganized the countryside into a nested hierarchy of five-family neighborhoods, five-neighborhood hamlets, and five-hamlet communities, each with a designated head—the so-called "three heads" system. In the late fifth and early sixth centuries, Northern Wei implemented a variety of measures intended to enhance central control.[75] Of these, the famous "Equitable Fields" farmland allocation system is exceptional enough to merit closer examination here.

Early Warring States Legalist experiments, from the fifth century B.C., may have included policies to ensure the maximum use of the available farmland by administratively allocating fields on a household basis. However, if certain early Legalist governments really did take an active role in registering and possibly even allocating land to small independent farm families during the Warring States period, this may have paradoxically laid the very foundations for the later emergence of a system of private land ownership in China.[76]

The extractive power of the Legalist Qin state, for example, had been based on a system of household registration and taxation of individual small family farms. However, whether or not the Qin state ever actively intervened to allocate equivalent amounts of cultivatable land to these families, none of this farmland ordinarily thereafter ever reverted back to the government for redistribution, and it naturally and fairly rapidly tended to become, therefore, at least de facto private property. The result was that by the time of the Han dynasty, Chinese farmers clearly held effective private possession of their own land; land was registered under their names and could be disposed of at their discretion.[77]

Private land ownership and an essentially free market in land sales under the Han dynasty, however, notoriously enabled some people to prosper more than others, and over the four centuries of the Han dynasty, a growing gap allegedly appeared between wealthy and poor villagers. Following the collapse of the unified Han empire in the second and third centuries, great landed estates made their appearance, although those in the south, in particular, were often operated for commercial profit and should not be presumed to be directly equivalent to the feudal manors of medieval Europe. This concentration of private landed wealth in the hands of a relatively small number of great families, with its consequent reduction of the imperial tax base of independent small farm families, is conventionally blamed for the catastrophic inability of the centralized imperial system to continue functioning effectively during this period.[78]

For some 400 years following the disintegration of the Han dynasty, governments in China were weak and divided. Surprisingly, however, despite the appearance of large private estates and the emasculation of many of the central governments during this interval, proposals for some kind of state regulation of land use remained a recurrent and possibly even increasing fixture of imperial administrative policy throughout the period of division. The Jin dynasty land law of 280, for example, attempted both to limit the maximum extent of private landholdings and to establish a fixed minimum amount of land on which each farmer-citizen was obliged to pay taxes.[79]

In addition, if private estates, subject to limited and often ineffectual imperial regulation, came to characterize the agrarian sector of the increasingly prosperous and commercialized Southern dynasty economy, the less economically developed Tuoba Xianbei nomadic conquest regime in the north moved to impose more direct imperial control. This initiative was inspired by the desire both "to ensure state tax revenues, and to maintain social stability by equalizing landed properties."[80] The policy had, in other words, a combination of what might be called idealistic Confucian and pragmatic Legalist motives.

Confucius, according to Dong Zhongshu,

> was not troubled by poverty, but was troubled instead by inequity. . . . With great wealth there is arrogance; with great poverty there is grief. Grief makes one steal; arrogance makes one cruel. These are the feelings of all people. The Sage sees, in these feelings of all people, where disorder breeds. Therefore he regulates the ways of men and distinguishes superiors and inferiors, causing the wealthy to have enough to manifest their nobility, but not to the point of arrogance, and the poor to have enough to nourish their lives without reaching the point of grief. Taking this as his rule he equalizes them, so that property is not lacking, but superiors and inferiors are mutually content. Therefore they are easy to rule.[81]

This Confucian pronouncement does not suggest absolute equality even as an ideal, but it does assert quite forcefully the responsibility of government to intervene to enforce a sense of economic justice. This humane Confucian philosophical concern for equity and benevolence meshed quite well with the Legalist desire to maximize state revenue from the tax base of registered households. The larger the number of small independent farming families, the more taxpayers the state could draw on. Around 477, illustrating this one small point of congruence between the otherwise normally quite divergent Confucian and Legalist perspectives, Li Anshi (d. 493) memorialized that "we wish to ensure that there is no idle land, and no aimless human effort; that assertive families do not monopolize the benefits of rich soil, and humble fellows also have a share of land."[82]

In the late fifth-century Northern Wei dynasty, murky old Confucian ideals combined with the practical needs of a centralizing seminomadic Tuoba Xianbei conquest regime in northern China to result in the formulation of what is known as the Equitable Fields system. This system, with modifications, was maintained in operation from its inauguration in 485 until about the middle of the eighth century. Although the Northern Wei dynasty itself eventually broke up, its successor states in northern China continued to implement many of its innovative procedures for the consolidation of state power, including the Equitable Fields arrangement. Such measures ultimately provided the Sui dynasty with the institutional mechanisms to field an enormous army and in 588 to fling 518,000 troops in an amphibious assault across the Yangzi River, overwhelm the last Southern dynasty, and resurrect the venerable ideal of a unified Chinese empire.[83]

Unified Sui soon succumbed to unified Tang, but Tang continued the Equitable Fields land system, and in 623 issued a new household registration law intended to "bind the farmers to the land" and stabilize the Tang tax base. Under the version of the Equitable Fields system in effect in the early Tang dynasty, a record of the population and land conditions was to be drawn up yearly in each administrative village. Empire-wide household registries were to be revised every three years. By Tang law, each adult male aged eighteen to sixty was to be allocated 100 *mu* of farmland, of which 80 was to be considered a revocable allocation and 20 was to become permanent property. More detailed special provisions were also made for varying land conditions, widows, and the infirm.[84]

Relatively abundant archaeological and other evidence now makes it clear, moreover, that the household registration and land redistribution laws actually were enforced through the middle of the Tang dynasty, although in a notably flexible manner. An important innovation of the Northern Wei and Sui-Tang Equitable Fields system made this land system more intrusive than any that even the First Emperor of Qin had envisioned a millennium before: it now contained provisions for the periodic reversion of allocated land back to the state, for redistribution, thus partially subverting the de facto private ownership of the land that had been the norm under all previous regulatory regimes in imperial China.[85]

In compiling their fifth- and sixth-century law codes, the Tuoba rulers of the Northern Wei dynasty consulted experts from every major region of China, drawing memories of the already ancient Han dynastic law together with more recent legal innovations. The codes of law that were promulgated by the Tuoba Xianbei Northern Wei dynasty subsequently formed the immediate precedent for legislation in the reunified Sui and Tang dynasties and established a lasting standard for all of East Asia. With some justice, the resulting Tang law has been said to occupy a place in East Asian history comparable to that of Roman law in the West.[86]

However, the portions of the administrative law code of the Northern Wei through early Sui-Tang period that dealt with the allocation of farmland were only imperfectly replicated elsewhere in East Asia (though, as we will see later, they were closely emulated in early Japan).[87] Even in China, the Equitable Fields land allocation procedures were rather atypical of general imperial practice and might be considered a special legacy of the peculiar seminomadic Tuoba Xianbei Northern Wei experience—almost a foreign imposition.

And yet, by the time the Equitable Fields land regulations were first issued, the Northern Wei court, despite its origins as an Altaic-speaking seminomadic frontier confederation, was deep in the midst of a quite conscious and comprehensive process of Sinification. This Sinification program reached a fever pitch during the reign of Emperor Xiaowen (r. 471–499), whose very (posthumous, Chinese-language) name is redolent of Confucian virtue—Xiaowen: filial and literate. In 483, his court (his active personal reign did not begin until the death of the empress dowager in 490) ordered a ban on same-surname marriage, a traditional Chinese taboo. In 484, the old imperial system of paying official salaries was restored to limit temptations toward official abuses. Also in 484, the Northern Wei adopted the thoroughly Chinese model of constructing a long wall to defend against the military threat from nomadic "northern barbarians." In 489, a Confucian temple was established at the capital, with obligatory seasonal sacrifices to Confucius as well as to the Tuoba imperial ancestors.

In 494, to the reported dissatisfaction of his subjects, the emperor forbade the wearing of Hu clothing. At least one modern scholar has concluded, however, not only that this degree was ineffective but that the direction of influence went the other way and that the "native Chinese" costume worn during the subsequent Chinese Sui, Tang, and Song dynasties originated with Tuoba Xianbei Northern Wei "barbarian" fashions.[88]

In 495, the emperor ordered the repair of Confucius' tomb and personally offered Confucian sacrifices. Also in 495, officials who used the Xianbei language at court were threatened with dismissal, the emperor supposedly arguing that "if names are not correct and speech not appropriate, ritual and music cannot flourish. Today I wish to abstain from all northern languages, and uniformly follow the correct [Chinese] pronunciations." That same year, the dynasty adopted standard units of measurement based on those described in the old Han dynasty records. The following year, in 496, members of the court were obliged to discard their Xianbei names in favor of Chinese-style surnames, and all ministers not actively engaged in military service were required to observe the Confucian three years of mourning for a deceased father.[89]

The Chinese sources in which this Sinification of the Tuoba Xianbei was recorded for posterity are naturally suspect of having a pro-Chinese bias, but there can be no mistaking the extremely thorough and self-conscious nature of the Sinification program attempted by the Northern Wei court at the end of the fifth century. As is typical of the Sinification process everywhere, these reforms included a mixture of practical administrative improvements designed to increase the efficiency of imperial government and other purely cultural changes whose substantive advantages are, perhaps, difficult for us to discern today. In constructing an ancestral temple and great hall of state at Datong, for example, the Northern Wei court dispatched a man to measure the foundations of the old Three Kingdoms Wei and Jin dynasty ruins so that their proportions would accord with precedent. The underlying motive for all these actions, furthermore, seems to have been to lay the groundwork for the conquest of the south and the reunification of the entire empire rather than the inherent attractiveness of Chinese culture itself.[90] This motivation merely underscores, however, the extent to which ethnicity is a plastic political tool rather than a permanent fact of nature.

One result of this determined Sinification campaign was that the "non-Chinese" Northern Wei dynasty could now claim to have become almost more "Chinese" than the ethnically purer Southern dynasty courts. Having adopted a "correct" standard of Chinese pronunciation, for example, one member of the Northern Wei court in 529 was able to ridicule the dialect-ridden spoken Chinese language of the south. In the realm of Confucian scholarship, the "non-Chinese" Northern dynasties in general were famous for adhering more closely

to Han dynasty Confucian standards than the "native Chinese" Southern dynasties, with their "new learning." Ironically, the eternally classic Chinese story of "Mulan" was probably originally a product of the
Sinified Tuoba Xianbei Northern Wei society of this period.[91]

By the early sixth century, the Northern Wei had become such a
thoroughly typical Chinese dynasty that it was possible for a visitor
from the south to report:

> Since the Jin and Song dynasties [317–479] we have called Luo-
> yang [the new Northern Wei capital] a wasteland, and from here
> said that everyone north of the Yangzi is a barbarian. Recently I
> went to Luoyang, and first realized that there are also well-bred
> families on the Central Plain. Propriety and justice flourish, and
> people and things are so abundant that I am unable to convey
> in words what you have not seen with your own eyes.[92]

The idea of Sinification, like the idea of westernization in modern times, provokes extreme reactions: both triumphal exultation,
from admirers of Chinese civilization, and angry denial that any such
thing ever happened from others. Both positions are untenable in extreme form; the truth, predictably, lies somewhere in between. Assimilation—understood to mean a process of becoming more alike—is
really "one of the most fundamental of social processes." However,
such assimilation is a complex process involving countless specific
choices made by unique individuals. It also typically involves adjust-
ments in the lifestyles of majority populations as well as minorities
and is seldom simply the inexorable digestion of entire ethnic blocs
by dominant majorities; and, even as a group of people may indeed
be assimilating toward some standard with regard to certain features
of their cultural practice, the very same people may simultaneously
"also be differentiating themselves"—accentuating their differences
from another population group—with regard to other aspects of their
cultural repertoire.[93] Consciousness of difference—and pride in the
maintenance of the outward symbols of that difference—is not uncommonly actively intensified by encounters with others.

The Sinification of the Tuoba Xianbei tends to be exaggerated
in our Chinese-language sources (there are no surviving Xianbei-
language histories) both because of the biases of their Chinese au-
thors and because of the nature of the language itself. Nothing com-

pletes the illusion of Sinification like the use of Chinese names and terminology in an entirely *kanji* text. The subjects of such histories inevitably become almost indistinguishable from any other "Chinese." The meritorious official Li Xian (502–569), to take one example, figured in Chinese history simply as just another Chinese gentleman until a tomb inscription was recently discovered disclosing his Tuoba Xianbei ancestry.[94]

As we have seen, to the extent that the Tuoba Xianbei elite really did adopt Chinese names, this practice began only at the end of the fifth century. Most of the earlier Chinese-style names of Xianbei people that populate the official dynastic history of the Northern Wei are, therefore, misleading anachronisms, dating from the sixth century.[95] This may greatly misrepresent the degree of foreignness that these figures exhibited at the time.

Moreover, sometimes the process of linguistic acculturation was reversed. As part of a general reaction against the extremity of the late Northern Wei Sinification measures, the old Xianbei surnames were deliberately restored under the subsequent Western Wei dynasty (534–557), beginning around 549, and Xianbei surnames were even bestowed as a favor on selected Chinese persons. To take one prominent example, the (supposedly Chinese) father of the man who would one day found the Sui dynasty and reunify "China" was awarded a non-Chinese surname for his services to the Northern Zhou dynasty (557–581). For a time in the sixth century, it seems to have been actively advantageous for Chinese people to learn to speak the Xianbei language. This Xianbei-ification phase proved to be fleeting, however. The new, non-Chinese surnames that had been so liberally bestowed on leading military officers under the Western Wei dynasty were soon re-replaced with Chinese names by the founder of the Sui dynasty only a generation later.[96]

With all the necessary caveats, after the fifth century the long-term adoption of Chinese-style names and the Chinese written language by many of the originally non-Chinese northern peoples probably did expedite an assimilation process that unmistakably did go forward, if in a somewhat halting and imperfect fashion, over the long duration of imperial history, but it was a slow process. Over 150 years elapsed between the first known, abortive Tuoba proposal to build a permanent Chinese-style walled capital for themselves in 339 and their relocation to the site of the old Han imperial capital at Luoyang in 494. Up until the move to Luoyang, at least, ethnic non-Chinese remained dominant in the Northern Wei government, although even then dynastic imperial interests were given precedence in the selection of officials over "ethnicity, class, cultural background, and historical ties with the tribal confederation of pre-dynastic times."[97]

Perhaps a million persons were relocated south onto the Central Plain at the time of the transfer of the Northern Wei capital from Datong to Luoyang in 494. This move split the preexisting Tuoba Xianbei population into two groups, one increasingly China oriented and "Chinese" and one remaining anchored north of the great loop of the Yellow River, especially in six garrisons located on the margin of the steppe. These northern Xianbei remained Xianbei in language and culture. They now found themselves politically marginalized, but they continued to hold the critical ingredient of military power: skill as mounted archers.[98] These fierce warriors were not pleased to find themselves relegated now to the margins.

Mounted archery was an inescapable feature of the lifestyle of the northwestern frontier, and frontiersmen were accordingly consistently prominent throughout the warfare of the Northern and Southern dynasties. One Xiongnu cavalry officer, for example, distinguished himself in the Western Jin imperial conquest of Three Kingdoms Wu in the third century.[99] The man named Hou Jing, who terrorized Southern dynasty Liang after 548 (and contributing much to the ultimate extinction of the Southern dynastic line in 589), was an accomplished mounted archer hailing from the Ordos region.[100] Horsemen from what is now Gansu Province, as we have already seen, founded the short-lived fourth-century Cheng-Han empire in Sichuan, and even as the Tuoba Xianbei rulers of the Northern Wei dynasty began to convert their state into a more thoroughly Chinese-style empire, it remained militarily advantageous for some of them to continue to cultivate the frontier ethos.

In the early fifth century, it is said that the Tuoba converted vast stretches of the Shaanxi-Gansu region into state pastureland, on which they grazed two million head of horses, half that number of camels, and innumerable cattle and sheep. In 450, when a group of ethnoculturally Chinese Northern Wei foot soldiers were captured by Southern dynasty forces and queried as to why they were fighting on behalf of barbarian (Tuoba Xianbei) rulers, they replied that they had been forcibly driven ahead on foot by the mounted Xianbei as a kind of human shield—"it is not that we dared rebel against the Middle Kingdom."[101]

A clear Xianbei-Chinese, ruler-subject dichotomy may be observed in operation here, but the difference was one more of lifestyle than of biological inheritance. An interesting parallel example of how an otherwise marginal frontier horse-breeding region can become politically dominant, thanks to the relative military advantage conferred by a mounted-archer warrior ethos—and, in this case, one that clearly does not permit any primordial racial explanation—may also be found in the case of Japan. There, government pastures were established in the northeastern Kantō frontier region (near modern Tokyo) in late prehistory and the early historical period for the purpose of supplying the newly solidifying Japanese state with horses for military and other uses. Immigrants from the continent seem to have been prominent in the early development of these pastures, but the specialization in mounted archery that naturally became characteristic of this region gradually generated a new and distinctively Japanese warrior class. The climactic twelfth-century confrontation between these rude warrior upstarts, who came to dominate the remainder of premodern Japanese history simply because of their unadorned coercive force, and the refined civil aristocracy of the old western capital is one of the most poignant themes in early medieval Japanese literature.[102]

In China, Xianbei (or Xianbei-ized) cavalry stationed on the Central Plain retained a separate identity—even sometimes physically separate military camps—until after the Sui reunification of the empire in the late sixth century. It was only when the Tang dynasty began requiring soldiers to spend three seasons of each year engaged in agricultural work, after 636, that the line of mutual distaste between mounted warrior and farmer began to dissolve, and the Xianbei subsequently disappeared from the Central Plain, absorbed into the general Chinese population.[103]

In the meantime, going the other way and showing that assimilation is not a one-way process, some previously Chinese people had become Xianbei. After the transfer of the Northern Wei capital to Central Plain Luoyang at the end of the fifth century, the glaring distinction was not so much between Chinese and Xianbei, conceived as permanently hereditary identities, as between opposing groups of people who had become either Chinese-ized or Xianbei-ized, with the direction of transformation being determined largely by their immediate environment. Within three generations after being exiled to a frontier garrison in the Ordos region, for example, the family of a certain Chinese attendant censor from the eastern Central Plain had come to consider themselves Xianbei and the Xianbei language their native tongue. The third-generation scion of this originally Chinese family, Gao Huan (d. 547), bitterly resented the Sinified hauteur of the Tuoba Xianbei imperial capital and participated in a violently conservative Xianbei reaction against the Northern Wei.[104]

After his move to the traditional Chinese heartland in Luoyang, the Tuoba Xianbei Northern Wei emperor supposedly favored Chinese Confucians, to the reported consternation of part of the imperial family and many of the old Xianbei subjects. Many Xianbei were uncomfortable with the Sinification program altogether. A rebellion soon erupted among the six northern frontier garrisons, which led indirectly to the overthrow of the dynasty. Within forty years of the transfer of the Northern Wei capital to Luoyang, Luoyang had lost its position as capital again, and its streets stood deserted.[105]

There was a general reaction against Sinification in the north after Emperor Xiaowen's reign. The last, short-lived Northern Wei monarch, Tuoba Xiu (r. 532–534 as Emperor Xiaowu), for example, revived an ancient steppe ritual for his coronation that involved his being lifted on a black felt rug by seven men.[106] The seminomadic Tuoba Xianbei non-Chinese self-identification had thus certainly not been extinguished even by a lengthy process of Sinification.

Yet it would be overly simplistic to take this military reaction as evidence of the general inappropriateness or impossibility of trying to turn Xianbei into Chinese. The more successfully the Xianbei court Sinified itself—the more Chinese, urban, and agriculturally based it became—the more militarily vulnerable it also became to nomadic mounted archers. The frontier garrisons, where the direction of assimilation had tended toward nomadification rather than Sinification, therefore remained crucial to the defense of the Northern Wei dynasty, even as they became progressively ever more marginal to the increasingly Chinese-style state and society as a whole. At the same time, as seminomadic warriors in their own right, these frontier garrisons themselves posed a potentially deadly threat to the dynasty. When the Sinified Northern Wei dynasty entered a protracted period of peace with the opposing steppe empire of the Rouran, lasting from 475 to 523, the apparent defensive importance of the frontier garrisons was diminished in the eyes of the court. The already troublesome frontier garrisons were consequently neglected and, feeling further alienated and impoverished, erupted in rebellion.[107]

The curious position of the Northern Wei dynasty within Chinese history is that it was simultaneously an alien nomadic conquest empire and one of the greater Chinese dynasties. Such ambiguity, and contradiction, is fundamental to the Northern Wei, and, whether or not the Northern Wei should be considered part of the direct orthodox line of sole imperial legitimacy in Chinese history, the only slightly less mixed Sino-barbarian northern dynasty known as Sui certainly stands foursquare in the line of legitimate succession. The Chinese empire was reunified in 589 by people who were at least partially foreigners.

The Sui dynasty reunified China, and when Sui was soon replaced by Tang in 618—the great Chinese dynasty that would serve as the immediate template for the emergence of independent states in Japan, Korea, and Vietnam—the coup was accomplished by yet another, very possibly Xianbei-language-speaking, northwestern frontier general from Shanxi and Inner Mongolia, the area that had served as the springboard for so many of China's culturally mixed Northern dynasties, including the Tuoba Xianbei Northern Wei.[108]

Before Vietnam

SOUTHERN YUE

The present configuration of the country we call Vietnam would have been unimaginable to anyone living during the time period covered in this book. Not only was the entire southern half of what is now Vietnam incorporated into the country only later, but neither the name Vietnam nor any recognizable Vietnamese identity referred to by some other name would have been discernable to people of this era. Vietnam simply did not exist yet. Instead, what is today northern Vietnam—the region centering around the Red River valley—was part of the Chinese empire. It was a peripheral part, to be sure, but there was no obvious ethnic or cultural frontier dividing what is now Vietnam from other parts of the southeastern-most administrative region of the empire, Lingnan—a region that included the modern Chinese provinces of Guangdong (Canton) and Guangxi as well as northern Vietnam.[1]

Lingnan (which means "south of the ridges"), on the other hand, was physically detached from the rest of the Chinese empire by an arc of low mountains. Long before Lingnan had ever been incorporated into China, it had been home to prehistoric communities of some sophistication who had mastered rice farming beginning no later than 2000 B.C. and the production of bronzes from as early as 1500 B.C. By the time of the so-called Dong Son archaeological phase, which flourished from approximately 500 to 300 B.C., people in the vicinity of modern northern Vietnam were familiar with iron technology and were producing a most remarkably characteristic type of bronze drum. This magnificent Dong Son culture was unique, but it had obvious cultural affiliations with a wide swath of what we now call Southeast Asia. Many of the new breakthrough technologies, including rice cultivation, seem to have filtered into the region from Yue or, in some cases, possibly Central Plain Chinese peoples living farther north.[2]

The earliest native Vietnamese histories, which date from the fourteenth century, speak of an independent Van-lang kingdom founded in the general area of Vietnam during the seventh century B.C. and surviving through eighteen generations of monarchs. This legendary account may be said to roughly coincide, furthermore, with the archaeologically discovered Dong Son culture. Modern Vietnamese scholars have been quick to identify this Van-lang with the origins of a Vietnamese "nation."[3]

As the archaeological record clearly attests, there undoubtedly was a vibrant and independent local culture in the region during this period, but these sketchy ancient Vietnamese legends were culled from somewhat hazy older Chinese sources, compiled mostly during the sixth and seventh centuries, and may not be very reliable. It is probably fairest to say that this archaeologically identified Dong Son culture was not exactly either Chinese or Vietnamese in the modern nationalist sense but rather a prehistoric local Yue (V: Viet) society that was becoming progressively more sophisticated through interaction with the earlier-blooming Yue and Central Plain states farther north.[4]

The earliest legends also go on to insist, in any case, that this Van-lang kingdom was "expelled" and replaced by an invading prince from (a place name usually associated with) what is now Sichuan Province in 257 B.C. who founded a new kingdom there called Au Lạc. The huge "spiral city" attributed to this prince at Co-loa is thought to have been the first great city in all of Lingnan and the entire Indochinese peninsula as well. Although this legendary event should not be imagined in terms of any sweeping elimination and replacement of the previously existing population, both the legend and the archaeological evidence from the remains of the city are suggestive of some discontinuity in the local culture and a new level of northern influence on the area of present-day northern Vietnam.[5] This is in keeping with our general picture of many different local prehistoric cultures being gradually transformed through interaction with the Central Plain core civilization.

We might add that while the genetic or "racial" composition of these societies probably often did exhibit a fairly high degree of local continuity over extended periods of time, the racial or genetic contribution to culture or civilization is presumed to be rather minimal. Physical attributes such as skin pigmentation are not considered to be culturally very significant, except where racial prejudice itself becomes a factor, which generally was not the case in ancient East Asia (although isolated examples of bigotry can undoubtedly be adduced).

In high antiquity, the entire Lingnan region, Guangdong and Guangxi as well as Vietnam, was completely beyond the pale of Bronze Age Chinese civilization. The First Emperor of Qin, however, motivated by a desire for the region's valuable exotic products, ordered a massive invasion of Lingnan in 214 B.C., allegedly conscripting a half million merchants and other "useless" fellows to garrison the newly conquered territory and digging canals to provision them. Within the area of present-day Vietnam, in particular, some degree of local self-rule seems to have long continued to be the norm. However, Lingnan was now, rather suddenly, part of the Chinese empire.[6]

Qin achieved an early pinnacle of imperial geographic expansion. However, Qin's rise and fall was meteoric. The centralized Qin imperial administration in what is now Yunnan Province, in the southwest, lasted scarcely a decade. In the southeast, three separate Yue kingdoms were resurrected amid the ruins of the shattered Qin empire: Eastern Ou in what is now southern Zhejiang Province, Min-Yue in Fujian Province, and Southern Yue in Guangdong, Guangxi, and northern Vietnam.[7]

The kings of Min-Yue claimed descent from the old native Yue royalty. Under Qin rule, these native potentates had been reduced to the status of commandery administrators, but because of their support for the successful founder of the Han dynasty during the subsequent civil wars, they were reenfeoffed by Han as autonomous princes in 201 B.C. In 138 B.C., Min-Yue attacked its northern neighbor, Eastern Ou, prompting an appeal for aid from Eastern Ou to the Han Son of Heaven. The Han defender-in-chief counseled that since their abandonment after the Qin dynasty, these kingdoms had never been subject to the empire and that, since it was only normal for the Yue people to engage in frequent internecine warfare, this should not be of concern to the Han Middle Kingdom. However, a counter argument prevailed that if the Son of Heaven did not come to the aid of small dependencies in their hours of need, "how could we treat the myriad kingdoms as our children?" A Han imperial army was sent by sea, dispatched from the region of modern Shaoxing in northern Zhejiang, and the Min-Yue troops withdrew.[8]

Despite this temporary reprieve, the independent Eastern Ou kingdom was utterly liquidated in 110 B.C., and the Han emperor allegedly transported the entire Yue population of Eastern Ou north to the lands between the Huai and Yangzi Rivers, leaving the former Eastern Ou lands vacant.[9] Their old territory in modern Zhejiang Province has subsequently become economically and demographically central to modern China, though it once was very foreign.

In 135 B.C., meanwhile, the expansionistic Min-Yue kingdom turned its attention south and invaded Southern Yue. A semi-independent Han prince in what is now Anhui Province wrote to (his nephew) the Han emperor, vigorously trying to dissuade the empire from military intervention in this war by offering the argument that "Yue is a land beyond this world, with a people who shear their hair and tattoo their bodies. It cannot be regulated by the laws of civilized countries."[10] Although the author of this epistle had ulterior motives—to prevent Han imperial military interference in his own domain—it is clear that the erstwhile Qin imperial territories in what is now southeastern China were still regarded as quite alien lands in the early Han dynasty. Yet the southernmost of these independent Yue kingdoms, Southern Yue, with its capital at modern Guangzhou (Canton), was actually not a "native" kingdom at all. The Southern Yue kingdom had been founded by an ex-Qin official who personally was of Central Plain extraction.

As the Qin world empire unraveled toward the end of the third century B.C., the desperately ill Qin commandant at Guangzhou (Canton, then called Panyu) confided to his subordinate Zhao Tuo (d. 137 B.C.) that

> the Middle Kingdom is in turmoil and we do not know from where peace will come. Heroes, rebelling against Qin, establish each other. Nanhai [the region whose capital Panyu was] is remote, but I fear that bandit soldiers will raid this far. I wish to raise troops and block up the new roads, in preparation. . . . Moreover, Panyu [Canton] occupies a strategic mountainous location. Relying upon Nanhai, east and west for several thou-

sand *li* we have the support of many people from the Middle Kingdom. This [place] is also the lord of a region, and can be used to establish an [independent] kingdom.[11]

Zhao Tuo took this advice and, following his mentor's death, in 208 B.C., established the independent kingdom of Southern Yue (C: Nan Yue; V: Nam-Viet), which survived for almost a century, though often as at least nominal vassals of the Han empire. Zhao Tuo was a native of the Central Plain, and he supposedly tempted his subjects with the attractions of Chinese higher culture. At the same time, he was also "transformed by the customs of the southern barbarians" and to some extent "went native," as they used to say.

The histories record a dramatic confrontation between Zhao Tuo and the Han imperial emissary Lu Jia (himself a man of Chu, once a somewhat marginal southern Chinese kingdom) in 196 B.C. in which Zhao greeted Lu like a Yue native, with his hair in a bun and squatting on the ground. Lu protested that Zhao had been born in the Middle Kingdom, with a family graveyard in what is now Hebei Province (near modern Beijing), and yet here he had unnaturally cast aside his civilized raiment to contend with the imperial Son of Heaven from "insignificant Yue." Sitting up abruptly, the story goes, Zhao apologized, explaining that long residence among barbarians had made him neglectful of courtesy. Needless to say, the conversation recorded in these histories cannot possibly be presumed to be scrupulously accurate, but the flavor of the dialogue may indeed be suggestive of roughly contemporary Chinese attitudes.[12]

The new king's subjects were described disparagingly as consisting of "no more than a few tens of thousands, all barbarians, precariously perched between the mountains and the sea, comparable to a single Han commandery." Former imperial administrators who had been in place at the time of the Qin disintegration formed the nucleus of this new Southern Yue government, but it is clear that the Sinified stratum of local society still constituted only a very thin layer. Archaeology confirms that Dong Son material culture survived in Vietnam for some time after the Qin conquest. Southern Yue cemeteries excavated by archaeologists in Canton reveal mixed Chinese- and Yue-style interments, sometimes with mixed furnishings in a single tomb, while (to date) no entirely native Yue graveyards have been found dating from the period of Southern Yue independence.

Despite its cultural pluralism, Southern Yue society was thus evidently rather integrated and cohesive.[13]

Southern Yue was a marginal state with a still largely un-Sinified indigenous population, leavened only by a scattering of settlers and former officials from the Central Plain proper; but it was nonetheless organized broadly along the lines of other Chinese states farther north. The third king of Southern Yue personally attended the Han imperial court and took a northern woman (from the Hebei area) as his concubine. After their son subsequently ascended the throne as the fourth king, amid growing popular disaffection, this woman pushed for a closer relationship with the Han empire, including a triennial audience with the Han emperor and the elimination of the need for passes at the border.

A Yue official who had served three Southern Yue kings in succession and who was reportedly personally even more popular than the current king was appalled at the prospect of this increased level of subordination to the Han empire, and in 113 B.C. he rose up in rebellion and killed the king, the king's mother, and the Han ambassadors. In the following year, the Han empire responded by dispatching 100,000 troops, crushing the rebellion, and in 111–110 B.C. reincorporating Lingnan directly into the empire for the first time since the Qin dynasty's fragmentation almost a century earlier. Thereafter, the lands that once constituted Southern Yue would always remain part of the Chinese empire, except for the far southernmost section, which achieved permanent independence in 939 and in 1802 finally came to be known as Vietnam (C: Yuenan, "south of Yue").[14]

Included in the vast Lingnan region that was brought under direct Han imperial administration in 110 B.C. was an island, nestled in the South China Sea between Guangzhou and modern Vietnam, which is known today as Hainan. In antiquity, Hainan island was sparsely inhabited by a mixed aboriginal population who reportedly "did not follow the virtuous teachings," carved decorative patterns into their cheeks, and passed pearls through their ears until their earlobes hung down to their shoulders. Although Hainan was now part of the Chinese empire, it suffered from continuous friction between Han dynasty officials and the natives.

One early Han governor of the southern portion of Hainan assessed a wide strip of cloth in tribute from the natives, provoking an uprising in which he was killed. His son returned with 10,000 men and subdued these natives, but the rare products that he continued to extract from them as imperial tribute kept the rebellion simmering, and in 46 B.C. the southern portion of the island had to be abandoned altogether—although an imperial foothold may have been retained on the northwestern shore.

Thereafter, Hainan island's position within the empire remained precarious. Around the year 460, for example, a great tribal chieftain in the Guangxi-Guangdong area surrendered to the then-current Southern dynasty and requested command of an imperial army to subjugate recalcitrant unsubmissive neighboring tribes. The officers whom he dispatched to conquer southern Hainan failed to do so, however, and revolted, killing him instead.

Even during the high Tang period, when Chinese imperial military power was possibly at its zenith, the imperial grip on Hainan continued to be rather tenuous. Tang dynasty Yai Prefecture, in the northeast of the island, had a registered population of only 819 households but held an imperial garrison and produced tribute for the empire in gold, silver, pearls, tortoiseshell, and other rarities. Neighboring Qiong Prefecture, which was detached from Yai in 631, had a registered population of only 649 households and relapsed under the control of rebellious tribesman from 667 to 789. Even today, Hainan is still something of a rough frontier province, described as recently as 1983 by the then-premier of the People's Republic of China as "the most underdeveloped region in the world."[15]

On the mainland to the west of Hainan, in the region of present-day Vietnam, fragmentary evidence suggests that as a reward for the alacrity with which they surrendered to Han forces, local chieftains were largely reconfirmed in their positions by the Han empire, and a degree of local Yue self-rule continued, as before, in that region. However, Lingnan, rather than Vietnam, was the key geographic region. The famous "native Vietnamese" rebellion of the Trung sisters in A.D. 40–42, for example, was not confined to what is now Vietnam but instead straddled the modern Sino-Vietnamese border—quite naturally since the pre-Chinese "natives" lived on both sides of a modern national border that simply did not exist at that time.[16]

IMPERIAL ENTREPÔT

The Trung sisters' rebellion was dealt with harshly. They were suppressed, and the bronze drums that were so characteristic of Dong Son culture and that had evidently symbolized the power of the na-

tive elite were confiscated and melted down. The old indigenous local chieftains disappear altogether thereafter, perhaps merging with
new arrivals from the north to generate a mixed new local elite. Henri
Maspero concludes that what is now Vietnam was transformed by this
military campaign from a Han imperial protectorate, with distinctive
native institutions and culture, into a part of the Chinese empire
proper.[17]

Beginning in the first century A.D., there seems to have been a
considerable influx of Han settlers coming into the Red River valley
region, some drawn by economic opportunity and others apparently
exiled criminals who were deliberately transported there by the imperial government. The cultural integration of the region into the
empire was accordingly accelerated.[18] By this time, a city on the Red
River known as Jiaozhi (later often called Jiaozhou), near present-day
Hanoi, had also emerged as possibly the Han empire's foremost maritime trading port.

In the third century A.D., Zhang Hua (232–300) reported that
there was no break in the traffic coming across the South Seas to Jiaozhi. Together with Canton (originally called Panyu, also known as
Nanhai, and eventually Guangzhou), Jiaozhi was one of the two great
cities of early imperial Lingnan, both of which were famous as places
where mercantile fortunes were easily made. However, precisely because early imperial interest in the region was so exhaustively focused
on the South Sea trade, the ultimate markets for the distribution of
whose commodities lay farther north, these two great cities in Lingnan served as little more than transshipment centers, having relatively little cultural or economic impact on the population of their
own hinterlands. The great cities were therefore enclaves of sophisticated Chinese civilization on the shores of a coastline whose interior
jungles remained largely tribal.[19]

The native customs and languages spoken in Lingnan were described as being highly diverse. Even after four centuries of imperial
rule, in 231 one official could still report that on Hainan island, outside the urban imperial administrative centers, men and women coupled (to the horror of Confucian moralists) without regard for their
parents' wishes at a festival in the eighth month, while in certain parts
of what is now Vietnam a custom like the levirate was practiced, and
in the extreme south men and women went about naked without
shame.[20] In other words, it would be possible to argue that 400 years

of Chinese rule in Lingnan had achieved little progress toward the Sinification of the population and that Vietnam in particular was still very "uncivilized."

It may be useful here to compare the experience of Vietnam under the Chinese empire, as of around 231, to Britain under Roman imperial rule, which had also lasted some four centuries, from the Claudian invasion of A.D. 43 to the British revolt and end of Roman rule in 409. Throughout the British islands, some version of Celtic seems to have remained the language of daily conversation for much of the population, and the conditions of rural life for many people seem to have been little changed from pre-Roman times even after four centuries of Roman occupation. Yet, on the other hand, many Britons did adopt the toga, Latin was widely spoken by those with some education, and Peter Salway believes that after the expulsion of Roman administration "there is no sign of pre-Roman tribal survival. . . . Britain had become so fundamentally integrated into the late Roman state that separation was fatal. . . . Its degree of Romanization had been too great, not too little."[21] The old, pre-Roman order could never be revived or probably even remembered clearly.

Despite much local continuity, Britain had been profoundly changed by four centuries of Roman presence. It is possible that Britain was regarded as strategically more important to the Roman empire than Vietnam had been to China, and more Roman troops may have been stationed there, but Jiaozhi was commercially more significant than London within the two respective empires. The most glaring difference between Roman Britain and Chinese Vietnam is that Chinese occupation of Vietnam was destined to continue for another 700 years (until 939), and, when it finally came, Vietnamese independence was not followed by catastrophic barbarian invasions like those of the Angles and Saxons, which utterly transformed post-Roman Britain along different lines and gave it, in a real sense, an entirely new beginning.[22] The Chinese imperial imprint on Vietnam was, in other words, both much longer in duration and less thoroughly erased afterward than the Roman mark on England.

Not only was the Red River valley area of modern Vietnam an integral part of imperial Lingnan, but it was initially the centerpiece of the imperial presence in Lingnan. As was the pattern in Roman Britain, the Chinese empire concentrated on developing the more fertile lowland portions of Lingnan while gradually squeezing the remaining defiantly independent native tribes up into inaccessible mountain areas (although low-lying marshes were also favorite tribal haunts). While the city of Canton had been the capital of Zhao Tuo's Southern Yue kingdom, that city was burnt and abandoned following Southern Yue's absorption into the Han empire. Afterward—possibly to escape the memory of Southern Yue independence but also because in Han times the Red River delta in what is now Vietnam was "much more thickly populated" than the Pearl River area near Canton—the Han dynasty chose a site near modern Hanoi for its administrative capital of Lingnan.[23] For the remaining three centuries of the Han dynasty, at least, a city in what is now Vietnam was the most important metropolis in all of southeastern China.

Within Lingnan, pre-Chinese tribal remnants were widespread, but they were at least as prominent in what is now Guangxi and Guangdong as they were in Vietnam. Shortly after the brief Western Jin reunification of the empire in 280, a general demobilization of local military forces throughout the empire was planned, but an imperial official based near modern Hanoi objected that there were still over 50,000 households of "unsubmissive" persons along the southern coast of Guangdong and another 10,000 in what is now Guangxi, while those who did submit to official regulation were scarcely 5,000 families. During the Southern dynasties period, Li and Liao aboriginal tribes reportedly proliferated amid the mountains of Guangdong, posing a perennial threat to the empire.[24]

In the hills of modern Guangdong and Guangxi Provinces, south of Canton City, Li tribesmen lived in widely scattered independent villages, referred to by imperial officials as "bandits." Along the modern Sino-Vietnamese border to the west, the cannibalistic Wuhu people prowled, allegedly attacking and eating solitary travelers whom they came upon. Between modern Guangdong and Guangxi Provinces lived the "wild Wenlang" (whose name in *kanji* is interestingly identical to the legendary Van-lang kingdom of Dong Son–era Vietnam, except they are now described here as "wild"), who slept in the forest without permanent homes, ate raw meat, and gathered incense for trade. In coastal Guangdong Province, there also seems to have been a lively slave trade in "natives" lasting into late Tang times.[25]

Unassimilated or partially assimilated tribespeople were obviously quite numerous in Lingnan throughout the period covered in this book, but there is no particular association between these native

tribes and the territory that eventually became Vietnam. Instead, the
Red River valley area of modern Vietnam at one time formed something of an oasis of Chinese civility.

ORPHAN EMPIRE

Jiaozhi and the Red River valley area were a haven for displaced Chinese refugees during the troubled final years of the Han dynasty. As
an island of stability amid the general collapse, however, the region
had little alternative but to assume the initiative in maintaining local
self-government since there was soon effectively no empire to which
to remain loyally subordinate.

The governor of Jiaozhi, from 187 to his death in 226, was named
Shi Xie (137–226). His ancestors supposedly were natives of Shandong Province who had fled south to Lingnan during the interregnum between Former and Later Han (A.D. 9–25). Such claims to
Central Plain ancestry are typical for southern notables, so the attribution should not be taken as necessarily accurate—but neither is it
inherently improbable. In fact, it is quite possibly true. In any case,
Shi Xie personally regarded Cangwu, near the border between modern Guangxi and Guangdong Provinces, to be his home, and his
father had served a term as governor of Ri'nan in modern central
Vietnam, so Shi Xie is probably best considered simply as a native of
Lingnan, which at that point was still officially a single unified region
of the empire, theoretically administered from Jiaozhi by a regional
inspector. Shi Xie had studied the classics as a child at the Han imperial capital, and he was a thoroughly Chinese-style figure.

The word "king" has even been applied to Shi Xie's tenure in
Jiaozhi. He was certainly effectively autonomous. His brothers and a
cousin served as governors in Guangxi and Guangdong, and the Shi
family came to exercise essentially independent dynastic rule throughout Lingnan. As has already been remarked, the parallel with the
Gongsun family's position in contemporary Liaodong is striking. Like
the Gongsuns, who are known to have continued submitting annual
reports to the Three Kingdoms Wei dynasty even while remaining effectively autonomous, Shi Xie also cautiously maintained an appearance of tributary submission to the rising power of the Three Kingdoms Wu dynasty headquartered to his north.[26]

After the news of Shi Xie's death reached the Three Kingdoms

Wu court in 226, Jiaozhou—the enormous Han imperial administrative "Jiao region" embracing all of Lingnan—was for the first time officially split, at approximately the modern Sino-Vietnamese border, into two smaller (though still quite large) regions, which were renamed Jiaozhou and Guangzhou. Since it was common practice in imperial China to designate both administrative areas and their capital cities by the same name, this was the historical origin of the Chinese name that is still used today for the city known in English as Canton: Guangzhou. The label Jiaozhou, then, referred (somewhat confusingly) to either or both the entire region of modern northern Vietnam and its administrative seat near modern Hanoi. Although Jiaozhou and Guangzhou were soon (briefly) reunited, after 264 the division was revived and made permanent.[27]

Jiaozhou, in the far south, was already proving intractable, distancing itself from Three Kingdoms Wu by proclaiming its allegiance instead to rival Chinese imperial dynasties farther north. During the lengthy period of division in China, the governments of the Southern dynasties tended to be dominated by émigré great families from the north who had fled the "barbarian" conquests of the Central Plain in the fourth century. Native southern Chinese of local importance tended to be deeply resentful of this émigré domination. In Jiaozhou, however, the situation was different. There, Shi Xie's forty-year period of quasi-independence at the end of Han had established a pattern of local great family self-rule.[28] This regional autonomy became gradually more pronounced and culminated in 541 when a local magnate named Ly Bi (d. 548) went into open rebellion against the Southern imperial Liang dynasty.

Ly's ancestors had supposedly moved to Lingnan from the Central Plain at the end of Former Han and over the centuries had been transformed into "native" southerners. Encouraged by some early military triumphs, Ly proclaimed himself "emperor of Southern Yue" (reviving the name of Zhao Tuo's old Southern Yue kingdom) in 544 and began to organize a Chinese-style imperial government. This proved premature, however, because Ly Bi was disastrously defeated by a Liang imperial army in 545–546 and died soon afterward. Ly's relatives and generals continued to fight a protracted guerrilla war from bases in remote and inaccessible locations until 550, when the Liang army was recalled to deal with more urgent military concerns farther north. The Liang dynasty was rapidly failing, and it would be replaced by the even weaker Chen dynasty in 557. For the remainder of the century, Jiaozhou stood apart from imperial rule under independent Ly family domination. In 602, however, an army from the newly reunified Sui dynasty smashed through to the Ly emperor's camp and compelled the resubmission of Jiaozhou.[29]

Since the end of the Han dynasty, the Red River valley area had thus enjoyed a lengthy tradition of imperial inattention, with only rarely active bursts of intervention from the empires of the north. This was capped by half a century of formal independence in name as well as a sovereign empire in its own right; and, although the Sui dynasty violently reestablished northern imperial authority in Jiaozhou in 602, Sui itself was soon overthrown by the Tang dynasty in 618, an event that presented fresh opportunities for local strongmen to assert their independence.

The Sui official who had been sent from the Central Plain around 616 to serve as governor of Jiaozhou was able to maintain firm local control there, but after the Sui dynasty collapsed, he inevitably did so on his own authority, until such time as the new Tang regime had reconstituted centralized imperial power sufficiently to be able to direct serious attention toward the remote regions of the extreme south. The Tang court eventually did dispatch a viceroy to supervise the region, but Tang also reconfirmed the former Sui governor of Jiaozhou as Tang grand area commander-in-chief. This man seems to have continued effectively dominating Jiaozhou until his death in 637. Yet, while Jiaozhou certainly enjoyed substantial autonomy throughout his tenure, it is noteworthy that he was not in any sense a local but rather a recent arrival from the Central Plain.[30] Vietnamese independence in this period took the form of strongman rule over a fragment of the Chinese empire.

Nor was this situation unique to Vietnam. Just north of Jiaozhou, in modern Guangxi Province, a tribal leader had been appointed governor at the end of the last Southern dynasty. He was succeeded by his son, and, with the aid of the tropical diseases that decimated invading Sui armies, they successfully resisted Sui attack. Instead of being directly subjugated by Sui, they were merely recruited as allied auxiliaries. In this capacity, they assisted Sui in its campaigns against Champa in the far south and Liaodong in the northeast. After Tang replaced Sui, they surrendered to Tang and were rewarded with renewed confirmation as local Tang dynasty commanders-in-chief.[31] These

strongmen were no less independent than the one in Vietnam (Jiaozhou) at this time and a lot more truly "native."

The situation in Canton was even more interesting. The out-
standing figure there was Feng Ang (d. 649). Feng claimed descent
from the rulers of the short-lived Northern Yan dynasty (408–437)
in the far northeast who had supposedly fled to Koguryŏ, and from
there a generation later returned to China by sea with 300 followers,
establishing themselves in the far south at Canton. Feng Ang's grand-
mother, known as the "lady of Qiao" (*Qiao guo furen*), sprang from a
family of hereditary Yue chieftains who had intermarried with the
Fengs. She played a decisive role in bringing Lingnan into the Sui dynasty with little resistance at the end of the sixth century, as a reward
for which her grandson Feng Ang was appointed as a Sui official.[32]

During the interval between effective assertions of Sui and Tang
imperial power, Feng Ang grabbed military control over much of
what is now Guangdong Province, Hainan Island, and a portion of
Guangxi. At the time, it was proposed to Feng that he should reclaim
Zhao Tuo's old title as "king of Southern Yue," but instead he more
cautiously submitted to Tang in 622. His submission must have been
fairly nominal, however, for Tang then "enfeoffed him as duke of the
state of Yue," and he was able to maintain a fair degree of de facto autonomy from his power base in Guangdong. Feng cultivated the personal style of a warrior chieftain—more like a Japanese samurai or a
European knight than a Chinese-style mandarin—and he was said to
possess over 10,000 servants and immense treasure. In the second
quarter of the seventh century, one of his kinsmen reportedly came
to the Tang imperial court followed by a barge filled with gold.[33]

The widespread phenomenon of hereditary local great family
domination in Lingnan was not suppressed until the last half of the
seventh century and the first half of the eighth; Feng family fortunes,
for example, seem to have suffered a nearly fatal blow only in 698.[34]
Compared to the wild Feng family enclave in Guangdong, Jiaozhou,
in what is now Vietnam, was a relatively sedate and Sinified part of the
Tang empire. It was also, however, increasingly something of an economic backwater.

Jiaozhi, in the Red River valley, had been the foremost city of
Han dynasty Lingnan, but its old rival, Canton city (Guangzhou), had
been resurrected after 226. Maritime trade, which increasingly involved the eastward-lying islands of Southeast Asia, was also increas-

ingly capable of navigating boldly across the sea directly to Canton rather than crawling timidly up the coast past Jiaozhou. Overland trade routes, which during the Han dynasty had passed more or less due north from Jiaozhi to the northwestern Han imperial capitals, shifted east to pass through Canton on their way to the new Southern dynastic capital near the site of modern Nanjing (Nanking). Canton was becoming relatively more important as a trading center than Jiaozhou. One modern scholar estimates that Canton surpassed Jiaozhou as a hub of international maritime trade in the seventh and eighth centuries. The Red River valley area, under any name, would never again regain its former commercial glory.[35]

Population movement into Lingnan from the northern imperial heartland during the Tang dynasty also tended to favor population growth in northern Guangdong over the extreme southernmost Red River valley area. By the time of the Sui dynasty (unified 589–618), the commandery containing Canton city already had a larger registered population than the one containing Jiaozhou—a reversal of the old Han dynasty relative balance.[36]

In addition, Jiaozhou was becoming something of an isolated salient of imperial power, surrounded by aggressive foreign enemies. The heavily Indianized Southeast Asian kingdom of Champa, on the southern border of Jiaozhou in what is now central Vietnam, had been a frequent military threat beginning especially in the fourth and fifth centuries. The Tang fortress at Jiaozhou was repeatedly sacked; in 767, for example, it fell to seaborne raiders from Java. From the mid-ninth century, Jiaozhou was also seriously menaced by the rise of the Nanzhao kingdom, located just to its northwest in modern Yunnan Province. Two Nanzhao seizures of Tang Jiaozhou reportedly resulted in 150,000 casualties.[37]

Jiaozhou was, furthermore, geographically cut off from the rest of the empire, accessible by land only through the bottleneck represented by the so-called Ghost Gate Pass (*gui men guan*) in modern Guangxi near the Guangdong border, where a pair of opposing rocks formed a kind of natural gateway. Because of Jiaozhou's insalubrious tropical climate, popular wisdom held it that those who ventured through the pass into the deep south "seldom returned alive." When Tang imperial attention was distracted by a disastrous rebellion in northern China during the mid-eighth century (that of An Lushan), tribal strongmen seized control over much of modern Guangxi Province, established several petty principalities, and severed land communication between the Tang urban centers at Canton and Jiaozhou from approximately 756 to 771.[38]

Jiaozhou also remained vulnerable to internal tribal rebellions, although not necessarily more so than other parts of Lingnan. In 687, for example, a protector-general was killed when his plan to impose the full Chinese tax rate on the Li tribesmen of Lingnan backfired and provoked a rebellion. He was besieged in Jiaozhou city with insufficient troops for his own defense and perished when the Feng family strongman at Canton maliciously withheld reinforcements.[39]

In recognition of the unique frontier conditions in Jiaozhou, in 679 Jiaozhou was separately made the seat of a Tang "protectorate of the peaceful south." This initiative was paralleled by the establishment of similar protectorates on each of the other principal imperial borders. The new protector-general of the "peaceful south" (C: Annan; V: Annam, which thus enters our vocabulary to become the standard pre-nineteenth-century name for Vietnam) was commissioned, in particular, to supervise "the pacification, subjugation, and patrol" of the non-Chinese tribes under his jurisdiction.[40]

However, late Tang dynasty Jiaozhou (or Annan) was threatened almost as much by mutinous imperial armies as it was by tribal unrest or foreign enemies. In 803, for example, imperial troops employed in improving the city's fortifications rebelled, expelling the protector-general. In 843, when the military commissioner of Annan put his troops to work restoring the walls, they mutinied again, burnt the city, plundered its treasury, and drove the commissioner back to Guangzhou. In 877, a garrison of Annan troops stationed in what is now Guangxi Province mutinied, driving out their surveillance commissioner. In 880, the army in the Jiaozhou capital mutinied once more, causing the military commissioner to flee from the city.[41]

Tang dynasty Jiaozhou was an unpopular posting. In 628, one great gentleman flatly refused a direct imperial appointment to govern Jiaozhou on the grounds that the climate there was so unhealthy that he could never return alive. Lingnan, in general, was still regarded as an exotic and forbidding place of exile. Isolated and surrounded by significant foreign military threats, with a reputation for often-fatal tropical diseases and increasingly overshadowed by the rise of Guangzhou (Canton), Jiaozhou was a growing imperial problem. Yet by the late eighth century, the Tang empire had many

troubles in many places. As late as 792, at least, one top imperial adviser could still argue against policies favoring Canton over Annan
(Jiaozhou), arguing that both were equally "the king's land."[42]

From the second half of the eighth century, many of the Tang
regional commands became effectively independent strongholds. In
904, a man named Liu Yin (d. 911) secured appointment as military
commissioner of Lingnan, with his base in the city of Canton. After
his death and the final demise of the Tang dynasty in 907, his younger
brother proclaimed the establishment of an independent new empire based at Canton in 917 that he called "Great Yue" (or "Great
Viet"), resurrecting the memory of Zhao Tuo's old independent Cantonese Southern Yue kingdom. A year later, however, he changed his
new empire's name to "(Southern) Han," obviously hoping to capi-
talize on memories of the much greater splendor and imperial legitimacy of the original Han dynasty, whose royal family's surname happened to be the same as his own.[43]

As Liu family power in Canton began to coalesce, the military
commissioner of Jiaozhou, Khuc Hao (d. 908), sent his son north to
Canton to reconnoiter. Succeeding to his father's position, this son
adroitly played off Cantonese (Southern) Han imperial power against
the various other upstart rival imperial dynasties of the north until
930, when (Southern) Han finally dispatched an army to crush this
Jiaozhou impertinence. The outcome was a bloody power struggle
in Jiaozhou that ended only in 938, when Ngo Quyen (d. 944)
seized local power, lured a (Southern) Han invasion fleet onto iron-
tipped stakes, annihilated it, and proclaimed himself king.[44] Vietnam
(though it was not yet known as Vietnam) was finally independent,
this time, as it turns out, permanently (almost).

During the course of more than a millennium of imperial rule,
the Red River valley area had already long enjoyed much de facto autonomy and occasionally openly proclaimed independence. Local
self-rule, however, in this case invariably meant not that all local
people governed themselves in some democratic fashion but merely
that they were ruled by families of local strongmen rather than remote northern emperors. That Vietnam was eventually able to become what we think of today as an entirely separate "nation," while
descendants of the originally very similar Yue (Viet) peoples of modern Zhejiang, Fujian, Guangdong, and Guangxi Provinces became
"Chinese" instead, was determined largely by factors of geography:

the Empire found it difficult and increasingly not worthwhile to project continuous effective administrative power into this awkward and remote salient.[45]

Both the ambition and the political tools to create an independent empire in Vietnam were provided by the experience of having long been part of the Chinese empire. Much as Western imperialism in modern times provoked a reaction in the form of worldwide anticolonial independence movements, the legacy of premodern imperial "Chinese rule . . . promoted Vietnamese nationalism,"[46] except that "nationalism" is not yet the right word for the tenth century. The rulers of newly independent Vietnam remained Chinese-style local great families, still scarcely any less "Chinese" than their counterparts in Canton but determined now to create their own All-under-Heaven in the south. The modern "nation" of Vietnam had yet to be imagined.

After Ngo Quyen seized control over the region in 938–939, he lived only five more years. Ngo family rule was challenged after Ngo Quyen's death by as many as a dozen local strongmen at a time, and it was not until the rise of Dinh Bo Linh (923–979) around 965 that a degree of unity was restored to the Red River valley. When the reunified Song dynasty (960–1279) in the north finally extended its newly recentralized Chinese imperial power as far south as Canton, in 971 Dinh Bo Linh's son, in Vietnam, was confirmed as Song military commissioner and protector-general, and in 975 Dinh Bo Linh himself was enfeoffed as "king of Jiaozhi commandery." Vietnamese autonomy was thus conceptualized, by the Chinese court at least, as still falling within the normal framework of the Sinocentric investiture system as an imperial vassal kingdom.[47]

This may have initially been intended simply as a temporary stopgap until such time as Song military power was strong enough to directly recapture Jiaozhou. Invasion was, in fact, contemplated by the second Song emperor, but he was dissuaded by an official's recommendation that "Jiaozhi is burning hot and pestilential; twenty to thirty percent of our troops will die before seeing combat. Even if we get it, we will be unable to hold it." In the end, the Song empire rested content with the nominal tributary submission of Vietnam, and, except for a brief interval of renewed military occupation during the early Ming, which proved to be extremely un-cost-effective, this would become the final Chinese imperial disposition toward Vietnam.[48]

The newly independent Vietnamese government replicated key

features of the Chinese order, establishing its own subvassals, bureaucratic network, and triennial Confucian examination system. After
independence, Vietnam long maintained many of the old Chinese
imperial standards of weights and measures and in commerce continued to employ Tang and Song money. Confucian culture flourished in Vietnam, it could almost be said, especially after its consolidation of political independence, and in the early centuries the two
monarchies were interchangeable enough that it was apparently not
uncommon for southern Chinese to emigrate to Vietnam and enter
government service there.[49]

At the same time, of course, this newly independent Vietnam
was in direct continuous contact with Southeast as well as East Asia.
As Vietnam gradually expanded its own imperial territory to the
south, occupying approximately the entire southern half of what is
now Vietnam between the sixteenth and the nineteenth centuries, its
population mix was also greatly enriched by the addition of Cham
and Khmer and various other non-Chinese and un-Sinified elements.
This greatly enlarged Vietnamese empire itself was politically divided
internally almost continually from 1527 to 1802. When, at the beginning of the nineteenth century, the great emperor Gia Long (r.
1802–1820) unified the entire region, with much foreign aid, from
his southern base at Saigon, he was in some senses "assembling a kingdom . . . that had never before existed."[50]

The quite conscious attempts of this new nineteenth-century
empire (which now for the first time finally begins to actually be known
by the name "Vietnam") to duplicate Chinese institutional models
have been pointedly contrasted to the simultaneous persistence there
of quite different popular native views. For example, the standard
Chinese title "emperor" (*Hoang-de* in Vietnamese pronunciation but
written with identical *kanji*) was officially employed in nineteenth-
century Vietnam alongside the native designation *Vua*, which has no
Chinese equivalent.[51]

However, such a distinction between elite high culture and local popular culture was normal—indeed, a fundamental expectation
of the premodern East Asian world—even within the Chinese empire
itself, although presumably to a somewhat lesser extent. In both Korea and Japan, there had also been a notably similar interplay between older native and newly introduced Chinese royal titles, at least
in early periods. Even in China proper, the ancient southern state of

Chu may also have observed a similar "parallel usage of indigenous and northern titles" for several centuries.[52]

Circumstances in nineteenth-century Vietnam were undeniably unique, but every place in East Asia was unique. It would be a misreading of the evidence (from a modern nationalist perspective that assumes the naturalness and immutability of ethnic nations) to conclude simply that such cultural layers are proof of the alien quality of Chinese influences, violating some eternal Vietnamese national essence, and therefore doomed to be rejected someday as unwelcome foreign impositions. In truth everything, everywhere, must have been either new or foreign once. Ho Chi Minh's modern Western-style title of "president," after 1945, was no less alien than the older Chinese-style title "emperor." Indeed, by the twentieth century, "emperors" had become part of Vietnamese tradition.

SEVEN

The Birth of Korea

CHINESE COLONIES

Documented Korean history begins in very much the same way that the written history of Vietnam began, with Chinese-language records of a newly dislodged fragment of the vast Qin world empire. Even before this time, the northeastern Warring States kingdom known as Yan had apparently already occupied and fortified a section of territory within what we now think of as Korea. When Qin conquered Yan and unified All-under-Heaven, Qin incorporated Yan's Korean territory as well. For logistical reasons, however, once the Han dynasty had reestablished centralized imperial administration following the disintegration of Qin, it pulled the northeastern imperial frontier back to the line formed by the Liao River. A dependent client state named Yan was resurrected beyond the river in Liaodong ("Liao East").

A close personal friend of the first Han emperor and fellow native villager was selected to be the first monarch of this revived Yan kingdom. However, when the emperor died in 195 B.C., this new king of Yan, fearing the empress dowager's intentions, fled amid the Xiongnu to become a Xiongnu prince. One of his ex-subordinates in Yan, named Wiman, together with some 1,000 followers, sought refuge elsewhere among the old Qin fortifications in what is now Korea. Dressing native style, with his hair up in a bun, he presided as king there over a growing population of mixed local tribespeople and Chinese refugees.[1]

Wiman's new kingdom in Korea was called Chosŏn. The question of whether it should be regarded as ethnically "Korean" or ethnically "Chinese" (or something else altogether) is a natural one and of considerable interest to modern Korean nationalists. It is also anachronistic.[2] These events were part of a broad tectonic process of interaction between the core civilizations of the Central Plain and all their neighboring peoples that eventually left Zhejiang, Guangzhou, and Hainan (and eventually even Manchuria) "Chinese" but Vietnam and Korea not. It is critical to a clear understanding of the origins of East Asia to realize that none of the modern nation-states of the region existed yet as such—not even "China" in the modern sense, although the limitations of our vocabulary may at times force us to use the modern English names.

Wiman is probably most accurately understood to have simply been a man from Yan. Much of his newly subject population is explicitly stated to have consisted of the former prehistoric natives of his new realm, located in what is now northern Korea. However, the basic ethnic difference between Yan, prehistoric northern Korea, and early imperial northeastern China may not have even been very great. According to Yang Xiong (53 B.C.–A.D. 18), in the Warring States period a single reasonably distinctive language (or dialect) had been spoken across the entire region stretching from just west of what is now Beijing to the northern half of what is now the Korean peninsula.[3]

We may surmise that Wiman did not think of himself as "Korean," but it is doubtful that he would have considered himself exactly as "Chinese," either, in the modern sense. If he has descendants still living today, they may well be Koreans now. Yet Yan had been one of the principal Chinese Warring States, and an early, though possibly somewhat peripheral, participant in the core Central Plain civilization. It was the subsequent interaction between the various prehistoric peoples living on the Korean peninsula and this Central Plain cultural and political core that would eventually combine to generate a distinctively Korean civilization.

If Wiman had ever been a direct Han imperial subject, he was one no longer. Instead, Wiman negotiated an understanding with the Han governor of Liaodong to act as an "external subject," as the ruler of a client buffer state responsible for securing the Han borders against barbarian raids, in exchange for which the Han empire provided Wiman with military and economic assistance in reducing his own native neighbors to dependence on him. However, Wiman's heirs developed minds of their own, and Chosŏn soon became known as a haven for refugees and expatriates from the Han empire.

When the third-generation king of Chosŏn, Ugŏ, killed the Han governor of Liaodong in 109 B.C., the Han emperor conscripted an army of condemned convicts and launched an invasion by both land and sea. Betrayed by its own officials, Chosŏn fell in 108 B.C. and was directly incorporated into the Han empire. The date, notably, coincides with the almost simultaneous imperial digestion of the Yue regions in what is now southeastern China and northern Vietnam. According to the third-century Chinese *Chronicles of the Three Kingdoms*, moreover, it was only after the establishment of direct Han imperial administration on the Korean peninsula that Chinese and non-Chinese (Han and Hu) began to be "gradually differentiated."[4]

The great series of Han military campaigns conducted under Emperor Wu that brought about the incorporation of both northern Korea and northern Vietnam into the empire were really targeted more especially against the Xiongnu nomadic confederation that confronted Han power from the northern steppes. This necessarily massive military effort put a heavy burden on the empire and all its citizens, and the wisdom of such an aggressive imperial policy has always been controversial. Later emperors sometimes, in a more Confucian vein, began to question the value of "troubling the common people for the sake of an empty reputation," as Tang Taizong phrased it in 631, in appreciation of the very real danger of imperial overstretch.[5]

After direct Han imperial administration was established in northern Korea, the Korean colonies' fortunes fluctuated considerably over the next four centuries. Although "Korea" is an English rather than a Korean name, our English word derives from an abbreviated form of the (apparently native) name already in use at this time for a Han dynasty imperial district in the northern portion of the peninsula: Gaogouli (K: Koguryŏ). By the second half of the second century A.D., as the Han dynasty was crumbling, Han citizens in Korea reportedly began fleeing in large numbers to the relative security provided by new native principalities that were emerging in the south and east of the peninsula, beyond the Han imperial jurisdiction.[6] During the long period of imperial disunity in China that followed, from the third century to the sixth, these native kingdoms consolidated their positions and effectively put an end to any possibility of Korea ever becoming "Chinese" like Canton (Guangdong) or Manchuria. They were now decisively Korean, but it still remained to be determined exactly what "Korean" would eventually mean.

Unlike the case of either Wiman's Chosŏn (in the area of Korea-Manchuria) or Zhao Tuo's Southern Yue (in the area of Canton-Vietnam) in the second century B.C. (and, indeed, the separatist regime in Vietnam after 939), these new Korean statelets were not simply breakaway representatives of the Central Plain civilization asserting local political independence but rather—with the obvious exception of Gongsun family rule in Liaodong from 190 to 238—genuinely "native" non-Chinese states. They were also very much conceived and organized, however, according to the model that had originally been pioneered on the Central Plain. Before the final consolidation of a unified, independent Korean kingdom in A.D. 675, no fewer than twenty full-scale Chinese imperial invasions of Korea would be launched, but the peninsula ultimately remained beyond the empire's permanent grasp. These early pre-Koreans steadfastly and successfully refused to be subjugated by the Chinese empire, but they could not, and apparently did not even wish to, completely escape its influence.[7]

NATIVE DIVERSITY

Four centuries of direct Chinese imperial rule can be expected to have left some mark on Korean culture. The first-century *Dynastic History of the Former Han* observed, for example, that while "the rural people eat and drink off of bamboo platters" in Han colonial areas, "in the cities they are inclined to imitate officials and merchants from the inner [more thoroughly Chinese] Commanderies, and often use cups and utensils to eat." Archaeological reports testify to a continuing visible material difference between natives and Chinese colonists in this period. However, such labels as "native Korean" and "Chinese" should be applied only with caution. In Roman northern Europe, under circumstances not dissimilar to the situation in Han dynasty Korea,

> when we examine the material evidence closely, categories such as "Roman," "provincial Roman," "native," "Celt," and "German" do not stand up to critical scrutiny. Instead we see patterns of infinite variability—every settlement and every cemetery is unique. From the time of the conquests on, there were no purely "Roman" nor purely "indigenous" sites—all show some degree of integration of features from different traditions.[8]

Not only did the "native" culture in Korea now begin to include elements introduced there from the Central Plain core (which was itself a complicated blend of earlier ingredients), but even the prehistoric native culture in the area of the Korean peninsula had already been "forged from diverse elements." Early pottery samples from the eastern coast of the peninsula resemble those from the Yue regions of southern China and Japan and are suggestive of ancient southern maritime links, while Neolithic pottery from the Korean west coast indicates affinities with northeastern China. Until as late as the seventh century A.D., moreover, the various native peoples who inhabited the Korean peninsula not only were politically divided but also spoke variant languages and practiced at least slightly different customs.[9]

There was no simple division in antiquity between China and Korea at the line formed by the Yalu River or even a neat triangular relationship among China, Korea, and Manchuria. Archaeological evidence suggests a close early cultural link between the inhabitants of Shandong peninsula, in what is now northern China proper, and Liaodong peninsula, which juts out toward it from Manchuria, from about 4000 B.C. These cultures, in turn, were somewhat distinct from the presumably proto-Chinese-speaking core prehistoric cultures of the western Central Plain. The last phase of this Neolithic period in both Shandong and Liaodong, terminating around 1700 B.C., may even be identified with the Dong Yi, or "eastern barbarians," who are mentioned in certain early Chinese texts.[10] Yet this same Shandong area would later be the birthplace of Confucius.

A multitude of tribes inhabited northeastern China and southern Manchuria in high antiquity, some of whom undoubtedly were ancestral to the later Koreans (as well as to many present-day Chinese people). A striking example of the early cultural links between what is now northeastern China, Manchuria, and the Korean peninsula is provided by the visual representation of the Korean Tan'gun foundation myth on the Chinese Wu family shrine in Han dynasty Shandong, dated A.D. 147.[11] In addition, while it is highly likely that there was much shifting of the prehistoric population within the Korean peninsula, the available archaeological evidence does not support simplistic theories of a single sweeping ethnic in-migration of some new "Korean" population group.

Megaliths and eventually bronzes begin to appear on the Korean peninsula after about 2000 B.C., but these may have been an indigenous development, perhaps influenced by ideas obtained from elsewhere, rather than evidence of the arrival of some hypothetical new "people." Despite a very strong modern Korean presumption that there must have been a single primordial proto-Korean ethnic group that migrated into the peninsula at some point to become the Korean nation (or "race"), what we think of today as the Korean people probably emerged from the mixing together of a variety of different communities that had inhabited the area in antiquity.[12] The genetic contributions of distant Stone Age ancestors, whether they all came from a single tribe or from many, in any case, must have been almost totally irrelevant to the historical development of a sophisticated Korean civilization.

In historical times, the ethnic mixture on the Korean peninsula included at least a sprinkling of persons from China proper. As the first imperial, Qin dynasty was convulsed by domestic rebellion toward the end of the third century B.C., tens of thousands of people from the northeastern corner of the Chinese empire reportedly sought refuge in Chosŏn (the name that is sometimes vaguely applied to prehistoric Manchuria-Korea). After the northern Korean peninsula was directly incorporated into the Han dynasty, four centuries of Chinese imperial rule must have brought more than a few permanent Han settlers to the region who were then left stranded by the demise of Chinese administration—and joined by still more refugees from the turmoil in the disintegrating imperial heartland after the end of the second century A.D.[13]

During the period of general collapse of centralized imperial authority in the fourth century especially, there seems to have been much fluidity among local strongmen, notably between the heavily Sinified Murong Xianbei rulers in Manchuria and the rising power known as Koguryŏ situated in Liaodong and the northern Korean peninsula.[14] Conditions fostered a certain interchangeability among the political elites of this era that was simply oblivious to modern national borders.

We are tempted to think of the rising, presumptively Korean statelet of Koguryŏ as filling the void left in northern Korea by the collapse of direct Chinese imperial rule, but this is something of an oversimplification. The rise of Koguryŏ, though it eventually did become a very great kingdom, was only gradual. There were still many little tribal communities scattered across the region. During a sixteen-year period toward the end of the third century, for example, the briefly reunified Western Jin dynasty in China reported receiving tribute emissaries from over 200 kingdoms of eastern barbarians, many, if not all, of whom were surely from the Korean peninsula. Even as late as the sixth century, our conventionalized portrait of three great rival Korean kingdoms in that age is, more accurately, complicated by the continued survival of numerous tiny principalities or other still-unaffiliated groups in the interstices between them.[15]

Koguryŏ and the nearly identical Puyŏ population farther north from which it claimed descent were at least as much Manchurian peoples as they were Korean (although neither designation conveys much meaning for this period apart from geographic location). A stone inscription placed on the northern (now Chinese) bank of the Yalu River in 414 to commemorate an especially renowned early king of Koguryŏ begins by proclaiming the great king's Puyŏ origins. The particular Puyŏ subgroup that at some point came to be known as Koguryŏ was itself initially further subdivided into five tribes or clans, and culturally these five Koguryŏ tribes must have been not very easily distinguishable from any other Puyŏ communities. At any rate, it was explicitly claimed that Koguryŏ preserved much of the old Puyŏ language and customs.[16]

Puyŏ itself, in turn, was far from being a pristine ethnic identity. The Puyŏ kingdom had reportedly arisen out of what had once been the old Yemaek homeland, and a third-century Chinese source remarks of Puyŏ that "the aged persons of that country themselves say that they are ancient refugees." Puyŏ has been called an "example of a state forming itself on the borders of China and evidently in imitation of China"—part of what may have been a very general phenomenon of secondary state formation taking place along the peripheries of the great early empires, such as Rome and China. Even Puyŏ's predecessor, Yemaek, on closer inspection proves to have been only a hyphenated label ("Ye" and "Maek") that began to be employed in Chinese-language writing from the time of the Han dynasty to designate, without any very great precision, some of the non-Chinese tribes of the northeast.[17]

Both Koguryŏ and Puyŏ were highly aristocratic societies, whose elite families maintained their own armor and weapons and waged war while their inferiors hauled supplies. Both sacrificed cattle to Heaven and augured the future from the shape of the beast's hooves. Koguryŏ, aside from being very warlike (in Chinese eyes) and having sturdy little ponies that were adept at clambering over mountains, was notable for its marriage practices. There were reported nightly songs and dances in their encampments during which men and women seduced each other without, from the highly moralistic and ritualistic Chinese Confucian perspective, any of the proper preliminary courtesies. Of particular interest was the marriage custom in which the bride's parents would construct a small house behind their own large one, where the young couple would live until their own children came of age. This is in striking contrast to the usual Chinese practice, which involved the young wife moving in with her husband's family.[18]

Puyŏ was the first of these to disappear. Sandwiched in between the rising military power of its own former colony Koguryŏ in the south and the Xianbei to the west, Puyŏ's position was precarious. It was prey to Murong Xianbei raiding from at least 285, and many of its people were eventually absorbed into the general northern Chinese population. What little remained of Puyŏ as an identifiable entity was finally engulfed by Koguryŏ in 494. The memory of Puyŏ did linger on, however. After Koguryŏ was itself destroyed by joint Tang Chinese and Sillan Korean forces in 668, a group of Koguryŏ refugees supposedly reorganized themselves, in Manchuria, into a new kingdom called Parhae (713–926), which claimed to have restored both the old territory of Koguryŏ and the ancient Puyŏ customs. Parhae, too, vanished eventually, and its subjects dissolved among the general Malgal (or Mohe, as the name would be pronounced in Mandarin) population of the region, who were in turn in some vaguely distant way ancestral to the Jurchen and thus ultimately to the more recent Manchus.[19]

Koguryŏ rose as an independent and, at its peak, notably powerful kingdom to take the place of the disintegrating Chinese imperial government in northern Korea and Manchuria. In the southern half of the Korean peninsula, which had never been directly administered by the Han Chinese empire, however, three quite different sociopolitical areas existed in this early period. These are the so-called Three (Korean) Han peoples—Mahan in the west, Chinhan in the east, and Pyŏnhan wedged in between along the south-central coast—who were themselves reportedly divided into no fewer than seventy-eight small "countries" during the period of the Later Han dynasty in China.[20]

A third-century Chinese account reported that these (Korean) Han peoples built their homes of earth and grass in the form of a tumulus or barrow, with a door at the top. The family lived together inside (most barbarously from a Confucian perspective) without distinctions as to age or sex. This style of housing has been described as being common later among the Tungusic-speaking peoples of the Manchurian region. After the end of the planting season in the spring and again after harvest in the fall, they would hold festivities involving sacrifices to their spirits, singing and dancing, and the consumption of much alcohol. "In their dances, several tens of people all arise and follow each other, stamping the earth and bending down and rising up, their hands and feet responding to each other, their rhythm resembling the 'Bell Dance.'"[21]

Virile youths supposedly proved their manhood by passing ropes and wooden sticks through the skin covering their spines. In Chinhan and Pyŏnhan, it was customary to artificially narrow the heads of newborn babies by pressing them with stones, and, in the style of Neolithic Japan and the Yue cultures of prehistoric southern China, the southern Koreans sometimes tattooed their bodies.[22] There were, in other words, multiple local populations in Korea at the dawn of history, and from all of these disparate elements three great Korean kingdoms gradually took shape. Finally, toward the end of our period, one kingdom unified them all.

SINGULAR KOREA

During the Later Han dynasty in China, Koguryŏ began to coalesce as a distinct polity in northern Korea and Manchuria. In the second century, Koguryŏ, perhaps driven by the inadequacy of its agricultural base in the mountains, repeatedly raided Han imperial installations in Manchuria. Around the year 209, in retaliation for successive raids, the Gongsun family warlords of Liaodong crushed Koguryŏ and set fire to its villages. The older brother of the Koguryŏ strongman, who had been passed over by his own people in the dynastic selection, reportedly then defected to the Gongsun (Chinese warlord) side with 30,000 followers. The little Koguryŏ kingdom was thus forced to start over and build a "new country," with a new capital at Hwando (also known as Kungnae-sŏng), on what is now the Chinese side of the Yalu River. This city was little different from numerous other fortified places that sprouted up everywhere across northern China during this great age of ethnic conflict and imperial division.[23]

In 244, the gathering power of the northern Chinese Three Kingdoms Wei dynasty, which in 238 had eliminated the independent Gongsun family base in Liaodong, spilled over into an attack on Koguryŏ, during which the Murong Xianbei grandfather of the founder of the Former Yan kingdom participated on the Chinese side and earned promotion to the Chinese imperial title of superior area commander-in-chief. A century later, in 342, the new Murong Xianbei state of Former Yan won a crushing victory over Koguryŏ, whose ruler reportedly fled the battlefield alone on horseback. Former Yan subsequently burnt the Koguryŏ palace at Hwando and seized over 50,000 Koguryŏ captives.

None of these victories was decisive, however. Koguryŏ was repeatedly resurgent and gradually began to reconfigure itself according to the developed Central Plain model. In 372–373, Koguryŏ reportedly constructed its first Chinese-style university, issued its first Chinese-style code of laws, and began experimenting with Buddhism. By 385, Koguryŏ raids on the Murong Xianbei had resumed, and eventually the Murong were forced to formally recognize Koguryŏ as a vassal monarchy.[24]

Koguryŏ was a rising power just as its rivals, the Murong Xianbei in western Manchuria, were being engulfed by their own cousins, the Tuoba Xianbei Northern Wei dynasty (to be precise, the Tuoba founder of the Northern Wei dynasty was a maternal nephew of the Murong founder of the Later Yan state), coming from further west, between 396 and 407. In a delicious irony, in 407 the last, short-lived Murong ruler of Later Yan (Murong Yun) was himself a man of Koguryŏ descent who had only been adopted into the Murong royal family and given the Murong surname.[25]

Under the distinguished military leadership of its great king Kwanggaet'o (r. 391–413), Koguryŏ took up the offensive against the faltering Murong kingdom to the west, established Koguryŏ power in Manchuria to approximately the line of the Liao River, and also began pushing southward down into the Korean peninsula. Kwanggaet'o's active career, according to the so-called Kwanggaet'o stele inscription, began with a raid into southern Manchuria in the fifth year of his reign (395), in which he defeated three tribes of 600 or 700 tents and captured innumerable cattle, horses, and sheep. When the Murong kingdom was replaced by the more awesome power of the Tuoba Northern Wei dynasty, however, Koguryŏ's westward ambitions were blocked, and from about 418 Koguryŏ began to refocus its attention increasingly southward down into the Korean peninsula.[26]

Koguryŏ was the first native kingdom to develop in Korea along the lines of the Central Plain Chinese model, and for a time, perhaps, it was the strongest. In the southwest, the realm known as Mahan was allegedly settled by tribesmen who had fled the encroaching power of Wiman's Chosŏn kingdom in the second century B.C. Whatever its origins, Mahan was initially not very cohesive. A third-century A.D. Chinese account describes Mahan as consisting of "over fifty countries," which were "scattered between the mountains and the sea," lacked walled cities, and were not very effectively coordinated with one another.[27]

Among these Mahan "countries" was one that came to be known as Paekche. According to legend, Paekche was founded, near the site of modern Seoul, by a son of the progenitor of Koguryŏ and shared with Koguryŏ a claim to Puyŏ royal origins. Modern scholars have regarded it as not altogether implausible that Paekche really was founded by a Puyŏ prince, probably sometime in the fourth century. A "foreign" origin for Paekche's royal house, which would have set them culturally somewhat apart from many of their own subjects, might help explain Paekche's exceptional receptivity to equally foreign Chinese influences later. It may also help explain why, during the Han dynasty, the people of Mahan were said to be unfamiliar with horseback riding but, by the time of the Tang dynasty Paekche, located in that same area, had become particularly noted for its custom of mounted archery. In any case, by the time the *Liang shu* was compiled in the early seventh century, it was possible to observe of Paekche that their "current language and ceremonial apparel are roughly the same as in Koguryŏ."[28]

The general picture that emerges throughout the region is one of ambitiously mobile leaders, claiming aristocratic descent, who established petty "kingdoms" at promising locations, perhaps bringing with them substantial followings and possibly also dominating preexisting local populations. Their "kingdoms" initially consisted of quite small city-states.

Although the earliest Korean records are already legend encrusted and cannot be trusted to be scrupulously accurate in every detail, the portrait they paint is nonetheless convincing in broad outline. No sooner, we are told, had the city that would become Paekche been founded than it was beset by Malgal raiders. On one early occasion, it is reported that the 200 Paekche soldiers who were deployed to repulse a group of Malgal invaders were badly defeated and took refuge on Chŏng Mok Mountain. Their king then personally led 100 picked cavalrymen to relieve the siege, forcing the Malgal to withdraw. While this particular incident may never have taken place as recorded, the extremely small scale of the conflict feels authentic. Mythic embellishment would presumably be more apt to inflate the numbers of warriors involved and the grandeur of the state rather than advertise such humble beginnings.

Shortly after this incident, the Paekche king determined to move his city—which must have effectively coincided with the better part of his "country"—to avoid further raiding. Two months later, he erected a palisade at the foot of Han Mountain and transferred the population of the city to the new location. The following month, he sent an emissary to announce the move to his Mahan overlord and staked out the frontiers of his new "country." Then he built more permanent walls and towers and on the new year formally shifted his seat of power. Four years later, marauding enemies burnt the old city. Again, the details in these early histories may be unreliable, but the image of a small-scale, movable "country" has the ring of verisimilitude.

As Paekche power slowly swelled, its Mahan overlord began to accuse Paekche of ingratitude for the original concession of a small plot of Mahan land on which to build their new homeland. In 369, according to our best reconstruction of the chronology, Paekche attacked and crushed its erstwhile Mahan overlord and transferred part of the urban Mahan population to a new home north of Han Mountain.[29]

Gradually, Paekche expanded from its humble beginnings, through almost incessant warfare, into a great kingdom, coming increasingly into conflict with the similarly rising powers of Silla to the east and Koguryŏ to the north. It has been observed that the known locations of Buddhist temples in Paekche are clustered into quite limited areas around its capital cities, indicating that higher culture, at least in Paekche, may have remained geographically somewhat constricted. However, by the time Paekche was finally destroyed by combined Tang and Sillan forces in 660–663, it reportedly boasted a population of 760,000 households in 200 cities and had become a substantial and sophisticated Chinese-style territorial kingdom.[30]

The Chinese Southern dynasties cultivated particularly close relations with Paekche as a strategic counter to the threat posed by the
Northern dynasties. In 415, for example, the Eastern Jin dynasty (in
southern China) invested Paekche with a variety of distinguished Chinese titles, including "king of Paekche." An analysis of the names of
Paekche's known ambassadors to the various southern Chinese empires during this period suggests, moreover, that many were actually
persons of Chinese ancestry—indicating, apparently, a significant
"Chinese" presence in fifth-century Paekche.[31]

If it is true, in general, that in the realm of art "the International
style of the Tang dynasty swept all before it in the [Korean] peninsula," these Chinese influences were especially vibrant for a time
in the kingdom of Paekche. In the early sixth century, even some
of the bricks in Paekche tombs were explicitly fabricated according
to Southern dynasty Chinese standards. The *Gua di zhi* (Annals En-
compassing the Earth), an early Tang era work thought to reflect
the accounts of contemporary eyewitnesses, reported that people in
Paekche were familiar with various Chinese pseudosciences, utilized
a Southern dynasty Chinese imperial calendar, and in their marriage
and mourning practices approximated the Chinese standard.[32]

The magnificent Wang Hŭng temple in Paekche was completed
in 634:

> The temple was near the water. Its ornamentation was grand
> and imposing. The king always rode a boat to the temple to of-
> fer incense. In the third month a pond was dug south of the Pal-
> ace, drawing in water for over twenty *li*. The four shores were
> planted with willows, and, in the midst of the water, large and
> small islands were constructed to resemble the [legendary Chi-
> nese] island of the immortals, Fangzhang.

Into this literally "willow pattern" Chinese-style landscape, in the
spring of 636

> the king led his various officials on an outing to the north bank
> of the Sabi River. On both shores wonderful caverns and strange
> rocks had been placed, and among them were wonderful flow-
> ers and extraordinary grasses—like a painting. The king drank
> wine and was utterly pleased. He strummed a stringed instru-

ment and sang to himself, while his attendants danced often. Contemporaries called the place "The Great King's Beach."[33]

A more sublime realization of one vision of Chinese high culture (it was "like a painting") could scarcely be imagined—especially as originally presented (in a native Korean history) in the classical Chinese language. It should be unnecessary to emphasize that Korea never became "Chinese" as a result of all these Chinese influences, but it is also undeniable that "much of what we now reckon as 'Korean culture' or 'Korean tradition'" was shaped, sometimes quite self-consciously, by elite Korean study of and admiration for the ancient civilizations of the Central Plain. Especially in the centuries after 1392, when these influences reached a peak, Korea became almost more thoroughly Confucian than China itself.[34] Paekche was an especially important early center of Chinese-style civilization on the Korean peninsula. From Paekche, in particular, these influences were then reexported to Japan.

The ultimate victor in the military-political struggle for supremacy on the Korean peninsula was Silla, a kingdom that originated in the southeastern region formerly known as Chinhan. In the third century, according to a contemporary Chinese account, Chinhan and Pyŏnhan held a combined total of twenty-four "countries," some with populations as small as 600 or 700 families. One account has Chinhan settled by descendants of primordial Chosŏn, in six "villages," among the mountain valleys of southeastern Korea. Many accounts insist, however, that Chinhan was also inhabited by refugees from Qin dynasty imperial China who were settled on an eastern grant of Mahan land and may have continued speaking the Qin (Chinese) language. Still other sources mention arrivals from Koguryŏ in the north and a claim that the founder of the Sillan royal house had fled there by sea from Paekche. What is clear is that the population of what would eventually become the Sillan state was, from the beginning, quite mixed.[35]

Silla's borders with Koguryŏ and Paekche were initially as "irregular as a dog's teeth," and it once was subordinate to Paekche, but Paekche's conscription for its continual wars with rival Koguryŏ pressed many of its people to flee to Silla, injecting Silla with increased strength and no doubt further complicating its population mix. The Sillan region was relatively remote, and Silla had little contact with China until the end of the sixth century.[36] However, Silla, too, was gradually transformed along Central Plain lines.

In 487, according to the *Samguk sagi,* Silla first established postal stations in the "four directions" and ordered officers to maintain "official roads." In 502, Silla banned human sacrifice at royal funerals. In 503, as previously discussed, the Chinese title "king" was adopted, as was a standardized way of writing the name Silla in the Chinese *(kanji)* script. In 504, Silla promulgated laws regulating mourning apparel—a central concern of the *li.* The use of Chinese-style posthumous royal titles began with the death of King Chijŭng in 514. In 520, Silla issued Chinese-style codes of penal and administrative law and regulated the order of official court dress. In 536, Chinese-style reign periods were implemented. By royal command, the compilation of a Chinese-style dynastic history for Silla began in 545.[37]

At the turn of the seventh century, the monk Wŏn'gwang promoted the secular Confucian precepts of loyalty to one's lord, filial piety to one's parents, and fidelity to friends—together with the more native Sillan virtue of fearlessness in battle and a Buddhist-inspired plea to at least be "selective" in killing living creatures. In 649 and 650, at the proposal of a monk who had traveled to Tang, the Sillan court adopted the clothing and reign periods of the "Middle Kingdom." Early Korean histories not uncommonly record dates using the reign periods of Chinese emperors as a benchmark presumably familiar to every literate East Asian (the Western system of dating from the birth of Christ—whether explicitly as the "year of our Lord," A.D., or euphemistically as the "common era," C.E.—was unknown in traditional East Asia). Members of the Sillan royal family were sent to study at the Tang capital beginning in 640. In 682, Silla established an academy of its own to promote Confucian learning and in 788 established a Confucian civil service examination system parallel to that of Tang.[38]

Tang influences on Sillan elite culture in the seventh and eighth centuries were sweeping. Notably, these Tang influences were a mixture of what we would today consider to be effective, pragmatic, technical "advances" and purely cultural and religious matters. In 706, for example, the Sillan government responded to a famine Chinese style, not only with distributions of grain but also with the construction of religious institutions and a general amnesty.[39] Chinese systems of posthumous titles and reign periods are difficult even to describe in

English and make little sense outside the traditional East Asian world order but were of critical importance within it (although they were also probably little understood even by Koreans beneath the level of the educated elite, who, in a sense, alone were civilized).

In 668, with Tang assistance, Silla completed the conquest of the Korean peninsula, and when Tang attempted to restore a measure of direct Chinese imperial administration on the peninsula, Silla drove the Tang army back to Manchuria in 676. The Korean peninsula was now unified for the first time and under native rule. Only the southern portions of the vanquished Manchurian-Korean Koguryŏ kingdom were incorporated into Silla, however. Much of Koguryŏ's former northern territory fell under Parhae and Malgal control instead. The frontier of the newly unified Korea's effective rule did not extend much above the site of modern Pyongyang, and the Yalu River did not become a reasonably firm northern border for the Korean state until about 1022, well after the end of the period under consideration here.[40]

Although the inhabitants of the Korean peninsula exhibited a broadly consistent pattern of steadily growing political independence from the Chinese empire throughout the period covered in this book, Korean contact and communication with China seems to have only increased in inverse proportion to the degree of Korean political independence. By the ninth century, long after the Sillan unification of an independent native Korean state, there was a notably strong Sillan presence in Tang China. Several Tang cities had "Sillan wards" or "Sillan villages" in the suburbs, and the Japanese pilgrim Ennin encountered Sillan boats carrying cargoes of charcoal inside China. Some ninety Sillans are known to have passed the Confucian civil service examinations in China during roughly the last century of the Tang dynasty. Koreans, in general, probably constituted the single most numerous group of foreign students in Tang China. It is possible to argue, though perhaps debatable, that following Silla's unification of the Korean peninsula in 668, Korea's relationship with the Tang empire paradoxically became even closer.[41]

As the *Samguk yusa* describes it, Silla's kings

> served the Middle Kingdom with the utmost sincerity. Embassies scaling [the mountains] and navigating [the seas] to pay court were without interruption. They constantly sent their children

to serve in the [Chinese] court's Imperial Bodyguard, and enter the academy to learn [the Chinese classics] by recitation, whereby they might inherit the example of the Sages, change the local customs of their vast wasteland, and become a country of *li* and *yi*.[42]

After the fall of the Tang dynasty in China in 907 and with the establishment of a new Koryŏ dynasty in Korea (918–1392), Sino-Korean relations entered a new era that is properly beyond the scope of this book. We may note, however, that these relations remained highly interactive, and the extent of Sinification can even be said to have increased appreciably, especially after the fourteenth century.

The attitude of the founder of the Koryŏ dynasty was ambiguous. We are told that he wanted to "emphasize Korea's unique culture and values" and assert that Korea was "no longer a satellite." However, at the same time, he also professed a commitment to the common East Asian standards of civilization. As he famously enjoined his heirs in 943,

We, in the east, have long admired the Tang style. Our literary matters, *li,* and music all follow their institutions. It is just that in various regions and different lands the people's natures are each different, and they need not lightly be made uniform.[43]

The result was an independent local Korean variant of East Asian civilization. Of the two earliest surviving Korean "national" histories, the *Samguk sagi* of 1145 and the *Samguk yusa* of 1280, the latter reflects what is said to be the more "Korea-centered" worldview of a Buddhist author who has even been called "a fervent nationalist."[44] Yet even the *Samguk yusa* was still written overwhelming in the classical Chinese language and sometimes uses the reign periods of Chinese emperors to date events on the Korean peninsula.

During the period of continent-wide Mongol domination in the thirteenth and fourteenth centuries, the heirs to the Koryŏ throne quite typically grew up in Beijing.[45] Since, at this time, Beijing was in some senses both a "Chinese" city and the capital of a vast non-Chinese Mongol empire, this only reemphasizes Korea's nested integration into the East Asian world and East Asia's own membership in a still larger planet.

When another new dynasty was established in Korea in 1392, the Yi or Chosŏn dynasty, which survived until the Japanese intrusion at the turn of the twentieth century, its formal dynastic name, Chosŏn, was bestowed on it in conscious reference to ancient Chinese written names for the region by none other than the emperor of Ming dynasty China. Chosŏn, thereafter, aggressively promoted neo-Confucian programs, with the result that, although Korea remained in many ways quite distinctively Korean, "by about the eighteenth century . . . Korea had become a normative Confucian society" whose people even eventually came to regard themselves sometimes "as more faithful to the Confucian tradition than the Chinese" themselves.[46]

Both because of their long-term political independence from the Chinese empire, lingering memories of quite different prehistoric cultural wellsprings, and simply because of a differing trajectory of historical evolution, Korea did not become "Chinese." Korea became Korean, which is only a tautology if you assume the end product as a self-evidently forgone conclusion or presume, as so many people do, simply that Korea "has always been that way." In reality, nothing has "always been that way," and Korean historical evolution could easily have followed many other conceivable—or now, to us, even inconceivable—courses, resulting in quite unrecognizably different present-day configurations. Despite the many distinctively Korean features of Korean civilization and to some extent as the result of a very deliberate choice that was often repeated and reaffirmed, Korean civilization evolved within an orbit of Confucian universals. The consequence is that Korea today is both sui generis—a uniquely attractive and remarkable Korean civilization—and in some ways what could almost be called the very epitome of an East Asian Confucian state.

EIGHT

Japan

INSULAR EAST ASIA

IMMIGRATION

From the perspective of the Chinese empire, the Japanese archipelago seemed to lie for an eternity "just off the coast of civilization."[1] The islands were literal outliers of the traditional East Asian world. Unlike either Korea or Vietnam, Japan did not share any contiguous borders with China, and no part of Japan was ever conquered by the Chinese empire. Chinese influences were correspondingly more indirect.

However, Japan's exposure to other, non-Chinese influence was also more limited. Korea, after all, abutted on Manchuria and was open to Siberia and the steppe world as well as the Central Plain. Vietnam forms a highly complex "epistemological watershed," simultaneously implicated in both East and Southeast Asian interaction spheres.[2] Japan was simply, in general, more isolated. Yet, unless we are willing to assume that the Japanese really are, as legend has it, divinely descended from the Sun Goddess, all human presence on the islands must be traced, ultimately, to continental origins. Isolation explains the relative slowness of early development in Japan; the incompleteness of that isolation brought people to the islands in the first place.

The Japanese islands were first drawn into the sphere of traditional East Asian higher civilization by immigrants from the Korean peninsula during the Qin-Han era. In Japan, these events coincide roughly with the epochal transition from the Jōmon to Yayoi periods of prehistory that sparked the rapid development of a sophisticated literate civilization in Japan, culminating by the time of the Tang dynasty, from what had been, in late Zhou and the Warring States era, still chiefly only preagricultural hunter-gatherer societies on the islands.[3]

Clearly, the rise of the Qin-Han empire on the mainland of East Asia set off a chain reaction that reached even faraway Japan. However, Japan's connection with the mainland did not really begin only at this time. Some modern Japanese scholars believe that the Chinese term "*Wo*" (J: *Wa*), which is the earliest written name for Japan, also may have been applied in early texts to some of the peoples of the Korean peninsula and possibly even what is now Indonesia. All these peoples, in turn, may be connected to the Yue populations of prehistoric southern China. Indeed, there is even a recent Chinese theory that the first known textual reference to Wo, in the *Shan hai jing* (a book that dates from the early Han dynasty but that incorporates earlier material), in which the land of Wo is described as being located south of the kingdom of Yan (in northeastern China and Manchuria) and subordinate to it, is actually only a variant designation for the Yue of southern China and not Japan at all.[4]

Physical proximity makes the route from Korea to the northern coast of Japan the most obvious direction for early traffic between the mainland and Japan. However, especially for the early, Jōmon phase of prehistoric culture in Japan, there are also tantalizing parallels with the Yue peoples of the south. These include the practice of intentional tooth extraction, tattooing, and certain shared or similar styles of jade and stone ornamentation. A third-century Chinese account emphasizes that, according to old folktales, some Japanese people themselves believed that their practice of tattooing faces and bodies derived from what is now Zhejiang Province in the People's Republic of China—the putative heartland of Yue culture.[5]

Connections with the Yue peoples of southern China link prehistoric Japan to the broader world of Southeast Asia, which may be thought of as radiating out from this Yue cultural zone. There is, for example, a fascinating early Japanese account of trial by ordeal, involving the plunging of hands into boiling water, attributed in the Japanese sources to A.D. 415, that is strikingly similar to practices ascribed by Chinese historians to roughly contemporary Funan in what is now Cambodia and southern Vietnam. Jar burials, which seem to have been an indigenous invention of island Southeast Asia, were also common in late Jōmon and Yayoi era Japan, indicating the possibility of some contact between Japan and the South Seas in late prehistory. Against the seeming improbability of such distant ocean voyages succeeding in primitive Stone Age vessels, we must set the undeniable fact that the South Sea islands really were settled somehow by peoples speaking Austronesian languages during the late Stone Age.[6]

Mounting Japanese archaeological evidence increasingly supports the theory that the early Jōmon hunter-gatherer Stone Age culture had some roots in the Yue cultural sphere of prehistoric southern China and Southeast Asia, while the subsequent Yayoi revolution in Japan was inspired by new waves of immigrants arriving through Korea from the north, beginning about 400 B.C. These new arrivals from the north, furthermore, either greatly outnumbered the earlier Jōmon inhabitants or soon outstripped them in number because of a "demographic explosion" touched off by the introduction of relatively intensive wet-field rice cultivation. Although estimates are controversial and most Japanese scholars prefer to minimize the number of immigrants, it has been speculated that as many as a million and possibly even more persons may have landed on the islands from the Korean peninsula during this last phase of Japanese prehistory.[7]

One important result of this process may have been the introduction or creation of a new linguistic environment in the islands. Many experts consider Japanese to be an Altaic language, whose "core" affiliation lies with the historic northern Puyŏ-Koguryŏ (-Paekche) languages of Manchuria-Korea, although Japanese may also have an underlying southern, perhaps Austronesian, substratum of some kind.[8] The similarities between modern Japanese and modern Korean are, it should be emphasized, rather faint, and the complete genealogy of the Japanese language would very likely be both unique and complicated, but its closest relatives surely lie to the north in Korea.

Immigrants from the Korean peninsula presumably introduced Altaic or, more broadly, Eurasiatic northern languages to the islands, laying the foundations for what became modern Japanese. At the same time, however, somewhat ironically these Altaic-speaking immigrants also initiated Japan's period of substantial interaction with the (non-Altaic, non-Eurasiatic speaking) Chinese core civilization. It is no coincidence that this happened during approximately the same time period that modern southern China, Korea, and Vietnam were also all first engulfed by Central Plain influences. The original, eponymous kingdom of Yue, for example, in the lower Yangzi River valley, was shattered by the more thoroughly Central Plain Chinese-style kingdom of Chu around the year 333 B.C.[9] Lingnan, including the northern parts of modern Vietnam, was conquered by the first emperor of Qin around 214 B.C., and Wiman's Chosŏn kingdom in Korea dates from approximately 194 B.C. Immigrants from the Korean peninsula then carried Central Plain influences to the Japanese islands along with their Altaic languages.

Nationalistically minded modern Japanese people like to imagine a powerful ancient Yamato state in the Japanese islands that quickly established supremacy over much of the Korean peninsula as a so-called Mimana colony, supposedly lasting from about the fourth century A.D. until 663. Equally nationalistic modern Koreans prefer to think, conversely, that Yamato, in Japan, was itself only a Korean colony. These mutually contradictory opinions are obviously fueled by bitter modern national rivalries and the malignant memory of Japan's very real early twentieth-century colonization of Korea. Yet a third, opposing nationalistic perspective is provided by those modern Chinese people who like to claim that Japan began as a direct Qin-Han era "colony" of China.[10]

Direct Chinese colonization of the Japanese islands is not supported by archaeological evidence, but it is possible that we may find a germ of truth in all three of these seemingly contradictory narratives—if only we can, for a moment, distance ourselves from prickly issues of modern national self-esteem. Neither Korea nor Japan could have begun as any kind of formal colony of the other, if only because extensive intermingling between peoples living in the two places we now call Korea and Japan dates from long before there were developed kingdoms in either location that could possibly have done any purposeful "colonizing." The evidence is overwhelming, however, that there really was a close cultural affinity between prehistoric Korea and prehistoric Japan,[11] and influences radiating out of the Central Plain core in China did provide the inspiration for higher civilization everywhere in traditional East Asia.

The principal direction of cultural flow and immigration in this early period was surely from the continent to Japan. Many of the key cultural and material technologies that were introduced to Japan in this period, notably literacy and codified law, were ultimately of Central Plain origin. Buddhism, of course, stems from points even farther west. Some of these ideas were of a more narrowly Korean provenance, however, such as the style of constructing solid cuirass armor for foot soldiers and "the southern Korean tradition of bloomery" metallurgy, based on the forging of iron (nearly all of which was physically imported to Japan from Korea until about 500) on an anvil with a small furnace rather than Chinese style in a large blast furnace. Korea was certainly the immediate point of embarkation for most continental influences on Japan, including even Chinese Confucianism. By the sixth century, there seems to have been a steady stream of so-called erudites in the "Five Confucian Classics" *(Gokyō Hakushi)* arriving in Japan from Paekche in Korea.[12]

If the direction of cultural flow was principally from Korea to Japan, it is also evident that the residents of the Japanese islands, going the other way, dabbled in military and political adventures on the Korean peninsula as well. The *Samguk sagi* records a raid by over 100 Wa (recall that Wa was the name used for Japan—though not necessarily exclusively what is now the country of Japan—in written texts - until the late seventh century, while Yamato at some point became a common native spoken designation) warships on the southeast Korean coast, which supposedly occurred in A.D. 14. The dates and presumably many of the details of the earliest events recorded in these histories may not be reliable, but the general picture of frequent raiding from the islands is credible.

Inter alia, there is a record of Wa "bandits" besieging the Sillan capital for five days in the summer of 393. After the Wa forces withdrew, the Sillan king intercepted them with 200 cavalrymen at Toksan and, catching them in a pincers maneuver with 1,000 pursing foot soldiers, annihilated the Wa force. In 408, the Sillan king was reportedly warned that Wa had established a military base on Tsushima Island, located strategically in the straits between Korea and Japan, and was stockpiling arms and supplies for attacks on Silla.[13]

In the meantime, Silla's southwestern Korean rival, Paekche, cultivated friendly diplomatic relations with Wa as an ally against the even more threatening northern Korean kingdom of Koguryŏ. To cement this alliance, King Asin (r. 392–405) reportedly sent his son and heir, who later ruled as King Chŏnji (r. 405–420), to the islands as a hostage in 397. After Asin's death, while the crown prince was still in Japan, the late king's brother assumed the regency but was then murdered by his own younger brother, who usurped the throne. The Wa court responded to these events in Paekche by returning Prince Chŏnji with 100 Wa guards, after which his own countrymen killed the usurper and welcomed Prince Chŏnji back to his rightful throne.

These events supposedly established a certain dominant Wa influence at the Paekche court.[14]

Wa military collaboration with Paekche in the wars against Koguryŏ during this period is documented by the Kwanggaet'o stone inscription of roughly 414. Although some scholars have darkly suspected modern Japanese imperialists of deliberately altering this inscription to support a claim to ancient Japanese rule in Korea, the text of this inscription (which is illegible in places and early rubbings of which were sometimes crudely and inaccurately enhanced) is really more consistent with a pattern of Japanese raiding on the peninsula rather than a stable Wa administrative presence. It is, in other words, consistent with what the native Korean histories themselves describe.[15]

In these incessant peninsular campaigns, Koguryŏ proved to be ascendant. However, growing military pressure from Koguryŏ only further cemented the military alliance between Paekche and Wa, and Japanese military activity on the peninsula in turn generated a flow of Paekche allies and Koguryŏ prisoners back to the islands.[16] This exchange greatly increased the Korean cultural influence in Japan.

A priest from Paekche was made the first official head of the Buddhist Church in Japan in 623. The nascent Buddhist *sangha* in sixth- to seventh-century Japan was heavily under the tutelage of immigrant priests from Paekche or Koguryŏ. Although Koreans in general were influential, it was Paekche especially that held the sixth- and seventh-century Japanese court in cultural thrall, and Paekche's own particular debt to Southern dynasty China established direct cultural ties between the elite Buddhist high culture of the Chinese Southern dynasties, Paekche, and Japan. Craftsmen coming from Paekche in 577 may have helped construct one of Japan's earliest Buddhist temples. In 612, two immigrants from Paekche, Nojagong and Mimaji, reportedly introduced Chinese gardening techniques and southern Chinese music and dance to the Japanese court.[17]

The final defeat of the combined Yamato and Paekche forces and the utter extinction of the Paekche kingdom at the hands of a Tang-Silla alliance in 660–663 permanently ended this Paekche connection, but in the short term also unleashed a new tide of refugee immigrants who continued to serve as important models of East Asian higher culture in Japan. Yamanoue Okura (660–773), for example, was a Korean who was exiled as a child to Japanese shores by the demise of Paekche and who subsequently became renowned as a composer of Japanese verse and served as a representative of the Japanese court to Tang China. Kuninaka Kimimaro (d. 774) was the grandson of a Paekche official who fled to Japan in 663. He was active in the fabrication of early Japanese Buddhist icons and in particular the casting of the great bronze buddha statue at Nara. Such talented immigrants as these, ironically, were vital to the early development of Japanese "national culture."[18]

Nor were these external influences exclusively limited to Paekche and Koguryŏ. There was at least some cultural exchange with Silla. The *Nihon shoki* relates the story of a fifth-century Japanese embassy to Silla (traditionally dated 414) in quest of skilled physicians to treat the ailing "Emperor Ingyō." During one, perhaps not unusual, raid on Sillan territory, ascribed by the *Nihon shoki* to 365 but probably really occurring in the early fifth century, the Japanese "took captive the people of four villages and returned with them."[19]

Even further afield, aside from the handful of Indians and other exotic westerners, discussed earlier, who may have arrived on Japanese shores as a spin-off from the "Indianization of Southeast Asia" and Buddhist missionary activity, in 544 a boatload of people from Manchuria or Siberia reportedly made landfall on an island off the northwestern coast of Honshū and spent the spring and summer fishing there to the horror of the local inhabitants. In 642, there is also a report from some attendants of the Paekche delegation to Japan that their ambassadors had thrown Kunlun diplomats into the ocean, presumably during their mutual approach to Japan. Since Kunlun was the generic *kanji* designation for Southeast Asians, this would seem to indicate some level of direct maritime contact between the Japanese archipelago and Southeast Asia at this time.[20]

The cultural implications of such contacts with Southeast Asia and Siberia were probably fairly limited, however, and often indirect. Records in the Shōsōin, for example, document the Japanese purchase of Southeast Asian ivory and aromatic woods only through the services of Sillan middlemen.[21] Most interactions were clearly with the East Asian world, first through Korea and later more directly by sea with the Sui-Tang empire. In addition, the incipient Japanese state also slowly asserted an increasingly centralized authority to regulate and monopolize all contact with the outside world for its own advantage. What had been in prehistory spontaneously private initiatives by independent small groups were increasingly preempted by an overarching Chinese-style governmental structure in Japan.

As we have already seen, the earliest contemporary Chinese account of prehistoric Japan, written in the third century, described people on the islands in the straits between Korea and Japan as voyaging by "boat north and south to trade for grain." It seems likely that fishermen and other seafaring groups established contact privately with the continent long before the rise of centralized Japanese political authority.[22] Substantial immigration from the continent had clearly been taking place haphazardly for centuries before there was any effective Japanese government to regulate such activity—before there even was a "Japan" in any meaningful sense.

The heavily mountainous terrain of the Japanese islands dictated that early immigrant settlements would fall into isolated valleys between which communications were predictably difficult and often as easily maintained by boat as overland. Prehistoric Japan was more of a maritime society than is often remembered today, and the ocean was as much an open highway for the early islanders as it was a barrier. Under these circumstances, it is quite possible that immigrant communities might have long maintained a sense of identification with and orientation toward their places of origin on the continent, perhaps even more than with their fellow islanders.[23]

A Sui imperial embassy to Wa in 608 reported, after crossing from Paekche, passing through several small "countries," "all of which were vassals of Wa." One of these, which has been identified as being located near modern Suō on the western end of Honshū facing the Inland Sea, was labeled by this embassy as "the country of the king of Qin" (the name of the first imperial Chinese dynasty), and it was reported that "their people are identical to the Chinese." One modern Japanese scholar suspects that this was a colony of immigrants from Silla, whose customs were heavily Sinified.[24]

In the prehistoric period, there was no overarching political power in Japan to coordinate these different local immigrant communities. Although some experts believe that the Yamato court began to harness transactions with the continent into a system of formal interstate diplomatic relations as early as the fourth century, other recent thinking in Japan suggests that the emergence of a truly centralized state there, capable of organizing and controlling immigrant groups, began only in the sixth century.[25] As late as 608 (in the seventh century), as we just saw, the Sui embassy still reported separate "countries" on the main Japanese island of Honshū that were merely "vassals" of Wa. Probably, there was a lengthy intermediate period of development during which the nucleus of a Yamato state, perhaps with hegemonic pretensions, existed but had not yet begin to exercise any kind of sweepingly effective governing power over the archipelago.

It was, in particular, control over maritime communications, stretching from the eastern Inland Sea to Korea, during the sixth century that helped leverage the incipient Yamato court into a privileged position over other regional chieftains elsewhere in the islands. By the eighth century, most of Japan had finally become "Japanese" in the sense of participating in a common cultural and political order. However, even then the northernmost island of Hokkaidō, southern portions of Kyūshū, Shikoku, and far northeastern regions of the main island remained at best peripheral. Extreme northeastern Honshū remained semiforeign and "independent of central control until . . . 1189"—indeed, to a surprising extent, even until the fifteenth century.[26]

The growing central authority of the early Japanese monarchs, up through the Nara period (710–784), owed much to the prestige they derived from control over the acquisition and distribution of *karamono* (literally, "Tang things"), or imported continental luxury goods. This state monopoly, in turn, was greatly facilitated by the imported Chinese political principle, much in force in contemporary Tang, that the only acceptable kind of foreign contact was the formal tribute embassy. Although a substantial amount of unofficial private trade seems to have continued throughout this period on the continent, Japan, especially during the eighth century up to about 762—after which unregulated private trade began to proliferate everywhere in East Asia—may have succeed rather remarkably (although even in Japan our textual sources probably paint an exaggerated picture) in reducing all forms of foreign contact to something of a state monopoly.[27]

Japan's state monopoly on foreign contact extended to control over immigrant communities as well. With the rise of the Yamato state, newly arriving groups of immigrants were given the new surnames Aya or Hata. The *kanji* with which these newly naturalized immigrant surnames were written refer to the Han and Qin dynasties of imperial China and reflect perhaps the widespread immigrant pretension to prestigious (often royal) Chinese origins, but the Japanese oral pronunciation of these Chinese graphs "probably derive directly from words in the languages of the southern Korean kingdoms."[28]

According to the *Nihon shoki*, in 471–472 the Aya and Hata immigrant families, who had previously been living scattered throughout Japan under the authority of local strongmen, for the first time were brought under central supervision. As Warring States–style Legalist methods of household registration began to be implemented in Japan, in 540 the *Nihon shoki* records the registration of no fewer than 7,053 households of Hata people.[29] While, as usual, the dates assigned to early events in the Korean and Japanese histories should be regarded with some skepticism, a process of consolidation and centralization was unmistakably taking place in which the mobilization of groups of skilled immigrants was critical to the success of the rising Yamato state.

Immigrants were assigned to supervise state finances in the sixth and seventh centuries, perhaps because of their presumed familiarity with the more sophisticated economic practices of the continent. The *Nihon shoki* records, for example, the story of an immigrant named (in Japanese) Hata no Ōtsuchi, who was appointed to the treasury by Emperor Kimmei (r. 539–571).[30]

Immigrants long enjoyed a virtual monopoly over the crucial skill of literacy. The inscription on the famous Eta-Funayama sword, for example, one of the earliest known examples of purposeful writing in Japan, was drafted by an immigrant with the highly Sino-Korean-appearing written name of Chang An (C: Zhang An; J: Chōan). In 572, another immigrant was reportedly the only person at the Japanese court able to read a certain document from Koguryŏ, after "all the scribes had been unable to read it for three days." The first president of Japan's university, in the late seventh century, was an immigrant, and many of its professors continued to be immigrants well into the eighth century. Of the nineteen people who are said to have participated in compiling the important Taihō legal codes at the start of the eighth century, eight or nine were apparently from immigrant families. In addition, immigrant family members were often called on to serve in embassies to the continent because of their presumed familiarity with foreign affairs and literacy.[31]

It is true that in the seventh and eighth centuries immigrants were often employed by the Japanese in relatively humble positions merely for their technical skills, while real power was retained by the native (or "more native," since ultimately all persons on the archipelago must be traced to continental origins at some time or other) nobility. However, some of the most significant figures in early Japanese history may have come from immigrant families. It is possible, though uncertain, for example, that the great Soga family, who dominated the court in the late sixth and early seventh centuries, were themselves originally immigrants. The emperor Kammu's (r. 781–806) mother was of Paekche descent, and persons claiming continental ancestry were prominent in court affairs in Japan throughout the Nara and into the early Heian (794–1185) periods.[32]

However, immigrant families in Japan were eventually given or took for themselves Japanese language names and, like the Xianbei in China after they acquired Chinese-language names, disappeared thereafter into the surrounding population. The immigrant families became Japanese families. It is likely that, for centuries, immigrants had already been surreptitiously immersing themselves in Japanese society by taking native-style names on their own initiative, but at the height of centralized Japanese imperial power in the mid-Nara period, there were also sweeping imperial grants of Japanese surnames. In 757, for example, it was decreed,

> Those people from Koguryŏ, Paekche, Silla, and others who have long desired the sagely transformation, and who have come and attached themselves to our customs, hoping to be bestowed with a surname, are all to be permitted one. Recording their household registers without *kabane* [titles of nobility] and family names is untenable in principle, and ought to be corrected.[33]

The result was that by the end of the eighth century, the names of immigrant families had become almost indistinguishable from those of any other Japanese.[34] In a real sense, they had all become "Japanese."

Afterward, from about 830, the naturalization of immigrants was little practiced in the archipelago, and the Japanese became noticeably less open to foreigners. By the fourteenth century, one famous Japanese author, while admitting that there had been many immigrants from the continent during the early historical era, could indignantly reject any suggestion that "the Japanese were of the same stock as the people of Korea" or China "since the Japanese are descendents of the *kami* [spirits] of heaven and earth."[35] Thus was the rise of a spirit of nationalism in Japan abetted by religious faith and historical amnesia and the foundations for an invidious early twentieth-century myth of racial purity and divine descent articulated.

BECOMING JAPANESE

Yet Japanese culture really is unique. Today, it is quite common practice not only to sharply distinguish "Japanese-style" *(wafū)* ways of doing and presenting things from "Western-style" *(yōfū)* but also sometimes from "Chinese-style" *(karafū)* as well. Indeed, the differences between Japan and China today may seem more obvious than the similarities. At least in part, these various cultural distinctions are preserved only by conscious artifice, yet they are real enough and lend considerable charm to travel in modern Japan. However, it does not necessarily follow that this distinctive "traditional" Japanese civilization must have descended unchanged in a continuous line from any one single homogenous "original" one, and not all "traditions" are necessarily really very old.[36]

Countless waves of fresh immigration from the continent at the dawn of Japanese history and the crucial early role of Central Plain influences in generating the first Japanese state make the origins of Japanese civilization quite heterogeneous and inextricable from the history of much of the rest of East Asia. Despite the wish of some modern folklorists to rediscover some aboriginal premodern Japanese *volk*, "complete, coherent and unchanging, continuously living everyday life under the sign of immutable custom," Japanese civilization has multiple roots and no single native origin, and Japanese civilization has never stopped evolving since that time. "It is difficult to identify any culturally specific traits that can be assigned to the Japanese population across the whole of its history," concludes one recent scholar.[37]

Chinese influences on early Japanese high culture were pervasive and ranged from the calendar to poetry, calligraphy, painting, architecture, music, and medicine. It could be argued, as Tsuda Sōkichi did, that the imported language and ideas of Chinese Confucianism remained foreign to the Japanese values system and were employed as little more than superficial decoration in the highly mannered early Japanese aristocratic circles. Tsuda (1873–1961), a famous iconoclast among early twentieth-century Japanese historians, was critical of any notion that Japanese culture was derivative of China's or indeed that there was any common "oriental culture."[38]

It has been commented on in Japan since at least the eighteenth century that the absence of *kun* pronunciations (native Japanese, as opposed to the *on*, or Chinese-style, readings) for the *kanji* designating the fundamental Confucian virtues of "humanity" *(jin)*, "justice" *(gi)*, "propriety" *(rei)*, "loyalty" *(chū)*, and "filial piety" *(kō)* is evidence of just how alien these Confucian virtues really were to Japan.[39] These were foreign Chinese loan words and therefore also foreign ideas for which there were arguably no native equivalents.

On the other hand, these alien virtues certainly do seem to have insinuated themselves rather successfully into "traditional" Japanese culture (some, such as loyalty, possibly more than others). One has to go back to the Stone Age to find a time when these may not have been part of the Japanese repertoire of ideas. In every corner of the world, new "foreign" practices periodically displace older native ones, as Christianity once replaced paganism throughout much of Europe. It would be absurd to claim that Christianity is therefore inappropriate and alien to Europe. Some discrepancy between local popular custom and the elite universal standards of high Confucianism was, furthermore, simply the normal expectation in premodern East Asia.

Still, it may be said with some justice that the ideas of Confucianism probably did emerge more spontaneously on the Central Plain of northern China than they did in either the Yue zone of what is now southern China, Japan, Korea, or Vietnam. Early Japanese society differed considerably from Central Plain standards (as did the old local Yue cultures of Zhejiang and Canton). In defiance of the patrilineal Chinese ideal, for example, eighth-century Japanese law made provisions for women's property rights. Literary evidence suggests that in Japan, until perhaps as late as the end of the twelfth century, it was common for a young married couple to move in together with the bride's family or for each to continue living separately with their own parents rather than follow the normal northern Chinese-style pattern of residence with the groom's family (known as virilocal marriage). As in Korea, the Chinese model of patrilineal descent and virilocal marriage would eventually triumph as "ideal" in Japan, but during the early centuries of Japan's incorporation into East Asia, Japanese social practice still continued to depart significantly from Chinese expectations.[40]

Rules against consanguinity in marriage were apparently less strict in ancient Japan than in China. Women, in general, were more prominent in early Japanese society than they have ever been in Chinese history. A disproportionate number of early Buddhist professionals in Japan, where there was a so-called shrine maiden tradition, were young unmarried women, in contrast to the Buddhist monastic practice in China, which was more typically masculine. Early Japanese records mention a striking number of female chieftains or dual-gender chiefly pairs. A late example of this dual-gender format, the team of Empress Suiko (r. 592–628) and her legendary regent Prince Shōtoku (573–621), also established a "precedent for the division of responsibility between the monarch who reigns and the regent who rules"—a remarkable pattern largely unknown in China that would become something of a peculiar fixture of Japanese history.[41]

The claim to imperial descent from the sun goddess Amaterasu, which is a central contention of both of the two earliest Japanese national histories; a traditional blurring of the distinction between religion and politics *(saisei-itchi);* and the mystical vision of the Japanese emperors as "manifest *kami,*" or deities, all give the monarchy in Japan a deeply religious dimension that has usually been absent from the more thoroughly secular Chinese empire, despite the continuing importance of (religiously flavored) ritual to the exercise of Confucian government even in China.[42]

The native Japanese religion, Shintō, is also quite distinctive. Yet even Shintō may not be quite as pristinely and uniquely Japanese as is commonly supposed. The conventional understanding that Shintō is "the indigenous religion of Japan, continuing in an unbroken line from prehistoric times down to the present," has been challenged recently by a revisionist contention that Shintō did not really emerge as a clearly "independent religion" in Japan until "modern times" and that "Japan's ancient popular beliefs were . . . merely a local brand of Taoism." In a speech attributed to 552, the *Nihon shoki* pits "the spirits of our country" against imported foreign Buddhism but defines these Japanese national spirits in a thoroughly Chinese written vocabulary, as consisting of "Heaven and Earth, the Soil and Grain [classic Chinese symbols of sovereignty], and the hundred and eighty spirits."[43]

The use of *kanji,* to say nothing of the classical Chinese language, in early Japanese texts meant that "in order to be written, Japan's traditions had virtually to be translated into Chinese first." The very name Shintō (the "Tao, or Way, of the spirits") is an excellent example. Shintō is, at best, a Sino-Japanese construction. The same combination of characters that is pronounced *shintō* in Japanese had already appeared in a purely Chinese context in the *Book of Changes,* long before writing had ever been introduced to Japan.[44] Shintō is, furthermore, primarily a written expression, intended for the eye and chosen for the meaning of its *kanji,* as is evident from the fact that in Japan it is invariably pronounced in Chinese-style (the modern Mandarin Chinese pronunciation, *shendao,* is still recognizably similar) rather than a native Japanese reading (such as *kami no michi*) that would presumably be more meaningful to Japanese ears.

At least a few immigrant families are known to have served as priests of the "native" Japanese religion in the early period, and the great shrine at Ise, which enjoys particularly sacred ties to the Japanese imperial house, is said by one modern Japanese historian to have practiced "popular religious usages" derived from "southern China." The most essential Shintō paraphernalia of the sacred Japanese imperial system—the cult of Amaterasu and the shrine at Ise—developed to maturity only in the seventh and eighth centuries, after the great age of immigration from the mainland and as part of the continentally inspired momentum toward state formation.[45]

Some of Japan's most cherished "native" traditions thus developed only through a dynamic process of interaction with the continent. This does not make them any less "Japanese," but it does demonstrates that Japanese-ness itself is the culmination of a long process of development rather than some primordial original essence.

The Japanese word for the specialized occupational groups, *be,* which are a rather distinctive feature of very early Japanese history, has been declared "a direct loanword . . . from early Tungusic" by Roy Andrew Miller. The *kanji* with which it is written, moreover (pronounced *bu* in modern Chinese), was employed in the early third century to refer in writing to the Xianbei tribal divisions that had settled at the northern edge of the Gulf of Bohai, just west of the Liao River, near the Korean peninsula. In the form of the compound *buqu,* it was a Han era Chinese imperial designation for a military unit, of a type that in the post-Han period notoriously fell under private control and came to be employed both as private work units and for private self-defense. However uniquely Japanese the institution of *be* may have been, in other words, it was not without important continental referents. William Wayne Farris suggests, significantly, that Japan's "first institutions of control—surnames, titles, ranks, and producer groups *(be)*—may all have had Korean roots."[46]

One of the more distinctive features of early Japanese society is the prominence of special lineage, or pseudolineage, groups known as *uji*. In contrast with contemporary China, which was notable for its mounting meritocratic pretensions and the eclipse of hereditary aristocracy, these *uji* are certainly distinctive enough. However, *uji* seem to have first been created beginning only in the fifth century through royal gifts of noble titles in recognition for service to the centralizing Yamato court.[47] However uniquely Japanese the form, this was part of Japan's state-building response to continental influences, and the written forms taken by all these new Japanese names, moreover, inevitably were recorded in imported continental *kanji*.

Toward the end of the seventh century, the Japanese state officially took for itself a new national name, Nihon (Japan), and its rulers a new title, *tennō* (heavenly sovereign). Although the word *"tennō"* varies somewhat from the standard Chinese imperial title *huangdi* (J: *kōtei*), both Nihon and *tennō* are specifically written expressions chosen for the significance of their *kanji* rather than words in the native Japanese spoken language. The complete range of standard Chinese imperial titles, moreover, were officially adopted in Japan, though none of the other titles ever became as pervasive as *tennō,* and all of them were originally employed only in writing: The commentary to an eighth-century law code specifies that in speech the Japanese monarchs continued to be designated by native Japanese oral titles such as *sumera mikoto.*[48]

Here, as often, our written Chinese-style textual sources mislead us, but the misdirection, too, is significant. It is most likely that Ōmi no Mifune (722–785)—or someone like him—in the late eighth century chose the Chinese-style royal posthumous names by which all the early "emperors" of Japan, from the legendary Jimmu (ascribed to 660–585 B.C.) to Kōnin (r. 770–781), have been known and revered by their loyal subjects for the last 1,000 years. In a real and powerful sense, Ōmi no Mifune thus invented a Chinese-style past for the new Japanese state and gave it antiquity and respectable institutional depth.[49]

Nor is it entirely appropriate even to distinguish this imported Chinese writing system from the native Japanese language. To be sure, the difference in spoken language among Chinese, Japanese, Korean, and Vietnamese today does form one of the most obvious markers of modern national identity in East Asia (and a serious obstacle to any scholar seeking to study more than one of these national traditions). It may also be true that different languages cannot ever mix together beyond the level of some borrowed vocabulary, except in the case of "the expedient languages of commerce such as Pidgins or Creoles," and even then only at the cost of "extensive degeneration of their grammatical structure."[50] This seems to imply that different linguistic traditions must remain eternally different.

It has seriously been hypothesized that "Japanese" really did begin, around the third century, just exactly as a kind of creolized lingua franca for use in communication for trade and other purposes between the various linguistic communities of prehistoric western Japan. Certainly, although mutual comprehension through speech was apparently possible everywhere from the Kantō in the east (near modern Tokyo) to central Kyūshū in the west in late fifth-century Japan, and although these Japanese spoken languages were apparently also already becoming distinct from those of the Korean peninsula (with whom they may once have enjoyed some similarity), contemporary inscriptions still preserve much local flavor, and translators were still required in the far northeast of the main island of Honshū to the end of the ninth century.[51] "Indeed, if we were to make mutual intelligibility the dividing line between 'language' and 'dialect,' it would be possible to say that in Japan there are still several different 'languages'" in existence even today.[52]

Regardless of how diverse the linguistic community in early Japan undeniably was, however, the long-term direction of linguistic evolution in premodern societies is generally expected to be toward ever greater diversity. Some scholars are, accordingly, more impressed by the relative lack of linguistic variety across the Japanese islands. They take this as confirmation of the sweeping "language replacement" that was presumably caused by Altaic-speaking immigrants from the northern mainland during the Yayoi period. "If such replacement had not happened, then we would expect the language(s) of the initial Pleistocene settlers of Japan to have split into hundreds of surviving local languages."[53]

The newly introduced Yayoi languages must have been, from the start, already far from thoroughly standardized, however. They gradually lost much resemblance to continental prototypes, absorbed vocabulary from the older indigenous populations, and were overlaid by repeated waves of still-newer imported vocabulary in a process that is continuing today. Among the newly introduced vocabulary items during the historic and late prehistoric periods, those from Chinese were notably important. In modern times, English and other Western languages have also made significant contributions. Today, for example, it is estimated that "quasi-English loanwords" make up nearly 10 percent of the ordinary Japanese vocabulary.[54] The linguistic impact of Chinese was much earlier and more pervasive.

Not unlike English, Chinese has always remained a foreign language throughout the islands of Japan. Indeed, the Chinese and Japanese languages are especially widely different from each other in grammar and in the tonal nature of Chinese speech. Yet Chinese graphs—*kanji*—were used to record written Japanese from the very beginning of literate civilization in the archipelago and are still normally used today in conjunction with the phonetic *kana*. The consequent borrowing of vocabulary and ideas has been extensive, and because these loan words arrived at the very beginning of Japan's literate, urban, metalworking civilization, there is at least a sense in which these "Chinese characters" are not really alien at all but rather an inextricable and legitimate part of the native tradition in Japan— much as the "Roman alphabet" became the "native" tool for writing English. Before *kanji*, there was no higher-level Japanese civilization, and Japanese civilization, in part because of *kanji*, is inescapably part of the larger East Asian whole.

There were, of course, vigorous earlier, preliterate Stone Age cultures in the Japanese islands, just as there were also flourishing prehistoric cultures in southern China, Korea, and Vietnam. However, those prehistoric societies have largely vanished now. The cultural continuity between hunter-gatherer Stone Age tribes and the present day must be rather thin. In important senses, what we can call Japanese civilization first appeared only in the sixth or even seventh century, together with the formation of the Yamato state and a structure of centralized authority based on the hereditary monarchy.[55]

Despite the lack of any kind of "immaculate conception" for Japanese civilization, something that is really possible only in mythology or religion anyway, the various peoples of the islands did gradually assemble, out of all these diverse components, a dazzlingly distinctive Japanese culture. Perhaps it is even normal for complex developed societies to be the result of intricate patterns of cultural cross-pollination. Thereafter, Japanese history charted an independent course, especially after the mid-Heian period. Yet the unique trajectory of Japanese history never completely took Japan away from its East Asian roots. Quite the opposite: it could be argued that in some ways Japanese civilization only drew closer to the Central Plain paradigm with time. Confucianism, in particular, is generally believed to have reached its self-conscious climax in Japan only in the seventeenth and eighteenth centuries.

A SEPARATE SUN — JAPAN'S ALL-UNDER-HEAVEN

Yamato sovereignty developed only gradually, through the wielding together of military power, religious awe, and administrative technologies introduced from the continent beginning perhaps around the sixth century. Although a sort of confederacy of "nested polities" may have already been emergent by as early as the fifth century, as late as the start of the seventh century many local chieftains may still have been little more than "autonomous allies of the king."[56]

On the mainland of East Asia, the reunification of the Chinese empire under the Sui dynasty in 589, after four centuries of almost continuous division, sent shock waves rolling across the region. The vigorous new Sui empire reclaimed command of the northern portions of what is now Vietnam, launched an invasion of Champa (in what is now central Vietnam), sent expeditions to an island that may have been Taiwan, and organized massive assaults on Korea. The Yamato court was stimulated by these developments to anxiously enter into a new phase of more intensive relations with the continent. Over a fourteen-year period, Yamato now sent no fewer than five official embassies to Sui; and, as Sui was replaced by Tang on the continent, the Japanese court continued to send literally thousands of persons on official missions to the Chinese empire up until the cancellation of the final embassy in 894.[57]

Historians agree that Japan's rapid implementation of ever more efficient methods of centralized administration in the seventh century was a strategic reaction to the rise of Sui-Tang power on the mainland and in particular to the emergency posed by the crushing military defeat of the Paekche-Wa alliance in 663. Four hundred Yamato warships were reportedly sunk in the defense of doomed Paekche in that climactic year.[58] In this time of crisis, the Yamato court felt a desperate need to organize effectively for self-defense, and the Chinese imperial model was the most effective political example available.

With the fall of Paekche, the old window onto continental culture that had existed since prehistory on the Korean peninsula was closed, and in its place a period of more direct interaction with the Chinese empire itself began. During the brief interval when Tang forces were garrisoned in newly unified Korea (before they were expelled by Silla), no fewer than six Chinese expeditions reached the shores of Japan between 664 and 672. By the 630s, the first Japanese scholars who had been sent to study in Sui China began returning home with firsthand reports on the conditions there.[59] All these developments combined to decisively reshape the monarchy in Japan.

The new Chinese-style imperial order in Japan was constructed around a series of codes of penal and administrative law, conventionally referred to by a pair of *kanji* that are pronounced *ritsuryō* in Japanese and *lüling* in Mandarin. The first of these vitally important new Japanese law codes purportedly dates from 668, but the oldest still-extant code was compiled only in 718. During roughly this period, the late seventh and early eighth centuries, the foundations for a centralized imperial state were laid in Japan on a base of systematic household registration that is uncoincidentally somewhat reminiscent of Warring States China.[60]

Household registrations in eighth-century Japan were updated every six years and served as the mechanism for the allocation of state farmland and the imposition of taxes and military conscription. The system was unmistakably based on Chinese precedents. With regard to the land law in particular, it has been estimated that 73 percent of the earliest surviving Japanese code was modeled, either closely or with some modifications, after the corresponding Chinese laws. (There is some danger of circular reasoning here, however, since the Tang administrative code survives today only in fragments and has been reconstructed by modern scholars with reference to the better-preserved Japanese texts.) Needless to say, moreover, the uniquely Japanese modifications are as significant as the commonalties.[61]

The Japanese did not simply copy Tang institutions. The Japanese farmland allocation system is best viewed as a wholly new system adapted to Japan with reference to the Tang and earlier Chinese models and professed ideals. Among the more significant departures from Tang precedent made by the Nara period Japanese land system were that in Japan both males and females were allocated farmland from early childhood, whereas in Tang only adult males were, and in Japan the system was strictly one of farming allocated state land, whereas in Tang China the system tended more toward the simple regulation of private landholding.[62]

The so-called *ritsuryō* system that was implemented in Japan in the seventh and eighth centuries is generally approached by modern historians, both in Japan and in the West, in terms of its practical achievements in administrative centralization, state building, systematic taxation, and military conscription.[63] These are the rational concerns of effective government, common to ancient Rome, ancient China, and every modern state. For precedent, seventh- and eighth-century Japan could look to the Legalist state-building efforts of Warring States and Qin China. However, a millennium had now elapsed since the time of the Warring States, and the contemporary Chinese example was not the rationalistic administrative machinery of Qin Legalism but the more thoroughly Confucianized, moralistic post-Qin orthodoxy.

To be sure, in traditional East Asia ancient precedents were normally valued above contemporary models, but Confucianism dominated the rhetoric of the idealized past even more thoroughly than it did the political reality of the present. Both contemporary Tang China and the textual world of the ancient sage kings presented by the (Confucian) classics held up a heavily Confucianized model for Japanese observation. Nor would Nara and early Heian period Japanese people necessarily see the distinction, however glaring it may seem to us today, between the practicably efficient administrative elements in the Chinese model and the seemingly impractical and moralistic Confucian ideal of government, in which "the King transforms the people with his virtue and promotes what is right."[64]

Early Japanese rulers seem to have been deeply taken by the Confucian idea of government by ritual example. According to the famous "Seventeen Article Constitution," ascribed to 604,

> all senior ministers and officials take the *li* [pronounced *rei* in Japanese] as fundamental. Their source for governing the people essentially consists of *li*. If superiors do not [follow] *li*, in-

feriors are disorderly. If inferiors lack *li,* there must necessarily be crime. Therefore, if all ministers possess *li,* the order of precedence is not confused. If the common people possess *li,* the state governs itself.[65]

Of course, the attribution of this important document to 604 is hotly disputed by modern scholars. We can be certain about the dates of few events in seventh-century Japan. However, since the "Seventeen Article Constitution" was inserted into the text of the *Nihon shoki,* it cannot possibly date from any later than the completion of that chronicle in 720. The Chinese-style reforms ascribed by the *Nihon shoki* to the seventh century may well be anachronistically dated, thereby distorting our record of the exact sequence of developments. However, even if the critics are entirely correct, the cumulative seventh-century transformation seems incontrovertible. *Nihon shoki* unquestionably does reflect at least some Japanese thinking by the beginning of the eighth century.

In addition, skepticism as to whether some of the reported seventh-century reforms were ever "really" implemented as opposed to merely being grandly proclaimed is itself an anachronistic misconception of seventh-century government in modern terms. From the Confucian perspective, emphasizing government by virtuous example, the distinction between "empty" proclamation and "actual" implementation would not have seemed as pertinent as it does to us today. The "Seventeen Article Constitution," after all, quite explicitly stated that the "source for governing the people essentially consists of *li,*" or ceremonial ritual.

There can be little doubt that Japan really was profoundly transformed over the course of the seventh century, and that these changes were driven by the experience of men who had traveled to the Sui-Tang empire on official embassies and who were determined to reproduce the idealized outlines of the Chinese empire in Japan.[66] The construction of a new palace, the adoption of a system of twelve court ranks distinguished by clothing (including some native Japanese clothing styles to emphasize the political autonomy of Japan's ritual order), and the drafting of the famous "Seventeen Article Constitution," all supposedly in 603–604, demonstrate a new attempt to represent the Yamato ruler as what Joan Piggott calls a Chinese-style "polestar" monarch: the "exemplary center" of a universal courtly culture displayed through Confucian propriety (li).[67] This Sinification process only accelerated as the seventh century wore on.

"All the ways of government take the li as foremost," proclaimed a Japanese empress in 707. "The principles of ruling the world and governing the people consist entirely" of ritual and music, in the words of a contemporary Japanese examination essay.[68] According to this Confucian line of reasoning, if rulers set a good ritual example, commoners will emulate it; and if commoners follow the ritual order of propriety, society becomes self-regulating, so that it truly becomes possible to govern well by not governing at all.

The ideal state envisioned by Miyoshi Kiyotsura (847–918) in 914, for example, was a classically Confucian order of simplicity, upright customs, and light tax and service obligations—a harmoniously hierarchical society in which "superiors shepherded inferiors with humanity, and inferiors upheld superiors with the utmost sincerity." For Miyoshi, the proliferation of laws and taxes could only have a harmful effect on this Confucian utopia.[69]

Although the ritsuryō regime in seventh- to eighth-century Japan was, by definition, based on legal codes, administrative law was intended to promote and enforce an ideal social order inspired by li and the ritual standards of Confucianism. Even the system of criminal law, based on Chinese models, had already been extensively Confucianized—for example, by the introduction of hierarchical status differentials into the penal sanctions.

The Japanese Nara era penal code recognized "eight atrocities" (hachi gyaku), closely parallel to the heavily Confucianized "ten abominations" of Chinese law, as especially heinous. Four of these, not surprisingly, involved different forms of treason or lèse-majesté—such as defecting, planning damage to the imperial tombs, forging the imperial seal, mispreparing imperial medication, or disrespect for imperial messengers.

However, because of the continuum in Confucian thought between lord and father, crimes of treason against the state shaded into "treachery" (akugyaku) against the family: assaulting or plotting to kill grandparents, parents, and other close relatives. Another atrocity, known as fudō ("not Tao"), referred to black magic, the murder of three or more innocent members of a single family, and dismemberment of victims' bodies. The seventh atrocity was the explicitly Confucian crime of being unfilial. "Injustice" (fugi) meant killing one's lord, killing a provincial governor, killing a teacher, or failing to properly mourn for a deceased husband.[70]

Good government in Nara, Japan, came to be conceived of as a balance of imperial virtue and bureaucratic diligence, held accountable by supernatural forces. In Japan, as in China, it was presumed that "virtuous government is a defense against evil; good words summon blessings." Thus, Sugawara no Fumitoki (899–981) could argue in 956 that the virtuous gestures of reducing the imperial consumption of delicacies and granting generous amnesties, indicative of the virtues of frugality and benevolence, could bring "timely beneficial rain." Between the years 708 and 886, Japanese emperors are known to have demonstrated their imperial benevolence by issuing at least 123 general pardons.[71]

The Japanese legal code held detailed provisions for the reporting of omens and natural disasters, since these were regarded as critical indications of imperial virtue. When earthquakes and floods ravaged numerous provinces in 888, an edict inquired, "What crime have the common people committed to repeatedly incur these misfortunes?" Calamitous anomalies were the imperial responsibility: "In my humble opinion, the seasons have been conferred on people by the labors of former Imperial majesties." In 705, for example, one emperor's proposed solution to the problem of unseasonal weather and crop failure was tax relief and the recitation of sutras in the Five Great Temples—both, equally, demonstrations of the imperial virtue that alone could change the weather.[72]

Aside from maintaining the stability of the seasons, the imperial government was also responsible for promoting a virtuous society. As in China, public and private virtue were linked by the presumed equivalence between political loyalty and filial piety. Filial children would also be loyal subjects. A Japanese decree of 757, for example, spoke of the "loyalty that is a transference from filial piety." According to one late eighth- or early ninth-century Japanese examination essay, "Although public and private are not equal, loyalty and filiality hang from each other. For spreading fame and establishing oneself, they may be considered one . . . inasmuch as those who are able to be filial to their parents transfer loyalty to their rulers."[73]

In 757, therefore, Empress Kōken (r. 749–758), in imitation of a recent Tang decree of 744, ordered that every household in the Japanese empire keep and study a copy of the Confucian *Classic of Filial*

Piety to promote the filial piety that was so essential to "governing the people and pacifying the country."[74] It is highly doubtful that this could possibly have literally been accomplished—the vast majority of the population could not read anyway—but a gap between the behavior of the central elite and distant commoners was fully consistent with Confucian theory. What mattered most was the correct moral and ritual posture adopted by the court.

By law, Japanese provincial governors were required to inspect the districts under their jurisdiction annually in order to promote those who were "fond of scholarship, respect the Tao, are filial and fraternal, loyal and honest, pure, and of exceptional conduct" and to discipline those were not. The early eighth-century Japanese court repeatedly issued commands that the homes of filial children, virtuous fellows, and chaste widows be marked and that tax exemptions or other rewards be provided for them.[75]

"For securing the rulers and governing the people, nothing is better than the *li*," declared Empress Kōken in 757, and, since causing the *li* to flourish was the task of the university, she awarded twenty *chō* of sustenance land to the students at that school. The Confucian civilizing process was preeminently a "transformation caused by teaching," and formal, text-based education was vital to its success. As Fujiwara no Muchimaro (680–737) observed at the turn of the eighth century,

> Now, schools are where men of ability meet, and where the transformation caused by kings originates. Managing a country and managing a family both depend on the teachings of the sages. Perfect loyalty and perfect filiality follow from this Tao.[76]

Karl Mannheim has written, "We belong to a group not only because we are born into it, not merely because we profess to belong to it, nor finally because we give it our loyalty and allegiance, but primarily because we see the world and certain things in the world the way it does." The *li* were core integrating ideals in premodern East Asia, providing educated East Asians with a common perspective and a common order. This was the significance of the alleged anonymous Chinese comment to the Japanese Ambassador Awata, around 702, that he had heard of the great land of Japan to the east of the sea as a "land of gentlemen," where "*li* and *yi* are sincerely practiced," and why a certain Chinese governor wrote of the Japanese monk Saichō (767–822) in 805 as "coming from a land of *li* and *yi*." It marks a claim of belonging to the same civilization—as does Sugawara no Michizane's (845–903) wistful remark, after attending a Confucian sacrifice and lecture on the *Classic of Filial Piety* in ninth-century Japan, that Confucius' spirit was "never far away."[77]

Two centuries previously, around 646, an exposition of the Confucian classics and performance of the same ritual that Sugawara no Michizane had found so deeply moving in Japan allegedly also impressed some obdurate tribal leaders in what is now Canton (Guangdong) so much that they "happily submitted."[78] These Confucian ritual practices were the common currency of East Asian high civilization, and it might not be suggesting too much to say that the renowned and courtly Japanese poet Sugawara was more fully versed in the Confucian arcana, more truly a proper Chinese-style Confucian gentleman, than these rough Cantonese tribespeople, although they lived in China and he lived in Japan.

However, Sugawara no Michizane did not become Chinese. He is, in fact, probably best known as the principal instigator of the termination of Japan's periodic official embassies to China in 894. This decision was taken more in response to specific changing circumstances than out of any desire to break utterly with the Chinese model. Yet, continued admiration for the Chinese model was not incongruent with a counter process we might call "Japanization."

Interaction with the continent had been essential to the emergence of a self-conscious "Japanese" identity in the first place. In general, everywhere, there is a tendency for globalizing international forces to also provoke counterreactions that may take the form of "exaggerated expressions of regional identity." As Peter Wells explains for the case of Roman northern Europe in the late first century, "While the elites adopted empire-wide styles . . . nonelites tended instead to reinforce their identities as members of traditional local groups," and a "divergence of local populations in their material culture" begins to manifest itself in the archaeological record there long before the collapse of Roman political authority.[79]

Japanese uniqueness was conceivable at all only in contrast to some conventional "other." The phrase the "spirit of Japan," ironically, first appears in Japanese literature (just after the end of the period covered in this book) in direct juxtaposition to a "background of Chinese learning." Even as a rich and uniquely Japanese "national culture" began to flourish by the later Heian period, it continued to be deeply impressed by Chinese calligraphic, literary, and other models. Without a Chinese example or contrasting foil, there could have been no native Japanese literature at all.[80]

Although "Western scholars have tended to belittle the importance of early Japan's civil service examinations and the schools that prepared men to take them," a fairly intact Confucian school system did function in Japan from the eighth century until as late as the twelfth. However, it is undeniable that the Japanese school system was ultimately less successful than its continental prototypes both in China and in Korea. In 914, Miyoshi Kiyotsura complained that the university had become an increasingly neglected "pit of disappointment" since so few of its students found official advancement based on academic merit.[81] The elaborate educational system prescribed by the *ritsuryō* codes eventually atrophied and disappeared.

Even earlier, the Chinese-inspired eighth-century Japanese *ritsuryō* rice land allocation system fell into desuetude, beginning after only half a century of operation, because of both widespread evasion of the regulations and the opening of new private fields outside the purview of the system. The last Empire-wide land allocation in Japan was conducted in 806. This gradual replacement of publicly administered farmland in Japan by private estates is frequently interpreted as being both a uniquely Japanese process and a critical stage in the rise of a "feudalism" in "medieval" Japan that roughly paralleled contemporary European phenomena.[82]

However, this failure of the Japanese *ritsuryō* "experiment of borrowing a foreign system of land tenure and taxation" was not simply "because it was too close a copy of the Chinese system" and therefore inappropriately alien to Japanese needs, as an earlier generation of scholarship too easily imagined.[83] We should recall that the Equitable Fields system had collapsed in China itself even earlier, by about 755. In addition, the Equitable Fields system had originally been at least a semiforeign, Tuoba Xianbei innovation in China too, one that was somewhat uncharacteristic of 2,000 years of Chinese imperial practice as a whole. The evolution of the agricultural economy in Japan, therefore, cannot be explained simply in terms of native versus foreign institutions but must be understood in terms of the appropriateness, feasibility, and attractiveness of certain specific practices under a variety of different and changing conditions.

As in Japan during the Heian period, great private estates also emerged in Tang China following the collapse of the Equitable Fields system. The details of this process were not, naturally enough, exactly the same as in Japan, but it is interesting to note that in both places these estates were referred to by an identical two-*kanji* expression, pronounced *shōen* in Japanese and *zhuangyuan* in Chinese.[84] The explanation for this verbal parallelism is, however, merely that these novel Japanese estates were given an old, well-known Chinese name.

The long-term structural pattern of historical development in Japan followed its own course. In China, a genuinely hereditary aristocracy never reappeared (a most peculiar examination-based meritocracy, the mandarinate, gradually emerged instead), and the imperial administrative machinery retained astonishing vitality. In China, the empire repeatedly disintegrated but was just as frequently restored. In contrast, Japan remained a highly aristocratic society, with an emerging samurai warrior elite that had no counterpart at all in imperial China.

In Japan, the line of emperors continued unbroken (after its initial fabrication according to the Chinese model), unlike the case in China, where there were frequent changes in the ruling family. However, the emperors of Japan were reduced to ceremonial impotence, and a physically and institutionally separate military government was established by the end of the twelfth century—known as the *bakufu* and headed by a so-called shogun—which sometimes acted more like the true functioning central government of Japan than the imperial court. Even this shogun was sometimes reduced to helplessness in the face of regional warrior leaders, who, as Ashikaga Yoshimasa (1435–1490) complained in 1482, "do as they please and do not follow orders. That means there can be no government."[85]

The course of Japanese history, in other words, evolved in significantly different directions than on the continent. History, in traditional East Asia, did not follow uniform rules. Yet it is interesting to note that the word "shogun" (C: *jiangjun*) is nothing more than the Japanese pronunciation of the old Chinese military title meaning "general." In earlier times, this same title had often been liberally bestowed on eastern tributary rulers by Chinese Sons of Heaven: sixth-century Chinese imperial "shoguns" were appointed, for example, in Paekche, Koguryŏ, and among the Khitan. *Bakufu* (C: *mufu*), furthermore, was a term commonly used in China since the Warring States period to designate "the headquarters of a military leader on campaign."[86] China, too, had its share of military strongmen.

Such linguistic links are trivial, no doubt, and none of this mini-
mizes the uniquely Japanese flavor of the shogunate. However, it does
illustrate something of the inescapability of the East Asian cultural orbit for premodern Japan. The Japanese adapted continental ideas
with wonderful elasticity and often made them unrecognizably their
own. Yet to truly savor Japanese history, it is necessary to appreciate
both the local peculiarities and the broader commonalties.

Elements of the core Central Plain civilization were so deeply
planted, at the very roots of each emerging local society in East Asia,
that it sometimes becomes almost meaningless to attempt to distinguish "native" from imported. Everywhere (including China), these
originally mixed, hybrid cultures subsequently developed according
to interactive dynamics all their own. Only within the borders of the
Chinese state did people become "Chinese," and even within China
proper there remained a remarkable amount of internal regional diversity. The core elements of Central Plain civilization disseminated
widely throughout East Asia without erasing the local cultures they
encountered. Like Hellenism in Mediterranean antiquity, Central
Plain civilization in traditional East Asia could be described as "a medium not necessarily antithetical to local or indigenous traditions. On
the contrary, it provided a new and more eloquent way of giving voice
to them."[87]

The more some early Japanese people came to think "like the
Chinese," ironically enough, the more they would naturally want to
envision Japan as a Middle Kingdom at the center of its own All-
under-Heaven, and the more intolerable Chinese imperial pretensions would come to seem. The promulgation of Chinese-style codes
of law and the issuance of Chinese-style calendars, reign periods, and
posthumous imperial names were inspired by a spirit of competitive
imitation in Japan; if the Chinese empire was *tianxia,* or "All-under-
Heaven," then a rival Japanese All-under-Heaven (J: *tenka*) would be
reproduced on the islands.[88]

Japan's adoption of Buddhism, and especially the casting of the
great bronze buddha statue at Nara in the eighth century, was also inspired by a desire to overtake their continental model. Even the construction of a Chinese-style capital city was intended to form the centerpiece of a competitively Chinese-style universal order. An order, in
724, for officials of the fifth rank and higher to tile the roofs of their
homes and paint their walls red and white—Chinese style, in contrast
to the Japanese tradition of unpainted wood and bark roofs—asked,

"If the [place where] ten-thousand kingdoms pay court is not so grand and imposing, how will we display [our imperial] virtue?"[89]

The imported Chinese vocabulary of government itself contained the seed for an explicit claim to universal rule. In the fifth century, at a time when the Yamato court was still actively sending tribute embassies to the continental Southern dynasties and literacy in the islands still largely in the hands of immigrant families, some of the earliest extant Japanese inscriptions already make the claim that the Yamato monarchs were "great Kings . . . governing All-under-Heaven."[90]

This was the only available political terminology for fully sovereign, centralized Chinese-style rule: the Chinese vocabulary in which Sons of Heaven had to describe themselves. The only alternative was the language of subordination, of "serving the great" as local vassals. In Japan, the selection of the "extremely Chinese" new imperial title *tennō* in the seventh century was designed to simultaneously proclaim the Japanese monarch's superiority over the mere "kings" of Korea and rivalry with the imperial Sons of Heaven in China.[91]

In the famous Chinese formula supposedly reiterated by the Japanese crown prince in 646, following the Taika coup d'état, "There are not twin suns in Heaven; there are not two kings in the state."[92] In the Chinese conception, there might be, simultaneously, many different kingdoms, but there could be only one *tianxia* and only one Son of Heaven to rule over all of it. "Therefore," the quotation continues, "only the *tennō* unifies All-under-Heaven, and can employ all of the people."

Following the logic of this pretension, the diplomatic credentials of the Yamato embassy that was sent to Sui in 607 were notoriously addressed from the "Son of Heaven in the place where the sun rises to the Son of Heaven in the place where the sun sets." Because such opposing claims to universal sovereignty were inherently mutually incompatible, Japanese ambassadors during this period may have sometimes been forced into the awkward position of having to secretly change or destroy some of the documents that they were charged with conveying between these two self-styled universal empires.[93]

Joan Piggott rejects the conventional English translation of *tennō* as "emperor," arguing that "the *tennō* of eighth-century Nihon did not conquer his realm, he had no standing army save some frontier forces, and the realm remained significantly segmented rather than vertically subjugated." This sounds reasonable enough, although it may underestimate the importance of the military in early Japan. However, military conquest may not be essential to the definition of an empire (especially a Confucian empire). In the sixteenth century, for example, prior to the acquisition of its own vast overseas colonies, England was already sometimes called an "empire" in order to emphasize its long tradition of independence and relative isolation from the continent of Europe. Such an application of the term would be quite pertinent to early Nihon, and if the most basic definition of "empire" designates the union of previously unrelated states or peoples under a common sovereign, then early Nihon really was an empire and even more clearly wanted to conceive itself in those terms: as a *zhongguo* (J: *chūgoku*), or middle kingdom, presiding over concentric circles of barbarian vassals.[94]

A Yamato embassy to Tang in 659 presented gifts of male and female Emishi barbarian captives from northern Honshū. In response to the Tang emperor's inquiry, the ambassador explained that there were three kinds of Emishi. Of the three, only the nearest, called "mature" or "ripe" Emishi, offered annual tribute to the Yamato court. These Emishi tribesmen of northern Honshū are continually represented in the Chinese-style Japanese national histories as offering tribute of local products to the Japanese court. In return, in 699, for example, 106 Emishi from Koshi no Michi no Shiri were bestowed with court titles as a grand gesture of imperial solicitude.[95] This was in the properly paternal model of a virtuous Son of Heaven presiding over all *tianxia*.

In addition to barbarians such as the Emishi, eighth-century Japanese texts also repeatedly tried to represent the newly unified Korean kingdom of Silla as a vassal state, obligated to submit tribute to the Japanese *tennō*. After attending the Japanese new year's court assembly in 706, for example, the Sillan ambassador was returned to his "vassal" realm with an imperial missive, in which "the *tennō* [with the Japanese phonetic reading "*sumera mikoto*" indicated] respectfully inquires about the Sillan king" and praises him for his "sincerity" and steady tribute.[96]

The attachment of a little Paekche court in exile, in permanent attendance on the Japanese sovereign after 667, gave added credibility to the picture of a Chinese-style emperor presiding over a universal All-under-Heaven. When "insignificant Silla," around 757, "gradually became deficient in the courtesy of a vassal," it was proposed to dispatch an armada to overawe the Korean kingdom, but this was countered by the wonderfully Confucian reply that it would be better to win their submission back peacefully through exposure to imperial "virtue and justice."[97]

The premodern Japanese rulers, in other words, accepted the Chinese imperial vision of *tianxia* but placed themselves in the center, as the Middle Kingdom, instead of China. Recognizing that "the local customs of one's native places are each different," the *tennō's* civilizing mission was then to spread Confucian high culture and "apportion ceremonial so that it trickles down to those on the eastern sea." Late seventh- and early eighth-century provincial governors in Japan have been described less as functional administrators, in the modern sense, than "cultural emissaries" sent to spread the literate civilization of the court throughout the countryside.[98]

In 710, for example, a man from Hyūga Province named Sō no Kimi Hosomaro received a grant of court rank in reward for "teaching in the wilderness, and taming it with the sagely transformation." In western Japan in the eighth and ninth centuries, the government conferred court rank on wealthy families who aided the sick and hungry in times of trouble.[99]

This was the eminently Confucian style of government by virtuous gesture. The spirit of Chinese civilization had been so thoroughly adopted and naturalized in Japan that by the fourteenth century it was even possible to argue that, since the time of Qin Shi huangdi's notorious book burning campaign in third-century B.C. China, "the complete works of Confucianism existed thereafter only in Japan."[100] The universal truths of Confucian civilization, in other words, had supposedly best been realized in Japan, even though they were, of course, still written in the classical Chinese language.

Conclusion

SINIFICATION AND ITS DISCONTENTS

In the year 755, a corpulent Tang general based in southern Man-churia named An Lushan (ca. 703–757), "calculating that he could take All-under-Heaven," rose up in rebellion against the dynasty. As if in preparation for this very moment, An Lushan had long been gathering strength, assembling mounted archers from among the northern tribes as well as building up the Tang imperial forces under his command. For, in addition to being a Tang official, An Lushan was also a Hu, born in a felt tent to an apparently Sogdian father and Turkic mother and reportedly conversant with several northern languages. "Secretly," before his rebellion, "he dispatched Hu merchants to travel all the Circuits [of the Tang empire], bringing in a million in riches annually."[1]

Modern scholarship has demonstrated that the traditional Chinese historical accounts of An Lushan are not very satisfactory, but the fact that they make so much of the foreign menace lurking behind his rebellion is itself significant. It was, at this particular time, quite normal for Tang regional military commissioners to be men of non-Chinese birth.[2] Yet this need only really mean frontiersmen with martial training, and An Lushan was now also a high-ranking Tang Chinese official with close ties to the imperial court. Uighur troops, far more thoroughly foreign to China than An Lushan, ironically proved essential to rescuing the dynasty from his rebellion. However, An Lushan's rebellion nonetheless marks the end of the old exuberant cosmopolitanism that had characterized the early Tang dynasty. The easy confidence that barbarians could be civilized and become Chinese yielded now to greater fear and suspicion.

Afterward, the Tang dynasty was restored, but its "financial machinery fell into such complete ruin as to become unsalvageable in its old form." The "former bases of rule had collapsed so thoroughly that the restoration seems on the surface little more than ritualistic." Whether it was because of the rebellion itself or some constellation of other factors, this mid-Tang rebellion of An Lushan marks a major watershed in the course of imperial Chinese history.[3]

Throughout Eurasia, whole new epochs were beginning. By Tang times, a continent-wide trading network had already infiltrated almost every corner of the Old World and woven it together into what was, to some extent, a single interdependent "civilization with many common factors." Although direct causal connections are difficult to discern, changes at one end of the continent were echoed by disruptions at the other. The great watershed indicated by An Lushan's rebellion in 755 in China coincides with the founding of the Frankish Carolingian dynasty in the far west in 751, the Abbasid caliphate in 747, and the Uighur empire on the steppe around 742.[4]

In East Asia, the period from An Lushan's rebellion to the end of the Tang in 907 witnessed the genuine end of an era. The last embassy to China from the Japanese islands was canceled in 894. On the Korean peninsula, Silla was replaced by Koryŏ in the years between 918 and 935. In Lingnan, the country we now call Vietnam gained permanent independence in 939. Everywhere, things were changing.

In China, the changes were permanent and profound. The very ideal of meticulous bureaucratic administration based on codified law gave way increasingly now to a self-consciously minimalist Confucian vision of government by moral example. In the short term, this may have helped unleash a burst of entrepreneurial energy that contributed to making "the Chinese economy after about 1100 the most advanced in the world."[5] Northern Wei and early Tang-style Equitable Fields land allocation disappeared, government regulation of business atrophied, and the later Chinese empire came to be characterized by the kind of noninterventionist economic policies admired by the eighteenth-century French physiocrats who first coined the term "laissez-faire."[6]

In the very long term, however, imperial vitality may have also been fatally compromised by the creeping failure to maintain even minimally effective standards of law and public services—including such extremely basic government functions as providing uniform systems of weights and measures and a standard currency, both of which proved to be more characteristic of earlier Chinese imperial dynasties than of the last ones. By the time the imperial system in China was over-thrown forever in 1912, Chinese revolutionary nationalists could ac-tually denounce the old empire not for any supposed despotism but rather for its failure to demand enough of the Chinese people to mold them into a competitively strong Western-style Chinese nation-state.[7]

Effective Tang administrative machinery did not disintegrate im-mediately, to be sure. As late as 845, the Japanese pilgrim Ennin could still report from remote Shandong Province that an imperial purge of Buddhism was being enforced there with the same thoroughness as in the capital.[8] Literally from its inception, however, the system of ad-ministration based on household registration experienced continu-ous decay, requiring constant applications of effort to rejuvenate it. Following Tang, the effort was largely abandoned. Never again would the Chinese empire aspire to its former level of direct bureaucratic micromanagement.

After the end of the Tang dynasty in 907, China, Japan, Korea, and Vietnam each followed their separate destinies. The trajectory of Japanese history after the early Heian period, for example, is in many ways notably divergent from that of late imperial China. Yet somehow all these East Asian regions became, if anything, more Confucian over the centuries. The broad harmony of East Asian higher civilization was not disturbed until the intrusion of the modern industrialized West in the nineteenth century.

This East Asian world had never existed in isolation. Tang China was surely more cosmopolitan—and less relatively isolated—than contemporary Western Europe was. Foreign trade, Buddhist mission-ary activity, and nomadic incursions from the steppe always connected East Asia to wider Eurasian horizons. However, these various outside influences were severely attenuated by the vast distances involved and by the opposing centrifugal expansive force of China's own supremely self-confident civilizing mission, which fully expected to transform the western regions rather than to be transformed by them. The teach-ers, after all, did not expect to be taught.

If East Asia was always part of wider planet, within East Asia there was also always a great deal of internal diversity. One might argue that Chinese influences on early Japan were scarcely any less limited and superficial than western influences were on China and, in turn, that the influence of the incipient Yamato court on some of the outlying corners of the Japanese archipelago also long remained rather weak. No two individual people are ever completely alike, yet at the same time all humanity is broadly similar. In choosing to focus on the East Asian region, we need to keep in mind the almost infinite number of layers of simultaneous commonality and diversity. Each is important. Yet in terms of elite high culture, premodern East Asia was a reasonably coherent whole, and it is especially important now not to allow this unity to be obscured by the blinders of modern nationalism.

Modern Vietnamese nationalists would like to believe that the 1,000 years of Chinese imperial rule in Vietnam were but "a temporary intrusion" into a continuously existing, pre- and post-Chinese occupation Vietnamese nation.[9] However, this perspective demands an essentially racial (or mystical) understanding of national identity. At the racial level, there undoubtedly was much genetic continuity in Vietnam, as in many other relatively isolated local pockets scattered throughout the world, from the Stone Age until the present day. There were also undoubtedly linguistic and other continuities in the local "folk culture" over extended periods of time. However, the independent Vietnamese state that emerged after the tenth century was in no sense a return to or a revival of the prehistoric local cultures of the region. Dong Son bronze drums, for example, do not suddenly reappear in the archaeological record. (If they had, it could have only been as a conscious archaism.) Nor was the newly independent tenth-century kingdom in the Red River valley quite yet the Vietnam we are familiar with today.

Bronze drums did, it is true, linger as a distinctly southern cultural motif for centuries. They continued to be displayed as treasured symbols of the wealth and power of local southern great families through Tang times and beyond, but in Canton (Guangdong), China.[10] Nor should this be surprising since the prehistoric inhabitants of both sides of the current Sino-Vietnamese border had once been virtually identical. Clearly, therefore, the present-day national differences between the southeastern-most regions of the People's Republic of China and Vietnam must be explained in terms of divergent trajectories of historical evolution rather than unchanging national character.

Moreover, much of Vietnam's own present borderline status, astride a somewhat hypothetical frontier between East and Southeast

Asia, is the result of the Sinified Vietnamese state's gradual absorption of Cham and Khmer and other population groups and regions as it expanded from its Red River origins south to the Mekong delta. In a sense, it could be argued that the frontier of Southeast Asia has retreated slowly south from the line of the Yangzi (in what is now central China) to the Mekong delta (in what is now southern Vietnam) over the course of the last 3,000 years. The case of Vietnam (and Guangxi-Guangdong) reminds us, moreover, that there are gradients of East Asian-ization: it was never an all-or-nothing proposition but, in fact, always a matter of cultural mixing, both unconscious and deliberate.

What I have here called East Asian-ization may also be defined as Sinification (or Sinicization), that is, Chinese-ization. There seems little doubt that the principal distinguishing common features of East Asian civilization—*kanji*, the imperial administrative system, Confucianism—can be traced mostly to ancient origins in the core area of the Central Plain in what is now northern China. East Asia developed in a notably lopsided fashion. Not only did China provide the original core civilization, but it has always formed by far the largest part of East Asia both geographically and demographically.

In 606, for example, the officially registered population of the Sui empire (which surely undercounts the real total) was forty-six million. By contrast, the best modern estimates of the population of the Japanese islands in the seventh century range from three to five and a half million. The registered population of Chinese Vietnam at the end of the seventh century (both literally and figuratively a fraction of the Chinese total) was a paltry 148,431 (down from almost a million 700 years earlier), although this number doubtlessly includes only a small proportion of the persons who actually lived there. Contemporary Korea's population is more uncertain, but the *Samguk sagi* reports 760,000 households in Paekche at the time of its destruction in 660–663 and 690,000 households sustaining 300,000 gentlemen-warriors *(sa)* for Koguryŏ at its seventh-century peak.[11] The ratio of households, or gentlemen, to the total population in Korea, as well as the fundamental reliability of these statistics, is a matter for conjecture, but it is clear that China dwarfed all its East Asian neighbors.

Yet Sinification in East Asia did not mean becoming "Chinese" anywhere except within the borders of the Chinese empire itself (where a great many people certainly did become Chinese). Elsewhere in East Asia, elements of Central Plain civilization merely overlay a complex mosaic of local diversity, functioning as something like international norms. If the acceptance of certain agreed-on common standards for elite East Asian higher civilization did tend to promote a degree of cultural convergence throughout the region, this may have acted as little more than a modest counterbalance to an opposing natural process of seemingly inexorable diversification. As elements of Central Plain civilization spread throughout East Asia and interacted with local prehistoric cultures, the resulting fusion generated several distinctively and gloriously new civilizations.

At the risk of conflating what are—it must be remembered—quite different biological and cultural processes, it is worth pausing to reflect that the Darwinian mechanism of natural selection, popularly known as "survival of the fittest," was primarily intended to explain not the winnowing out of uncompetitive species through extinction but rather "the origin of [entirely new] species" through a plausible mechanism of evolution from common ancestors. Darwinian evolution is, fundamentally, a process of diversification. "This tendency in the large groups to go on increasing in size and diverging in character, together with the almost inevitable contingency of much extinction, explains the arrangement of all the forms of life, in groups subordinate to groups, all within a few great classes, which we now see everywhere around us," wrote Darwin.[12]

Humanity is a notably successful species that has spread across the planet and diversified spectacularly. Current theory suggests that not only people but also human language originated in Africa approximately 150,000 to 200,000 years ago.[13] The unmistakable long-term trend of human evolution has been toward greater diversity. This diversification can, however, be partially or temporarily reversed by improved communication, colonization or conquest, and the emergence and spread of overridingly powerful new methods and technologies. Successful new practices can spread rapidly, and local communities that fail to adopt them may run the risk of extinction.

Out of the crucial Neolithic breakthrough to settled agriculture that took place in what is now China emerged the classical Bronze Age states and civilizations of the Central Plain, and eventually a mighty Chinese empire that swallowed up most of modern China, and for a time also northern Korea and Vietnam. Through the complex historical evolutionary process that has been the central theme of this book, this core East Asian civilization then helped sire new and uniquely different Japanese, Korean, and Vietnamese civilizations.

Even in this diluted sense, however, Sinification is a concept that many people find objectionable. The civilizing mission is, after all, another name for cultural imperialism, and its progress implies a winner and many losers: one "civilization" and many "barbarisms." Not only is this distasteful to some people, but the very process itself virtually guarantees that it will provoke counterreactions that must ultimately qualify its success.

An all too obvious modern parallel is the twentieth-century phenomenon of global Westernization, which has alternately been regarded as a universally inevitable mechanical process, glorified as "progress," hotly refuted, or sadly lamented. An astute anthropologist such as Joy Hendry, deeply immersed in the study of modern Japanese society, can conclude that theories "about the convergence of industrial societies" are "now largely discredited," yet popular opinion in the United States in the post–Cold War era now seems firmly convinced that the new millennium will bring "the end of history" in an inexorable process of global "coca-colonization." As is so often the case, the truth probably lies somewhere in between the most extreme positions.[14]

Benjamin Barber has sensationally explored the dialectical interdependence between global convergence and local reaction in a book titled *Jihad vs. McWorld.* Quintessentially American fast-food chains have, in recent years, successfully proliferated throughout much of East Asia, where their often-considerable appeal is precisely as purveyors of "a 'taste' of America." Yet they also, unsurprisingly, have undergone a process of "localization" while taking root in East Asian markets. The experience of "McDonald's in Beijing" suggests to at least one thoughtful observer that at the dawn of the twenty-first century still, "the emerging global culture is marked by diversity rather than uniformity."[15]

Cultural interaction is and always has been quite natural. The very illusion of universal laws or patterns of historical evolution is made possible in the first place chiefly by the sharing and resultant dispersion of ideas and practices among scattered population groups, creating certain broad similarities in their development. Typically, moreover, cultural exchange is also at least temporarily somewhat lopsided—more one direction than the other—either because of imbalances of raw power, which are also quite normal, or simply as the result of fickle twists of fashion. However, cultural interaction never results in complete and perfect copying of one culture by another, even in those relatively rare cases were exact copying is seriously intended.

The matrix of circumstances is always too complicated for simple copying. Too many different people and too many different considerations must be involved. The slate can never be wiped perfectly clean, and in no case has cultural interaction ever taken place between two previously entirely discrete, closed, static, and homogeneous "native" cultures. Instead, there has been an uneven and halting but broadly continuous ebb and flow of global migration, trade, and other interaction extending back in time to the very origins of humanity, which we presume now to have been in Africa some 200,000 years ago. Ethnic identities shift and change eternally in response to changing circumstances. These new ethnicities are then, typically, wishfully reimagined to be primordial since that provides a comforting illusion of stability for people who might otherwise feel "buffeted by uncertainties."[16]

Given the natural dynamics of all human interactions, with their unpredictable twists and perpetual imbalances (the "balance of nature" is maintained only by constant teetering), it would be strange if phenomena such as Sinification and Westernization did not happen. It would also be naive (although this seems to be exactly what most people always do suppose) to expect any such "-ization" to ever be comprehensive and complete. For the premodern period, one recent survey concludes that "generally speaking, . . . large-scale conversion to foreign cultural standards occurred only when powerful political, social, or economic incentives encouraged it—and even then it led universally to syncretism rather than to outright, wholesale adoption of a foreign cultural tradition."[17] Cultural "-ization" is a fairly common phenomenon, but it is almost never total, and the results can be surprising.

One of America's leading Korea experts, Bruce Cumings, protests that "Korea was never 'Sinicized.' . . . The real story is indigenous Korea and the unstinting Koreanization of foreign influence, not vice versa." He is, of course, correct (although his point is reminiscent of the old quibble about whether a glass of water is half full or half empty). David Pollack makes a similar case for Japan. Instead of passively being "influenced" by China, the Japanese actively engaged in "selecting foreign cultural elements and synthesizing them into the native culture." However, as Pollack also observes at an even higher level of sophistication, "what we can perceive as a 'native' process is itself . . . already the product of countless earlier syntheses."[18]

Neither Korea nor Japan was simply Chinese-ized, nor is it, conversely, sufficient to say that a handful of Chinese motifs, more modestly, were selected for Korean-ization or Japan-ization. Instead, Korea and Japan (and China too) are the end products (actually, still unfinished works in progress) rather than the starting points of the process. In the beginning, there was no Korea or Japan—nor even a China, either. At the risk of much oversimplification, we might say that Sinification, along the lines of the early Central Plain Chinese states and the later empire, was the force that gradually shaped the various emerging civilizations of East Asia out of what had once been a mosaic of Stone Age tribes. Their final differences are, in part, the very product of their sustained interaction.

The use of terminology such as "Sinification" or the "Confucianization of Korea," it must be confessed, does imply a relatively one-sided process of interaction. There was a gross disparity in size (and degree of antiquity) between China and Korea, as the Korean diplomatic expression *sadae* (serving the great) makes painfully clear. However, again, though "China" may be older than "Korea," neither was primordial. Both the Chinese and the Korean states, each of whose borders were defined more by politics than by nature, evolved together interactively over many centuries to give rise to an East Asian world in which Korea was admittedly the smaller of the two states but no less a creatively active participant. In the case of Korea, the real story is one of the creation of an "indigenous" Korea through a long process of evolution and interaction—with other proto-Koreans, the Chinese empire, and beyond.

It makes little sense to even speak of "Korea," except as a conventional label for a piece of real estate, prior to the fusion together of Sillan, Paekchean, Koguryŏan, and Tang elements that occurred at the time of the creation of the first unified Korean kingdom in the seventh century.[19] Thereafter, Korea continued to change. The point has already been well established that it was only under the concluding Yi (or Chosŏn) dynasty, which lasted from 1392 to the end of the premodern period, that Korea finally became what may be called a paradigmatic Confucian society. Even then, it managed to be paradigmatic while remaining unique.

If one were to design, from the wide array of available options, an abstraction and call it the Confucian state, the resulting configuration might more closely resemble late premodern Korea than China itself. Yet even in this most Confucian of places, Confucian standards were fully applied only to the elite Korean *yangban* class, which comprised no more than 10 percent of the total Korean population: "The Confucianization of Korean society is an upper-class phenomenon."[20]

So it was also, to some extent, everywhere. Unlike modern international exchanges, which often involve genuinely popular mass culture, communications in antiquity tended to link ruling elites together without reaching downward much to the larger numbers of the common people.[21] However, this again merely confirms the Chinese expectation of a single universal elite high culture, with multiple local popular cultures everywhere. In the case of a high-traffic area such as the Korean peninsula, it might be added that there probably was substantial mixing of even basic, commoner population groups, at least in the early period.

In the case of Japan, as a mature Japanese state first emerged in the seventh and eighth centuries, conscious emulation of Chinese standards may be said to have pertained almost exclusively to public acts of state. Chinese fashions gradually spread, however. By the ninth century, there was something of a vogue for Chinese-style cuisine among the Japanese elite. In 818, Sugawara no Kiyogimi (770–842) proposed mandating the wearing of Chinese-style clothing in Japan at national events and that Tang-style plaques be hung over the doors of all public buildings. In addition, there can be no mistaking the profound influence of Chinese literary models on the Heian era aristocratic Japanese ideal of gentlemanly behavior.[22]

Yet again, this was very much a standard only for the aristocracy, and even at that elite level, early Japanese literary works, such as the eleventh-century *Tale of Genji*, depict a society more comfortable with casual sexual contact, and exhibiting much greater gender equality, than one would expect from an austerely patriarchal Confucian society, prizing idealized self-restraint.[23] However, by now we should expect Sinification to be an open-ended dialogue between local customs and international East Asian norms and not some simple duplication of everything Chinese. Even the loftiest members of the elite were tied simultaneously both to the universal elite standards and to the peculiar local practices of their homes.

Even within what we are inclined to think of as a single national culture, there has never been a single completely uniform cultural "system of fixed ideas." Culture is, instead, always more of "an ongoing conversation," a dialogue within the framework provided by "a common language," and perhaps a relatively stable "horizon" of shared values and assumptions.[24] "The notion of a single national culture, shaping the community and embracing all its people, is an admirable one whose principal shortcoming is its remoteness from historical fact."[25] Monolithic national cultures are a myth.

Above the level of uniquely individual persons and diversely multicultural states, however, in early East Asia the written language that we know as classical Chinese (and the use of *kanji* even more broadly) did provide nearly all literate people, literally, with a common language and a shared literature. The books—Confucian, Buddhist, and other—that were transmitted in this language bequeathed a distinctive ideological horizon on the entire East Asian world. Nor was this exclusively limited to the relatively few people who were literate since those persons often served as examples for others.

The notion of "nation" was weak or nonexistent in premodern East Asia, especially in a *zhongguo* whose self-image was of a universal center. Japan at least, by contrast, was an island chain on the periphery of the traditional East Asian world. It was probably always relatively difficult to take talk of *tenka* in Japan entirely seriously. A certain whiff of incipient nationalism has even sometimes been detected in premodern Japan. Yet it is still most accurate to say, even for Japan, that "the core population here termed 'Japanese' almost certainly did not see itself as a single ethnos until the twentieth century." "The modern Japanese nation state . . . is an artificial construct whose boundaries were drawn in the second half of the nineteenth century. Those boundaries enclosed within the nation state a wide range of groups with different dialects, lifestyles and beliefs."[26]

The idea of the nation-state is so deeply ingrained in our own conceptual horizon today that it is difficult for us to acknowledge the awkward fact that there are no perfectly homogeneous nations and no absolutely native cultures anywhere. All nations are historical constructions—none have simply "always been that way"—and "native" is always, at best, a matter of relative priority. "There is no culture that has existed 'since time immemorial' and no people that is aboriginal in terms of their contemporary culture with a specific piece of real estate."[27]

On the other hand, there is also no denying the extraordinary continuity of Chinese civilization over several thousand years. While Chinese high civilization shaped the emergence of East Asian civilization in general, an opposing factor of resistance to Chinese culture—and especially to political control by specific Chinese governments—has also been a driving force in the formulation of historical East Asia. Much as "the rise of Rome may be conceived as an instance of a successful native reaction against foreign pressures" and Roman conquest itself subsequently provoked secondary native reactions against Rome, the various states or countries of East Asia both imitated and resisted the Chinese empire and, by domesticating various elements of that Chinese model, were able to create independent new varieties of East Asian civilization.[28]

"The paradox of civilizing projects is that they can . . . turn back on themselves."[29] In modern times, Western global imperialism and the urge to modernize have stimulated reactive anticolonial independence movements in many places and have given rise to many thoroughly new (Western-style) nations. Because the pernicious concept of race based on immutable physical differences was nonexistent (or, at least, relatively undeveloped) in premodern East Asia, it may have been easier for foreigners to really become Tang dynasty "Chinese" than it was for, say, an early twentieth-century Indochinese (Vietnamese) colonial subject to be accepted as fully "French." However, on the other hand, few ordinary Tang Chinese villagers had any hope of ever becoming "as civilized" as the great literati, and the overweening *Mission Civilisatrice* of Central Plain high culture did stimulate counterreactions.

An Oedipal impulse to reject parental models even as one imitates them is, perhaps, only human—especially when the model to be imitated defines itself precisely as the pinnacle of a hierarchy. Hierarchic pinnacles can be duplicated only by being toppled and replaced or through the elaboration of parallel rival hierarchies. Replicating the model entails rejecting its authority. There can only be one Son of Heaven. The more thoroughly Sinified the new East Asian states became, the more fiercely independent they might also want to be, and the more inclined they might be to aspire to become self-contained imperial All-under-Heavens of their own.

Furthermore, sometimes imitation is simply the most effective device to rebuff a foreign challenge. "Just as Meiji Japan, Petrine Russia, late Qing China, or the late Ottoman empire felt compelled to adopt Western technologies to avoid European political domination, many tribal groups and border dynasties in East Asia have used similar strategies to avoid Chinese political domination, although the armaments they borrowed were more likely to be the instruments of imperial bureaucracy than of war."[30]

In modern Japan, the globalizing process known as "internationalization" *(kokusaika)*—which is often understood to mean Westernization or even Americanization—often also provokes in reaction a nostalgic yearning for the old native place *(furusato)*. Ironically, "native place" is an almost universal East Asian expression. *Furusato* is pronounced *kohyang* in Korean and *guxiang* in Mandarin but is written with identical *kanji* and conveys essentially identical sentiments. Also ironically, it turns out that modern internationalization is not really "antithetical to 'Japanese culture'; rather, it is both a product of and central to the ongoing (since the Meiji period) formation of a *Japanese national cultural identity.*"[31] In a similar (though not identical) way, the premodern Sinification of Japan, Korea, and Vietnam was inextricable from the original formation of local national cultural identities. The maturation of the East Asian region as a whole coincided with the maturation of its separate major internal divisions.

It is noteworthy that the period when East Asian states were most actively learning from the Chinese model coincides with the most protracted period of division and imperial weakness within China itself, the so-called Six Dynasties (or Northern and Southern dynasties), that lie between the great unified empires of Han and Tang.[32] Political division in China provided unique opportunities for diplomatic interaction in the region and independent state formation. It also made China less menacing to its neighbors. However, it was the very menace of a powerfully reunified Sui-Tang empire in China that drove the formation of Chinese-style independent states in Korea and Japan to completion in the seventh and eighth centuries.

It is also ironic that the period of most intensive Chinese-style state formation in Japan, from about the sixth through the ninth century, coincided with the most tightly restricted phase of physical movement to and from the continent. Before the rise of a Japanese state, there had been a period of unregulated and apparently surprisingly massive immigration. After the tenth century, there was a growing volume of private commercial exchange.[33] Yet during the key phase of intensive and fairly conscious Sinification, the Japanese empire claimed a royal monopoly on all traffic with the continent. This, too, was the Chinese model.

The view from Chang'an, as of A.D. 700, was of a Tang-centered Chinese world that extended east to Korea, south to Cambodia, west to Persia and Tibet, and north to the steppe and forests of Manchuria. "Together, these are the approachable barbarians; beyond them are inaccessible lands."[34] Japan was almost beyond the notice of even the most knowledgeable residents of Tang Chang'an. The view from Nara, Japan, in the eighth century, on the other hand, would have been informed by Chinese texts and Chinese knowledge, but Nara would have been the self-proclaimed imperial center, and from the perspective of each of these universal centers, everything else faded imperceptibly into barbarism at the edges.

ENDNOTES

CHAPTER ONE

1. Isaacs, *Scratches on Our Minds,* p. 37.
2. Ronald Takaki, p. 502. March, p. 23.
3. Herodotus, pp. 211, 247–248, 250.
4. Diamond, p. 417. The territories that became the Federation of Malaysia (in 1963) fall outside the perimeter of traditional Chinese influence, and Malaysia is presumably included here by mistake. However, British colonial Malaya was extensively transformed by modern Chinese immigration in the nineteenth to twentieth centuries. See Freedman, "The Chinese in Southeast Asia."
5. Iriye, p. 19. See also Huntington, pp. 86–88; Frank.
6. Tsien, p. 2.
7. See, for example, Maddison.
8. Su Bingqi, p. 144, insists that Chinese civilization did not develop in isolation. Chang, pp. 40–42, remains skeptical of the "out of Africa" hypothesis, however, noting that "time and again the theme of the African origin of human evolution has been put forward only to be retracted later."
9. McNeill, *Rise of the West,* p. 324.
10. For Japan, see Kornicki, p. 382. See also Jansen, pp. 4, note 6, and 76–77. The situation in Korea is discussed in Robinson, pp. 26, 89–90. For Vietnam, see DeFrancis, *Colonialism,* pp. 77–81, 99–100, 110–111, 131–134, 140–142, 145–149; Jamieson, pp. 68–71. A discussion of the "Literary Revolution" in May Fourth–era China may be found in Grieder, pp. 75–88.
11. Jansen, pp. 93–94.

CHAPTER TWO

1. Chang, pp. 55, 59.
2. Boltz, pp. 75, 123.
3. For early mention of *zhongguo,* see *Shang shu zhengdu,* 4.186; Hsu and

Linduff, pp. 96–99. For the surprising lack of a Chinese name for premodern China, see John Fitzgerald, "Nationless State," p. 67; *Awakening China*, p. 117. For Japan as a self-styled Middle Kingdom, see *Nihon shoki*, 14.371; Han Sheng, *Yimin yanjiu*, pp. 9–10. For Vietnam, see Woodside, pp. 18–19. The search for a modern Japanese-language name for China is surveyed in Fogel.

4. Loewe, "Heritage," p. 994; Zhao Shichao, p. 12.

5. Hsu and Linduff, pp. 152–153, 224, 382–383.

6. Eberhard, *Local Cultures*, pp. 13–14, 19–20, 24; Falkenhausen, "Regionalist Paradigm," pp. 198–199; Kuang Shiyuan, pp. 12–14; Li Xueqin, p. 12; Su Bingqi, pp. 28–32.

7. Gele; Zhou Zhenhe, p. 60. See also Ng-Quinn, pp. 42, 57.

8. Pulleyblank, "The Chinese and Their Neighbors," pp. 423, 459; Pulleyblank, "Zou and Lu," pp. 41, 52–54. The origins of Xia culture are suggested in Han Jianye, pp. 121–123.

9. Chang, p. 64; Hsu and Linduff, pp. 8–9, 12–17; Li Donghua, *Haiyang fazhan*, p. 23; *Rongzhai suibi*, 5.64; Zhang Boquan, "'Zhonghua yiti,'" pp. 2–3; Zhao Shichao, p. 45.

10. Hsu, "Spring and Autumn," p. 550. "The Concept of State in Ancient China" is sketched in Wu Xize, p. 1.

11. The *Shuo wen* is quoted in Zhang Yufa, pp. 48–49. The reference to "different customs" comes from *Huai nan zi*, 6.9a. For a portrait of the warring states as incipient "nations," see Shi Nianhai, p. 9; Yan Gengwang, "Zhanguo shidai." On the consolidation of territorial kingdoms, see Zang Zhifei, pp. 71–72; Zhao Shichao, pp. 259, 263.

12. Li Xueqin, pp. 175–176; Lin Jianming, *Shehui wenming*, pp. 11–12, 23–28. For marital practices in Yan, see *Han shu*, 28b.1657. The *Guan zi* quotation is from 14.3b–4a.

13. Blakekey, "Geography of Chu," p. 10; Gao Zhixi, pp. 25, 277, 360–361, 402.

14. *Han shu*, 28b.1665; *Shi ji*, 40.1697.

15. Falkenhausen, "Waning," p. 514. On claims to Chinese descent, see Cao Shibang.

16. Blakeley, "Geography of Chu," p. 9. Peters, "Towns and Trade," pp. 105, 108–109; Xu Shaohua, pp. 21, 24, 26–32.

17. *Han shu*, 28b.1668. Gao Zhixi, pp. 389–392, 399, 405–406, 410–411.

18. On the *Chu ci*, see Hawkes, pp. 19–20; Waters, p. 12.

19. *Xun zi*, 4.12b.

20. *Zhan guo ce*, 30.9a.

21. *Lü shi chunqiu jinzhu jinyi*, 13.350; 20.644–645. *Shi ji*, 6.239, 6.283. Zhang Binglin, pp. 39, 41, 43, 48.

22. Du Zhengsheng, "'Bianhu qimin'," p. 77; Hsu, "Development of Statehood," pp. 98–100.

23. See Kosambi, pp. 133–165.

24. *Shi ji*, 15.685. For the early development of Legalism in Wei, see *Jin shu*, 30.922; Hori Tsuyoshi, pp. 15–16.

25. Lewis, p. 18. For Qin's drive toward wealth and power, see *Shi ji*, 29.1408. See also *Shang jun shu zhuyi*, 11.96. On the modern Japanese revival of this slogan, see Samuels, p. 35.

26. *Zhan guo ce*, 3.9b. An Zuozhang, pp. 35–39; He Qinggu, "Siying gongshangye," p. 31.

27. *Shi ji*, 15.708; 6.289; 5.203, 15.723–724, 68.2232. On household registration, see Du Zhengsheng, "'Bianhu qimin,'" pp. 77–111; Yang Kuan, p. 191.

28. Gao Mingshi, "Yunmeng Qin jian," p. 37; Lin Jianming, "Qin-Han shi bufen," pp. 89–91.

29. An Zuozhang, pp. 30–31; Lin Ganquan, p. 210; Ōba Osamu, *Qin-Han fazhi*, p. 41; Yu Zongfa, pp. 93–98.

30. *Shi ji*, 6.245. See Hori Toshikazu, *Chūgoku to kodai higashi Ajia*, pp. 56–58; Yü Ying-shih, "Han Foreign Relations," pp. 377–378.

31. *Shi ji*, 6.239. Ding Yihua; Lin Jianming, *Shehui wenming*, p. 24.

32. *Shi ji*, 15.686. Zheng Dekun, p. 102. For attachment to local customs, see Gao Mingshi, "Yunmeng Qin jian," pp. 38–39; Li Xueqin, p. 345.

33. Yuan Zhongyi, "Qin Shihuang ling de kaogu ziliao," pp. 60, 66. On the First Emperor's tomb, see also Li Xueqin, p. 203; Liu Yunhui, p. 7; Wu and Zhang, pp. 19, 89. Dong Zhongshu's judgments are expressed in *Han shu*, 56.2504, 56.2510–2511. The *Shi ji* (15.758) entry for 209 B.C. reads, "All the commanderies and districts rebelled."

34. Derk Bodde, p. 20. Liu Zongyuan (773–819), "Fengjian lun" (On the Appointment of a Nobility), in *Liu Hedong quanji*, 3.33.

35. Zhang Boquan, *Xianbei*, pp. 103–104. *Shi ji*, 6.239.

36. *Hou-Han shu*, 85.2809. On the assimilation of the Yue, see Li Dong-hua, *Haiyang fazhan*, pp. 26–32.

37. Bellwood, pp. 97, 112; Meng Wentong, p. 17; Norman and Mei, pp. 274, 276–280, 295; Rao Zongyi, pp. 618–620; *Yan tie lun*, 5.71.

38. Peters, "Tattooed Faces," pp. 1, 7, 9, 12; Rao Zongyi, p. 612; *Tong dian*, 188.1006.

39. Customs farther west are sketched in *Han shu*, 95.3837; Meng Wentong, p. 20. For the Yue, see *Annam chi luoc*, 1.41. Maritime proclivities are noted in *Yue jue shu*, 8.122–123. For the spread of tattooing, see Wang Jinlin, *Han-Tang wenhua*, p. 148. On rice cultivation, see Higham, pp. 70–71, 76, 309; Bellwood, pp. 206, 208; Suwa Haruo, pp. 62–63. Chang, pp. 46–47, reports radiocarbon dating of domesticated rice in what is now south China to 8000 B.C.

40. Bellwood, pp. 92, 105, 110–111, 214, 255, 258, 311; Coedès, pp. 8–10; Higham, pp. 1, 246, 297; Lü Shipeng, p. 3; Shaffer, pp. 5–7; Wyatt, p. 3.

41. Rao Zongyi, p. 615.

42. *Han shu*, 28b.1668, 28b.1666. McNeill, *Plagues and Peoples*, pp. 30, 86, 89. In the early Han dynasty, Sima Qian estimated that the northwestern

region around the capital was home to 30 percent of the empire's population and 60 percent of its wealth. *Shi ji,* 129.3262. For the eighth-century population distribution, see Yang Yuan, pp. 414–418.

43. Zhou Lin, pp. 55–57.

44. *Yan tie lun,* 8.123.

45. *Hou-Han shu,* 18.693. *Lun heng,* 19.8b.

46. Gardiner, *Early History of Korea,* p. 24. On increasing regional and ethnic integration, see Huang Lie, p. 86; Kanō Naosada, "Kanbō to sono shūhen," p. 37.

47. On Diwu Lun, see Bielenstein, "Restoration," pt. 3, p. 148 (see also pp. 79–80); *Kuaiji zhi,* 2.9b; Miyakawa Hisayuki, "Confucianization of South China," p. 30. Dialects are discussed in Pulleyblank, "The Chinese and Their Neighbors," p. 415.

48. Bielenstein, "The Census of China," p. 141; Duan Tali, p. 180; Luo Tonghua, *Han dai de liumin wenti,* pp. 42–43; Zhou Lin, p. 55.

49. *Sui shu,* 31.897, 31.887.

50. On the status of ethnic non-Chinese within the empire, see Tang Changru, "Jin dai beijing gezu 'bianluan,'" p. 138; Yü Ying-shih, *Trade and Expansion,* pp. 85–86, 203; Zhu Dawei, p. 60. The example of naturalization is from *Dong-Han huiyao,* 39.570. For the Trung sisters, see *Tong dian,* 188.1006; Taylor, *Birth of Vietnam,* pp. 37–41.

51. For Tian Yizong, see *Shui jing zhu,* 30.578. On Kang Sengyuan, consult *Gao seng zhuan,* 4.94.

52. *Xin Tang shu,* 2.31, 2.33. Fu Lecheng, "Tang dai Yi-Xia guannian," p. 213; Fu Lecheng, "Tang xing wenhua," p. 257.

53. *Zizhi tongjian jinzhu,* 198.117. Hu Rulei, p. 40; Lin Tianwei, p. 74.

54. *Annam chi luoc,* 9.126; Chen Shangsheng; Imaeda Jirō; Lin Wenyue, pp. 382–384; Reischauer, *Ennin's Travels,* pp. 277–278; Xie Haiping, p. 78; *Xin Tang shu,* 135.4576–4578, 220.6209, 225a.6425.

55. Arakawa Masaharu, p. 192; Ikeda On, "Dong-Ya gudai jizhang," pp. 108–109; Xue Zongzheng, p. 53. *Fozu tongji,* 41; T.49.378c; Liu Xinru, *Silk and Religion,* p. 183.

56. Backus, p. 6; *Xin Tang shu,* 43b.1119; Yü Ying-shih, *Trade and Expansion,* pp. 71–73; *Zizhi tongjian,* 198.114.

57. *Xin Tang shu,* 43b.1119–1120, 1137–1138, 1140, 1144–1145. On *jimi zhou,* see Pan Yihong, "Settlement Policies," pp. 66–69; Schafer, *Vermilion Bird,* p. 71.

58. James Watson, p. 86. For modern population figures, see Dittmer and Kim, p. 10, note 28. On the broad commonality of Chinese culture, see Cohen, pp. 90–91.

59. Bielenstein, "Colonization of Fukien," pp. 110–111; Faure and Siu, p. 5; Zhou Zhenhe, p. 60; Zhu Dawei, p. 59.

60. Kennedy, p. xvi. Compare Elvin, chap. 1, "Empires and Their Size," pp. 17–22.

61. De Crespigny, *To Establish Peace,* pp. 124–125, 356–357.

62. "Mountain-dwelling recluses" are mentioned in *Shui jing zhu*, 40.754. Zhuge Ke's complaint is from *San guo zhi*, 64.1431. On subordination to local great families, see Hou Wailu, pp. 28–29; Uchida Gifu, p. 48; Wang Zhongluo, "Wei-Jin fengjian lun," pp. 63–64.

63. Wright, "The Sui Dynasty," p. 49. On Jiangnan customs, compare *Han shu*, 28b.1666, with *Shi ji*, 129.3268, 3270, and with *Sui shu*, 31.886.

64. For immodest wives, see *Sui shu*, 31.887; Miyakawa, "Confucianization of South China," p. 42. The persistence of uxorilocal marriage in Jiangnan is documented in Eastman, p. 31.

65. *Liu Hedong quanji*, 30.328; *Xin Tang shu*, 168.5133.

66. *Fozu tongji*, 39; T.49.368a. The entry is dated 672.

67. *Dong-Han huiyao*, 39.569–570; *Nan shi*, 79.1980; *Song shu*, 97.2399; *Sui shu*, 31.897.

68. *Huayang guo zhi*, 9.510; *Jin shu*, 121.3047; *Tong dian*, 187.999.

69. *Hou-Han shu*, 87.2878.

70. *Quan Jin wen*, 78.1908–1909; *Song shu*, 31.901–902; *Tong dian*, 187.999; "Touhuang za lu" (Miscellaneous Records of Flight to the Wilds), in *Taiping guangji*, 269.2112.

71. *Xin Tang shu*, 3.70, 3.72, 4.95, 4.109, 5.122, 5.124, 6.157, 175–176, 207.5857, 222c.6329; *Zizhi tongjian*, 224.180–181.

72. *Tang huiyao*, 100.1798; *Xin Tang shu*, 182.5367.

CHAPTER THREE

1. See Ames, p. 191.

2. *Xin Tang shu*, 201.5733.

3. *Xin Tang shu*, 94.3829.

4. Qian Mu fiercely defends the superiority of Chinese imperial institutions in "Zhonguo lishi shang de zhengzhi zhidu."

5. Jensen, pp. 5, 23, 28.

6. *Meng zi zhushu*, 14b.114.

7. *Lunyu zhushu*, 16.64. *Chunqiu fanlu*, 2.2a.

8. *Yan tie lun*, 8.121.

9. *Chunqiu fanlu*, 15.2b–3a. The Prince of Huai nan, 135 B.C., quoted in *Annam chi luoc*, 5.114. *Song shu*, 14.358.

10. See, for example, *Cefu yuangui*, 963.11326.

11. *Sui shu*, 81.1829.

12. *Chunqiu fanlu*, 13.3a–b. Usami Kazuhiro, pp. 140–142. *Zang Rongxu Jin shu*, 14.10b.

13. Fujiwara Atsumitsu (1063–1145), in *Honchō zokumonzui*, 2.483–484.

14. See Munro, pp. 110–112.

15. Dong Zhongshu, quoted in *Han shu*, 56.2521.

16. "Wuli lun," 7a.

17. *Shuo yuan*, 1.2b.

18. *Jiu Tang shu*, 21.815.

19. *Chunqiu fanlu*, 6.4b–5a.
20. *Huan zi xinlun*, 7b. *Huai nan zi*, 6.3a, annotation.
21. *Chunqiu fanlu*, 4.1a, 14.1b.
22. See Lewis, pp. 222–224.
23. *Han shu*, 56.2501. *Chunqiu fanlu*, 1.7a. See also Queen, pp. 127–162; Usami Kazuhiro, pp. 144–145.
24. *Han shu*, 56.2502; *Chunqiu fanlu*, 11.5a, 12.6b.
25. *Chunqiu fanlu*, 3.9a. For "natural law," see Li Jiafu, pp. 34, 38. See also Ōsumi Kiyoharu, pp. 135–137.
26. Hua Yougen, pp. 59–60.
27. On compulsory mourning, see Zhu Zongbin, pp. 110–111. For the third-century law code, see *Jin shu*, 30.927; Pan Wusu, pp. 16–17; Kamiya Noriko, "Shin jidai ni okeru irei shingi," p. 49. On the "ten abominations," see Hua Yougen, p. 63. For the *Six Statutes*, see Yan Gengwang, "Lüelun Tang Liudian," pp. 421, 424, 427. See also Liu Baiji, pp. 276, 278; Ōsumi Kiyoharu, p. 134; Wang Jiahua, *Rujia sixiang*, pp. 227–229.
28. *Xin Tang shu*, 102.3984; *Kun xue jiwen*, 12.997.
29. For Han, see Nishijima Sadao, *Kokusai kankyō*, pp. 22–23. For Tang, see Shi Dongchu, *Zhong-Ri Fojiao*, p. 288. For Taizong's doubts concerning omens, see *Zhenguan zhengyao*, 10.449–450. The emperor is constantly depicted hunting in the "Basic Annals" of the *Xin Tang shu*.
30. *Xin Tang shu*, 2.28–30, 2.39.
31. On welfare provisions, see Hulsewé, "Han China," pp. 271, 284–285. For critical modern evaluations, see Ray Huang, p. 34; Somers, "Time, Space, and Structure," p. 989.
32. Sansom, pp. 197–198; Morris, *Shining Prince*, pp. 84–85.
33. De Crespigny, *To Establish Peace*, p. xxx. *Zhenguan zhengyao*, 10.455.
34. *Mission civilisatrice*, or "civilizing mission," was the nineteenth-century French moral justification for imperialism. See Duiker, p. 31.
35. Lewis, p. 338.
36. *Lunyu zhushu*, 17.69. On art and politics, see Kraus, p. x. On the sociopolitical rise of the literati, see, for example, Yu Yingshi, *Zhishi jieceng*, p. 115; Mao Hanguang, *Zhonggu shehui*, pp. 78–80, 84, 88–90; Watanabe Yoshihiro, "'Bungaku' no seijiteki senyō," p. 50.
37. *Hong ming ji*, 14.9b
38. *Shishuo xinyu jiaojian*, chap. 2, no. 29, pp. 49–50.
39. *Qiaozi faxun*, p. 2b. On *li*, see Fehl, pp. ix, 213; He Liankui, pp. 11–12; Zhang Boquan, p. 2; Zheng Dekun, p. 30.
40. For the barbarization of Chinese, see *Chunqiu Gongyang zhuan zhushu*, 24.133. For Vietnam, see *Quoc-su di-bien*, 3.346; Zhu Yunying, p. 299.
41. Soothill, p. 219. Fehl, p. 213. He Liankui, pp. 7, 14.
42. McMullen, p. 29; Wechsler, p. 9.
43. Watson, trans., *Hsün Tzu* [Xun Zi], p. 71. Legge, trans., *Lî Kî*, vol. 28, p. 236.
44. Ge Jianping, p. 71; *Nian er shi zhaji*, 20.438; Qian Mu, "Xueshu

wenhua," pp. 138–139; Shigezawa Toshirō, pp. 7–8; Yoshikawa Tadao, pp. 32, 136.

45. Fehl, p. 219. Ōsumi Kiyoharu, p. 131. Qian Mu, "Xueshu wenhua," pp. 139–140, 165.

46. Gao Mingshi, *Jiaoyuquan*, pp. 5–6; Kaji Nobuyuki, p. 146; Watanabe Shinichirō, "Kōkyō no kokka ron," pp. 403–404, 409. On the stability of the Confucian imperial package, see Jin Guantao and Liu Qingfeng, pp. 50–51.

47. *Lü shi chunqiu*, 20.642–643.

48. "Yuan dao" (The Sources of the Tao), in *Han Changli quanji*, 11.173. *Xin Tang shu*, 56.1407. *Ruijū kokushi*, 79.425.

49. *Xin Tang shu*, 216a.6072. Lydia Liu, p. 240; March, p. 35; Mather, "Conflict," p. 34.

50. See Dennerline, pp. 8–9.

51. Wang Gungwu, "The Chinese Urge to Civilize," pp. 4, 6.

52. Wheatley, pp. 124–125.

53. Woodside, p. 199.

54. Pollack, p. 68; Seidensticker, trans., *The Tale of Genji*, p. 182.

55. *Li ji jinzhu jinyi*, 5.230–231. *Koryŏ sa*, 93.16a; Deuchler, p. 30. James Watson, p. 89. See also Cohen, pp. 92, 96–97; March, p. 13.

56. *Honchō zokumonzui*, 3.516.

57. *Sui shu*, 84.1874. *Nihon shoki*, 25.252.

58. Chen Shangsheng, p. 166.

59. *Han shu*, 28b.1640.

60. *Li ji jinzhu jinyi*, 18.594. Gao Mingshi, *Jiaoyuquan*, pp. 102–103. *Han shu*, 56.2512.

61. Gao Mingshi, *Jiaoyuquan*, pp. 67, 71–72, 86–93; Wang Zhoukun, p. 113. For Kūkai, see Ienaga Saburō, ed., *Nihon Bukkyōshi*, p. 201; Yang Zengwen, p. 129. For the shift to private education, see Jo-shui Chen, pp. 48, 62; Lü Simian, *Du shi zhaji*, pp. 1088–1097; McMullen, pp. 30–31.

62. *Jin wen gui*, 4.14a; *Jin shu*, 68.1825. *Wenxian tongkao*, 12.124; *Hou-Han shu*, treatise 28.3624. See also Ch'en Ch'i-yün, *Life and Reflections*, p. 23; Hsü, "Roles of the Literati," p. 189; Okazaki Fumio, *Gi-Shin Nanbokuchō*, p. 551; Ueda Sanae, p. 112.

63. Beckwith, pp. 180–182. Goodman, pp. 8, 17–18. For the availability of books in early medieval Europe and China, compare Okazaki Fumio, *Gi-Shin Nanbokuchō*, p. 546, with Diringer, p. 259.

64. Zhou Zhenhe, p. 64. *Dong-Han huiyao*, 11.165. *Hou-Han shu*, 76.2462; *Han yuan*, transcript, p. 56, note. For education as a tool of assimilation, see Lü Simian, *Du shi zhaji*, pp. 1100–1102; Herman.

65. Wang Chengwen, "Tang-dai 'nan xuan,'" pp. 95–96. *Zizhi tongjian*, 249.568.

66. Armstrong, pp. 5, 7. The allusion is to Benedict Anderson's famous title *Imagined Communities: Reflections on the Origin and Spread of Nationalism.*

67. See Okazaki Fumio, *Gi-Shin Nanbokuchō*, p. 126; Yu Yingshi, "Minzu yishi," p. 3.

68. See Hori Toshikazu, *Chūgoku to kodai higashi Ajia*, pp. 37–39, 43, 45; Su Bingqi, pp. 2–3; Xie Haiping, pp. 324–327.

69. *Chunqiu Zuo zhuan zhengyi*, 26.1901.

70. Jiang Tong, "Xi Rong lun" (On Moving the Rong), in *Quan Jin wen*, 106.2069. "Yuan dao," in *Han Changli quanji*, 11.174. *Huai nan zi*, 11.4b; Ames, p. 17.

71. "Hua xin" (The Chinese Mind), in *(Qin ding) Quan Tang wen*, 767.10094.

72. Huntington, p. 310. *Nan shi*, 78.1953; *Liang shu*, 54.789.

73. For Champa, see *Dai Viet su ky toan thu*, ngoai ky, 5.157. For tribute relations, see Kikuchi Hideo, p. 25.

74. Kim Ch'ungnyŏl, pp. 46–48; *Samguk sagi*, vol. 1, p. 95 (Silla Basic Annals 5); Xie Haiping, pp. 135, 137, 292–293; *Xin Tang shu*, 198.5636.

75. *Tang hui yao*, 36.777–778; Don Lee, pp. 46–50.

76. Gao Mingshi, *Jiaoyuquan*, pp. 5–7.

77. Arano Yasunori et al., pp. 6, 12; Nishijima Sadao, "Roku-hachi"; Wang Zhenping, *Han-Tang Zhong-Ri guanxi*, p. 16, note 61; Xu Xianyao, "Sui-Wo bangjiao," p. 499.

78. *Jiu Tang shu*, 9.15a.

79. Nishijima Sadao, "Roku-hachi," p. 278; Xia Yingyuan, p. 122.

80. Han Sheng, "'Wei fa Baiji,'" p. 40; Wang Zhenping, *Han-Tang Zhong-Ri guanxi*, pp. 36–41; *Zizhi tongjian*, 136.731.

81. *Wei shu*, 100.2218. *Xin Tang shu*, 43b.1135. Victor Xiong, p. 340.

82. Duara, p. 785. *Wei shu*, 1.1; *Zizhi tongjian*, 140.68. Cao Shibang, p. 30.

83. Lü Shipeng, p. 5; Rao Zongyi, pp. 609, 617–618; *Wu-Yue chunqiu*, 6.1a, 6.4a–4b. For an attempt to trace the Vietnamese to origins in northern China, see He Guangyue, p. 95.

84. Wang Chengwen, "Tang-dai 'nan xuan,'" p. 96. Backus, pp. 7–8. Siu, pp. 22–23.

85. "Wei zhi," extracted in *Taiping yulan*, 782.3595. Suwa Haruo, pp. 58–59. For Saichō, see "Eizan Daishiden," vol. 5, appendix, p. 1; *Genkō shakusho*, 1.32.

86. *Samguk yusa*, 1; T.49.962a; *Han yuan*, transcript, p. 33, note. Nelson, *Archaeology of Korea*, pp. 156–157. For nationalistic repudiation, see Schmid, pp. 33–34.

87. Wang Zhenping, *Han-Tang Zhong-Ri guanxi*, pp. 40–41. *Liang shu*, 54.802. Huang Zhilian, p. 24.

88. Wang Liping, p. 7.

89. For Silla, see Nishijima Sadao, *Kokusai kankyō*, p. 69.

90. Kawakatsu Yoshio, *Chūgoku no rekishi*, p. 52; Nishijima Sadao, "Roku-hachi," p. 237; Suzuki Yasutami, pp. 208–212; Ueda Masaaki, *Kikajin*, p. 150; Xu Xianyao, "Dongya wenxian," pt. 3, p. 17. Hori Toshikazu (*Chūgoku to kodai higashi Ajia*, pp. 157–158) has tabulated the Chinese titles with which Japanese rulers were invested between 421 and 502.

91. Kikuchi Hideo, pp. 12–13; Nishijima Sadao, "Roku-hachi," pp. 239, 271; Ōmachi Ken, pp. 320–321.

92. *Sui shu,* 81.1826–1827; *Xin Tang shu,* 220.6208. See also Cao Xian'gun, p. 22.

93. Huang Zhilian, p. 33; Mōri Hisashi, p. 6; Nishijima Sadao, "Roku-hachi," p. 236; Wang Yi, p. 22.

94. Bingham, p. 38; Huang Zhilian, pp. 29–31; Kim Tal-su, p. 52–53; Nishijima Sadao, "Roku-hachi," pp. 245–247; Pan Yihong, *Son of Heaven,* pp. 108–111; Wang Liping, pp. 8–9. For Turfan, see Victor Xiong, p. 338.

95. Suzuki Yasutami, pp. 202, 204, 207–208.

96. Sŏ Yŏngsu, p. 12. Edwards (pp. 33–34, 42) describes the frontier control regulations of the last Chinese dynasty, the Qing, as marked by "substantive equality and reciprocity, coupled with Sinocentric hierarchy in form." On the inapplicability of modern conceptions, see Wang Zhenping, *Han-Tang Zhong-Ri guanxi,* pp. 33–34; Kikuchi Hideo, pp. 59–62.

97. On *sadae,* see Cumings, pp. 54–55; Robinson, pp. 27, 33–34, 36.

98. *Samguk sagi,* vol. 1, pp. 109–110, 120–121 (Sillan Basic Annals 5–6); vol. 2, pp. 342–343 (Yŏl chŏn 4).

99. For Eurasiatic, see Greenberg, pp. 1–3, 279–281.

100. On Vietnamese as an Austroasiatic language, see Norman and Mei, p. 295. For French colonial views of it as "a Chinese patois," see DeFrancis, *Colonialism,* pp. 5, 142.

101. For the Phoenicians, see Bentley, pp. 22–23. For Chinese, see Hsu and Linduff, p. 31.

102. Gao Mingshi, *Jiaoyuquan,* p. 359.

103. See the discussion of nineteenth-century Japanese perceptions of *kanbun* in Howland, p. 46.

104. DeFrancis, *Chinese Language,* p. 133. Boltz, p. 122. Hannas, p. 9.

105. On the fallacy of linear evolution and the contingent character of historical development, see Gould, pp. 28–35, 48, 51, 283.

106. Hannas, pp. 247–252.

107. Ramsey, p. 4.

108. For a valiant attempt to disentangle *kanji* from prevailing Western assumptions, see Hansen, pp. 373–375, 388–389, 396–397.

109. Quotations are from Hannas, pp. 113, 186–201.

110. Woodside, p. 50. See also SarDesai, p. 17.

111. *Yan shi jiaxun,* 7.1a. For early Han languages, see Zhang Yufa, p. 18.

112. Zhang Yufa, p. 20.

113. On elite standards of pronunciation, see Li Yuancheng, p. 73; Mather, "A Note on the Dialects," p. 248; Miyazaki Ichisada, *Kyūhin kanjinhō,* p. 186; Zhou Yiliang, pp. 62–63. For the *Qieyun,* see Pulleyblank, *Middle Chinese,* p. 130.

114. *Shoku Nihongi,* 10.232–233. On the monolingual Greeks, see Momigliano, p. 13. Owen Lattimore ("Chinese Turkistan," p. 194) observed that,

in his experience, Chinese people seldom were conversant in central Asian languages.

115. *Nihon shoki,* 30.411, 417. *Ryō no gige,* 1.39. Lin Wenyue, p. 385; *Shoku Nihongi,* 35.82. Regarding yearly ordinands, see Hayami Tasuku, p. 145; *Ruijū sandai kyaku,* 2.76; Yang Zengwen, pp. 93–94.

116. Ramsey, pp. 118–120.

117. Ury, p. 347. See also Piggott, *Kingship,* p. 176.

118. *Chen shu,* 34.473. Lewis, p. 339.

119. Piggott, *Kingship,* p. 100. The Chinese-style date engraved on the Inariyama sword is interpreted as indicating either 471 or 531. See Anazawa and Manome, pp. 375, 383–384; Seeley, pp. 16, 19–23.

120. Cranston, pp. 453–454; Ishida Ichirō, p. 28; Seki Akira, p. 32; Ueda Masaaki, *Ronkyū,* pp. 15, 17; Wang Jiahua, *Rujia sixiang,* pp. 3–5. For alleged evidence of the Paekche language on the Inariyama sword, see Wontack Hong, pp. 83–84.

121. Borgen, p. 74; Gao Mingshi, *Jiaoyuquan,* p. 389; Lin Wenyue, pp. 372, 377.

122. Borgen, p. 16; Pollack, pp. 26–27, 228. See also Ienaga Saburō, "Asuka, hakuhō bunka," p. 345.

123. Piggot, *Kingship,* p. 226. On *semmyō,* see *Shoku Nihongi,* "Introduction," p. 7.

124. Pollack, p. 19; Seeley, p. ix. See also Hannas, p. 28.

125. Gao Mingshi, *Jiaoyuquan,* p. 27; Ueda Masaaki, *Kikajin,* pp. 75–76, 79; Ueda Masaaki, *Ronkyū,* p. 3.

126. For *Genji,* see Wang Jiahua, *Rujia sixiang,* p. 342. For the nineteenth-century decline of classical Chinese in Japan, see Kornicki, p. 16. For a "common literature," see Howland, p. 7.

127. *Samguk sagi,* vol. 1, p. 126 (Sillan Basic Annals 6); *Tang hui yao,* 99.1770, 100.1792. See also Amino Yoshihiko, *Nihon shakai,* vol. 1, pp. 108–109; Ōba Osamu, "Nitchū bunka kōryūshi," p. 26; Piggott, *Kingship,* pp. 143–144; Wang Zhenping, *Han-Tang Zhong-Ri guanxi,* p. 1, note 3. The old label Wa is of obscure origin but may represent an attempt to transcribe some indigenous name in *kanji,* according to Roy Andrew Miller, *Japanese Language,* p. 11. The derogatory use of Wa as "a deliberate pejorative" in China does not seem to have begun until Ming times. See Howland, p. 22.

128. Lewin, "Japanese and Korean," p. 407.

129. *Samguk sagi,* vol. 2, p. 355 (Yŏl chŏn 4). *San guo zhi,* 30.852.

130. For the start of record keeping in Paekche, see *Samguk sagi,* vol. 2, p. 34 (Paekche Basic Annals 2). For vernacular poems, see Kichung Kim, pp. 5, 13.

131. On early Korean surnames, see Haboush, "Confucianization," p. 99; *Samguk sagi,* vol. 1, p. 23 (Sillan Basic Annals 1).

132. *Samguk sagi,* vol. 1, pp. 16, 72 (Sillan Basic Annals 1, 4); *Samguk sagi,* vol. 2, p. 250 (treatise 7). Kitō Kiyoaki, pp. 77–80.

133. Ki-baik Lee, p. 43.

134. Hannas, pp. 54–56, 65, 77, 126–127, 183. For Vietnam, see also DeFrancis, *Colonialism*, p. 8.

135. Lewis, p. 339. See Gao Mingshi, *Jiaoyuquan*, p. 64.

136. The Confucian scholar Kangsu was called on to perform valuable diplomatic services for the Sillan king in the seventh century. See *Samguk sagi*, vol. 2, p. 378 (Yŏl chŏn 6). For Shi Le, see *Deng Can Jin ji*, p. 15a; *Shishuo xinyu jiaojian*, p. 216. On Helian Bobo, see Barfield, pp. 119–120; *Jin shu*, 130.3208; Li Zefen, *Liang-Jin nanbeichao*, vol. 1, pp. 123–127; *Nian er shi zhaji*, 8.161.

137. On Turfan, see Roy Andrew Miller, trans., *Accounts of Western Nations*, p. 7; Zhang Guangda, "Lun Sui-Tang shiqi," pp. 282–283. For Dunhuang, see Strickmann, p. 61.

138. *Chu Sanzang jiji*, 1.12.

139. *Gao seng zhuan*, 1.5–6, 2.30–31, 2.39; *Wei shu*, 114.3031. For a meticulous analysis of the problems involved in just one translation project, see Boucher.

140. The point is well established; but see, for example, Ienaga Saburō, ed., *Nihon Bukkyōshi*, pp. 30–31.

CHAPTER FOUR

1. *Xin Tang shu*, 3.66. *Han shu*, 1b.65. See also Luo Tonghua, *Han dai de liumin*, pp. 78–80; Twitchett, "The T'ang Market System."

2. See *Han shu*, 24a.1128; *Jin wen gui*, 4.13a; *Yan shi jiaxun*, 1.11b–12a.

3. *Samguk sagi*, vol. 2, p. 174 (treatise 2).

4. Cheng Xilin, pp. 83–84, 88, 90–92; *Tang lü shuyi*, 8.124–128; *Tang huiyao*, 86.1579, 1581, 1583. For the estimated number of officials, see Han Guopan, *Juntian zhidu*, p. 239. The edict of 627 is from *Xin Tang shu*, 2.27.

5. *Samguk sagi*, vol. 1, pp. 35, 67, 72 (Sillan Basic Annals 1, 3, 4).

6. *Samguk sagi*, vol. 2, p. 62 (Paekche Basic Annals 4).

7. Amino Yoshihiko, *Nihon shakai*, vol. 1, p. 139, note; Wheatley and See, p. 154.

8. Edict dated 711, in *Shoku Nihongi*, 5.172–173. See also 6.194–195.

9. Farris, "Trade, Money, and Merchants," pp. 309, 313–318. McCullough, "The Capital," pp. 162, 164.

10. Farris, *Population, Disease, and Land*, pp. 142–144; Farris, "Trade, Money, and Merchants," p. 322. On "agricultural fundamentalism," see Amino Yoshihiko, "Emperor, Rice, and Commoners," pp. 237–238. For examples of petty commerce, see *Nihon ryōiki*, 1.212–213, item 12; 1.217, item 21; 1.220, item 27; 3.281–282, item 26. This book is described in Nakamura, trans., pp. vi, 3.

11. Nippon Gakujutsu Shinkōkai, trans., "Introduction," p. xxxvi. For the

Yue, see *Annam chi luoc,* 1.41. This traditional Yue stereotype is supported by modern archaeological evidence. See Huang and Sun, pp. 47, 50–51. For early Japan, see also Amino Yoshihiko, "Emperor, Rice, and Commoners"; Holcombe, "Trade-Buddhism."

12. *San guo zhi,* 30.854. The shell trade is discussed in Hudson, p. 189. For prehistoric boats, see Hanihara Kazurō, pp. 176–178. Ledyard, "Galloping Along with the Horseriders," p. 231.

13. Enomoto Junichi, pp. 170, 172–173; Piggott, *Kingship,* pp. 56–57, 71, 100; Ueda Masaaki, *Ronkyū,* pp. 101–103. *Nihon shoki,* 19.79.

14. Amino Yoshihiko, *Nihon shakai,* vol. 1, p. 163. McCullough, "The Capital," pp. 168–169.

15. The report dated 842 is from *Ruijū sandai kyaku,* 18.570. Lee Sungsi, pp. 160–166, 174–184. For the award of cloth, see *Shoku Nihongi,* vol. 4, 29.220–221. On late Tang private trade, see Huang Yuese, "'Da-Tang shang ren,'" p. 47; Ōba Osamu, *Nitchū kankeishi,* p. 310.

16. For Han Sichuan, see *Han shu,* 95.3838. The rebellion is described in Liu Xinru, *Silk and Religion,* p. 191. On Tang Guangdong, see "Touhuang za lu" (Miscellaneous Records of Flight to the Wilds), in *Taiping guangji,* 269.2112.

17. For the collapse of the Equitable Fields system, see *Xin Tang shu,* 51.1341–1342, 52.1351. On tax exemptions in 754, see Wang Jinlin, *Nara bunka,* p. 218; Yang Yuan, p. 390. On registration of women, see Deng Xiaonan, pp. 91–93; Twitchett, *Financial Administration,* p. 8; Yang Yuan, pp. 389, 421. On flexible implementation of the Equitable Fields system, see Han Guopan, *Juntian zhidu,* p. 70; Liu Baiji, p. 65; Yoshida Takashi, p. 47; Zhao and Chen, p. 43.

18. Wu Hui, p. 36.

19. Hsu, "Development of Statehood," pp. 110–111.

20. Angus Maddison (pp. 13, 38–40) estimates that China's economic performance surpassed Europe's following the disintegration of Rome around the fifth century and thereafter remained "the world's leading economy in terms of per capita income . . . until the fifteenth century" and in terms of total size until as recently as the 1890s.

21. Watson, trans., *Records,* vol. 2, p. 477; *Shi ji,* 129.3253–3254.

22. See, for example, Paper, trans., pp. 55–56.

23. *Nan shi,* 77.1940.

24. *Xin Tang shu,* 7.184; *Tang hui yao,* 86.1582.

25. *Shi ji,* 129.3282–3283. On Qin era commerce, see He Qinggu, "Qin Shihuang"; Lu Ying.

26. Gao Zhixi, pp. 316–317, 389.

27. Liu Xinru, *Silk and Religion,* pp. 9, 49–50.

28. *Han shu,* 28b.1671. McNeill, *The Rise of the West,* p. 296. For overland communication, see Rhie, p. 13; Tang Yongtong, pp. 33, 57–61.

29. *Song shu,* 97.2399. For the development of South Sea trade during

the Southern dynasties, see Kenneth Hall, pp. 20, 26–27; Haneda Akira, p. 116; Liu Shufen, "Liuchao Nanhai," p. 341.

30. "Nanzhou yiwu zhi" (A Record of Strange Things from the South) (third century), in *Taiping yulan*, 769.3543. For Lop Nor, see Elizabeth Barber, p. 84.

31. Liu Shufen, "Liuchao Nanhai," p. 317. On the dearth of tribute embassies, see *Tong dian*, 188.1007; *Liang shu*, 54.783; *Nan shi*, 78.1947.

32. Rhie, pp. 101–103. Monks arriving by sea are surveyed in Feng Chengjun, pp. 31–35; Wu and Zheng, pp. 25–26, 39.

33. *Jin zhongxing shu* (History of the Jin [Dynastic] Revival) (fifth century), quoted in *Chu xue ji*, 8.192. On corruption in those ports, see *Jin shu*, 37.1087, 90.2341, 97.2546; *Tong dian*, 188.1008.

34. Li Donghua, *Haiyang fazhan*, p. 88. A connection between commercial activity and weakening official supervision is noted in Liu Shufen, "San zhi liu shiji," p. 205. On the Southern dynasty economy, see Du Shousu, p. 486; Han Guopan, *Wei-Jin nanbeichao*, pp. 208–210, 386–405; Hua Zhisun, pp. 15–16; Wang Zhongluo, *Wei-Jin nanbeichao*, p. 496. For the population of the capital, see Li Xu, pp. 12–13.

35. Kawakatsu Yoshio, *Chūgoku no rekishi*, pp. 267–268; Kawakatsu, "Kahei keizai," p. 369.

36. *Sui shu*, 64.1519.

37. Taizong's decree is in *Cefu yuangui*, 504.6047–6048. The description of Guangzhou is from "Tō dai-oshō tōseiden," p. 902. For ninth-century profits, see *Xin Tang shu*, 225c.6454.

38. On travel documents, see Tonami and Takeda, pp. 234–237; Yü Ying-shih, *Trade and Expansion*, pp. 123–128. For Ennin, see Reischauer, *Ennin's Travels*, pp. 24–26.

39. *Tang hui yao*, 86.1579, 1581; *Tang lü shuyi*, 8.128. See Arakawa Masaharu, p. 171.

40. Thompson, pp. 10–15. See also Sinor, "Inner Asian Warriors," p. 143.

41. *Annam chi luoc*, 3.78, 4.93, 6.153–154, 11.270; *Han shu*, 95.3848.

42. *Jin shu*, 57.1559.

43. *Zizhi tongjian*, 253.734. For Uighur moneylenders, see Mackerras, p. 49.

44. Feng Chengjun, p. 51; Kenneth Hall, p. 42; *Nanhai jigui neifa zhuan jiaozhu*, 1.17–18; Wang Gungwu, "Nanhai Trade," pp. 43–44, 103.

45. The Indian ships are mentioned in *Gao seng zhuan*, 2.50. Arab and Sillan shipping is discussed in Hodges and Whitehouse, p. 149; Reischauer, *Ennin's Travels*, pp. 286–287; Wang Gungwu, "Nanhai Trade," p. 103. On Chang Po-go, see Ki-baik Lee, pp. 94–96; *Samguk sagi*, vol. 2, pp. 351–352 (Yŏl chŏn 4).

46. Liu Xinru describes the "seven treasures" in *Ancient India*, pp. 100–101, 176. For the trade in "holy things," see Wang Gungwu, "Nanhai Trade," pp. 53–55, 113. See also Klimburg, p. 32, for overland trade.

47. *Chu sanzang jiji,* 13.512–513; *Gao seng zhuan,* 1.10–11; *Fozu tongji,* 35; T.49.331c. See also Gao Guanru, p. 210.

48. Tang Yongtong, pp. 88–89, 95–98. *Haedong kosŭng chŏn,* appendix, p. 65; Peter Lee, trans., *Lives,* pp. 36–37.

49. Gombrich, pp. 3, 137–139; Sherman Lee, pp. 139–140, 145–150; Rhie, pp. 23–25, 261–263.

50. *Chu Sanzang jiji,* 14.552.

51. These are central concerns in Jerry Bentley's fascinating book (p. 6).

52. Rhie, pp. 71–94, 427. On the Roman-style fresco, see Sherman Lee, pp. 152–153. For Persian motifs in early Japanese art, see Shi Jiaming, p. 40; Munsterberg, p. 53. South China Indigo is discussed in Han Sheng, *Yimin yanjiu,* p. 221. The epidemic is traced in Twitchett, "Population," pp. 42–52.

53. Liu Xinru, *Silk and Religion,* pp. 188–189, 192–193. On the Tang international style, see Sherman Lee, pp. 156, 171–188.

54. The claim for Sui era Buddhist popularity comes from *Fozu tongji,* 39; T.49.359b. The initial Chinese reaction to Buddhism is discussed in Mori Mikisaburō, "Chūgoku chishikijin," pp. 88–89; Qu Xiaoqiang, pp. 189–190.

55. Emperor Wu's donation is described in Gernet, p. 243. King Chinhŭng may be found in *Samguk sagi,* vol. 1, p. 80 (Sillan Basic Annals 4). For tonsured emperors in Japan, see John Hall, "Kyoto," pp. 20–22; Hurst, p. 87. On the Great Eastern Temple, see Piggott, *Kingship,* p. 263.

56. Michihata Ryōshū, "Dengyō Daishi," pp. 365, 368–371, 375.

57. *Fozu tongji,* 38; T.49.355a. On animal sacrifice in China, see Kleeman, p. 185.

58. The decree of 517 is in *Fozu tongji,* 37; T.49.349b. That of 692 is in *Fozu tongji,* 39; T.49.369c.

59. For the ban of 529, see *Samguk sagi,* vol. 1, p. 75 (Sillan Basic Annals 4). For that of 599, see *Samguk yusa,* 3; T.49.988b; Best, "Tales of Three Paekche Monks," p. 143.

60. Buddho-Taoist cross-fertilization is discussed in Hu Shih, "Buddhistic Influence," p. 149; Robinet, pp. 151, 153–155, 191–195, 203, 260; Zürcher, "Buddhist Influence," p. 143; Zürcher, "'Prince Moonlight,'" p. 47. On print technology, see Carter, pp. 26–28, 38–41, 59–62; Mair, p. 736; Pelliot, pp. 33–34, 37–41, 50; Twitchett, *Printing,* pp. 13–14. Indian literary influences are itemized in Sun Changwu, pp. 178–179, 188–190; Strickmann, p. 56. Parallels between monasteries and academies are discussed in Walton, pp. 15–16, 102–103.

61. Jiang Weiqiao, pp. 1, 4; Jin'ichi Konishi, p. 8; Mair and Mei, pp. 380, 430, 435–444.

62. Kamata Shigeo, p. 36.

63. *Gao seng zhuan,* 1.1.

64. The "red-moustached Abhidharma master" is from *Fozu tongji,* 36; T.49.342c. The Kashmiri monk who came by sea is in *Chu sanzang jiji,* 14.543; *Fozu tongji,* 36; T.49.344b.

65. See Xie Haiping, pp. 149–161, 329–330. The eighth-century monk with occult skills is from *Zizhi tongjian*, 208.591. On Amoghavajra and Kūkai, see *Fozu tongji*, 40; T.49.373c; Kamata Shigeo, pp. 201–202, 206, 209–210; Qu Xiaoqiang, p. 96.

66. *Haedong kosŭng chŏn*, appendix, p. 67; Peter Lee, trans., *Lives*, p. 45; *Samguk sagi*, vol. 2, p. 37 (Paekche Basic Annals 2); *Samguk yusa*, 3; T.49.986a. Tamura Enchō ("Kudara bukkyōshi," pp. 311–312, 320–322) challenges this story and prefers to date the introduction of Buddhism to Paekche to the early sixth century instead. For Korean travel to India, see *Haedong kosŭng chŏn*, appendix, pp. 82–84; Hong Soon-chang, p. 97; Kamata Shigeo, p. 11.

67. *Nihon shoki*, 25.256. Aston, trans., vol. 2, p. 246, note 8. For Bodhisena, see *Genkō shakusho*, 15.224; Kamata Shigeo, pp. 166, 277; "Nan Tenjiku baramon sōjō hi," p. 887.

68. Ray, pp. 8, 153–154; Coedès, pp. 19–21.

69. Pollock, pp. 6, 10–12.

70. *Liang shu*, 54.787–788; *Nan shi*, 78.1951.

71. Pollock, pp. 32–33. For an Indian perspective, see Kosambi, pp. 166–176.

72. See Bellwood, pp. 137–138.

73. Coedès, pp. 10, 48; Pollock, p. 12.

74. Coedès, pp. 17, 56; Kenneth Hall, p. 59; *Liang shu*, 54.789; Ray, p. 160; *Taiping yulan*, 786.3613; *Tong dian*, 188.1008.

75. Coedès, p. 36; Kenneth Hall, pp. 48–77; Mabbett and Chandler, pp. 63–64, 66–77; Ray, pp. 101, 159–160; Shaffer, pp. 18–36. McNeill, *Plagues and Peoples*, pp. 112–113.

76. Coedès, p. 41; *Liang shu*, 54.798; *Tang huiyao*, 100.1786. For the gift from Paekche, see *Nihon shoki*, 19.59.

77. *Cefu yuangui*, 959.11289; *Liang shu*, 54.787. For the location of Dunxun, see Groeneveldt, pp. 119–121; Kenneth Hall, pp. 64–67.

78. Bellwood, p. 122; Coedès, pp. 65, 81; Kenneth Hall, p. 78; *Tong dian*, 188.1010; Wang Gungwu, "Nanhai Trade," p. 97.

79. *Cefu yuangui*, 959.11288; *Nan shi*, 78.1949; *Taiping yulan*, 786.3611. On the possible island origins of the Chams, see Higham, pp. 304–308.

80. Examples of Sino-Cham conflict are *Liang shu*, 54.785; *Nan shi*, 78.1949. For the Champa-ization of a group of Chinese people, see *Shui jing zhu*, 36.680. Champa's eighteenth-century demise is cited in SarDesai, p. 6.

81. See Wang Gungwu, "Nanhai Trade," p. 114.

82. Coedès, p. 34.

83. See Mair, pp. 722–725; Asanga Tilakaratne, pp. 116–117.

84. Bellwood, pp. 137–138; Coedès, pp. 23, 63–64; Ray, pp. 132–134, 136, 199–200.

85. Snellgrove, p. 330; Xie Haiping, pp. 164–165.

86. Mather, trans., p. 50; *Shishuo xinyu jiaojian*, p. 55. See also *Gao seng zhuan*, 1.21.

87. Kūkai's principal teacher was the Chinese Huiguo. See Dai Fanyu, p. 75. For Ennin, see Reischauer, *Ennin's Travels*, pp. 176-177; Reischauer, trans., *Ennin's Diary*, p. 289; Xie Haiping, p. 178, note 8.

88. Weinstein, "Beginnings," p. 179. On Kūkai's studies with western monks, see *Genkō shakusho*, 1.37; Yang Zengwen, p. 126. On Kūkai's Sanskrit, see also Dai Fanyu, p. 82; Ienaga Saburō, ed., *Nihon Bukkyōshi*, p. 192. For rare Japanese and Korean ventures farther west, see *Genkō shakusho*, 16.234-235; *Samguk yusa*, 4; T.49.1004a-b.

89. Zhi Dun is described in Demiéville, "La pénétration," p. 32. On Yijing, see Sun Changwu, p. 81. For a discussion of Southern dynasty Sanskrit studies, see Mair and Mei, pp. 389-391. On the "essentially Chinese" nature of Chan (Zen) as just one example of the Sinification of Buddhism, see Demiéville, "Le bouddhisme chinois," p. 394.

90. *Ebyō Tendai gishū*, vol. 3, p. 363.

91. Kamata Shigeo, p. 255; Liu Xinru, *Ancient India*, pp. 124, 144; Luo Zongzhen, pp. 101, 241, 257; Sun Changwu, pp. 199-201.

92. Michihata Ryōshū ("Chūgoku bukkyō," pp. 291-292, 306-308) comments on the exotic appearance of western monks. For Chinese debates over the acceptability of foreign Buddhism, see *Fozu tongji*, 38; T.49.358b; *Guang hong ming ji*, 10.2a-b; *Hong ming ji*, 7.1b-2a, 5b-6a; *Nan shi*, 75.1875-77.

93. For the cosmopolitan monasteries of seventh-century Britain, see Wailes and Zoll, pp. 31-33.

94. Gao Guanru, p. 200. On the Japanese establishment, see *Genkō shakusho*, 1.28, 16.231; *Nihon shoki*, 22.164-165.

95. "Tō dai-oshō tōseiden," p. 896. Yang Zengwen, p. 80.

96. Shi Dongchu (*Zhong-Ri Fojiao*, pp. 184-185) miscounts his own list as twenty-seven. Saichō's catalog dedication is in "Dengyō daishi shōrai mokuroku," p. 368.

97. For the embassy of 541, see *Nan shi*, 7.216; *Samguk sagi*, vol. 2, pp. 64-65 (Paekche Basic Annals 4). On the Paekche-Liang connection, see also Kamata Shigeo, p. 110. Regarding Silla's adoption of Chinese clothing, see *Samguk yusa*, 4; T.49.1005c.

98. For Ganjin, see Chen Shuifeng, pp. 92-93. The role of temples as early centers of continental culture is discussed in Ienaga Saburō, "Asuka, hakuhō bunka," pp. 336-337; Lin Tianwei, p. 123; Tsuji Zennosuke, *Nihon Bukkyōshi*, p. 107; Wang Jinlin, *Han-Tang wenhua*, p. 259. On the Monk Min, see *Nihon shoki*, 25.243-244; Yokota Ken'ichi, pp. 168-169, 171.

99. Wang Jinlin, *Han-Tang wenhua*, p. 261; Wang Jinlin, "Tō dai bukkyō," p. 603; Yang Zengwen, p. 13.

100. Chinese apocryphal texts are discussed in Swanson, pp. 42, 44; Kyoko Tokuno, p. 33. For Sogdian texts, see Sinor, "Languages," pp. 3, 10. On painting, see Sherman Lee, pp. 151-152, 155.

101. The Uighur conversion to Manichaeism is discussed in Mackerras,

p. 9. On the Chinese Buddhist mission to Tibet, see Fazun, pp. 134, 138; *Fozu tongji*, 41; T.49.379a; Qu Xiaoqiang, p. 122; Snellgrove, pp. 44, 445–446.

CHAPTER FIVE

1. Barfield, pp. 16–20.

2. On central Asia as a "nodal center," see Gills and Frank, pp. 19, 23; Zhang Guangda, "Gu dai Ou-Ya," p. 380. The quotations are from Grousset, pp. xxii–xxiii. On the natural division of the region between oasis and nomadic economies, see Yu Taishan, pp. 72–73.

3. Klimburg, p. 29. Sinor, "Languages and Cultural Interchange," p. 3. Lipman, p. 18.

4. Zhao Shichao, p. 62; Xie Haiping, pp. 2–7.

5. *Nanhai jigui neifa zhuan*, 2.91. *San guo zhi*, 30.832, note 1, and 30.836, note 1. Ying Shao, quoted in *Han yuan*, transcript, p. 23. See also *Hou-Han shu*, 48.1609–1610.

6. Amory, pp. 19–21. See also Geary, pp. 39–43. On the cultural uniformity of the steppe, see William Watson, pp. 98–99. On seminomadism, see Lattimore, "Caravan Routes," pp. 61–62.

7. McNeill, *Rise of the West*, pp. 234–238. Jettmar, pp. 148–149.

8. Boodberg, "Turk, Aryan and Chinese," pp. 13–16. *Jin shu*, 97.2549. Musset, p. 20.

9. Di Cosmo, p. 1106. On the early inhabitants of the Tarim basin, see Elizabeth Barber, especially pp. 202, 211–212; Grousset, pp. 50–53.

10. Grousset, pp. 189–190. On "The Altaic Problem," see Greenberg, pp. 11–21; Roy Andrew Miller, *Japanese and the Other Altaic Languages*, pp. 6, 44–45; Roy Andrew Miller, "Linguistic Evidence," p. 104; Nichols, p. 4.

11. Wells, pp. 116–117.

12. Crossley, pp. 6, 26–27, 211–212.

13. *Wei shu*, 114.3025. For Kushāna, see Snellgrove, pp. 47–48, 326, 330.

14. For the Xiongnu, see Yü Ying-shih, "Han Foreign Relations," pp. 383–405. On the "five Hu," see Kuang Shiyuan, p. 323. For the Ruan-ruan, see *Nan shi*, 79.1986–1987.

15. *Wei shu*, 103.2289.

16. Pulleyblank, "The Chinese and Their Neighbors," pp. 454–455; Sinor, "Establishment and Dissolution of the Türk Empire," pp. 285, 288, 290–291, 296, 315; Sinor, "Some Components of the Civilization of the Türks," pp. 145, 147, 156–157. On the origins of the Tujue empire and its culture, see Yu Taishan, pp. 104, 260–266.

17. Mackerras, p. 1, note 1, and p. 8.

18. Barfield, pp. 90, 104–105, 112.

19. Mackerras, p. 14.

20. *Han ji*, 14.137. On north-south communication, see Higham, p. 181.

21. Backus, p. 25.

22. On Tibet, see Backus, pp. 24, 28; Beckwith, pp. 168–172; Pan Yi-hong, *Son of Heaven*, pp. 231–261, 322–341; Snellgrove, pp. 351, 358; Stein, *Tibetan Civilization*, pp. 27–29, 56–62; Wang Xiaopu, pp. 14–18; *Xin Tang shu*, 3.68, 37.960, 216a.6071. Beckwith (pp. 5–8) denies any affiliation between the Qiang and Tibetans.

23. Backus, pp. 47–52; Luce, trans., pp. 78–80.

24. For a summary of Tibet's contemporary situation, see Oksenberg, pp. 54–55, 77–84.

25. Geary, pp. 43, 50–57; Goffart, pp. 13, 25; Musset, p. 12; Wells, pp. 102, 112–114.

26. Musset, pp. 27–28.

27. Amory, pp. 40–41, 86, 102–108, 278, 310; Musset, p. 46; Pirenne, pp. 38–40, 46. On the "ethnogenesis" of the Goths, see also Geary, pp. 62–73.

28. Thompson, pp. 45–50, 56, 93. Musset, p. 145: "rex Theodericus, . . . custos libertatis et propagator Romani nominis."

29. Pirenne, pp. 53–54, 142.

30. Amory, pp. 3–6; Goffart, p. 5; Musset, p. 121; Van Dam, p. 332; Wells, p. 260.

31. Geary, pp. 226–231; Musset, pp. 126–128, 149.

32. Hodges and Whitehouse, pp. 32–33, 52. Pirenne, pp. 163, 185, 197, 266.

33. *Wei shu*, 181.2733. He Ziquan, *Wei-Jin nanbeichao*, p. 90; Hong Tao, p. 6.

34. *Jin shu*, 62.1680.

35. Li Zefen, *Liang-Jin nanbeichao*, vol. 1, pp. 1–12, 80.

36. Ma Changshou, pp. 7–8, 36. Shao Taixin (pp. 50–74, 233–234) examines the Han settlements beyond the Yellow River.

37. *Shi ji*, 123.3167.

38. Psarras, p. 5.

39. Lattimore, "Origins of the Great Wall of China," p. 115. Di Cosmo, pp. 1095, 1100, 1109, 1116.

40. On Ma Yuan, see *Hou-Han shu*, 24.828; *Dong guan Han ji*, 12.1a. For the second-century complaint, see *Hou-Han shu*, 90.2991.

41. *Jin shu*, 97.2548–2549; Pan Yihong, "Settlement Policies," pp. 54–55, 76; *Zizhi tongjian*, 67.27.

42. For the nineteen "kinds," see *Jin shu*, 97.2549–2550. The complaint of 300 is from *Quan Jin wen*, 106.2070. On subordination, see Amory, p. 25 (for Rome); Tonami and Takeda, p. 125; Yoshida Fudōmaro, p. 214.

43. *San guo zhi*, 30.858–859, quoting the *Wei lüe*.

44. De Crespigny, trans., *To Establish Peace*, pp. xxvi–xxvii, xxxii–xxxiii. For the rise of strongmen, see Zhuge Liang's comment in *San guo zhi*, 35.912. On mounted auxiliaries, see He Ziquan, *Wei-Jin nanbeichao*, p. 53.

45. See Zhang Xiong, p. 58.

46. Cai Xuehai, pp. 44, 51; Barfield, p. 99; Honey, pp. 119–134; Hong

Tao, p. 7; Li Zefen, *Liang-Jin nanbeichao*, vol. 1, pp. 88–90; Yü Ying-shih, *Trade and Expansion*, pp. 209–211.

47. Population estimates are from Bielenstein, "Census," pp. 145–146, 158; *Jin shu*, 26.791; Ni Jinsheng, "Wu-Hu luan Hua qianye," pp. 39, 42; Wang Zhongluo, *Wei-Jin nanbeichao*, p. 345. On fortifications, see *Jin shu*, 114.2926; Liu Shufen, "Zhucheng yundong," pp. 371, 373. The Yellow River pirates are from *Jin shu*, 63.1714.

48. Tian Yuqing, *Dong Jin menfa*, pp. 28–35.

49. Zhang Ping is from *Jin shu*, 110.2839–2840. Liu Chou's story is in *Cao Jiazhi Jin ji*, 4a.

50. Li Zefen, *Liang-Jin nanbeichao*, vol. 1, pp. 81, 85–87. The annexation of Sichuan by the preimperial state of Qin is described in detail by Sage.

51. This account of the Cheng-Han empire is drawn from *Huayang guo zhi*, 8.445, 8.459–460, 8.464–465, 9.483–484; *Jin shu*, 120.3022–3023, 120.3028–3029, 121.3035–3036, 121.3039.

52. *Jin shu*, 102.2665; Zhang Xiong, p. 60.

53. *Jin shu*, 104.2707, 2709; *Wei shu*, 95.2047–2048. Honey (pp. 134–149) surveys Shi Le's career.

54. *Jin shu*, 105.2735–2737, 2748, 2751.

55. *Jin shu*, 107.2795; Hong Tao, p. 14; Ma Changshou, p. 18; Zhang Xiong, p. 60.

56. Schreiber, vol. 14, p. 374–375.

57. *Jin shu*, 108.2813. See Schreiber, vol. 14, p. 416, and vol. 15.1, pp. 124–125.

58. Cheng Zhangcan, pp. 34–36.

59. Lattimore, "Chinese Turkistan," p. 196. Cai Xuehai, p. 49; C. P. Fitzgerald; So and Bunker, pp. 29, 86–87, 129, no. 46.

60. Fu Lecheng, "Tang xing wenhua," pp. 257–259; Lin Enxian, pp. 581–591; Pulleyblank, "The An Lu-shan Rebellion," pp. 37–39; Wang and Zhao, "Sui Yangdi," pp. 72, 76; Xie Haiping, pp. 428–429, 432.

61. Li Donghua, *Haiyang fazhan*, p. 180.

62. De Crespigny, trans., *To Establish Peace*, pp. 58–59, 61; Gardiner, *Early History of Korea*, pp. 24–25; Huang Zhilian, p. 28; Li Donghua, *Haiyang fazhan*, pp. 83–84, 90–96.

63. *San guo zhi*, 30.842; *Zizhi tongjian*, 64.21. See Lü Simian, *Du shi zhaji*, p. 887.

64. De Crespigny, "Three Kingdoms," pt. 1, pp. 35–36; Gardiner, *Early History of Korea*, p. 26; Gardiner, "Kung-sun Warlords," pt. 6, pp. 172–174; Li Donghua, *Haiyang fazhan*, pp. 95, 102.

65. *Hou-Han shu*, 90.2985; Liu Xueyao, pp. 49, 51, map, p. 55. On the grotto temple, see Tonami and Takeda, pp. 116–118; Wan Shengnan, p. 251; *Wei shu*, 108a.2738. For a similar Manchu expedition in 1677 to locate their lost homeland "in the midst of a thickly forested uninhabited region," see Crossley, p. 103; Rawski, pp. 73, 85.

66. *Jin shu*, 108.2803; *Xu Han shu* (Continued History of the Han), by

Sima Biao, quoted in *Han yuan,* transcript, p. 22, note. See also Yu Taishan, pp. 78-79.

67. *Shiliu guo chunqiu jibu,* 23.403; Tang Changru, "Jin dai beijing gezu," pp. 176-178.

68. *Jin shu,* 97.2537-2539; *Liang shu,* 54.810; *Xin Tang shu,* 221a.6224-6228. See Liu Xueyao, pp. 102-105.

69. *Wei shu,* 13.325. For early Tuoba history, see Holmgren, *Annals of Tai,* pp. 7-11; Pan Yihong, *Son of Heaven,* pp. 44-45; Yu Taishan, p. 80.

70. *Fozu tongji,* 39; T.49.361b. By the end of the fifth century, at least, Northern Wei emperors were claiming to be the legitimate successors to Chinese imperial titles. See Wang Xiaoyan, p. 262. A sixth-century history commissioned by the rival Southern dynasty Liang, on the other hand, predictably dismissed Northern Wei as a barbarian state. See Shigezawa Toshirō, pp. 14-15.

71. *Wei shu,* 1.4-5, 114.3030. *Sui shu,* 32.947.

72. Boodberg, "The Language of the T'o-Pa Wei," p. 239; Liu Xueyao, pp. 83-86; Pulleyblank, "The Chinese and Their Neighbors," pp. 452-453. Chen Sanping (p. 48) observes that the Tuoba language "obviously had both Turkic and (proto-) Mongolian elements."

73. *Hou-Han shu,* 90.2985-2986. For tribal confederations, see Ma Changshou, p. 14.

74. *Wei shu,* 2.31-33. On resettlement, see Liu Jingcheng, pp. 30, 32; Ma Changshou, p. 47.

75. Han Guopan, *Juntian zhidu,* pp. 82-88; Mao Hanguang, *Zhonggu shehui,* pp. 20-21; *Zizhi tongjian,* 136.738, 743-744.

76. Du Zhengsheng, "Cong fengjian zhi," pp. 399, 402, 405, 407; Kimura Masao, pp. 168-169.

77. On the Qin economy, see Gao Shangzhi, pp. 25-26; Liu Chunfan, pp. 5-14; Yang Kuan, pp. 188-190 and notes. For the Han dynasty, see Du Zhengsheng, "Cong fengjian zhi," p. 383.

78. On Han village inequality, see Luo Tonghua, "Zheng li linbu shi lun," pp. 16-17, 33, 36-40. On post-Han estates, see Huang Renyu, pp. 111-112, 127; Liu Shufen, "San zhi liu shiji," p. 225; Liu Yuhuang, p. 116.

79. Gao Min, *Qin-Han,* pp. 194-195; Holcombe, "Administrative State," pp. 16-18; Zhao and Chen, pp. 28-29.

80. Victor Xiong, p. 377. See also Miyazaki Ichisada, "Chūgoku shijō no shōen," p. 32.

81. *Chunqiu fanlu,* 8.1a.

82. *Tong dian,* 1.12-13.

83. For the place of Confucian ideals in the *juntian* system, see Hori Toshikazu, *Kindensei,* chap. 1. For the Sui mobilization, see *Zizhi tongjian,* 176.806, 814-815.

84. Liu Baiji, p. 66; *Tang lü shuyi,* 13.173; Wang Jinlin, *Nara bunka,* pp. 28, 214-215; *Xin Tang shu,* 51.1342-1343. For the somewhat different Northern Wei regulations of 485, see *Wei shu,* 110.2853-2855.

85. Han Guopan, *Juntian zhidu*, pp. 20, 181, 185–219; Hori Toshikazu, *Kindensei*, pp. 154–155; Ikeda On, "Jizhang guanjian," p. 103; Twitchett, *Financial Administration*, pp. 5–9; Zhao and Chen, p. 41.

86. Chen Yinke, *Sui-Tang zhidu*, pp. 108–123. On Tang law, see Yang Tingfu, p. 172.

87. Kurihara Masuo, pp. 142–143.

88. Liu Xueyao, pp. 256–259.

89. The Northern Wei Sinification program is presented in Wang Xiaoyan, pp. 252, 254–263; *Wei shu*, 21a.536; *Zizhi tongjian*, 135.722, 136.729–731, 139.25, 140.49, 51–52, 66, 69.

90. For architectural orthodoxy, see Ma Changshou, p. 67. On the issue of motive, see Holmgren, "Race and Class," pp. 113–114.

91. *Luoyang qielan ji*, 2.102; Jenner, trans., p. 201. For standards of Confucian scholarship, see Kuwahara Jitsuzō, p. 110. On "Mulan," see Wan Shengnan, pp. 283–286.

92. *Luoyang qielan ji*, 2.105; Jenner, trans., p. 203.

93. Banton, pp. 31, 50–51.

94. Han Sheng, "Wubi he cun," p. 103.

95. Holmgren, *Annals of Tai*, p. 12; Yao Weiyuan, introduction, p. 4.

96. Ma Changshou, p. 108; Pan Yihong, *Son of Heaven*, pp. 34–35, 98; *Sui shu*, 1.1; Yang Cuiwei, p. 70.

97. Holmgren, "Composition," pp. 115–116, 120, 151; Liu Shufen, "Zhucheng yundong," pp. 362–363; Liu Xueyao, p. 260.

98. Ma Changshou, pp. 70, 75; Waldron, pp. 43–44.

99. *Jin shu*, 97.2550.

100. *Liang shu*, 56.833.

101. *Wei shu*, 110.2857. *Song shu*, 77.1985.

102. Hudson, pp. 192–193. On the courtier-warrior contrast in literature, see Varley, *Warriors of Japan*, pp. 91–92, 109–111.

103. Ma Changshou, pp. 74, 105–107, 109.

104. Wan Shengnan, pp. 290–291. Ma Changshou, pp. 75–76, 81–82, 86–88.

105. Jenner, trans., p. v; Tonami and Takeda, pp. 124–125; *Wei shu*, 14.360; *Zizhi tongjian*, 140.73.

106. Boodberg, "Marginalia," p. 308; Pan Guojian, pp. 137–138.

107. Pan Guojian, pp. 135, 149–150, 154–155, 213–214.

108. Chen Sanping, pp. 52–55; *Nian er shi zhaji*, 15.319–320; Somers, "Time, Space, and Structure," p. 972; *Xin Tang shu*, 1.1–2.

CHAPTER SIX

1. The relationships between Vietnam, Lingnan, and early imperial China are explored in Holcombe, "China's Deep South."

2. Bellwood, p. 269; Higham, pp. 37–38, 90, 94, 96, 108–109, 324; Lü Shipeng, p. 2.

3. *Viet su luoc,* 1.1a. The nationalist appropriation of Van-lang is discussed in Taylor, *Birth of Vietnam,* pp. 3–4.

4. On the sketchy early records, see Maspero, "Van-lang," pp. 2–4, 7–8; Rao Zongyi, p. 628. For an archaeological approach, see Higham, pp. 133–134.

5. *Dai Viet su ky toan thu,* ngoai ky, 1.100; *Shui jing zhu,* 37.694; *Viet su luoc,* 1.1a. For a modern discussion, see Lü Shipeng, p. 14; Higham, p. 122; Taylor, *Birth of Vietnam,* pp. 16–17, 21, 23.

6. *Shui jing zhu,* 37.693–694; *Tong dian,* 188.1005. On the Qin conquest, see *Annam chi luoc,* 4.93; *Huainan zi,* 18.16a; *Shi ji,* 6.253. It is uncertain how far into modern Vietnam the Qin conquests extended. See Lü Shipeng, pp. 25–26.

7. On Yunnan, see *Han shu,* 95.3838. For the Yue kingdoms, see Li Donghua, *Haiyang fazhan,* p. 31.

8. *Han ji,* 10.97–98; *Han shu,* 95.3859–3860; *Tong dian,* 186.995.

9. *Han shu,* 95.3860, 3863. Almost certainly this measure was applied only to the population of the major urban centers in Eastern Ou. See Lü Simian, *Du shi zhaji,* p. 582.

10. *Annam chi luoc,* 5.113. On this writer's motives, see Le Blanc, p. 23.

11. *Shi ji,* 113.2967. See also *Shui jing zhu,* 37.708.

12. *Annam chi luoc,* 3.78, 14.324; *Han ji,* 4.34; *Han shu,* 95.3848; *Lun heng,* 2.15a.

13. *Han ji,* 4.34. The archaeological evidence is assessed in Bellwood, p. 271; Huang and Sun, p. 51.

14. *Annam chi luoc,* 1.17, 11.271–272, 15.341–342; *Han ji,* 14.137–138; *Han shu,* 95.3854–3855, 3857, 3859; *Viet su luoc,* 1.3a. The story of how "Vietnam" got its name is related in Anderson, pp. 157–158; Woodside, p. 120.

15. For Hainan, see *Han shu,* 28b.1670; *Nan shi,* 78.1951; *Shui jing zhu,* 36.688; *Taiping yulan,* 172.972; *Tong dian,* 188.1006; *Xin Tang shu,* 3.66, 43a.1100. The premier is quoted in Kemenade, p. 186. For Hainan today, see also Feng Chongyi.

16. *Annam chi luoc,* 4.93–94. *Tong dian,* 188.1006.

17. *Dong guan Han ji,* 12.3a; Holmgren, *Chinese Colonization,* pp. 16–21; Maspero, "Ma Yuan," pp. 18–19, 27.

18. Holmgren, *Chinese Colonization,* pp. 2, 62; Maspero, "Ma Yuan," p. 12. For Han dynasty banishment of criminals to Vietnam, see *Annam chi luoc,* 5.118.

19. *Bo wu zhi,* 1.2a; Feng Chengjun, p. 35; Li Donghua, *Haiyang fazhan,* p. 154; Liu Shufen, "Liuchao Nanhai," p. 338; *Sui shu,* 31.887–888.

20. *San guo zhi,* 53.1251–1252; Taylor,.*Birth of Vietnam,* pp. 75–76.

21. Blair, pp. 118–119; Salway, pp. 3, 18–19, 119, 354–355, 360.

22. Aside from place names (and Latin borrowings), for example, the modern English language retains scarcely fifteen or sixteen British words that pre-date the Germanic invasions. See Musset, p. 104.

23. Holmgren, *Chinese Colonization,* p. 64; Lü Shipeng, p. 48; Wang Gungwu, "Nanhai Trade," pp. 17–18.

24. *Jin shu,* 57.1560; *Nan shi,* 78.1951.

25. For the Li "bandits," see "Nanzhou yiwu zhi," in *Taiping yulan,* 785.3609. For cannibals, see "Nanzhou yiwu zhi," in *Taiping yulan,* 786.3611. *Tong dian,* 188.1005, places the land of the cannibals to the west of modern Vietnam. For the "wild Wenlang," see "Linyi ji" (Champa Chronicle), in *Taiping yulan,* 172.971. On the Guangdong slave trade, see *Han Changli quanji,* 33.416; *Liang shu,* 33.470; *Xin Tang shu,* 163.5009.

26. *Annam chi luoc,* 7.171–172; *Viet su luoc,* 1.4b–5a. For the parallel with Liaodong, see Ōba Osamu, *Nitchū kankeishi,* pp. 49, 63, 94. Wu suspicion was not assuaged by Shi Xie's offerings of exotic tribute or even by a Shi son sent as hostage. Since an independent Lingnan was intolerable to the Wu regime, it dispatched one of its own officers to act as a superior inspector for the region. In 217, this man moved the official capital of Lingnan from Shi Xie's family stronghold at Jiaozhi back to the site of Zhao Tuo's old city at Canton, constructed a new walled city there, and began to pacify and assemble the "Hundred Yue" people. *Shui jing zhu,* 37.708.

27. *Annam chi luoc,* 7.173; *Dai Viet su ky toan thu,* ngoai ky, 4.137–139.

28. On émigré domination, see Wu Xianqing, "Nanchao dazu," p. 4; Zhou Yiliang, pp. 55–56, 58. For local resentment of these émigrés, see Han Guopan, *Wei-Jin nanbeichao,* p. 176; Ōkawa Fujio, p. 534. For Jiaozhou's relative autonomy, see Holmgren, *Chinese Colonization,* pp. 115, 119, 129–130; Lü Shipeng, pp. 58, 62.

29. *Dai viet su ky toan thu,* ngoai ky, 4.147–153. For the Sui reconquest, see also *Sui shu,* 53.1357–1358.

30. *Dai viet su ky toan thu,* ngoai ky, 5.158; *Xin Tang shu,* 90.3777–3778.

31. *Xin Tang shu,* 222c.6326.

32. *Sui shu,* 80.1800–1803.

33. *Xin Tang shu,* 110.4112–4114; *Zizhi tongjian,* 193.932–933.

34. Wang Chengwen, "Tang-dai 'nan xuan,'" pp. 97–98.

35. Li Donghua, *Haiyang fazhan,* pp. 150–154; Lü Shipeng, pp. 103, 119.

36. On population movement, see Li Qingxin, p. 80. For relative population, compare *Sui shu,* 31.880 with 31.885.

37. *Annam chi luoc,* 10.265–266; *Dai viet su ky toan thu,* ngoai ky, 5.158–160, 165; Taylor, *Birth of Vietnam,* pp. 198–199. For Cham raids, see *Jin shu,* 8.193; *Liang shu,* 54.785; *Nan shi,* 78.1949; *Tong dian,* 188.1008.

38. For "Ghost Gate Pass," see "Shi dao zhi" (A Record of the Ten Circuits), in *Taiping yulan,* 172.970; *Xin Tang shu,* 43a.1109. For eighth-century tribal uprisings, see Taylor, *Birth of Vietnam,* pp. 196–200; *Xin Tang shu,* 6.157, 175–176; 222c.6329; *Zizhi tongjian,* 224.180–181.

39. *Annam chi luoc,* 9.212–213; *Dai viet su ky toan thu,* ngoai ky, 5.159; *Viet su luoc,* 1.9b–10a; *Xin Tang shu,* 4.86, 201.5732–5733.

40. *Tong dian,* 32.186; *Xin Tang shu,* 43a.1111.

41. *Dai viet su ky toan thu,* ngoai ky, 5.161–162, 169; *Xin Tang shu,* 9.267, 170.5175.

42. *Annam chi luoc,* 9.208–209; *Dai viet su ky toan thu,* ngoai ky, 5.158–159. For exile to Lingnan, see, for example, *Xin Tang shu,* 4.88, 5.133. On the policy advice of 792, see *Zizhi tongjian,* 234.596.

43. *Zizhi tongjian,* 270.242, 263. On Tang regional commands, see *Xin Tang shu,* 64.1759.

44. *Annam chi luoc,* 4.99–100; *Dai viet su ky toan thu,* ngoai ky, 5.169–171; *Viet su luoc,* 1.13b–14b. See also Lü Shipeng, pp. 140, 142.

45. See Lü Shipeng, p. 3.

46. SarDesai, p. 17.

47. *Annam chi luoc,* 11.278, 282; *Viet su luoc,* 1.15b–16a. See also Sar-Desai, p. 20; Taylor, *Birth of Vietnam,* pp. 275–295.

48. *Annam chi luoc,* 16.381. On the costly Ming reoccupation of Vietnam, see Levathes, pp. 159, 168.

49. *Annam chi luoc,* 14.324, 329; Gao Mingshi, *Jiaoyuquan,* p. 40; Woodside, p. 8.

50. Taylor, "Surface Orientations," p. 966.

51. Woodside, pp. 10, 12–13.

52. Blakeley, "Chu Society," pp. 53–54. Korean and Japanese nomenclature are discussed elsewhere in this book.

CHAPTER SEVEN

1. *Han ji,* 14.139; *Han shu,* 95.3863–3864; *Samguk yusa,* 1; T.49.962a; *Shi ji,* 93.2637–2639, 115.2985.

2. See Ki-baik Lee, pp. 16–17. For a discussion of early Korean ethnicity, see also Cumings, pp. 30–31.

3. On this so-called northern Yan language, see Hsu and Linduff, p. 201; Ma Changshou, pp. 11, 34–35; Yan Gengwang, "Yang Xiong," map, p. 85.

4. *Han ji,* 14.139; *Han shu,* 95.3864–3867; *Samguk yusa,* 1; T.49.962a–b. *San guo zhi,* 30.848.

5. Loewe, "Campaigns of Han Wu-ti," pp. 77, 104–105. For Tang Taizong, see *Zizhi tongjian,* 193.932.

6. *San guo zhi,* 30.851. On the name "Korea," see Cumings, p. 23; *Hou-Han shu,* treatise 23.3529; Yü Ying-shih, "Han Foreign Relations," p. 449.

7. Huang Zhilian, pp. 59–60.

8. *Han shu,* 28b.1658. Hong Soon-chang, p. 43. Nelson, *Archaeology of Korea,* p. 5. Wells, p. 264.

9. Nelson, "Politics of Ethnicity," pp. 221, 225. Kim Tal-su, pp. 54–55.

10. Li Donghua, *Haiyang fazhan,* pp. 10–12, 79.

11. Peter Lee, ed., *Sourcebook,* pp. 4–5.

12. Kim Tal-su, p. 41; Nelson, *Archaeology,* pp. 58, 108–110, 161–163; Nelson, "Politics of Ethnicity," pp. 218, 223. More typically, Hong Soon-chang

(pp. 3–5) sees the origins of the Korean people among Altaic-speaking agriculturists from northern China who conquered the peninsula, possibly expelling its previous inhabitants, sometime after 2000 B.C.

13. Kim Tal-su, p. 44; Lewin, *Aya und Hata,* p. 6; Ma Changshou, pp. 37–38; *San guo zhi,* 30.848; Xia Yingyuan, pp. 94–97.

14. Gardiner, *Early History of Korea,* pp. 39–41; *Han yuan,* transcript, p. 36, note; Kawakatsu Yoshio, *Chūgoku no rekishi,* pp. 47–51.

15. Kitō Kiyoaki, p. 86; Lü Simian, *Du shi zhaji,* pp. 885–887; Ōba Osamu, *Nitchū kankeishi,* pp. 59–60.

16. Gardiner, *Early History of Korea,* pp. 29–30; Huang Zhilian, p. 5; Lewin, *Aya und Hata,* p. 6; *Liang shu,* 54.801; *Samguk yusa* 1; T.49.963c; Wang Jianqun, p. 202. On the languages of the Puyŏ group, see Lewin, "Japanese and Korean," pp. 407–408.

17. Puyŏ was located in former Yemaek territory, according to *Jin shu,* 97.2532; *Shan hai jing,* 6.293, note. On the Yemaek, see Lin Yun. Quotations are from *San guo zhi,* 30.841; Pulleyblank, "The Chinese and Their Neighbors," pp. 443–444.

18. *Han yuan,* transcript, pp. 27, 35, notes; *Liang shu,* 54.802; *San guo zhi,* 30.841, 843–844. Conventional Chinese marriage patterns are surveyed in Eastman, pp. 24–31.

19. For Puyŏ's fate, see Hong Soon-chang, p. 46; *Hou Han shu,* 85.2810; Yao Weiyuan, pp. 269–270. Regarding the origins of Parhae, see Kim Tal-su, pp. 56–57; *Samguk yusa* 1; T. 49.963a, note. For the dissolution of Parhae, see Crossley, p. 15.

20. Huang Zhilian, pp. 20–21; Lewin, *Aya und Hata,* pp. 6–7.

21. *Han yuan,* transcript, p. 29, note; *San guo zhi,* 30.851–852. For the homes of Tungusic-speaking peoples, see Crossley, p. 19.

22. *San guo zhi,* 30.852–853.

23. Gardiner, "The Kung-sun Warlords," vol. 5, pp. 85–89; *Liang shu,* 54.802; *San guo zhi,* 30.843, 845. On Hwando as an example of the northern fortified cities of this age, see Liu Shufen, "Zhucheng yundong," pp. 389–391.

24. For the vicissitudes and gradual consolidation of the Koguryŏ state, see *Han yuan,* transcript, p. 36, note; *Liang shu,* 54.803; Ōba Osamu, *Nitchū kankeishi,* p. 72; *Samguk sagi,* vol. 1, p. 345 (Koguryŏ Basic Annals 6); *Shiliu guo chunqiu,* 23.401, 24.415.

25. *Jin shu,* 124.3108; *Samguk sagi,* vol. 1, p. 348 (Koguryŏ Basic Annals 6); *Shiliu guo chunqiu,* 47.570. On intermarriage between the Tuoba and Murong Xianbei leaders, see Wan Shengnan, pp. 253–254. On the rising Tuoba threat to the Murong, see Liu Xueyao, pp. 142–143.

26. Han Sheng, "'Wei fa Baiji,'" pp. 38–39. For the Kwanggaet'o stele, see Wang Jianqun, pp. 208–210. A balanced appraisal of this controversial inscription may be found in Farris, *Sacred Texts,* p. 115.

27. *San guo zhi,* 30.849–851. For refugee settlement, see *Samguk yusa* 1; T. 49.962b.

28. For Paekche's Puyŏ origins, see *Samguk sagi*, vol. 2, p. 10 (Paekche Basic Annals 1); *Han yuan*, transcript, p. 44, note. Modern assessments include Best, "Diplomatic and Cultural Contacts," pp. 444–446; Gardiner, *Early History of Korea*, p. 45; Ledyard, "Horseriders," p. 234. On horseback riding, compare *Han yuan*, transcript, pp. 29, 46, notes. Quotation from *Liang shu*, 54.805.

29. The preceding narratives are all drawn from *Samguk sagi*, vol. 2, pp. 10–12 (Paekche Basic Annals 1). For the date 369, see Ki-baik Lee, p. 37.

30. For growing friction with Silla, see *Samguk sagi*, vol. 2, p. 19 (Paekche Basic Annals 1). Tamura Enchō comments on the distribution of Paekchean temples in "Kudara bukkyōshi," pp. 334–336. For the Paekche population as of 660–663, see *Samguk sagi*, vol. 2, p. 80 (Paekche Basic Annals 6), and p. 232 (treatise 6).

31. Best, "Diplomatic and Cultural Contacts," pp. 491–492; Han Sheng, "'Wei fa Baiji,'" pp. 40–41, 43; Ōba Osamu, *Nitchū kankeishi*, p. 92; Mōri Hisashi, pp. 7–8; *Samguk sagi*, vol. 2, p. 42 (Paekche Basic Annals 3).

32. Sherman Lee, p. 163. On tomb bricks, see Best, "Tales of Three Paekche Monks," pp. 147–148; Tamura Enchō, "Kudara bukkyōshi," p. 322. Extract from the *Gua di zhi*, quoted in *Han yuan*, transcript, p. 46, note. For information about this text, see Huang Yuese, "Zhong-Han-Ri guanxi," p. 2

33. *Samguk sagi*, vol. 2, p. 71 (Paekche Basic Annals 5).

34. Cumings, pp. 48–49.

35. *Samguk sagi*, vol. 1, pp. 16–17 (Sillan Basic Annals 1); *Samguk yusa* 1; T. 49.964b; *San guo zhi*, 30.852. For Paekche origins of the Sillan royal house, see Huang Zhilian, p. 22; *Sui shu*, 81.1820. On the third-century population, see *San guo zhi*, 30.853.

36. *Han yuan*, transcript, p. 42, note; Mōri Hisashi, p. 9; *Samguk sagi*, vol. 2, p. 40 (Paekche Basic Annals 3), and p. 187 (treatise 3).

37. *Samguk sagi*, vol. 1, pp. 67, 72–73, 75, 78 (Sillan Basic Annals 3–4).

38. For Wŏn'gwang's secular precepts, see Ki-baik Lee, p. 55; *Samguk sagi*, vol. 2, p. 372 (Yŏl chŏn 5); *Samguk yusa*, 4; T.49.1003a. For the proposals of 649–650, see *Samguk sagi*, vol. 1, p. 103 (Sillan Basic Annals 5); *Samguk yusa*, 4; T.49.1005c. On education, see Wang Zhoukun, pp. 110, 113.

39. *Samguk yusa*, 2; T.49.974a. For a recitation of Tang influences on early Korea, see Wang Yi, pp. 86–91.

40. Ledyard, "Yin and Yang," p. 323; Rogers, "National Consciousness," p. 152; *Samguk sagi*, vol. 2, p. 230 (treatise 6).

41. Chen Shangsheng, pp. 161–162, 164; Ikeda On, "Zui-Tō sekai," p. 6; Zhang Yonglu, p. 238.

42. *Samguk yusa*, 2; T.49.978b.

43. *Koryŏ sa*, 2.15b; Peter Lee, trans., *Sourcebook*, p. 264. For Koryŏ's somewhat ambivalent relationship to China, see Fang Yaguang, p. 166; Huang Zhilian, pp. 65–68; Ledyard, "Yin and Yang," pp. 313, 343; Rogers, "National Consciousness," p. 158; Yang Tingfu, pp. 185–187.

44. Kichung Kim, p. 51.

45. Ledyard, "Yin and Yang," p. 325.

46. Haboush, "Confucianization," pp. 84–85. On the selection of the name Chosŏn, see Cumings, p. 46; Robinson, pp. 16, 25–26.

CHAPTER EIGHT

1. Howland, p. 12.

2. Taylor, "Surface Orientations," p. 972.

3. Keiji Imamura, pp. 127, 216–223; Kitō Kiyoaki, p. 245.

4. Suwa Haruo, p. 56; Wang Zhenping, *Han-Tang Zhong-Ri guanxi*, p. 2, note 4. The theory concerning *Shan hai jing* is discussed in Wang Jinlin, *Han-Tang wenhua*, pp. 46–47. See *Shan hai jing jiaozhu*, 12.321.

5. Suwa Haruo, pp. 60–61; Wang Jinlin, *Han-Tang wenhua*, pp. 48, 148–150. *Wei lüe*, quoted in *Han yuan*, transcript, pp. 50–51, note.

6. *Nihon shoki*, 13.340. Compare *Cefu yuangui*, 959.11288, for Funan. On jar burials, see Bellwood, pp. 306–307.

7. Farris, *Sacred Texts*, p. 25; Hanihara Kazurō, pp. 157, 169, 173; Ikeda On, "Zui-Tō sekai," p. 4; Keiji Imamura, pp. 155–160; Katayama Kazumichi, pp. 23–24.

8. Lewin, "Japanese and Korean," pp. 395, 405–408. Greenberg, pp. 11–21, 280–281, distinguishes Korean-Japanese-Ainu from Altaic but includes both categories within Eurasiatic.

9. *Shi ji*, 41.1751. Cross-reference for dating purposes with 15.728.

10. For opposing Japanese and Korean views, see Farris, *Sacred Texts*, pp. 56, 106. For a Chinese example, see Shi Dongchu, *Zhong-Ri Fojiao*, p. 8.

11. See Saitō Tadashi, p. 15.

12. Farris, "Korean Connection," pp. 3–4, 6; Farris, *Sacred Texts*, pp. 72–77. On the Confucian erudites from Korea, see Tsuji Zennosuke, *Nihon bunka shi*, p. 124.

13. *Samguk sagi*, vol. 1, pp. 20, 57, 59 (Sillan Basic Annals 1, 3).

14. *Samguk sagi*, vol. 2, pp. 40, 42 (Paekche Basic Annals 3). See also Suzuki Yasutami, p. 202.

15. Wang Jianqun, pp. 181–184.

16. See Naobayashi Futai, p. 49. For a mid-seventh-century example of a Paekche monk who returned with the Wa army to Japan, see *Genkō shakusho*, 9.134.

17. *Genkō shakusho*, 16.231; Mōri Hisashi, pp. 12–23; *Nihon shoki*, 22.164–165; Xia Yingyuan, p. 117. The connections among Japan, Paekche, and Southern dynasty China are evaluated in Saitō Tadashi, p. 245; Sonoda Kōyū, pp. 366, 370; Yoshimura Rei. On the arrivals of 577, see Tamura Enchō, "Kudara bukkyōshi," pp. 330–331. For Mimaji and Nojagong, see Best, "Diplomatic and Cultural Contacts," p. 475; *Nihon shoki*, 22.155–156.

18. Roy Andrew Miller, "Yamato and Paekche," p. 4. *Shoku Nihongi*, 33.442; Ueda Masaaki, *Kikajin*, pp. 10–11.

19. *Nihon shoki*, 13.339, 11.312; Han Sheng, *Yimin yanjiu*, p. 18.

20. *Nihon shoki*, 19.70, 24.190.

21. Kitō Kiyoaki, p. 155.

22. *San guo zhi*, 30.854. See Ueda Masaaki, *Ronkyū*, pp. 101–103.

23. See Naobayashi Futai, p. 46; Piggott, *Kingship*, p. 12.

24. *Sui shu*, 81.1827. Hirano Kunio, pp. 145–146.

25. Compare Hirano Kunio, pp. 160–161, and Kitō Kiyoaki, pp. 20, 256–257.

26. Amino Yoshihiko, *Nihon shakai*, vol. 1, pp. 74–77, 114, 158–159; Hudson, pp. 204–205, 221–224; William McCullough, "Heian court," pp. 30–32.

27. Enomoto Junichi, pp. 170, 172–173; Lee Sungsi, pp. 107–108, 123–124, 160–166, 174–184; Piggott, *Kingship*, pp. 36, 100. For the increase in private trade in Tang after the mid-eighth century, see Jie Yongqiang, p. 99.

28. Farris, *Sacred Texts*, p. 100; Ueda Masaaki, *Kikajin*, p. 26.

29. *Nihon shoki*, 14.385–386, 19.51.

30. *Nihon shoki*, 19.49–50. See Ueda Masaaki, *Kikajin*, pp. 137–139.

31. Borgen, p. 71; Farris, *Sacred Texts*, p. 105; Kitō Kiyoaki, p. 261; Ueda Masaaki, *Kikajin*, p. 133. For the Eta-Funayama sword, see Anazawa and Manome, pp. 392–393. The incident involving scribes is from *Nihon shoki*, 20.102.

32. On low-level technical employment, see Kiley, "A Note on the Surnames," p. 177. For Soga, Kammu, and other examples, see Kitō Kiyoaki, p. 271; Ueda Masaaki, *Kikajin*, pp. 12, 14, 16–17, 19, 173–174.

33. *Shoku Nihongi*, 20.184.

34. Kiley, "A Note on the Surnames," pp. 177–178, 184–185.

35. Kitabatake Chikafusa (1293–1354), in Varley, trans., *Chronicle*, pp. 104–105. For the virtual cessation of immigration after 830, see Ueda Masaaki, *Kikajin*, p. 176.

36. For fascinating cases of "The Invention of Tradition" as a general phenomenon, see Hobsbawm and Ranger.

37. Harootunian, p. 144. Hudson, p. 236.

38. Tsuda Sōkichi, pp. 18, 128, 132–134. On Tsuda's iconoclasm and the prewar ultranationalist reaction to it, see Mitchell, pp. 298–299; Tanaka, pp. 4–5, 279–281. Shi Dongchu surveys Tang influences on Japan in *Zhong-Ri Fojiao*, pp. 285–349.

39. See Zhu Yunying, p. 39.

40. Hsiao Kung-chuan (p. 54) maintains that as late as the fourth century B.C., Confucian learning was still largely foreign to the Yangzi River area of what is now southern (or even central) China. Ebrey ("The Chinese Family," pp. 45, 83) sketches the emergence of Confucian society in the north. On women's property rights and marriage patterns in early Japan, see Amino Yoshihiko, *Nihon shakai*, vol. 1, pp. 130–131; McCullough, "Japanese Marriage Institutions." For more recent Japanese marriage patterns, see Befu, pp. 1329–1330.

41. Kitagawa, "The Shadow of the Sun," pp. 104–105. Consanguinity is

discussed in McCullough, "Japanese Marriage Institutions," pp. 135–136; Tsuji Zennosuke, *Nihon bunka shi*, pp. 128–129. On shrine maidens, see Hayami Tasuku, pp. 41–42; Satō Hiroo, p. 82. For female chieftains, see Piggott, *Kingship*, p. 39.

42. On *saisei-itchi*, see Kitagawa, "*Matsuri*," p.117. On "manifest *kami*," see Kitagawa, "The Shadow of the Sun," p. 110.

43. Kuroda, pp. 1, 3, 5–6, 19–20. *Nihon shoki*, 19.77–78.

44. Kamstra, p. 55. The *Book of Changes* (*Zhou yi zhengyi*, 3.36) says, "The sage uses way of the spirits [C: *shendao;* J: *shintō*] to exert cultural influence, and All-Under-Heaven obeys."

45. For Ise, see Piggott, *Japanese Kingship*, p. 62. For immigrant priests, see Ueda Masaaki, *Kikajin*, pp. 141–142. See also Ienaga Saburō, ed., *Nihon Bukkyōshi*, p. 112.

46. Farris, *Sacred Texts*, p. 235. Roy Andrew Miller, "Linguistic Evidence," p. 113. Han Sheng (*Yimin yanjiu*, pp. 22–23) traces the Japanese *be* system, via the Korean peninsula, to roots in Northern and Southern dynasty *buqu*. For Xianbei tribal divisions, see *Jin shu*, 108.2803. On *buqu*, see Wang Yitong, p. 152.

47. Piggott, *Kingship*, p. 55. See also Inoue Mitsusada, "Ritsuryō kokkagun," p. 132.

48. *Ryō no gige*, 6.205. See also Takikawa Masajirō, pp. 324–325; Yamao Yukihisa, *Ni-Chō kankei*, p. 467.

49. See Shi Dongchu, *Zhong-Ri Fojiao*, p. 292; *Shoku Nihongi*, vol. 3, p. 493, supplementary note 18.21.

50. Lewin, "Japanese and Korean," pp. 405–406.

51. Maher, pp. 31–32, 34, 39–41; Yamao Yukihisa, *Ni-Chō kankei*, pp. 494, 498. On the incipient linguistic differentiation from southern Korea, see Ueda Masaaki, *Ronkyū*, p. 15.

52. Roy Andrew Miller, *The Japanese Language*, p. 147.

53. Hudson, pp. 4, 82–102.

54. Stanlaw, p. 61.

55. See McCormack, pp. 267–268; Yamao Yukihisa, *Ni-Chō kankei*, p. 493.

56. Piggott, *Kingship*, pp. 45, 62, 96–99. See also Kitagawa, "The Shadow of the Sun," p. 100; Wheatley and See, p. 91.

57. Wang Zhenping, *Han-Tang Zhong-Ri guanxi*, p. 3; Yang Tingfu, p. 174. For the Sui expedition to an island tentatively identified as Taiwan, see Bingham, p. 25; Wang Gungwu, "Nanhai," pp. 64–65; Wang Liping, pp. 12–14.

58. On the naval battle, see *Samguk sagi*, vol. 2, p. 81 (Paekche Basic Annals 6). For a sampling of historical assessments, see Arano Yasunori, pp. 18–19; Batten, "Foreign Threat," pp. 200, 208–219; Inoue Mitsusada, "Ritsuryō kokkagun," pp. 138–140; Seki Akira, pp. 28–29, 31.

59. Mōri Hisashi, pp. 26–28; Suzuki Hideo, p. 334.

60. Gao Mingshi, *Jiaoyuquan*, pp. 42–43; Naoki Kōjirō, pp. 221, 231–241; Ōmachi Ken, p. 325.

61. On household registration in early Japan, see Chen Shuifeng, p. 85;

Hayakawa Jirō, p. 16. For the text of the Nara land law, consult *Ryō no gige*, 3.107, 110. Shi Lihua (pp. 48–49, 56) has a detailed comparison between the Tang and Nara land laws. On the use of Japanese material to reconstruct the Tang code, see Gao Mingshi, *Jiaoyuquan*, p. 43. The reconstructed text of the Tang land law is translated in Twitchett, *Financial Administration*, pp. 124–135.

62. Ōmachi Ken, p. 333; Wang Jinlin, *Nara bunka*, p. 210; Yamamoto Yukihiko, p. 33.

63. For examples, see Hayakawa Shōhachi, pp. 214–215; Farris, *Population*, p. 17. Yoshida Takashi (p. 41) argues that the Japanese system emphasized practical functions over ideals.

64. Ishida Ichirō, p. 42; Wang Jiahua, *Rujia sixiang*, p. 233.

65. *Nihon shoki*, 22.142–143.

66. Inoue Mitsusada, *Nihon kodai kokka*, p. 15; Lin Wenyue, p. 372.

67. Piggott, *Kingship*, pp. 82–92; Suzuki Yasutami, p. 226.

68. *Shoku Nihongi*, 4.124–127. *Keikokushū*, 20.381.

69. "Iken jūni kajō" (Twelve Suggestions), in *Honchō monzui chūshaku*, 2.233, 2.239.

70. *Ritsu*, 1.2–4. For ritual in administrative law, see Gao Mingshi, *Jiaoyuquan*, p. 58; Takikawa Masajirō, pp. 305, 323–333; Yamao Yukihisa, "Shomin no shūzoku," p. 95. On criminal law, see Wang Jiahua, *Nitchū jugaku*, pp. 78–84.

71. On Nara conceptions, see Fujiwara Masami, pp. 48–49. Sugawara no Fumitoki's argument is recorded in *Honchō monzui chūshaku*, 2.154–158. Pardons are tabulated in *Ruijū kokushi*, 86.501–510.

72. On omens, see Takikawa Masajirō, p. 330; Farris, *Population*, p. 52. The edict of 888 is from *Ruijū sandai kyaku*, 17.525–26. For the solution of 705, see *Shoku Nihongi*, 3.84–85.

73. The decree of 757 comes from *Shoku Nihongi*, 20.174–175. The examination essay is reproduced in *Keikokushū*, 20.375–76.

74. *Shoku Nihongi*, 20.182–183. For the Tang precedent, see *Xin Tang shu*, 5.144.

75. *Ryō no gige*, 2.102–103. *Shoku Nihongi*, 2.60–61; 4.128–129; 5.184–185; 6.216–219.

76. The award of 757 is in *Ruijū kokushi*, 107.59. Fujiwara no Muchimaro's observation comes from "Kaden," pt. 2, p. 882.

77. Mannheim, p. 19. On the "land of gentlemen," see *Shoku Nihongi*, 3.80–81. For Saichō, see "Dengyō daishi shōrai mokuroku," p. 382. Sugawara no Michizane's remark comes from *Honchō monzui*, 9.210.

78. *Xin Tang shu*, 112.4160; Miyakawa Hisayuki, "Confucianization," p. 40.

79. Wells, pp. 193–194. For Sugawara's role in terminating the embassy of 894, see Borgen, pp. 240–253.

80. For the "spirit of Japan," see Pollack, pp. 58–59. Chinese models for Heian "national culture" are enumerated in Enomoto Junichi, pp. 154–159.

81. Borgen, pp. 69–88; Shi Jiaming, p. 42; Wang Jiahua, *Rujia sixiang*, pp. 39–43. Miyoshi Kiyotsura is quoted from *Honchō monzui*, 2.285.

82. On the breakdown of the Japanese land allocation system, see Kiley, "Provincial administration," p. 278; Shi Jiaming, p. 40; Yamamoto Yukihiko, pp. 39–40; Yoshida Takashi, p. 217. For its pivotal role in "the gradual emergence of a feudal style of government," see Duus, pp. 31–36.

83. Sansom, pp. 103–104.

84. For the rise of "*shōen*" in mid-Tang China, see Qiu Tiansheng, p. 7.

85. Hayashiya Tatsusaburō, p. 22. For the shogunate, see John Whitney Hall, *Government and Local Power*, pp. 152–154, 200–201, 359–360.

86. Examples of investiture with the title of *shogun* are in Mōri Hisashi, p. 8; Wang Liping, p. 7. For *bakufu*, see Hucker, pp. 336–337; *Cefu yuangui*, 716.8511.

87. Bowersock, p. 7.

88. Piggott, *Kingship*, p. 167; Tsuji Zennosuke, *Nihon bunka shi*, pp. 257–273; Yoshida Takashi, p. 29.

89. *Shoku Nihongi*, 9.156–157. See also Piggott, *Kingship*, p. 244. For Buddhism, see Tsuji Zennosuke, *Nihon bukkyōshi*, pp. 109, 113.

90. Anazawa and Manome, p. 382; Nishijima Sadao, *Kokusai kankyō*, pp. 76–80; Wang Jinlin, *Han-Tang wenhua*, pp. 158–159.

91. Ishida Ichirō, p. 37.

92. *Nihon shoki*, 25.233.

93. *Sui shu*, 81.1827. Xu Xianyao ("Sui-Wo bangjiao xinkao," pp. 529–530) discusses the awkward predicament in which this put ambassadors.

94. Piggott, *Kingship*, pp. 8–9. On England, see Canny, p. 1. For Japan's self-image as a Chinese-style Middle Kingdom, see Morris-Suzuki, "Descent," p. 83; Zhu Yunying, pp. 286–287.

95. *Shoku Nihongi*, 1.10–11, 16–17. The embassy of 659 is recorded in *Nihon shoki*, 26.270–271.

96. *Shoku Nihongi*, 3.92–95. See Yamao Yukihisa, *Ni-Chō kankei*, pp. 474–475.

97. *Keikokushū*, 20.354, 356. On the Paekche court in exile, see Piggott, *Kingship*, p. 117.

98. The "trickle down" theory is Fujiwara Atsumitsu's (1063–1145), from *Honchō zokumonzui*, 3.516. Piggott (*Kingship*, pp. 153–154) calls the governors "cultural emissaries."

99. *Shoku Nihongi*, 5.160–161. Nishibeppu Ganjitsu, p. 431.

100. Varley, trans., *Chronicle*, pp. 10, 91.

CHAPTER NINE

1. For An Lushan, see *Xin Tang shu*, 225a.6411–6421.

2. Pulleyblank, *Background*, pp. 7–23. Pan Yihong (*Son of Heaven*, p. 155) writes that "except for Jiannan, all the Military Commissioners were non-Chinese."

3. Peterson, pp. 151–152. Institutional changes in the wake of An Lushan's rebellion are detailed by Liu Houbin. For a survey of the profound social, political, and economic transformations that began in the mid-Tang, see Qiu Tiansheng.

4. Beckwith, pp. 177–178, 182, 192.

5. Elvin, preface.

6. On the reduced expectations of late imperial government, see Eastman, pp. 133–134; Hartwell, pp. 395, 404; Schirokauer and Hymes, pp. 2–3, 12–31, 48–51; Twitchett, "Introduction," pp. 18–19. Mungello (pp. 89–90) credits contemporary China for inspiring the French expression "laissez-faire." The precise origins of the term are obscure, but it is commonly attributed to the school known as the physiocrats, among whom Francois Quesnay, in his admiring *Le despotisme de la Chine* (1767), did insist on the existence of so-called natural laws, to which "men can add nothing but confusion." In particular, he argued, "the natural policy with respect to commerce, then, is free and extensive competition" (translated in Maverick, pp. 274, 296). This foreshadows Adam Smith's later (1776) "invisible hand."

7. The atrophy of imperial public service is discussed in Eastman, pp. 107–112. For the modern nationalist critique, see Bergère, pp. 371–372; John Fitzgerald, "Misconceived Revolution," p. 326.

8. Reischauer, *Ennin's Travels,* p. 268.

9. Taylor, *Birth of Vietnam,* p. 4.

10. Wang Chengwen, "Liu zu Hui Neng," p. 13.

11. For Sui China, see Twitchett, "Population," p. 35; Zhao and Chen, pp. 137, 145, table 3.2. For Japan, see Farris, *Population,* p. 8. For Vietnam, see Taylor, *Birth of Vietnam,* pp. 176–181. For Korea, see *Samguk sagi,* vol. 1, p. 413 (Koguryŏ Basic Annals 10), vol. 2, p. 80 (Paekche Basic Annals 6), and pp. 230, 232 (treatise 6); *Xin Tang shu,* 220.6197.

12. Darwin, p. 735.

13. Cavalli-Sforza, pp. 104, 106, 108–109.

14. Hendry, p. 348. "The End of History" was the title of a controversial article (and, later, book) by Francis Fukuyama.

15. Yunxiang Yan, pp. 72–76.

16. Keyes, pp. 27–28.

17. Bentley, p. 19

18. Cumings, pp. 19–20. Pollack, p. 57.

19. Kim Tal-su, p. 64.

20. Deuchler, pp. 12–14. See Haboush, "Confucianization," p. 85.

21. Kitō Kiyoaki, p. 149.

22. Ienaga Saburō ("Asuka, hakuhō bunka," p. 343) describes the limited early spread of continental forms. For later Chinese-style fashions in Japan, see Lin Wenyue, p. 373; Helen McCullough, *Brocade,* pp. 1–72; Song Qi, p. 43.

23. Wang Jiahua, *Rujia sixiang,* pp. 266–270.

24. Madsen, pp. 210, 214.

25. Emerson, p. 149.
26. Hudson, p. 13. Morris-Suzuki, "Descent," p. 82.
27. Kohl and Ttsetskhladze, pp. 150–151.
28. For Rome, see McNeill, *Rise of the West,* pp. 313–314.
29. Harrell, p. 35.
30. Dunnell, p. 9.
31. Robertson, p. 128.
32. Kawakatsu Yoshio, *Chūgoku no rekishi,* pp. 54–55.
33. Ikeda On, "Zui-Tō sekai," pp. 4–5.
34. *Tang hui yao,* 100.1798. See also Wang Gungwu, "Nanhai Trade," p. 92, note 14.

SELECT BIBLIOGRAPHY

CLASSICAL EAST ASIAN SOURCES CITED
(ALPHABETIZED BY TITLE)

Annam chi luoc (A Brief Chronicle of Vietnam). By Le Tac. 1340; Beijing: Zhonghua shuju, 1995.

Bo wu zhi (An Account of Many Things). By Zhang Hua (232–300). Taibei: Taiwan Zhonghua shuju, 1983.

Cao Jiazhi Jin ji (Chronicle of the Jin Dynasty, by Cao Jiazhi). *Jin ji jiben.* Ed. by Tang Qiu. 4th century; N.p.: Guangya shuju congshu, n.d.

Cefu yuangui (The Great Tortoise of Archives). Ca. 1012; Taibei: Taiwan Zhonghua shuju, 1981.

Chen shu (Dynastic History of the Chen). By Yao Silian. 636; Beijing: Zhonghua shuju, 1972.

Chu Sanzang jiji (Collected Records from the Tripitaka). By Seng You. 515; Beijing: Zhonghua shuju, 1995.

Chu xue ji (Record of Initial Learning). Ed. by Xu Jian (659–729). Beijing: Zhonghua shuju, 1962.

Chunqiu fanlu (Luxuriant Gems of the Spring and Autumn). By Dong Zhongshu (ca. 195–105 B.C.). Taibei: Taiwan Zhonghua shuju, 1965.

Chunqiu Gongyang zhuan, zhushu (The Annotated Gongyang Commentary to the Spring and Autumn Annals). *Shi san jing zhushu.* Ed. by Ruan Yuan (1764–1849). Taibei: Dahua shuju, 1982.

Chunqiu Zuo zhuan, zhengyi (The Correct Meaning of the Zuo Commentary to the Spring and Autumn Annals). *Shi san jing zhushu.* Ed. by Ruan Yuan (1764–1849). Taibei: Dahua shuju, 1982.

Da Tang liudian (Six Canons of Great Tang). Guyi Congshu photocopy of 1134 ed. 738; Beijing: Zhonghua shuju, 1984.

Dai Viet su ky toan thu (Complete Historical Records of Great Vietnam). By Ngo Si Lien. 1479; Tokyo: Tōkyō daigaku tōyō bunka kenkyūsho fuzoku, 1986.

Deng Can Jin ji (Annals of the Jin Dynasty, by Deng Can). *Jin ji jiben.* Ed. by Tang Qiu. 4th century; N.p.: Guangya shuju congshu, n.d.

"Dengyō daishi shōrai mokuroku" (Catalog [of Books] Brought [to Japan] by Saichō). *Dengyō daishi zenshū.* 805; Tokyo: Sekai seiten kankō kyōkai, 1989.

Dong guan Han ji (Eastern Library Chronicle of the Han Dynasty). Attributed to Liu Zhen. Ca. 175; Taibei: Taiwan Zhonghua shuju, 1965.

Dong-Han huiyao (Institutes of the Eastern Han). By Xu Tianlin. 13th century; Shanghai: Shanghai guji chubanshe, 1978.

Ebyō Tendai gishū (Collection [Documenting] the Dependence on Tiantai Doctrine of All the Sects of Great Tang and Silla). By Saichō. *Dengyō daishi zenshū.* 813; Tokyo: Sekai seiten kankō kyōkai, 1989.

"Eizan Daishiden" (Biography of the Great Master of Mt. Hiei). By Ichijō Chū. *Dengyō daishi zenshū.* 9th century; Tokyo: Sekai seiten kankō kyōkai, 1989.

Fozu tongji (Complete Record of the Buddha and Patriarchs). By Zhipan. *Da Zangjing* (Photo-reprint of the Taishō Tripitaka). T.49. 1269; Taibei: Zhonghua Fojiao wenhuaguan, 1957.

Gao seng zhuan (Biographies of Eminent Monks). By Huijiao. Ca. 530; Taibei: Huiwentang, 1987.

Genkō shakusho (History of Buddhism [Compiled during] the Genkō Era). By Kokan Shiren. Shintei zōho kokushi taikei, vol. 31. Ca. 1322; Tokyo: Yoshikawa kōbunkan, 1930.

Guan zi (Master Guan). Attributed to Guan Zhong (d. 645 B.C.). Taibei: Taiwan Zhonghua shuju, 1965.

Guang hong ming ji (Extended Collection Expanding Illumination). By Daoxuan (596–667). Taibei: Taiwan Zhonghua shuju, 1966.

Haedong kosŭng chŏn (Biographies of Eminent Monks from East of the Sea [Korea]). By Kakhun. Reprinted in Chang Hwi-ok. *Haedong kosŭng chŏn yŏn'gu.* 1215; Seoul: Minjoksa, 1991.

Han Changli quanji (Collected Works of Han Yu). By Han Yu (768–824). Beijing: Zhongguo shudian, 1991.

Han ji (Chronicles of the Han Dynasty). By Xun Yue. A.D. 200; Taibei: Taiwan shangwu yinshuguan, 1974.

Han shu (Dynastic History of the [Former] Han). By Ban Gu (A.D. 32–93). Beijing: Zhonghua shuju, 1962.

Han yuan (Literary Collection). By Zhang Chujin. 660; Tokyo: Yoshikawa kōbunkan, 1977.

Honchō monzui, chūshaku (The Annotated Essential Literature of Our Dynasty). Attributed to Fujiwara no Akihira (989–1066). Ed. by Kakimura Shigematsu. Ca. 1037–1045; Tokyo: Fuzambō, 1968.

Honchō zokumonzui (Continued Essential Writings of Our Dynasty). Edition attributed to Fujiwara no Suetsuna. Kōchū Nihon bungaku taikei, vol. 24. 12th century; Tokyo: Kokumin tosho, 1927.

Hong ming ji (Collection Expanding Illumination). By Seng You (435–518). Taibei: Taiwan Zhonghua shuju, 1983.

Hou-Han shu (Dynastic History of the Later Han). By Fan Ye (398–445). Beijing: Zhonghua shuju, 1965.

Huai nan zi (The Master from Huai nan). Attributed to Liu An. 139 B.C.; Taibei: Taiwan Zhonghua shuju, 1965.

Huan zi xinlun (New Discourse of Master Huan). By Huan Tan (43 B.C.–A.D. 28). Taibei: Taiwan Zhonghua shuju, 1976.

Huayang guo zhi, jiaobu tuzhu (The Revised and Supplemented Chronicles of the States South of Mount Hua [in Sichuan], with Notes and Maps). By Chang Qu (291–361). Shanghai: Shanghai guji chubanshe, 1987.

Jin shu (Dynastic History of the Jin). Ed. by Fang Xuanling. 644; Beijing: Zhonghua shuju, 1974.

Jin wen gui (Return to Jin Literature). Ed. by Zhong Xing. Ca. 1600; Taibei: Taiwan shangwu yinshuguan, 1973.

Jiu Tang shu (Old Dynastic History of the Tang). By Liu Xu (887–946). Beijing: Zhonghua shuju, 1975.

"Kaden" ([Fujiwara] Family Biography). *Nara ibun.* Ed. by Takeuchi Rizō. Ca. 764; Tokyo: Tōkyōdō shuppan, 1962.

Keikokushū (Collection for Ordering the State). Ed. by Yoshimine no Yasuyo et al. Kōchū Nihon bungaku taikei, vol. 24. 827; Tokyo: Kokumin tosho, 1927.

Koryŏ sa (History of Koryŏ). By Chŏng In-ji. 1451; Seoul: Kyŏngin munhwasa, 1981.

Kuaiji zhi ([Local] Gazetteer for Kuaiji [Commandery]). By Shi Su. 1201; Shaoxing, 1926.

Kun xue jiwen (Tidings of Difficult Learning). By Wang Yinglin (1223–1296). Shanghai: Shangwu yinshuguan, 1935.

Li ji, jinzhu jinyi (The Newly Annotated and Translated Book of Rites). Ed. by Wang Meng'ou. Taibei: Taiwan shangwu yinshuguan, 1984.

Liang shu (Dynastic History of the Liang). By Yao Silian (557–637). Beijing: Zhonghua shuju, 1973.

Liu Hedong quanji (The Collected Works of Liu Zongyuan). By Liu Zongyuan (773–819). Beijing: Zhongguo shudian, 1991.

Lü shi chunqiu, jinzhu jinyi (The Newly Annotated and Newly Interpreted Spring and Autumn of Master Lü). Annotated by Lin Pinshi. Ca. 239 B.C.; Taibei: Taiwan shangwu yinshuguan, 1989.

Lun heng (Balancing of Essays). By Wang Chong. A.D. 82; Taibei: Taiwan Zhonghua shuju, 1981.

Lunyu zhushu (The Annotated Analects). *Shi san jing zhushu.* Ed. by Ruan Yuan (1764–1849). Taibei: Dahua shuju, 1982.

Luoyang qielan ji (A Record of Buddhist Temples in Luoyang). By Yang Xuanzhi. Ca. 550; Beijing: Zhonghua shuju, 1991.

Meng zi zhushu (The Annotated Mencius). *Shi san jing zhushu.* Ed. by Ruan Yuan (1764–1849). 4th century B.C.; Taibei: Dahua shuju, 1982.

Nanhai jigui neifa zhuan, jiaozhu (An Annotated Record of a Return from the South Seas with the Inner [i.e., Buddhist] Doctrines). By Yijing (635–713). Beijing: Zhonghua shuju, 1995.

Nan shi (History of the Southern Dynasties). By Li Yanshou. Ca. 629; Beijing: Zhonghua shuju, 1975.

"Nan Tenjiku baramon sōjō hi" (Inscription for the Brahmin High Priest from Southern India). *Nara ibun.* Ed. by Takeuchi Rizō. Tokyo: Tōkyōdō shuppan, 1967.

Nian er shi zhaji (Notes to Twenty-Two Histories). By Zhao Yi. 1795; Taibei: Huashi chubanshe, 1977.

Nihon ryōiki (Tales of the Miraculous in Japan). By Keikai (Kyōkai). Shin Nihon koten bungaku taikei, vol. 30. Ca. 800; Tokyo: Iwanami shoten, 1996.

Nihon shoki (Chronicles of Japan). Shintei zōho kokushi taikei (fukyūban). 720; Tokyo: Yoshikawa kōbunkan, 1993.

Qiaozi faxun (Model Instructions of Master Qiao). By Qiao Zhou (201–270). *Yuhan shanfang ji yishu.* Ed. by Ma Guohan. N.p.: Chunan xiangyuantang, 1884.

(Qin ding) Quan Tang wen ([Imperially Commissioned] Complete Writings of the Tang Dynasty). Ed. by Dong Gao. 1814; Taibei: Datong shuju, 1979.

Quan Jin wen (Complete Writings of the Jin Dynasty). *Quan shanggu, Sandai, Qin, Han, Sanguo Liuchao wen.* Ed. by Yan Kejun (1762–1843). Kyoto: Chūbun shuppansha, 1981.

Quoc-su di-bien (Posthumous National History [of the Nguyen Dynasty]). By Phan Thuc-truc. 1852; Hong Kong: Chinese University, Xin-Ya yanjiusuo, 1965.

Ritsu (The [Yōrō] Penal Code). Compiled by Fujiwara no Fuhito et al. Shintei zōho kokushi taikei, vol. 22. 718; Yoshikawa kōbunkan, 1966.

Rongzhai suibi (Miscellaneous Notes from a Capacious Studio). By Hong Mai (1123–1202). Taibei: Dali chubanshe, 1981.

Ruijū kokushi (Categorized National Histories). Compiled by Sugawara no Michizane. Shintei zōho kokushi taikei, vols. 5–6. Ca. 892; Yoshikawa kōbunkan, 1965.

Ruijū sandai kyaku (Categorized Regulations from Three Reigns). Shintei zōho kokushi taikei, vol. 25. Tokyo: Yoshikawa kōbunkan, 1965.

Ryō no gige (Commentary to the [Yōrō] Administrative Code). By Kiyowara no Natsuno. Shintei zōho kokushi taikei (fukyūban). 833; Tokyo: Yoshikawa kōbunkan, 1972.

Samguk sagi (Historical Record of the Three [Korean] Kingdoms). By Kim Pusik. Annotated trans. by Ch'oe Ho. 1145; Seoul: Hongsin munhwasa, 1994.

Samguk yusa (Memorabilia from the Three [Korean] Kingdoms). By Iryŏn.

Da Zangjing (Photo-reprint of Taishō Tripitaka). T.49. 1280; Taibei: Zhonghua Fojiao wenhuaguan, 1957.

San guo zhi (Chronicles of the [Chinese] Three Kingdoms). By Chen Shou (233–297). Beijing: Zhonghua shuju, 1959.

Shan hai jing, jiaozhu (Annotated Classic of the Mountains and Seas). Ed. by Yuan Ke. Shanghai: Shanghai guji chubanshe, 1980.

Shang jun shu, zhuyi (The Annotated and Interpreted Book of Lord Shang). Annotated by Gao Heng. Ca. 3rd century B.C.; Beijing: Zhonghua shuju, 1974.

Shang shu zhengdu (Correct Reading of the Book of Documents). Ed. by Zeng Yunqian. Hong Kong: Zhonghua shuju, 1972.

Shi ji (Records of the Grand Historian). By Sima Qian (145–ca. 90 B.C.). Beijing: Zhonghua shuju, 1959.

Shiliu guo chunqiu, jibu (The Supplemented Spring and Autumn of the Sixteen Kingdoms). By Cui Hong (d. 525). *Ye shi jingpin,* vol. 1. Changsha: Yuelu shushe, 1996.

Shishuo xinyu, jiaojian (Revised Commentary to A New Account of Tales of the World). By Liu Yiqing (403–444). Modern ed. by Xu Zhen'e. Hong Kong: Zhonghua shuju, 1987.

Shoku Nihongi (Continued Chronicles of Japan). Ed. by Sugano no Mamichi et al. Shin Nihon koten bungaku taikei, vol. 12. 797; Tokyo: Iwanami shoten, 1989.

Shui jing zhu (Annotated Classic of Rivers). By Li Daoyuan. Ca. 520; Shanghai: Shanghai guji chubanshe, 1990.

Shuihudi Qin mu zhujian (Bamboo Documents from the Qin Grave at Shuihudi). Ed. by Shuihudi Qin mu zhujian zhengli xiaozu. Beijing: Wenwu chubanshe, 1978.

Shuo yuan (Garden of Sayings). By Liu Xiang (77–6 B.C.). Taibei: Taiwan Zhonghua shuju, 1977.

Song shu (Dynastic History of the [Liu-]Song). By Shen Yue (441–513). Beijing: Zhonghua shuju, 1974.

Sui shu (Dynastic History of the Sui). By Wei Zheng (580–643). Beijing: Zhonghua shuju, 1973.

Taiping guangji (Extensive Records [Assembled during] the Taiping Era [976–984]). 978; Beijing: Zhonghua shuju, 1981.

Taiping yulan ([Encyclopedia Assembled for] Imperial Inspection during the Taiping Era). 983; Taibei: Taiwan shangwu yinshuguan, 1980.

Tang huiyao (Institutes of Tang). By Wang Pu (922–982). Taibei: Taiwan shangwu yinshuguan, 1968.

Tang lü shuyi (An Annotated Discussion of the Tang Penal Code). Compiled by Changsun Wuji. A.D. 653; Taibei: Taiwan shangwu yinshuguan, 1990.

"Tō dai-oshō tōseiden" (Record of the Great Tang Priest's Eastward Expedition). By Ōmi no Mifune (722–785). *Nara ibun.* Ed. by Takeuchi Rizō. Tokyo: Tōkyōdō shuppan, 1967.

Tong dian (Comprehensive Canons). By Du You (735–812). Beijing: Zhonghua shuju, 1984.

Tōrei shūi (Collected Fragments of the Tang Administrative Code). Compiled
by Niida Noboru. 1933; Tōkyō daigaku shuppankai, 1964.

Viet su luoc (A Brief History of Vietnam). Anonymous. Shoushan'ge congshu,
1; Baibu congshu jicheng, series 52. 14th century; Taibei: Yiwen yinshuguan, 1968.

Wei shu (Dynastic History of the [Northern] Wei). By Wei Shou (506–572).
Beijing: Zhonghua shuju, 1974.

Wenxian tongkao (Thorough Examination of Literary Offerings). By Ma
Duanlin. 13th century; Shanghai: Shangwu yinshuguan, 1936.

"Wuli lun" (On the Principles of Things). By Yang Quan. *Longxi jingshe congshu*. Ed. by Zheng Guoxun. 3rd century; Shanghai: Shanghai guji shudian, 1962.

Wu-Yue chunqiu (Annals of Wu and Yue). By Zhao Ye. 1st century; Taibei:
Taiwan Zhonghua shuju, 1980.

Xin Tang shu (New Dynastic History of the Tang). By Ouyang Xiu (1007–
1072) and Song Qi. Beijing: Zhonghua shuju, 1975.

Xun zi (Master Xun). By Xun Qing (313–238 B.C.). Taibei: Taiwan Zhonghua shuju, 1965.

Yan shi jiaxun (Family Instructions for the Yan Clan). By Yan Zhitui (531–
591). Taibei: Taiwan Zhonghua shuju, 1974.

Yan tie lun (Discourses on Salt and Iron). By Huan Kuan. 81 B.C.; Shanghai:
Shanghai guji chubanshe, 1990.

Yue jue shu (The Book of Peerless Yue). Anonymous. *Ye shi jingpin*, vol. 1. 1st
century; Changsha: Yuelu shushe, 1996.

Zang Rongxu Jin shu (History of the Jin Dynasty, by Zang Rongxu). *Jiu jia jiu
Jin shu jiben*. Ed. by Tang Qiu. Late 5th century; N.p.: Guangya shuju
congshu, n.d.

Zhan guo ce (Intrigues of the Warring States). Attributed to Liu Xiang (77–
6 B.C.). Taibei: Taiwan Zhonghua shuju, 1965.

Zhenguan zhengyao (Essentials of Government from the Zhenguan Reign Period [627–650]). By Wu Jing. Ca. 707; Taibei: Hongye shuju, 1990.

Zhou yi zhengyi (The Correct Meaning of the Book of Changes). *Shi san jing
zhushu*. Ed. by Ruan Yuan (1764–1849). Taibei: Dahua shuju, 1982.

Zizhi tongjian, jinzhu (A New Commentary to the Comprehensive Mirror
for Aid in Governance). By Sima Guang (1019–1086). Taibei: Taiwan
shangwu yinshuguan, 1966.

MODERN SOURCES (CITED, OR ESPECIALLY RELEVANT)

Ames, Roger T. *The Art of Rulership: A Study of Ancient Chinese Political Thought.*
Albany: State University of New York Press, 1994.

Amino Yoshihiko. "Emperor, Rice, and Commoners." *Multicultural Japan: Pa-*

laeolithic to Postmodern. Ed. by Donald Denoon et al. Cambridge: Cambridge University Press, 1996.

————. *Nihon shakai no rekishi* (A History of Japanese Society). 3 vols. Tokyo: Iwanami shoten, 1997.

Amory, Patrick. *People and Identity in Ostrogothic Italy, 489–554.* Cambridge: Cambridge University Press, 1997.

An Zuozhang. "Cong Shuihudi Qin mu zhujian kan Qin-dai de nongye jingji" (The Agricultural Economy of the Qin Dynasty as Seen from the Bamboo Tablets in the Qin Grave at Shuihudi). *Qin-Han shi luncong,* vol. 1. Xi'an: Shaanxi renmin chubanshe, 1981.

Anazawa Wakou and Manome Jun'ichi. "Two Inscribed Swords from Japanese Tumuli: Discoveries and Research on Finds from the Sakitama-Inariyama and Eta-Funayama Tumuli." *Windows on the Japanese Past: Studies in Archaeology and Prehistory.* Ed. by Richard J. Pearson et al. Ann Arbor: Center for Japanese Studies, University of Michigan, 1986.

Anderson, Benedict. *Imagined Communities: Reflections on the Origin and Spread of Nationalism.* 1983; London: Verso, 1991.

Arakawa Masaharu. "Tō teikoku to Sogudo jin no kōeki katsudō" (The Tang Empire and Sogdian Commercial Activity). *Tōyōshi-kenkyū,* 56.3 (1997).

Arano Yasunori, Ishii Masatoshi, and Murai Shōsuke. "Jiki kubun ron" (On Periodization). *Ajia no naka no Nihonshi, 1, Ajia to Nihon.* Tokyo: Tōkyō daigaku shuppankai, 1992.

Armstrong, John A. *Nations before Nationalism.* Chapel Hill: University of North Carolina Press, 1982.

Asakawa, Kan'ichi. *The Early Institutional Life of Japan: A Study in the Reform of 645 A.D.* New York: Paragon Book Reprint Corp., 1963.

Aston, W. G., trans. *Nihongi: Chronicles of Japan from the Earliest Times to A.D. 697.* 1896; Rutland: Charles E. Tuttle Company, 1972.

Backus, Charles. *The Nan-Chao Kingdom and T'ang China's Southwestern Frontier.* Cambridge: Cambridge University Press, 1981.

Bai Cuiqin. "Wei-Jin nanbeichao minzuguan chutan" (An Initial Inquiry into the Ethnic Views of the Wei-Jin, Northern and Southern Dynasties). *Minzu yanjiu* (1993.5).

Balazs, Etienne. *Chinese Civilization and Bureaucracy.* H. M. Wright, trans. New Haven, Conn.: Yale University Press, 1964.

Banton, Michael. "The Direction and Speed of Ethnic Change." *Ethnic Change.* Ed. by Charles F. Keyes. Seattle: University of Washington Press, 1981.

Barber, Benjamin R. *Jihad vs. McWorld.* New York: Times Books, 1995.

Barber, Elizabeth Wayland. *The Mummies of Ürümchi.* New York: W. W. Norton, 1999.

Barfield, Thomas J. *The Perilous Frontier: Nomadic Empires and China, 221 B.C. to A.D. 1757.* Cambridge, Mass.: Blackwell Publishers, 1989.

Barnes, Gina L. *China Korea and Japan: The Rise of Civilization in East Asia.* London: Thames and Hudson, 1993.

Batten, Bruce L. "Foreign Threat and Domestic Reform: The Emergence of the *Ritsuryō* State." *Monumenta Nipponica,* 41.2 (1986).

———. "Provincial Administration in Early Japan: From *Ritsuryō kokka* to *Ōchō kokka.*" *Harvard Journal of Asiatic Studies,* 53.1 (1993).

Beckwith, Christopher I. *The Tibetan Empire in Central Asia: A History of the Struggle for Great Power among Tibetans, Turks, Arabs, and Chinese during the Early Middle Ages.* Princeton, N.J.: Princeton University Press, 1987.

Befu, Harumi. "Patrilineal Descent and Personal Kindred in Japan." *American Anthropologist,* 65.6 (1963).

Bellwood, Peter. *Prehistory of the Indo-Malaysian Archipelago.* 1985; Honolulu: University of Hawai'i Press, 1997.

Bentley, Jerry H. *Old World Encounters: Cross-Cultural Contacts and Exchanges in Pre-Modern Times.* New York: Oxford University Press, 1993.

Bergère, Marie-Claire. *Sun Yat-sen.* Trans. by Janet Lloyd. 1994; Stanford, Calif.: Stanford University Press, 1998.

Best, Jonathan W. "Diplomatic and Cultural Contacts between Paekche and China." *Harvard Journal of Asiatic Studies,* 42.2 (1982).

———. "Tales of Three Paekche Monks Who Traveled Afar in Search of the Law." *Harvard Journal of Asiatic Studies,* 51.1 (1991).

Bielenstein, Hans. "The Census of China during the Period 2–742 A.D." *Bulletin of the Museum of Far Eastern Antiquities,* 19 (1947).

———. "The Chinese Colonization of Fukien until the End of T'ang." *Studia Serica Berhard Karlgren Dedicata.* Ed. by Søren Egerod and Else Glahn. Copenhagen: Ejnar Munksgaard, 1959.

———. "The Restoration of the Han Dynasty, 3." *Bulletin of the Museum of Far Eastern Antiquities,* 39.2 (1967).

Bingham, Woodbridge. *The Founding of the T'ang Dynasty: The Fall of Sui and Rise of T'ang, A Preliminary Survey.* 1941; New York: Octagon Books, 1970.

Blair, Peter Hunter. *Roman Britain and Early England, 55 B.C.–A.D. 871.* New York: W. W. Norton, 1963.

Blakeley, Barry B. "Chu Society and State: Image versus Reality." *Defining Chu: Image and Reality in Ancient China.* Ed. by Constance A. Cook and John S. Major. Honolulu: University of Hawai'i Press, 1999.

———. "The Geography of Chu." *Defining Chu: Image and Reality in Ancient China.* Ed. by Constance A. Cook and John S. Major. Honolulu: University of Hawai'i Press, 1999.

Bodde, Derk. "The State and Empire of Ch'in." *The Cambridge History of China. Vol. 1: The Ch'in and Han Empires, 221 B.C.–A.D. 220.* Ed. by Denis Twitchett and Michael Loewe. Cambridge: Cambridge University Press, 1986.

Bol, Peter K. *"This Culture of Ours": Intellectual Transitions in T'ang and Sung China.* Stanford, Calif.: Stanford University Press, 1992.

Boltz, William G. "Language and Writing." *The Cambridge History of Ancient*

China: From the Origins of Civilization to 221 B.C. Ed. by Michael Loewe and Edward L. Shaughnessy. Cambridge: Cambridge University Press, 1999.

Boodberg, Peter A. "The Language of the T'o-Pa Wei." *Selected Works of Peter A. Boodberg.* Ed. by Alvin P. Cohen. 1936; Berkeley and Los Angeles: University of California Press, 1979.

———. "Marginalia to the Histories of the Northern Dynasties." *Selected Works of Peter A. Boodberg.* Ed. by Alvin P. Cohen. 1938–1939; Berkeley and Los Angeles: University of California Press, 1979.

———. "Turk, Aryan and Chinese in Ancient Asia." *Selected Works of Peter A. Boodberg.* Ed. by Alvin P. Cohen. 1942; Berkeley and Los Angeles: University of California Press, 1979.

Borgen, Robert. *Sugawara no Michizane and the Early Heian Court.* Cambridge, Mass.: Harvard University Press, 1986.

Boucher, Daniel. "Gāndhārī and the Early Chinese Buddhist Translations Reconsidered: The Case of the *Saddharmapuṇḍarīkasūtra.*" *Journal of the American Oriental Society,* 118.4 (1998).

Bowersock, G. W. *Hellenism in Late Antiquity.* Ann Arbor: University of Michigan Press, 1990.

Buswell, Robert E., Jr. "Introduction: Prolegomenon to the Study of Buddhist Apocryphal Scriptures." *Chinese Buddhist Apocrypha.* Ed. by Robert E Buswell, Jr. Honolulu: University of Hawai'i Press, 1990.

Cai Xuehai. "Xi-Jin zhongzu bianluan xilun" (An Analysis of Ethnic Strife in the Western Jin). *Guoli bianyiguan guankan,* 15.2 (1986).

Canny, Nicholas. "The Origins of Empire: An Introduction." *The Oxford History of the British Empire. Vol. 1: The Origins of Empire: British Overseas Enterprise to the Close of the Seventeenth Century.* Ed. by Nicholas Canny. Oxford: Oxford University Press, 1998.

Cao Gecheng. "Zhou-dai cunshe tudi zhidu de yanbian" (The Evolution of Zhou Dynasty Village Land Systems). *Beifang luncong* (1984.1).

Cao Shibang. "Shi cheng 'wu hu yuan chu Zhongguo sheng wang zhi hou' de laiyuan" (The Origins of the Assertion in the Histories That "The Five Hu [Peoples] Sprang from Descendants of the Chinese Sage Kings"). *Shihuo yue kan,* new series, 4.9 (1974).

Cao Xian'gun. "Riben Ruxue de fazhan" (The Development of Japanese Confucianism). *Zhong-Ri wenhua lunji, xubian 1.* Ed. by Zhang Qiyun. Taibei: Zhonghua wenhua chuban shiye weiyuanhui, 1958.

Carter, Thomas Francis. *The Invention of Printing in China and Its Spread Westward.* Rev. by L. Carrington Goodrich. 1925; New York: The Ronald Press, 1955.

Cavalli-Sforza, Luigi Luca. "Genes, Peoples and Languages." *Scientific American* (Nov. 1991).

Chang, Kwang-chih. "China on the Eve of the Historical Period." *The Cambridge History of Ancient China: From the Origins of Civilization to 221 B.C.*

Ed. by Michael Loewe and Edward L. Shaughnessy. Cambridge: Cambridge University Press, 1999.

Char, S. V. R. "Dharmaraksha—A Short Biography." *Chinese Culture*, 23.3 (1982).

———. "Methods and Principles Used in Translating the Buddhist Tripitika into Chinese." *Chinese Culture*, 32.3 (1991).

Ch'en, Ch'i-yün (Chen Qiyun). *Hsün Yüeh (A.D. 148–209): The Life and Reflections of an Early Medieval Confucian*. Cambridge: Cambridge University Press, 1975.

———. *Hsün Yüeh and the Mind of Late Han China*. Princeton, N.J.: Princeton University Press, 1980.

Chen, Jo-shui. *Liu Tsung-yüan and Intellectual Change in T'ang China, 773–819*. Cambridge: Cambridge University Press, 1992.

Ch'en, Kenneth K. S. *Buddhism in China: A Historical Survey*. Princeton, N.J.: Princeton University Press, 1964.

Chen Qiyun (Ch'en Ch'i-yün). "Wei-Jin nanbeichao shiqi Zhongguo zhishi fenzi de tese" (The Special Characteristics of Chinese Intellectuals in the Wei-Jin, Northern and Southern Dynasties Period). *Guoji Hanxue huiyi lunwenji: lishi kaogu zu*. Taibei: Zhongyang yanjiuyuan, 1981.

———. "Zhongguo zhonggu 'shizu zhengzhi' kaolun zhi yi (yuanyuan lun)" (An Examination into Medieval Chinese "Literati Politics" [on Their Origins]). *Xin-Ya xuebao*, 12 (1977).

Chen, Sanping. "A-gan Revisited—The Tuoba's Cultural and Political Heritage." *Journal of Asian History*, 30.1 (1996).

Chen Shangsheng. "Tang-dai de Xinluo qiaomin shequ" (Communities of Korean Resident Aliens in the Tang Dynasty). *Lishi yanjiu* (1996.1).

Chen Shaodi. "Qin guo zhongnong zhengce jianlun: Shang Yang Qin lü yu Yunmeng chutu Qin lü de bijiao yanjiu zhi yi" (A Brief Discussion of the Qin State Policy of Emphasizing Agriculture: One Comparative Study of Shang Yang's Qin Laws with the Qin Laws Excavated from Yunmeng). *Qin-Han shi luncong*, vol. 3. Xi'an: Shaanxi renmin chubanshe, 1986.

Chen Shuifeng. *Riben wenming kaihua shi lüe* (A Brief History of the Development of Japanese Civilization). 1967; Taibei: Taiwan shangwu yinshuguan, 1993.

Chen Shuliang. *Liuchao yanshui* (Misty Waters of the Six Dynasties). Bejing: Xiandai chubanshe, 1990.

Chen Xiaojiang. "San guo shidai de renkou yidong" (Population Movement in the Three Kingdoms Period). *Shihuo banyuekan*, 1.3 (1935).

Chen Yinke. *Sui-Tang zhidu yuanyuan lüelun gao* (Draft Study of the Origins of Sui-Tang Institutions). 1944; Taibei: Taiwan shangwu yinshuguan, 1994.

———. "Tianshidao yu binhai diyu zhi guanxi" (The Way of the Heavenly Masters and Its Relationship to the Region Near the Sea). *Chen Yinke xiansheng wenshi lunji*, vol. 1. 1933; Hong Kong: Wenwen chubanshe, 1972.

Chen Yong. "Liu Yu yu Jin-Song zhi ji de hanmen shizu" (Liu Yu and the Poor Literati at the time of the Jin-Song Transition). *Lishi yanjiu* (1984.6).

Cheng Xilin. "Han-Tang guosuo yu Zhong-Ri guosuo bijiao" (Han-Tang Border Passes and a Comparison of Chinese and Japanese Border Passes). *Dunhuang yanjiu* (1998.1).

Cheng Zhangcan. *Shizu yu Liuchao wenxue* (The Hereditary Elite and Six Dynasties Literature). Harbin: Heilongjiang jiaoyu chubanshe, 1998.

Chin, Frank Fa-ken. "The Element of Regionalism in Medieval China: Observations on the Founding of the Eastern Chin." *Actes du XXIXe congrès international des orientalistes; Chine ancienne.* Paris, 1977.

Chu Ke. "Gudai Zhong-Chao liang-guo de shuji jiaoliu" (Exchange of Books between China and Korea in Antiquity). *Shulin zhanggu, xubian.* Ed. by Yun Ruxin. Hong Kong: Zhongshan tushu, 1973.

Ch'ü T'ung-Tsu. "Chinese Class Structure and Its Ideology." *Chinese Thought and Institutions.* Ed. by John K. Fairbank. Chicago: University of Chicago Press, 1957.

Coedès, George. *The Indianized States of Southeast Asia.* Trans. by Susan Brown Cowing. 1944; Honolulu: East-West Center Press, 1968.

Cohen, Myron L. "Being Chinese: The Peripheralization of Traditional Identity." *The Living Tree: The Changing Meaning of Being Chinese Today.* Ed. by Tu Wei-ming. Stanford, Calif.: Stanford University Press, 1994.

Collcutt, Martin. "The Legacy of Confucianism in Japan." *The East Asian Region: Confucian Heritage and Its Modern Adaptation.* Ed. by Gilbert Rozman. Princeton, N.J.: Princeton University Press, 1991.

Connery, Christopher Leigh. *The Empire of the Text: Writing and Authority in Early Imperial China.* Lanham, Md.: Rowman and Littlefield, 1998.

Cotterell, Arthur. *East Asia: From Chinese Predominance to the Rise of the Pacific Rim.* New York: Oxford University Press, 1993.

Cranston, Edwin A. "Asuka and Nara Culture: Literacy, Literature, and Music." *The Cambridge History of Japan. Vol. 1: Ancient Japan.* Ed. by John Whitney Hall. Cambridge: Cambridge University Press, 1993.

Creel, Herrlee Glessner. "The Eclectics of Han Thought." *The Making of China: Main Themes in Premodern Chinese History.* Ed. by Chun-shu Chang. Englewood Cliffs, N.J.: Prentice Hall, 1975.

Crossley, Pamela Kyle. *The Manchus.* Cambridge: Blackwell Publishers, 1997.

Crowell, William G. "Northern Émigrés and the Problems of Census Registration under the Eastern Jin and Southern Dynasties." *State and Society in Early Medieval China.* Ed. by Albert E. Dien. Stanford, Calif.: Stanford University Press, 1990.

Cumings, Bruce. *Korea's Place in the Sun: A Modern History.* New York: W. W. Norton, 1997.

Dai Fanyu. "Tang-dai Qinglongsi zhi jiaoxue yu Riben wenhua" (The Teachings of Tang Dynasty Qinglong Monastery and Japanese Culture). *Zhong-Ri Fojiao guanxi yanjiu.* Ed. by Zhang Mantao. 1956; Taibei: Dacheng wenhua chubanshe, 1978.

Darwin, Charles. *The Origin of Species by Charles Darwin: A Variorum Text.* Ed. by Morse Peckham. 1859; Philadelphia: University of Pennsylvania Press, 1959.

de Bary, Wm. Theodore. *East Asian Civilizations: A Dialogue in Five Stages.* Cambridge, Mass.: Harvard University Press, 1988.

de Crespigny, Rafe. *Generals of the South: The Foundation and Early History of the Three Kingdoms State of Wu.* Canberra: Australian National University, Faculty of Asian Studies Monographs No. 16, 1990.

————. *Northern Frontier: The Policies and Strategy of the Later Han Empire.* Canberra: Australian National University, Faculty of Asian Studies Monographs No. 4, 1984.

————. "Prefectures and Population in South China in the First Three Centuries A.D." *Zhongyang yanjiuyuan, lishi yuyan yanjiusuo jikan,* 40 (1968).

————. "The Three Kingdoms and Western Jin: A History of China in the Third Century A.D." *East Asian History,* 1 and 2 (1991).

————, trans. *To Establish Peace: Being the Chronicle of Later Han for the Years 189 to 220 A.D. as Recorded in Chapters 59 to 69 of the Zizhi tongjian of Sima Guang.* Canberra: Australian National University, 1996.

DeFrancis, John. *The Chinese Language: Fact and Fantasy.* Honolulu: University of Hawai'i Press, 1984.

————. *Colonialism and Language Policy in Viet Nam.* The Hague: Mouton Publishers, 1977.

Demiéville, Paul. "Le bouddhisme chinois." *Choix d'études bouddhiques (1929–1970).* 1970; Leiden: E. J. Brill, 1973.

————. "La pénétration du bouddhisme dans la tradition philosophique chinoise." *Cahiers d'histoire mondiale,* 3 (1956).

Deng Xiaonan. "Women in Turfan during the Sixth to Eighth Centuries: A Look at their Activities Outside the Home." *Journal of Asian Studies,* 58.1 (1999).

Dennerline, Jerry. *Qian Mu and the World of Seven Mansions.* New Haven, Conn.: Yale University Press, 1988.

Deuchler, Martina. *The Confucian Transformation of Korea: A Study of Society and Ideology.* Cambridge, Mass.: Harvard University Press, 1992.

Di Cosmo, Nicola. "Ancient Inner Asian Nomads: Their Economic Basis and Its Significance in Chinese History." *Journal of Asian Studies,* 53.4 (1994).

Diamond, Jared. *Guns, Germs, and Steel: The Fates of Human Societies.* New York: W. W. Norton, 1999.

Dien, Albert. "A New Look at the Xianbei and Their Impact on Chinese Culture." *Ancient Mortuary Traditions of China: Papers on Chinese Ceramic Funerary Sculptures.* Ed. by George Kuwayama. Los Angeles: Los Angeles County Museum of Art, 1991.

Dikötter, Frank. *The Discourse of Race in Modern China*. Stanford, Calif.: Stanford University Press, 1992.

Ding Yihua. "Qin shihuang de zhenggang xuanyan he xinli jilu: Qin shihuang dong xun keshi wenci pingyi" (The First Emperor of Qin's Statement of His Principles of Government and Psychological Record: A Critical Evaluation of the Language of the Stone Inscriptions from the First Emperor of Qin's Eastern Circuits). *Qin ling Qin yong yanjiu dongtai* (1992.1).

Diringer, David. *The Book before Printing: Ancient, Medieval and Oriental*. Reprint; Dover, 1982.

Dittmer, Lowell, and Kim, Samuel S. "In Search of a Theory of National Identity." *China's Quest for National Identity*. Ed. by Lowell Dittmer and Samuel S. Kim. Ithaca, N.Y.: Cornell University Press, 1993.

Dohi Yoshikazu. "A Study of a Fragmentary Tun-Huang District Land Allotment Record from the T'ien-pao Period of the T'ang Dynasty with Regard to the Problem of Land Reallotment." *Memoirs of the Research Department of the Toyo Bunko*, 42 (1984).

Du Shousu. "Wei-Jin nanbeichao de shehui jingji ji qi sixiang dongxiang" (The Social-Economy of the Wei, Jin, Northern and Southern Dynasties, and Their Intellectual Inclinations). *Wenxun yuekan*, 8.4 (1948).

Du Zhengsheng. "'Bianhu qimin' de chuxian ji qi lishi yiyi: bianhu qimin de yanjiu zhi yi" (The Appearance of the "Registration of Commoner Households" and Its Historical Significance: A Study of the Registration of Commoner Households). *Zhongyang yanjiuyuan, Lishi yuyan yanjiusuo jikan*, 54.3 (1983).

———. "Cong fengjian zhi dao junxian zhi de tudi quanshu wenti" (The Question of Property Rights, from the [Zhou] Feudal System to the [Imperial] System of Commanderies and Districts). *Shihuo yuekan*, new series, 14.9–10 (1985).

Duan Tali. "Shilun San guo shiqi dong-Wu dui Lingnan de kaifa yu zhili" (An Examination of Eastern Wu's Development and Administration of Lingnan during the Three Kingdoms Period). *Nanjing daxue xuebao: zhexue, renwen, she ke ban* (1999.1).

Duara, Prasenjit. "Bifurcating Linear History: Nation and Histories in China and India." *Positions: East Asia Cultures Critique*, 1.3 (1993).

Duiker, William J. *Vietnam: Revolution in Transition*. 2nd ed. Boulder, Colo.: Westview Press, 1995.

Dull, Jack L. "Determining Orthodoxy: Imperial Roles." *Imperial Rulership and Cultural Change in Traditional China*. Ed. by Frederick P. Brandauer and Chun-chieh Huang. Seattle: University of Washington Press, 1994.

———. "The Evolution of Government in China." *Heritage of China: Contemporary Perspectives on Chinese Civilization*. Ed. by Paul S. Ropp. Berkeley and Los Angeles: University of California Press, 1990.

Dunnell, Ruth W. *The Great State of White and High: Buddhism and State Forma-*

tion in Eleventh-Century Xia. Honolulu: University of Hawai'i Press, 1996.

Duus, Peter. *Feudalism in Japan.* 2nd ed. New York: Alfred A. Knopf, 1976.

Eastman, Lloyd E. *Family, Fields, and Ancestors: Constancy and Change in China's Social and Economic History, 1550–1949.* New York: Oxford University Press, 1988.

Eberhard, Wolfram. *Conquerors and Rulers: Social Forces in Mediaeval China.* Leiden: E. J. Brill, 1952.

————. *The Local Cultures of South and East China.* Trans. by Alide Eberhard. Leiden: E. J. Brill, 1968.

————. "The Political Function of Astronomy and Astronomers in Han China." *Chinese Thought and Institutions.* Ed. by John K. Fairbank. Chicago: University of Chicago Press, 1957.

Ebrey, Patricia Buckley. *The Aristocratic Families of Early Imperial China: A Case Study of the Po-Ling Ts'ui Family.* Cambridge: Cambridge University Press, 1978.

————. "The Chinese Family and the Spread of Confucian Values." *The East Asian Region: Confucian Heritage and Its Modern Adaptation.* Ed. by Gilbert Rozman. Princeton, N.J.: Princeton University Press, 1991.

————. "The Economic and Social History of Later Han." *The Cambridge History of China. Vol. 1: The Ch'in and Han Empires, 221 B.C.–A.D. 220.* Ed. by Denis Twitchett and Michael Loewe. Cambridge: Cambridge University Press, 1986.

————. "Estate and Family Management in the Later Han as Seen in the *Monthly Instructions for the Four Classes of People.*" *Journal of the Economic and Social History of the Orient,* 17.2 (1974).

————. "Towards a Better Understanding of the Late Han Upper Class." *State and Society in Early Medieval China.* Ed. by Albert E. Dien. Stanford, Calif.: Stanford University Press, 1990.

Edwards, R. Randle. "Imperial China's Border Control Law." *Journal of Chinese Law,* 1.1 (1987).

Eisenstadt, S. N. *The Political Systems of Empires.* New York: The Free Press of Glencoe, 1963.

Elvin, Mark. *The Pattern of the Chinese Past: A Social and Economic Interpretation.* Stanford, Calif.: Stanford University Press, 1973.

Emerson, Rupert. *From Empire to Nation: The Rise to Self-Assertion of Asian and African Peoples.* Cambridge, Mass.: Harvard University Press, 1960.

Enomoto Junichi. "'Kokufū bunka' to Chūgoku bunka: bunka inyū ni okeru chōkō to bōeki" ("National Culture" and Chinese Culture: Tribute and Trade in the Importation of Culture). *Kodai o kangaeru: Tō to Nihon.* Ed. by Ikeda On. Tokyo: Yoshikawa Kōbunkan, 1992.

Falkenhausen, Lothar Von. "The Regionalist Paradigm in Chinese Archaeology." *Nationalism, Politics, and the Practice of Archaeology.* Ed. by Philip L. Kohl and Clare Fawcett. Cambridge: Cambridge University Press, 1995.

———. "The Waning of the Bronze Age: Material Culture and Social Developments, 770–481 B.C." *The Cambridge History of Ancient China: From the Origins of Civilization to 221 B.C.* Ed. by Michael Loewe and Edward L. Shaughnessy. Cambridge: Cambridge University Press, 1999.

Fan Ning. "Lun Wei-Jin shidai zhishifenzi de sixiang fenhua ji qi shehui genyuan" (On the Differentiation of the Thought of Intellectuals in the Wei-Jin Period and Its Social Origins). *Lishi yanjiu* (1955.4).

Fang Litian. *Wei-Jin nanbeichao Fojiao luncong* (Collected Essays on Wei-Jin, Northern and Southern Dynasties Buddhism). Beijing: Zhonghua shuju, 1982.

Fang Xun. "Tang-dai Zhongguo he Yazhou ge zu de wenhua jiaoliu" (Cultural Exchange between China and Each of the Peoples of Asia during the Tang Dynasty). *Sui-Tang shi yanjiu lunji, xueshu wenhua pian.* Ed. by He Guanbiao. 1956; Hong Kong: Shixue yanjiuhui, 1979.

Fang Yaguang. *Tang-dai dui wai kaifang chutan* (A Preliminary Investigation of the Tang Dynasty's Opening to the Outside). Hefei: Huangshan shushe, 1998.

Farris, William Wayne. "Ancient Japan's Korean Connection." *Korean Studies,* 20 (1996).

———. *Heavenly Warriors: The Evolution of Japan's Military, 500–1300.* Cambridge, Mass.: Harvard University Press, 1992.

———. *Population, Disease, and Land in Early Japan, 645–900.* Cambridge, Mass.: Harvard University Press, 1985.

———. *Sacred Texts and Buried Treasures: Issues in the Historical Archaeology of Ancient Japan.* Honolulu: University of Hawai'i Press, 1998.

———. "Trade, Money, and Merchants in Nara Japan." *Monumenta Nipponica,* 53.3 (1998).

Faure, David, and Siu, Helen F. "Introduction." *Down to Earth: The Territorial Bond in South China.* Ed. by Faure and Siu. Stanford, Calif.: Stanford University Press, 1995.

Fazun. "Xizang qian-hong-qi Fojiao" (The Early Period of the Flourishing of Tibetan Buddhism). *Zhongguo Fojiao, 1.* Ed. by Zhongguo Fojiao Xiehui. Shanghai: Dongfang chuban zhongxin, 1980.

Fehl, Noah Edward. *Li: Rites and Propriety in Literature and Life: A Perspective for a Cultural History of Ancient China.* Hong Kong: Chinese University, 1971.

Feng Chengjun. *Zhongguo Nanyang jiaotong shi* (A History of Chinese Communication with the South Seas). 1937; Taibei: Taiwan shangwu yinshuguan, 1993.

Feng Chongyi. "Seeking Lost Codes in the Wilderness: The Search for a Hainanese Culture." *China Quarterly,* 160 (1999).

Feng Tianyu. "Luan shi liebian: Wei-Jin nanbeichao wenhua chuyi" (An Age of Anarchy and Division: My Humble Views on Wei-Jin, Northern and Southern Dynasties Culture). *Zhongguo wenhua yanjiu* (winter 1994).

Fitzgerald, C. P. *Barbarian Beds: The Origin of the Chair in China.* Canberra: The Australian National University, 1965.

Fitzgerald, John. *Awakening China: Politics, Culture, and Class in the Nationalist Revolution.* Stanford, Calif.: Stanford University Press, 1996.

———. "The Misconceived Revolution: State and Society in China's Nationalist Revolution, 1923–26." *Journal of Asian Studies,* 49.2 (1990).

———. "The Nationless State: The Search for a Nation in Modern Chinese Nationalism." *Chinese Nationalism.* Ed. by Jonathan Unger. Armonk, N.Y.: M. E. Sharpe, 1996.

Fletcher, Joseph. "The Mongols: Ecological and Social Perspectives." *Harvard Journal of Asiatic Studies,* 46.1 (1986).

Fogel, Joshua A. "The Sino-Japanese Controversy over *Shina* as a Toponym for China." *The Cultural Dimension of Sino-Japanese Relations: Essays on the Nineteenth and Twentieth Centuries.* Joshua A. Fogel. 1989; Armonk, N.Y.: M. E. Sharpe, 1995.

Frank, Andre Gunder. *ReOrient: Global Economy in the Asian Age.* Berkeley and Los Angeles: University of California Press, 1998.

Freedman, Maurice. "The Chinese in Southeast Asia: A Longer View." *The Study of Chinese Society: Essays by Maurice Freedman.* Ed. by G. William Skinner. 1964; Stanford, Calif.: Stanford University Press, 1979.

Friday, Karl F. *Hired Swords: The Rise of Private Warrior Power in Early Japan.* Stanford, Calif.: Stanford University Press, 1992.

Fu Kehui. "Wei-Jin nanchao huangji zhi yanjiu" (Studies of the Yellow Registers in Wei-Jin and the Southern Dynasties). *Shandong daxue xuebao: zhe she ban* (1989.1).

Fu Lecheng. "Tang-dai Yi-Xia guannian zhi yanbian" (The Evolution of the Concept of Chinese and Barbarians in the Tang Dynasty). *Han-Tang shi lunji.* 1962; Taibei: Lianjing chuban, 1977.

———. "Tang-xing wenhua yu Song-xing wenhua" (Tang-Style Culture and Song-Style Culture). *Tang-dai yanjiu lunji,* vol. 1. Ed. by Zhongguo Tang-dai xuehui. 1972; Taibei: Xin wenfeng chuban, 1992.

Fujiwara Masami. "Rekishi no naka no shōchō sekai: kodai Nihon no shūkyō shi ni okeru Bukkyō, Jukyō, Jingi, Tennō" (The Symbolic World in History: Buddhism, Confucianism, the Deities of Heaven and Earth, and the Emperor in Ancient Japanese Religious History). *Bukkyō shigaku kenkyū,* 28.1 (1985).

Fujiyoshi Masumi. "Zui-Tō Bukkyō e no shikaku" (Viewpoints on Sui-Tang Buddhism). *Chūgoku chūseishi kenkyū: Rikuchō, Zui, Tō no shakai to bunka.* Ed. by Chūgoku chūseishi kenkyūkai. Tokyo: Tōkai daigaku shuppankai, 1970.

Fukuyama, Francis. "The End of History." *National Interest,* 16 (1989).

Fumimasa-Bunga Fukui. "Buddhism and the Structure of *Ch'ing-t'an* ('Pure Discourses')—A Note on Sino-Indian Intercourse." *Chinese Culture,* 10.2 (1969).

Gao Guanru. "Zhong-wai Fojiao guanxi shilüe" (A Brief History of Sino-Foreign Buddhist Relations). *Zhongguo Fojiao, 1*. Shanghai: Dongfang chuban zhongxin, 1980.

Gao Min. "Cao-Wei shijia zhidu de xingcheng yu yanbian" (The Formation and Evolution of the Cao-Wei System of Military Families). *Lishi yanjiu* (1989.5).

———. *Qin-Han Wei-Jin nanbeichao tudi zhidu yanjiu* (Studies of the Land Systems of the Qin, Han, Wei, Jin, and Northern and Southern Dynasties). Kaifeng: Zhongzhou guji chubanshe, 1986.

———. "Wei-Jin nanbeichao fuyi huomian de duixiang yu tiaojian" (The Targets and Terms of Tax and Labor Exemptions in the Wei-Jin, Northern and Southern Dynasties). *Jiang-Han luntan* (1990.6).

Gao Mingshi. "Lun Wude dao Zhenguan lüling zhidu de chengli: Tang-chao li guo zhengce de yanjiu zhi er" (On the Establishment of Penal and Administrative Systems from the Wude to Zhenguan Reign Periods [618–650]: A Second Study of Tang Dynasty Policies for the Founding of the State). *Han xue yanjiu*, 11.1 (1993).

———. *Tang-dai Dongya jiaoyuquan de xingcheng: Dongya shijie xingcheng shi de yi cemian* (The Formation of an East Asian Educational Sphere in the Tang Dynasty: One Side of the History of the Formation of the East Asian World). Taibei: Guoli bianyiguan Zhonghua congshu bianshen weiyuanhui, 1984.

———. "Yunmeng Qin jian yu Qin-Han shi yanjiu: yi Riben de yanjiu chengguo wei zhongxin" (The Qin Documents from Yunmeng and the Study of Qin-Han History: Taking the Results of Japanese Research as Central). *Shihuo yuekan*, new series, 11.3 (1981).

Gao Shangzhi. "Qin jian lüwen zhong de 'shou tian'" ("Receipt of Fields" in the Qin Document Legal Texts). *Qin-Han shi luncong*, vol. 3. Xi'an: Shaanxi renmin chubanshe, 1986.

Gao Zhixi. *Chu wenhua de nan jian* (The Southward Penetration of Chu Culture). Wuhan: Hubei jiaoyu chubanshe, 1995.

Gardiner, Kenneth H. J. *The Early History of Korea: The Historical Development of the Peninsula up to the Introduction of Buddhism in the Fourth Century A.D.* Honolulu: University of Hawai'i Press, 1969.

———. "The Kung-sun Warlords of Liao-Tung (189–238)." *Papers on Far Eastern History*, 5 and 6 (1972).

———, and de Crespigny, R. R. C. "T'an-shih-huai and the Hsien-pi Tribes of the Second Century A.D." *Papers on Far Eastern History*, 15 (1977).

Ge Jianping. "Dong-Jin nanchao shehui zhong de jiating lunchang" (Family Ethics in Eastern Jin and Southern Dynasty Society). *Zhongshan daxue xuebao (zhexue, shehui, kexue ban)* (1990.3).

Geary, Patrick J. *Before France and Germany: The Creation and Transformation of the Merovingian World.* Oxford: Oxford University Press, 1988.

Gele. "Zhonghua da di shang de san da kaogu wenhua xitong he minzu xitong"(The Three Great Archaeological-Cultural Systems and Ethnic Systems of Greater China). *Zhongshan daxue xuebao: zhexue, shehui, kexue ban* (1987.4).

Gernet, Jacques. *Buddhism in Chinese Society: An Economic History from the Fifth to the Tenth Centuries.* Trans. by Franciscus Verellen. 1956; New York: Columbia University Press, 1995.

Gills, Barry K., and Frank, Andre Gunder. "The Cumulation of Accumulation: Theses and Research Agenda for 5000 Years of World System History." *Dialectical Anthropology,* 15.1 (1990).

Goffart, Walter. *Barbarians and Romans, A.D. 418–584: The Techniques of Accommodation.* Princeton, N.J.: Princeton University Press, 1980.

Gombrich, Richard F. *Theravāda Buddhism: A Social History from Ancient Benares to Modern Colombo.* London: Routledge and Kegan Paul, 1988.

Gong Weiying. "Gu Qin, Chu, liang-zu tongyuan shuzheng" (A Point-by-Point Demonstration of the Common Origins of the Ancient Qin and Chu Peoples). *Shixue yuekan* (1999.2).

Goodman, Howard L. *Ts'ao P'i Transcendent: The Political Culture of Dynasty-Founding in China at the End of the Han.* Seattle: Scripta Serica, 1998.

Gould, Stephen Jay. *Wonderful Life: The Burgess Shale and the Nature of History.* New York: W. W. Norton, 1989.

Grafflin, Dennis. "The Great Family in Medieval South China." *Harvard Journal of Asiatic Studies,* 41.1 (1981).

———. "Reinventing China: Pseudobureaucracy in the Early Southern Dynasties." *State and Society in Early Medieval China.* Ed. by Albert E. Dien. Stanford, Calif.: Stanford University Press, 1990.

Greenberg, Joseph H. *Indo-European and Its Closest Relatives: The Eurasiatic Language Family. Vol. 1: Grammar.* Stanford, Calif.: Stanford University Press, 2000.

Grieder, Jerome B. *Hu Shih and the Chinese Renaissance: Liberalism in the Chinese Revolution, 1917–1937.* Cambridge, Mass.: Harvard University Press, 1970.

Groeneveldt, Willem Pieter. *Notes on the Malay Archipelago and Malacca, Compiled from Chinese Sources.* Batavia, 1876.

Groner, Paul. *Saichō: the Establishment of the Japanese Tendai School.* Seoul: Berkeley Buddhist Studies Series, 1984.

Grousset, René. *The Empire of the Steppes: A History of Central Asia.* Trans. by Naomi Walford. 1939; New Brunswick, N.J.: Rutgers University Press, 1994.

Gu Jiguang. *Fubing zhidu kaoshi* (An Explanation of the Garrison-Militia System). 1962; Taibei: Hongwenguan chubanshe, 1985.

———. "Liuchao menfa" (Six Dynasties Great Families). *Guoli Wuhan daxue wen-zhe jikan,* 5.4 (1936).

Gu Mingjian (Gu Jiegang). *Qin-Han de fangshi yu rusheng* (Occultists and Confucians of the Qin and Han). 1933; Taibei: Liren shuju, 1985.

Haboush, JaHyun Kim. "The Confucianization of Korean Society." *The East*

Asian Region: Confucian Heritage and Its Modern Adaptation. Ed. by Gilbert Rozman. Princeton, N.J.: Princeton University Press, 1991.

———. "Filial Emotions and Filial Values: Changing Patterns in the Discourse of Filiality in Late Chosŏn Korea." *Harvard Journal of Asiatic Studies,* 55.1 (1995).

Hall, John Whitney. *Government and Local Power in Japan, 500 to 1700: A Study Based on Bizen Province.* Princeton, N.J.: Princeton University Press, 1966.

———. "Kyoto as Historical Background." *Medieval Japan: Essays in Institutional History.* Ed. by John W. Hall and Jeffrey P. Mass. 1974; Stanford, Calif.: Stanford University Press, 1988.

Hall, Kenneth R. *Maritime Trade and State Development in Early Southeast Asia.* Honolulu: University of Hawai'i Press, 1985.

Han Fuzhi. "Dong-Han de xuanju" (The Selection System of the Eastern Han). *Guoli Taiwan daxue lishi xuexi xuebao,* 4 (1977).

Han Guopan. *Beichao Sui-Tang de juntian zhidu* (The Equitable Fields System of the Northern Dynasties, Sui, and Tang). Shanghai: Shanghai renmin chubanshe, 1984.

———. "Nanbeichao Sui-Tang yu Baiji Xinluo de wanglai" (Northern and Southern Dynasty, Sui-Tang, Intercourse with Paekche and Silla). *Lishi yanjiu* (1994.2).

———. *Nanchao jingji shi tan* (Probing the Southern Dynasty Economy). Shanghai: Shanghai renmin chubanshe, 1963.

———. *Wei-Jin nanbeichao shi gang* (An Outline of Wei, Jin, Northern and Southern Dynasty History). Beijing: Renmin chubanshe, 1983.

Han Jianye. "Xia wenhua de qiyuan yu fazhan jieduan" (The Origins and Stages of Development of Xia Culture). *Beijing daxue xuebao: zhe she ban* (1997.4).

Han Sheng. *Riben gudai de dalu yimin yanjiu* (A Study of Japan's Ancient Mainland Immigrants). Taibei: Wenjin chubanshe, 1995.

———. "'Wei fa Baiji' yu Nanbeichao shiqi Dongya guoji guanxi" ([Northern] Wei's Chastisement of Paekche, and East Asian International Relations in the Northern and Southern Dynasties Period). *Lishi yanjiu* (1995.3).

———. "Wei-Jin, Sui-Tang, de wubi he cun" (Defensive Walls and Villages of the Wei-Jin and Sui-Tang [Dynasties]). *Xiamen daxue xuebao: zhe she ban* (1997.2).

Haneda Akira. "Tō-zai kōtsū" (East-West Communication). *Kizoku shakai.* Ed. by Kyōdai tōyōshi kankōkai. Osaka: Sōgensha, 1981.

Hanihara Kazurō. *Nihonjin no naritachi* (The Formation of the Japanese People). Kyoto: Jinbun shoin, 1995.

Hannas, William C. *Asia's Orthographic Dilemma.* Honolulu: University of Hawai'i Press, 1997.

Hansen, Chad. "Chinese Ideographs and Western Ideas." *Journal of Asian Studies,* 52.2 (1993).

Harootunian, H. D. "Figuring the Folk: History, Poetics, and Representation." *Mirror of Modernity: Invented Traditions of Modern Japan.* Ed. by Stephen Vlastos. Berkeley and Los Angeles: University of California Press, 1998.

Harrell, Stevan. "Introduction: Civilizing Projects and the Reaction to Them." *Cultural Encounters on China's Ethnic Frontiers.* Ed. by Stevan Harrell. Seattle: University of Washington Press, 1995.

Hartwell, Robert M. "Demographic, Political, and Social Transformations of China, 750–1550." *Harvard Journal of Asiatic Studies,* 42.2 (1982).

Hashimoto Hokei. "The Philosophic Influence of *Vimalakīrti-Nirdeśa Sūtra* upon Chinese Culture." *Actes du XXIXe congrès international des orientalistes; Chine ancienne.* Paris, 1977.

Hawkes, David, trans. *The Songs of the South: An Anthology of Ancient Chinese Poems by Qu Yuan and Other Poets.* Harmondsworth: Penguin Books, 1985.

Hayakawa Jirō. "Ōchō jidai shōen seido hassei no shozentai" (Various Preconditions for the Emergence of the Estate System in the Dynastic Era). *Nihon hōkensei no shakai to kokka,* vol. 1. Ed. by Toda Yoshimi. Tokyo: Azekura shobō, 1973.

Hayakawa Shōhachi. "Ritsuryō sei no keisei" (The Formation of the Ritsuryō System). *Iwanami kōza: Nihon rekishi 2; kodai 2.* Tokyo: Iwanami shoten, 1975.

Hayami Tasuku. *Nihon Bukkyōshi: kodai* (A History of Japanese Buddhism: Antiquity). Tokyo: Yoshikawa kōbunkan, 1986.

Hayashiya Tatsusaburō. "Kyoto in the Muromachi Age." *Japan in the Muromachi Age.* Ed. by John Whitney Hall and Toyoda Takeshi. Berkeley and Los Angeles: University of California Press, 1977.

He Changqun. *Han-Tang jian fengjian de guoyou tudi zhi yu juntian zhi* (The Feudal System of State Landownership and the Equitable Fields System between Han and Tang). Shanghai: Shanghai renmin chubanshe, 1958.

He Guangyue. *Bai Yue yuanliu shi* (A History of the Origins of the Hundred Yue). Nanchang: Jiangxi jiaoyu chubanshe, 1989.

He Liancheng et al. *Zhongguo jingji guanli sixiang shi* (A History of Chinese Thought concerning Economic Management). Xi'an: Xibei daxue chubanshe, 1988.

He Liankui. *Zhongguo li su yanjiu* (Studies of Chinese Rituals and Customs). Taibei: Taiwan Zhonghua shuju, 1978.

He Qimin. "Han-Jin bianju zhong de zhongyuan shifeng" (The Literati Style in the Central Plain amid the Changing Circumstances from Han to Jin). *Zhongguo lishi xuehui shixue jikan,* 5 (1973).

He Qinggu. "Lun zhan'guo shangye de fazhan" (On the Development of Warring States Commerce). *Zhongguo shi yanjiu* (1981.2).

———. "Qin Shihuang shidai de siying gongshangye" (Private Handicrafts and Trade in the Age of the First Emperor of Qin). *Wenbo,* 38 (1990.5).

He Ziquan (Ho Tzu-ch'üan). "Liang-Han haozu fazhan de san ge shiqi"

(Three Periods in the Development of Magnates during the Two Han Dynasties). *Qin-Han shi luncong,* vol. 3. Xi'an: Shaanxi renmin chubanshe, 1986.

————. "Nanbeichao shiqi nan-bei Ruxue fengshang bu tong de yuanyuan" (The Origins of the Difference between Confucian Fashions in North and South in the Northern and Southern Dynasties Period). *Jinian Chen Yinke xiansheng danchen bai nian xueshu lunwenji.* Ed. by Beijing daxue Zhongguo zhonggushi yanjiu zhongxin. 1983; Beijing: Beijing daxue chubanshe, 1989.

————. "San guo shiqi nong-cun jingji de pohuai yu fuxing" (The Destruction and Revival of the Village Economy during the Three Kingdoms Period). *Shihuo banyuekan,* 1.5 (1935).

————. *Wei-Jin nanbeichao shi lüe* (A Brief History of the Wei, Jin, Northern and Southern Dynasties). Shanghai: Shanghai renmin chubanshe, 1958.

————. "Wei-Jin shiqi zhuangyuan jingji de chuxing" (The Incipient Manorial Economy of the Wei and Jin Period). *Shihuo banyuekan,* 1.1 (1934).

Hendry, Joy. "Japan: The Anthropology of Modernity." *Asia's Cultural Mosaic: An Anthropological Introduction.* Ed. by Grant Evans. New York: Prentice Hall, 1993.

Herman, John E. "Empire in the Southwest: Early Qing Reforms to the Native Chieftain System." *Journal of Asian Studies,* 56.1 (1997).

Herodotus. *The Histories.* Trans. by Robin Waterfield. Oxford: Oxford University Press, 1998.

Hesselink, Reinier H. "The Introduction of the Art of Mounted Archery into Japan." *Transactions of the Asiatic Society of Japan,* 4th series, 6 (1991).

Higashi Shinji. "Go-Kan jidai no senkyo to chihō shakai" ([Bureaucratic] Selection and the Local Society of Later Han Times). *Tōyōshi-kenkyū,* 46.2 (1987).

Higham, Charles. *The Bronze Age of Southeast Asia.* Cambridge: Cambridge University Press, 1996.

Hirai Masashi. "Kandai ni okeru juka kanryō no kugyō-sō e no shinjun" (The Infiltration of Confucian Officials into the High Ranks of Officialdom in the Han Dynasty). *Rekishi ni okeru minshū to bunka—Sakai Tadao sensei koki shukuga kinen ronshū.* Tokyo: Kokusho kankokai, 1982.

Hirano Kunio. *Kikajin to kodai kokka* (Naturalized Persons and the Ancient State). Tokyo: Yoshikawa kōbunkan, 1993.

Hobsbawm, Eric, and Ranger, Terence, eds. *The Invention of Tradition.* Cambridge: Cambridge University Press, 1983.

Hodges, Richard, and Whitehouse, David. *Mohammed, Charlemagne and the Origins of Europe: Archaeology and the Pirenne Thesis.* London: Gerald Duckworth, 1983.

Holcombe, Charles. "The Administrative State in Early Imperial China and Japan." *Studies in Chinese History,* 5 (1995).

————. "The Bonds of Empire: Liberty in Early Medieval China." *The Historian*, 54.4 (1992).

————. "Early Imperial China's Deep South: The Viet Regions through Tang Times." *T'ang Studies*, 15–16 (1997–98).

————. "The Exemplar State: Ideology, Self-Cultivation, and Power in Fourth Century China." *Harvard Journal of Asiatic Studies*, 49.1 (June 1989).

————. "Re-Imagining China: The Chinese Identity Crisis at the Start of the Southern Dynasties Period." *Journal of the American Oriental Society*, 115.1 (1995).

————. "*Ritsuryō* Confucianism," *Harvard Journal of Asiatic Studies*, 57.2 (1997).

————. *In the Shadow of the Han: Literati Thought and Society at the Beginning of the Southern Dynasties*. Honolulu: University of Hawai'i Press, 1994.

————. "Trade-Buddhism: Maritime Trade, Immigration, and the Buddhist Landfall in Early Japan." *Journal of the American Oriental Society*, 119.2 (1999).

Holmgren, Jennifer. *Annals of Tai: Early T'o-Pa History according to the First Chapter of the Wei-Shu*. Canberra: Faculty of Asian Studies, Australian National University Press, 1982.

————. *Chinese Colonization of Northern Vietnam: Administrative Geography and Political Development in the Tongking Delta, First to Sixth Centuries A.D.* Canberra: Australian National University, 1980.

————. "The Composition of the Early Wei Bureaucratic Elite as Background to Emperor Kao-tsu's Reforms (423–490 A.D.)." *Journal of Asian History*, 27 (1993).

————. "The Lu Clan of Tai Commandery and Their Contribution to the T'o-Pa State of Northern Wei in the Fifth Century." *T'oung Pao*, 69.4–5 (1983).

————. "The Making of an Élite: Local Politics and Social Relations in Northeastern China during the Fifth Century A.D." *Papers on Far Eastern History*, 30 (1984).

————. "Northern Wei as a Conquest Dynasty: Current Perceptions; Past Scholarship." *Papers on Far Eastern History*, 40 (1989).

————. "Race and Class in Fifth Century China: The Emperor Kao-tsu's Marriage Reform." *Early Medieval China*, 2 (1995–96).

Holzman, Donald. "Les débuts du système médiéval de choix et de classement des fonctionnaires: Les neuf categories et l'impartial et juste." *Mélanges publiés par l'institut des hautes études chinoises*, vol. 1. Paris: University of Paris, 1957.

Honey, David B. "Sinification as Statecraft in Conquest Dynasties of China: Two Early Medieval Case Studies." *Journal of Asian History*, 30.2 (1996).

Hong Soon-chang. *Kankoku kodai no rekishi* (Ancient Korean History). Tokyo: Yoshikawa kōbunkan, 1992.

Hong Tao. *San Qin shi* (A History of the Three [Former, Later, and Western] Qin [Dynasties]). Shanghai: Fudan daxue chubanshe, 1992.

Hong, Wontack. *Paekche of Korea and the Origin of Yamato Japan.* Seoul: Kudara International, 1994.

Hong Xiuping. "Fojiao banruo sixiang de chuanru he Wei-Jin xuanxue de chansheng" (The Introduction of Buddhist Prajñā Thought and the Birth of Wei and Jin Xuanxue). *Nanjing daxue xuebao (zhexue, shehui kexue),* 1985, supplement.

Hori Toshikazu. *Chūgoku to kodai higashi Ajia sekai: Chūka teki sekai to shominzoku* (China and the Ancient East Asian World: The Chinese World and the Various Nations). Tokyo: Iwanami shoten, 1993.

————. *Kindensei no kenkū: Chūgoku kodai kokka no tochi seisaku to tochi shoyūsei* (Studies of the Equitable Fields System: Land Policy and Land Ownership Systems of the Ancient Chinese State). Tokyo: Iwanami shoten, 1975.

Hori Tsuyoshi. *Qin-Han fazhi shi lunkao* (A Study of the History of Qin-Han Legal Systems). Beijing: Falü chubanshe, 1988.

Hoshino Eiki. "Nihon Bukkyō no minshūka to girei shūzoku" (The Popularization of Japanese Buddhism and Ceremonial Custom). *Kōza: Bukkyō no juyō to henyō, 6: Nihon hen.* Ed. by Yamaori Tetsuo. Tokyo: Kōsei shuppansha, 1991.

Hou Wailu. "Zhongguo fengjian shehui tudi suoyouzhi xingshi de wenti: Zhongguo fengjian shehui fazhan guilü shangdui zhi yi" (The Problem of the Form of Land Ownership in Chinese Feudal Society: An Exchange Concerning the Laws of Development of Chinese Feudal Society). *Lishi yanjiu* (1954.1).

Hou Xudong. "Jinnian liyong Dunhuang Tulufan wenshu yanjiu Wei-Jin nanbeichao shi gaikuang" (The Status of Research in Recent Years into Wei-Jin, Northern and Southern Dynasty History Using Documents from Dunhuang and Turfan). *Zhongguo shi yanjiu dongtai* (1992.5).

Howland, D. R. *Borders of Chinese Civilization: Geography and History at Empire's End.* Durham, N.C.: Duke University Press, 1996.

Hsiao, Kung-chuan. *A History of Chinese Political Thought. Vol. 1: From the Beginnings to the Sixth Century A.D.* Trans. by F. W. Mote. 1945; Princeton, N.J.: Princeton University Press, 1979.

Hsu, Cho-yun. "Development of Statehood: From Eastern Chou to Han." *Zhongyang yanjiuyuan, Lishi yuyan yanjiusuo jikan,* 57.1 (1986).

————. "The Roles of the Literati and Regionalism in the Fall of the Han Dynasty." *The Collapse of Ancient States and Institutions.* Ed. by Norman Yoffee and George L. Cowgill. Tucson: University of Arizona Press, 1988.

————. "The Spring and Autumn Period." *The Cambridge History of Ancient China: From the Origins of Civilization to 221 B.C.* Ed. by Michael Loewe and Edward L. Shaughnessy. Cambridge: Cambridge University Press, 1999.

———, and Linduff, Katheryn M. *Western Chou Civilization.* New Haven, Conn.: Yale University Press, 1988.

Hu Rulei. "Tang-dai Zhong-Ri wenhua jiaoliu gaodu fazhan de shehui zhengzhi tiaojian" (Social and Political Conditions for the High Degree of Development in Cultural Exchanges between China and Japan during the Tang Dynasty). *Gudai Zhong-Han-Ri guanxi yanjiu.* Ed. by Lin Tianwei and Huang Yuese. Hong Kong: Centre of Asian Studies, University of Hong Kong, 1987.

Hu Shih. "Buddhistic Influence on Chinese Religious Life." *The Chinese Social and Political Science Review,* 9.1 (1925).

———. "The Establishment of Confucianism as a State Religion during the Han Dynasty." *Journal of the North China Branch of the Royal Asiatic Society,* 60 (1929).

———. "The Indianization of China: A Case Study in Cultural Borrowing." *Independence, Convergence, and Borrowing in Institutions, Thought, and Art.* Cambridge, Mass.: Harvard University Press, 1937.

Hua Yougen. "Xi-Han de li-fa jiehe ji qi zai Zhongguo falü shi shang de diwei" (The Western Han Unification of Ritual and Law and Its Place in Chinese Legal History). *Fudan xuebao: she ke ban* (1995.6).

Hua Zhisun. "Wei-Jin nanbeichao zhi jingji zhuangkuang" (The Economic Situation of the Wei, Jin, Northern and Southern Dynasties). *Zhongguo jingji,* 2.9 (1934).

Huang Chongyue and Sun Xiao. "Huanan gu Yuezu dui Zhonghua minzu wenhua de lishi gongxian" (The Historical Contribution of the Ancient Yue People of South China to Chinese National Culture). *Wenbo* (1998.3).

Huang Lie. "Wei-Jin nanbeichao minzu guanxi de jige lilun wenti" (Several Theoretical Problems Concerning Ethnic Relations during the Wei, Jin, Northern and Southern Dynasties). *Lishi yanjiu* (1985.3).

Huang, Ray. *China: A Macro History.* 1988; Armonk, N.Y.: M. E. Sharpe, 1990.

Huang Renyu (Ray). *Hexun he pan tan Zhongguo lishi* (Discussing Chinese History from the Banks of the Hudson River). Taibei: Shibao wenhua chuban, 1989.

Huang Yuese. "'Da-Tang shang ren' Li Yanxiao yu jiu shiji Zhong-Ri guanxi" (The "Great Tang Merchant" Li Yanxiao and Sino-Japanese Relations in the Ninth-Century). *Lishi yanjiu* (1993.4).

———. "Luelun gudai Zhong-Han-Ri guanxi yanjiu: dai xu" (A Brief Essay on the Study of Ancient Chinese, Korean, and Japanese Relations: In Place of an Introduction). *Gudai Zhong-Han-Ri guanxi yanjiu.* Ed. by Lin Tianwei and Huang Yuese. Hong Kong: University of Hong Kong, Centre of Asian Studies, 1987.

Huang Zhilian. *Tian chao lizhi tixi yanjiu (zhong juan): Dong-Ya de liyi shijie—Zhongguo fengjian wangchao yu Chaoxian bandao guanxi xingtai lun* (["Pax Sinica"] Studies in the System of the Heavenly Court's Rule by Propriety [vol. 2]: The East Asian Ceremonial World—On the Form of Relations between the Chinese Feudal Monarchy and the Korean Peninsula). Beijing: Zhongguo renmin daxue chubanshe, 1994.

Hucker, Charles O. *A Dictionary of Official Titles in Imperial China.* Stanford, Calif.: Stanford University Press, 1985.

Hudson, Mark J. *Ruins of Identity: Ethnogenesis in the Japanese Islands.* Honolulu: University of Hawai'i Press, 1999.

Hulsewé, A. F. P. "Ch'in and Han Law." *The Cambridge History of China. Vol. 1: The Ch'in and Han Empires, 221 B.C.–A.D. 220.* Ed. by Denis Twitchett and Michael Loewe. Cambridge: Cambridge University Press, 1986.

————. "Han China—A Proto 'Welfare State'? Fragments of Han Law Discovered in North-West China." *T'oung Pao,* 73.4–5 (1987).

————. *Remnants of Ch'in Law: An Annotated Translation of the Ch'in Legal and Administrative Rules of the 3rd Century B.C. Discovered in Yün-meng Prefecture, Hu-pei Province, in 1975.* Leiden: E. J. Brill, 1985.

Huntington, Samuel P. *The Clash of Civilizations and the Remaking of World Order.* New York: Simon and Schuster, 1996.

Hurst, G. Cameron III. "The Development of the *Insei*: A Problem in Japanese History and Historiography." *Medieval Japan: Essays in Institutional History.* Ed. by John W. Hall and Jeffrey P. Mass. 1974; Stanford, Calif.: Stanford University Press, 1988.

Ienaga Saburō. "Asuka, hakuhō bunka" (The Culture of the Asuka and Hakuhō Periods [7th Century]). *Iwanami kōza, Nihon rekishi II, kodai, 2.* Tokyo: Iwanami shoten, 1962.

————, ed. *Nihon Bukkyōshi: kodai hen* (A History of Japanese Buddhism: Antiquity). Tokyo: Hōzōkan, 1967.

Ikeda On. "Dong-Ya gudai jizhang guanjian" (A Partial View of [Household] Registration in Ancient East Asia). *Gudai Zhong-Han-Ri guanxi yanjiu.* Ed. by Lin Tianwei and Huang Yuese. Hong Kong: Centre of Asian Studies, University of Hong Kong, 1987.

————. "T'ang Household Registers and Related Documents." *Perspectives on the T'ang.* Ed. by Arthur F. Wright and Denis Twitchett. New Haven, Conn.: Yale University Press, 1973.

————. "Zui-Tō sekai to Nihon" (The Sui-Tang World and Japan). *Kodai o kangaeru: Tō to Nihon.* Ed. by Ikeda On. Tokyo: Yoshikawa kōbunkan, 1992.

Imaeda Jirō. *Tōdai bunka no kōsatsu (1): Abe no Nakamaro kenkyū* (Considerations of Tang Dynasty Culture 1: A Study of Abe no Nakamaro). Tokyo: Kōbundō shuppansha, 1979.

Imamura, Keiji. *Prehistoric Japan: New Perspectives on Insular East Asia.* Honolulu: University of Hawai'i Press, 1996.

Inaba Ichirō. "Chū-Tō ni okeru shin jugaku undō no ichi kōsatsu: Ryū Chiki no keisho hihan to Tan, Chō, Riku shi no *shunjū*-gaku" (An Examination of the New Confucian Studies Movement in Mid-Tang: Liu Zhiji's Criticism of the Classics and the *Spring and Autumn* Studies of Messrs Dan, Zhao, and Lu). *Chūgoku chūseishi kenkyū: Rikuchō, Zui, Tō no shakai to bunka.* Ed. by Chūgoku chūseishi kenkyūkai. Tokyo: Tōkai daigaku shuppankai, 1970.

————. "Kandai ni okeru minkan chitsujo no keisei—iwayuru gōzoku o chū-shin to suru" (The Formation of Private Order in the Han Dynasty—Centering around the So-Called Magnates). *Chūgoku kizokusei shakai no kenkyū.* Ed. by Kawakatsu Yoshio and Tonami Mamoru. Kyoto: Kyōto daigaku jinbun kagaku kenkyū sho, 1987.

Inoue Mitsusada. *Nihon kodai kokka no kenkyū* (Studies of the Ancient Japanese State). Tokyo: Iwanami shoten, 1965.

————. "Ritsuryō kokkagun no keisei" (The Formation of a Cluster of *Ritsuryō* States). *Inoue Mitsusada chosakushū*, vol. 5. 1971; Tokyo: Iwanami shoten, 1986.

Iriye, Akira. *China and Japan in the Global Setting.* Cambridge, Mass.: Harvard University Press, 1992.

Isaacs, Harold R. *Idols of the Tribe: Group Identity and Political Change.* New York: Harper and Row, 1975.

————. *Scratches on Our Minds: American Views of China and India.* 1958; Armonk, N.Y.: M. E. Sharpe, 1980.

Ishida Ichirō. *Nihon shisō shi gairon* (An Outline History of Japanese Thought). Tokyo: Yoshikawa kōbunkan, 1963.

Ishigami Eiichi. "Hikaku ritsuryō-sei ron: joron" (On Comparative Ritsuryō Systems: Introductory Remarks). *Ajia no naka no Nihonshi, 1, Ajia to Nihon.* Ed. by Arano Yasunori et al. Tokyo: Tōkyō daigaku shuppankai, 1992.

Ishimoda Shō. "Nihon kodai ni okeru kokusai ishiki ni tsuite: kodai kizoku no baai" (Concerning International Consciousness in Ancient Japan: The Case of the Ancient Aristocracy). *Shisō,* 454 (1962).

Jamieson, Neil L. *Understanding Vietnam.* Berkeley and Los Angeles: University of California Press, 1993.

Jansen, Marius B. *China in the Tokugawa World.* Cambridge, Mass.: Harvard University Press, 1992.

Jenner, W. J. F., trans. *Memories of Loyang: Yang Hsüan-chih and the Lost Capital (493–534).* Oxford: Clarendon Press, 1981.

Jensen, Lionel M. *Manufacturing Confucianism: Chinese Traditions and Universal Civilization.* Durham, N.C.: Duke University Press, 1997.

Jettmar, Karl. "The Altai before the Turks." *Museum of Far Eastern Antiquities, Bulletin,* 23 (1951).

Jiang Boqin. "Zhongguo tiankezhi, buquzhi yu Yingguo weilanzhi de bijiao yanjiu" (A Comparative Study of China's Guest Farmer and Private Retainer Systems with English Villeinage). *Lishi yanjiu* (1984.4).

Jiang Fuya. "Dong-Jin nanchao de da tudi suoyouzhi" (The Large Landholding System of the Eastern Jin and Southern Dynasties). *Jianghai xuekan* (1992.2).

Jiang Weiqiao. "Liuchao wenxue yu Fojiao yingxiang" (Six Dynasties Literature and Buddhist Influences). *Guoxue lunheng* (1935.6).

Jie Yongqiang. "Tang-dai de waishang" (Tang Dynasty Foreign Trade). *Jinyang xuekan* (1995.1).

Jin Fagen. *Yongjia luan hou beifang de haozu* (Northern Magnates after the Yongjia Disturbances [307–313]). Taibei: Taiwan shangwu yinshuguan, 1964.

Jin Guantao and Liu Qingfeng. *Xingsheng yu weiji: lun Zhongguo fengjian shehui de chao-wending jiegou* (Prosperity and Crisis: On the Super-Stable Structure of Chinese Feudal Society). 1982; Taibei: Tianshan chubanshe, 1987.

Jin Jiarui. "Dong-Jin nanchao da dizhu de tudi zhanyou yu laodongli de bianzhi" (The Occupation of Land and Organization of Labor by Great Landlords in the Eastern Jin and Southern Dynasties). *Shixue yuekan*, 1 (1957).

Jin Mei and Zhang Zhongqiu. "Da Tang lüling yu Tang-dai jingji fanrong guanxi zhi yanjiu" (Studies in the Relationship between the Legal Code of the Great Tang Dynasty and Tang Dynasty Economic Prosperity). *Nanjing daxue xuebao: zhexue, renwen, she ke ban* (1990.2).

Johnson, David G. *The Medieval Chinese Oligarchy.* Boulder, Colo.: Westview Press, 1977.

Kaji Nobuyuki. *Chūgoku shisō kara mita Nihon shisō shi kenkyū* (Studies in the History of Japanese Thought as Seen from Chinese Thought). Tokyo: Yoshikawa Kōbunkan, 1985.

Kamata Shigeo. *Bukkyō denrai* (The Introduction of Buddhism). Tokyo: Kodansha, 1995.

Kamiya Noriko. "Shin jidai ni okeru irei shingi: sono genreishugiteki seikaku" (An Investigation of Violations of the Rites in the Jin Period: Its Character of Strict Ritualism). *Tōyō gakuhō*, 67.3–4 (1986).

———. "Shin jidai ni okeru ōhō to karei" (Royal Law and Family Ritual in the Jin Period). *Tōyō gakuhō*, 60.1–2 (1978).

Kamstra, J. H. *Encounter or Syncretism: The Initial Growth of Japanese Buddhism.* Leiden: E. J. Brill, 1967.

Kanō Naosada. "Go-Kan matsu chihō gōzoku no dōkō: chihō bunkenka to gōzoku" (The Trend Towards Local Magnates at the End of the Later Han: Local Separatism and the Magnates). *Chūgoku chūsei shi kenkyū: Rikuchō, Zui, Tō no shakai to bunka.* Ed. by Utsunomiya Kiyoyoshi. Tokyo: Tōkai daigaku shuppankai, 1970.

———. "Kanbō to sono shūhen: Kōnan bunka no ichi kōsatsu" (Gan Bao and His Milieu: An Investigation of Jiangnan Culture). *Kodaigaku*, 18.1 (1972).

Katayama Kazumichi. "The Japanese as an Asia-Pacific Population." *Multi-*

cultural Japan: Palaeolithic to Postmodern. Ed. by Donald Denoon et al. Cambridge: Cambridge University Press, 1996.

Kawakatsu Yoshio. "L'aristocratie et la société féodale au début des Six Dynasties." *Zinbun,* 17 (1981).

———. *Chūgoku no rekishi: 3, Gi-Shin nanbokuchō* (Chinese History: 3, the Wei, Jin, Northern and Southern Dynasties). Tokyo: Kōdansha, 1981.

———. "La décadence de l'aristocratie chinoise sous les dynasties du sud." *Acta Asiatica,* 21 (1971).

———. "Kahei keizai no shinten to Kō Kei no ran" (The Development of a Money Economy and Hou Jing's Rebellion). *Rikuchō kizokusei shakai no kenkyū.* 1962; Tokyo: Iwanami shoten, 1982.

Kemenade, Willem Van. *China, Hong Kong, Taiwan, Inc.* Trans. by Diane Webb. New York: Vintage Books, 1998.

Kennedy, Paul. *The Rise and Fall of the Great Powers: Economic Change and Military Conflict from 1500 to 2000.* New York: Random House, 1987.

Keyes, Charles F. "The Dialectics of Ethnic Change." *Ethnic Change.* Ed. by Charles F. Keyes. Seattle: University of Washington Press, 1981.

Kikuchi Hideo. "Sōsetsu: kenkyū shiteki kaiko to tenbō" (Introduction: Historical Retrospective and Prospects for Research). *Zui-Tō teikoku to higashi Ajia sekai.* Ed. by Tōdaishi kenkyūkai. Tokyo: Kūko shoin, 1979.

Kikuchi Yasuaki. *Nihon kodai tochi shoyū no kenkyū* (Studies in Ancient Japanese Landownership). Tokyo: Tōkyō daigaku shuppankai, 1969.

Kiley, Cornelius J. "A Note on the Surnames of Immigrant Officials in Nara Japan." *Harvard Journal of Asiatic Studies,* 29 (1969).

———. "Provincial Administration and Land Tenure in Early Heian." *The Cambridge History of Japan.* Vol. 2: *Heian Japan.* Ed. by Donald H. Shively and William H. McCullough. Cambridge: Cambridge University Press, 1999.

———. "State and Dynasty in Archaic Yamato." *Journal of Asian Studies,* 33.1 (1973).

Kim Ch'ungnyōl. *Gaoli Ruxue sixiang shi* (A History of Koryŏ Confucian Thought). Taibei: Dongda tushu, 1992.

Kim, Kichung. *An Introduction to Classical Korean Literature: From Hyangga to P'ansori.* Armonk, N.Y.: M. E. Sharpe, 1996.

Kim Minsoo. "Tō-Shin seiken no seiritsu katei—Shiba Ei (Gen tei) no furyō o chūshin toshite" (The Process of Formation of Eastern Jin Political Authority—Centering around Sima Rui's [Emperor Yuan's] Administration). *Tōyōshi-kenkyū,* 48.2 (1989).

Kim Tal-su. *Chōsen: minzoku, rekishi, bunka* (Korea: Nation, History, and Culture). 1958: Tokyo: Iwanami shoten, 1985.

Kimura Eiichi. "The New Confucianism and Taoism in China and Japan from the Fourth to the Thirteenth Centuries A.D." *Cahiers D'Histoire Mondiale,* 5.4 (1960).

Kimura Masao. "Mōshi no seiji setsu: sono rekishi teki igi" (Mencius' Well

Field Doctrine: Its Historical Significance). *Yamazaki Sensei taikan kinen tōyōshigaku ronshū.* Ed. by Yamazaki Sensei taikan kinenkai. Tokyo: Tōkyō kyōiku daigaku bungakubu tōyōshigaku kenkyū shitsunai, 1967.

Kinbara Osamu. "Ping'an-chao shiren yu Bohai shi" (Heian Court Poets and the Ambassadors from Parhae). *Zhongguo bijiao wenxue.* Shanghai: Shanghai waiyu jiaoyu chubanshe, 1991.1.

Kishida Tomoko. "Ō Tō: Zui matsu no 'daiju'" (Wang Tong [584–617]: a "Great Confucian" of Late Sui). *Chūgoku shisōshi.* Ed. by Hihara Toshikuni. Tokyo: Perikan sha, 1987.

Kitagawa, Joseph M. "*Matsuri* and *Matsuri-goto:* Religion and State in Early Japan." *On Understanding Japanese Religion.* Joseph M. Kitagawa. 1979; Princeton, N.J.: Princeton University Press, 1987.

———. "The Shadow of the Sun: A Glimpse of the Fujiwara and the Imperial Families in Japan." *On Understanding Japanese Religion.* Joseph M. Kitagawa. 1982; Princeton, N.J.: Princeton University Press, 1987.

Kitamura Yoshikazu. "Zenkan matsu no kairei ni tsuite" (Concerning the Ritual Modifications at the End of Former Han). *Nippon-Chūgoku gakkaihō,* 33 (1981).

Kitō Kiyoaki. *Yamato chōtei to higashi Ajia.* (The Yamato Court and East Asia). Tokyo: Yoshikawa kōbunkan, 1994.

Kleeman, Terry F. "Licentious Cults and Bloody Victuals: Sacrifice, Reciprocity, and Violence in Traditional China." *Asia Major,* 3rd series, 7.1 (1994).

Klimburg, Maximilian. "The Setting: The Western Trans-Himalayan Crossroads." *The Silk Route and the Diamond Path: Esoteric Buddhist Art on the Trans-Himalayan Trade Routes.* Ed. by Deborah E. Klimburg-Salter. Los Angeles: UCLA Art Council, 1982.

Kobayashi Yasuko. *Kōkaido ō to "Wa no go ō"* (King Kwanggaet'o [of Koguryŏ, r. 391–413] and the "Five Kings of Yamato"). Tokyo: Bungei shunjū, 1996.

Kohl, Philip L., and Tsetskhladze, Gocha R. "Nationalism, Politics, and the Practice of Archaeology in the Caucasus." *Nationalism, Politics, and the Practice of Archaeology.* Ed. by Philip L. Kohl and Clare Fawcett. Cambridge: Cambridge University Press, 1995.

Kojima Tsuyoshi. "Chūgoku Jukyōshi no aratana kenkyū shikaku ni tsuite" (Concerning a New Research Angle on the History of Chinese Confucianism). *Shisō,* 805 (1991.7).

Kominami Ichirō. "Rikuchō, Zui, Tō shōsetsushi no tenkai to Bukkyō shinkō" (The Development of the History of Fiction in the Six Dynasties, Sui and T'ang, and Buddhist Belief). *Chūgoku chūsei no shūkyō to bunka* (1982.3).

Konishi, Jin'ichi. *A History of Japanese Literature. Vol. 2: The Early Middle Ages.* Trans. by Aileen Gatten. Princeton, N.J.: Princeton University Press, 1986.

Kornicki, Peter. *The Book in Japan: A Cultural History from the Beginnings to the Nineteenth Century.* Leiden: E. J. Brill, 1998.

Kosambi, D. D. *The Culture and Civilization of Ancient India in Historical Outline.* London: Routledge and Kegan Paul, 1965.

Kraus, Richard Curt. *Brushes with Power: Modern Politics and the Chinese Art of Calligraphy.* Berkeley and Los Angeles: University of California Press, 1991.

Kuang Li'an. "Wei-Jin mendi shili zhuanyi yu zhi-luan zhi guanxi" (The Transferal of Social Status and Power in Wei and Jin and Its Relationship to Order and Disorder). *Shixue huikan,* 8 (1977).

Kuang Shiyuan. *Guo shi lunheng, di yi ce: Xian-Qin zhi Sui-Tang pian* (Deliberations on National History. Vol. 1: Pre-Qin through Sui-Tang). Revised ed.; Taibei: Liren shuju, 1995.

Kubozoe Yoshifumi. "Gi-Shin nanbokuchō ni okeru chihōkan no honsekichi ninyō ni tsuite" (Concerning the Employment of Local Officials in Their Original Places of Registration in the Wei, Jin, Northern and Southern Dynasties). *Shigaku-zasshi,* 83.1 (1974).

Kurihara Masuo. "Shichi, hasseiki no higashi Ajia sekai" (The East Asian World of the Seventh to Eighth Centuries). *Zui-Tō teikoku to higashi Ajia sekai.* Ed. by Tōdaishi kenkyūkai. Tokyo: Kūko shoin, 1979.

Kuroda Toshio. "Shinto in the History of Japanese Religion." *Journal of Japanese Studies,* 7.1 (1981).

Kuwahara Jitsuzō. "Shin shitsu no nan-to to nanpō no kaihatsu" (The Southward Passage of the House of Jin and the Development of the South). *Tōyōshi setsuen.* Kyoto: Kōbundo insatsubu, 1927.

Kuwayama Shōshin. "How Xuanzang Learned about Nālandā." *Tang China and Beyond: Studies on East Asia from the Seventh to the Tenth Century.* Ed. by Antonino Forte. Kyoto: Istituto Italiano di Cultura, Scuola di Studi sull'Asia Orientale, 1988.

Lao Gan (Lao Kan). *Qin-Han shi* (Qin-Han History). Taibei: Zhongguo wenhua daxue, 1986.

———. *Wei-Jin nanbeichao shi* (A History of the Wei, Jin, Northern and Southern Dynasties). Taibei: Zhongguo wenhua daxue, 1980.

Lao Kan (Lao Gan). "Population and Geography in the Two Han Dynasties." *Chinese Social History.* Ed. by E-tu Zen Sun and John DeFrancis. Washington, D.C.: American Council of Learned Societies, 1956.

Lattimore, Owen. "Caravan Routes of Inner Asia." *Studies in Frontier History: Collected Papers, 1928–1958.* 1928; London: Oxford University Press, 1962.

———. "Chinese Turkistan." *Studies in Frontier History: Collected Papers, 1928–1958.* 1933; London: Oxford University Press, 1962.

———. *Inner Asian Frontiers of China.* New York: American Geographical Society, 1940.

———. "Origins of the Great Wall of China: A Frontier Concept in Theory

and Practice." *Studies in Frontier History: Collected Papers, 1928–1958.*
1937; London: Oxford University Press, 1962.

Le Blanc, Charles. *Huai-Nan Tzu: Philosophical Synthesis in Early Han Thought.*
Hong Kong: Hong Kong University Press, 1985.

Ledyard, Gari. "Galloping Along with the Horseriders: Looking for the
Founders of Japan." *Journal of Japanese Studies*, 1.2 (1975).

———. "Yin and Yang in the China-Manchuria-Korea Triangle." *China
among Equals: the Middle Kingdom and Its Neighbors, 10th–14th Centuries.*
Ed. by Morris Rossabi. Berkeley and Los Angeles: University of California Press, 1983.

Legge, James, trans. *The Lî Kî.* Oxford: Clarendon Press, 1885.

———. *A Record of Buddhistic Kingdoms: Being an Account by the Chinese Monk
Fâ-hien of His Travels in India and Ceylon (A.D. 399–414) in Search of the
Buddhist Books of Discipline.* Reprint; San Francisco: Chinese Materials
Center, 1975.

Lee, Don Y. *The History of Early Relations between China and Tibet: From Chiu
T'ang-shu, a Documentary Survey.* Bloomington, Ind.: Eastern Press,
1981.

Lee, Ki-baik. *A New History of Korea.* Trans. by Edward W. Wagner. Cambridge,
Mass.: Harvard University Press, 1984.

Lee, Peter H., trans. *Lives of Eminent Korean Monks: The Haedong Kosŭng Chŏn.*
Cambridge, Mass.: Harvard University Press, 1969.

———, ed. *Sourcebook of Korean Civilization. Vol. 1: From Early Times to the Sixteenth Century.* New York: Columbia University Press, 1993.

Lee, Sherman E. *A History of Far Eastern Art.* 5th ed. New York: Prentice Hall,
1994.

Lee Sungsi. *Higashi Ajia no ōken to kōeki: Shōsōin no hōmotsu ga kita mō hitotsu no
michi* (East Asian Sovereign Power and Trade: Another Route for the
Arrival of the Treasures in the Shōsōin). Tokyo: Aoki shoten, 1997.

Levathes, Louise. *When China Ruled the Seas: The Treasure Fleet of the Dragon
Throne, 1405–1433.* New York: Oxford University Press, 1994.

Levenson, Joseph R. "The Province, the Nation, and the World: The Problem of Chinese Identity." *Approaches to Modern Chinese History.* Ed. by Albert Feuerwerker et al. Berkeley and Los Angeles: University of California Press, 1967.

Lewin, Bruno. *Aya und Hata: Bevölkerungsgruppen altjapans kontinentaler Her-
kunft.* Wiesbaden: Otto Harrassowitz, 1962.

———. "Japanese and Korean: The Problems and History of a Linguistic
Comparison." *Journal of Japanese Studies*, 2.2 (1976).

Lewis, Mark Edward. *Writing and Authority in Early China.* Albany: State University of New York Press, 1999.

Li Donghua. "Han-Sui jian Zhongguo nanhai jiaotong zhi yanbian" (The
Evolution of Chinese Communications with the South Seas from Han
to Sui). *Zhongguo lishi xuehui, shixue jikan*, 11 (1979).

———. *Zhongguo haiyang fazhan guanjian shi, di, ge'an yanjiu, (gudai pian)* (Case Studies in Key Times and Places in China's Maritime Development [Antiquity]). Taibei: Da'an chubanshe, 1990.

Li Jiafu. *Zhongguo fazhi shi* (A History of Chinese Legal Institutions). Taibei: Lianjing chuban, 1988.

Li Qingxin. "Huangfu zhi shan bu, yanyi zhi liang di: lun Tang dai Yue bei diqu de jingji yu wenhua" (A Part of the Wilderness Made Good—the Barren Lands of the Far South: On the Economy and Culture of the Northern Yue [Guangdong] Region in the Tang Dynasty). *Guangdong shehui kexue* (1998.1).

Li Shi. "Tang Taizong yu dongnan wenren" (Emperor Taizong of Tang [r. 626–649] and the Southeastern Literati). *Zhongguo shi yanjiu* (1997.2).

Li Shijie. "Dong-Jin shidai zhi Fojiao sixiang" (Buddhist Thought of the Eastern Jin Era). *Wei-Jin nanbeichao Fojiao xiaoshi.* Ed. by Huang Chanhua et al. Taibei: Dacheng wenhua chubanshe, 1979.

Li Xing. "Dong-Jin jinglüe zhongyuan zhi jingguo" (The Eastern Jin Experience at Managing the Central Plain). *Wenshi zazhi,* 1.7 (1941).

Li Xu. "Wei-Jin nanbeichao shi zhengzhi jingji zhongxin de zhuanyi" (The Transfer of Political and Economic Centers in Wei, Jin, Northern and Southern Dynasty Times). *Shihuo banyuekan,* 1.1 (1934).

Li Xueqin. *Dong Zhou yu Qin-dai wenming* (Eastern Zhou and Qin Dynasty Civilization). Beijing: Wenwu chubanshe, 1984.

Li Yan. "San jiao zhengheng yu Tang-dai de xueshu fazhan" (The Struggle for Supremacy among the Three Doctrines and the Development of Learning in the Tang Dynasty). *Shehui kexuejia* (1994.5).

Li Yuancheng. "Liang-Jin nanchao shehui jieji kao" (An Investigation of Social Classes in the Two Jin and Southern Dynasties). *Wenshi zazhi,* 5.5–6 (1945).

Li Zefen. *Liang-Jin nanbeichao lishi lunwen ji* (Collected Essays on the History of the Two Jin, Northern and Southern Dynasties). Taibei: Taiwan shangwu yinshuguan, 1987.

———. *Zhong-Ri guanxi shi* (A History of Sino-Japanese Relations). Taibei: Taiwan Zhonghua shuju, 1982.

Liebenthal, Walter. "Chinese Buddhism during the 4th and 5th Centuries." *Monumenta Nipponica,* 11.1 (1955).

Lin Enxian. "Tujue wenhua ji qi dui Tang-chao zhi yingxiang" (Türk Culture and Its Influence on the Tang Dynasty). *Tang-dai yanjiu lunji,* vol. 1. Ed. by Zhongguo Tang-dai xuehui. 1972; Taibei: Xin wenfeng chuban gongsi, 1992.

Lin Ganquan. "Lun Qin-Han fengjian guojia de nongye zhengce: guanyu zhengzhi quanli yu jingji fazhan guanxi de kaocha" (On the Agricultural Policies of the Feudal State in Qin and Han: An Investigation into the Relationship between Political Authority and Economic Development). *Di shiliu jie guoji lishi kexue da hui: Zhongguo xuezhe lunwenji.* Ed. by Zhang Lianfang. Beijing: Zhonghua shuju, 1985.

Lin Jianming. *Qin-Han shehui wenming* (Qin-Han Society and Civilization). Xi'an: Xibei daxue chubanshe, 1985.

———. "Qin-Han shi bufen" (Section on Qin-Han History). *Zhongguo gudai shi daodu* (Reader's Guide to Ancient Chinese History). Ed. by Xiao Li and Li Guihai. Shanghai: Wenhui chubanshe, 1991.

Lin Shimin. "Tang-dai dongfang haishi huodong yu Mingzhou gang" (Eastern Maritime Activity in the Tang Dynasty and Mingzhou [Ningbo] Harbor). *Zhedong wenhua luncong*. Ed by Dong Yi'an. Beijing: Zhongyang bianyi chubanshe, 1995.

Lin Tianwei. *Sui-Tang shi xin lun* (New Essays on Sui-Tang History). Taibei: Donghua shuju, 1978.

Lin Wenyue. "Tang-dai wenhua dui Riben Ping'an wentan zhi yingxiang: cong Riben qian Tang shi shidai dao *Bai shi wenji* zhi dong chuan" (The Influence of Tang Dynasty Culture on Heian Japanese Literary Circles: From the Time of the Japanese Embassies to Tang to the Eastward Transmission of the *Literary Collection of Mr. Bai* [Bo Juyi]). *Zhong-gu wenxue luncong*. Taibei: Da'an chubanshe, 1989.

Lin Yun. "Shuo 'Mo'" (An Explication of "*Mo*" [*Maek*, as in *Yemaek*]. *Shixue jikan* (1999.4)

Lipman, Jonathan N. *Familiar Strangers: A History of Muslims in Northwest China*. Seattle: University of Washington Press, 1997.

Liu Baiji. *Tang-dai zhengjiao shi* (A History of Governmental Teachings in the Tang Dynasty). Revised ed. Taibei: Taiwan Zhonghua shuju, 1974.

Liu Chunfan. "Qin zhuanzhi zhuyi zhongyang jiquanzhi de jingji jichu" (The Economic Foundations for the System of Centralized Power in Qin Autocracy). *Qin-Han shi luncong*, vol. 3. Xi'an: Shaanxi renmin chubanshe, 1986.

Liu Guijie. "Xuanxue sixiang yu banruo sixiang zhi jiaorong" (The Blending Together of Xuanxue Thought with Prajñā Thought). *Guoli bianyiguan guankan,* 9.1 (1980).

Liu Houbin. "An-Shi zhi luan yu Tang-dai zhengzhi tizhi de yanjin" (The Rebellions of An Lushan and Shi Siming and the Evolution of Tang Political Systems). *Zhongguo shi yanjiu* (1999.2).

Liu Jingcheng. "Lun Bei-Wei juntian zhi de chansheng" (On the Birth of the Northern Wei Equitable Fields System). *Guizhou shifan daxue xuebao: she ke ban* (1993.4).

Liu, Lydia H. *Translingual Practice: Literature, National Culture, and Translated Modernity—China, 1900–1937*. Stanford, Calif.: Stanford University Press, 1995.

Liu Shufen. "Liuchao Jiankang de jingji jichu" (The Economic Foundations of Six Dynasties Jiankang [Nanking]). *Shihuo yuekan,* 12.10–11 (1983).

———. "Liuchao Nanhai maoyi de kaizhan" (The Development of South Sea Trade in the Six Dynasties). *Liuchao de chengshi yu shehui*. Taibei: Taiwan xuesheng shuju, 1992.

———. "San zhi liu shiji Zhe-dong diqu de jingji fazhan" (The Economic Development of the Eastern Zhejiang Region in the 3rd–6th Centuries). *Liuchao de chengshi yu shehui.* 1987; Taibei: Taiwan xuesheng shuju, 1992.

———. "Wei-Jin beichao de zhucheng yundong" (The City-Building Movement of the Wei, Jin, and Northern Dynasties). *Liuchao de chengshi yu shehui.* Taibei: Taiwan xuesheng shuju, 1992.

Liu Xinru. *Ancient India and Ancient China: Trade and Religious Exchanges A.D. 1–600.* Delhi: Oxford University Press, 1988.

———. *Silk and Religion: An Exploration of Material Life and the Thought of People, A.D. 600–1200.* Delhi: Oxford University Press, 1998.

Liu Xueyao. *Xianbei shi lun* (Essays in Xianbei History). Taibei: Nantian shuju, 1994.

Liu Yuhuang. "Lun Han-Jin-nanchao de fengjian zhuangyuan zhidu" (On the Feudal Manorial System of the Han, Jin, and Southern Dynasties). *Lishi yanjiu* (1962.3).

Liu Yunhui. *Qin shi huang ling zhi mi* (The Riddle of the First Emperor of Qin's Tomb). Shaanxi Province: Xibei daxue chubanshe, 1987.

Loewe, Michael. "The Campaigns of Han Wu-ti." *Chinese Ways in Warfare.* Ed. by Frank A. Kierman, Jr., and John K. Fairbank. Cambridge, Mass.: Harvard University Press, 1974.

———. *Crisis and Conflict in Han China: 104 B.C. to A.D. 9.* London: George Allen and Unwin, 1974.

———. "The Heritage Left to the Empires." *The Cambridge History of Ancient China: From the Origins of Civilization to 221 B.C.* Ed. by Michael Loewe and Edward L. Shaughnessy. Cambridge: Cambridge University Press, 1999.

Lü Shipeng. *Bei shu shiqi de Yuenan: Zhong-Yue guanxi shi zhi yi* (Vietnam in the Period of Subordination to the North: A History of Sino-Vietnamese Relations). Hong Kong: Chinese University of Hong Kong, Southeast Asia Studies Section, 1964.

Lü Simian. *Du shi zhaji* (Commentaries on Reading History). Shanghai: Guji chubanshe, 1982.

———. *Xian Qin shi* (Pre-Qin History). 1941; Hong Kong: Taiping shuju, 1968.

Lu Yaodong. *Cong Pingcheng dao Luoyang: Tuoba Wei wenhua zhuanbian de licheng* (From Pingcheng to Luoyang: The Process of Tuoba Wei Cultural Transformation). Taibei: Lianjing chuban, 1979.

Luce, Gordon H., trans. *Man Shu (Book of the Southern Barbarians).* By Fan Ch'o. Ca. 860; Ithaca, N.Y.: Cornell University Press, 1961.

Luo Tonghua. *Han-dai de liumin wenti* (The Han Dynasty Refugee Problem). Taibei: Taiwan xuesheng shuju, 1989.

———. "Zheng li linbu shi lun: Han dai renkou yilailü yu pin fu chaju zhi yanjiu" (An Examination of the Granary Records of Zheng Administrative Village: Studies in the Rate of Dependency and the Gap between Poverty and Wealth in the Han Dynasty Population). *Xin shi xue,* 3.1 (1992).

Luo Zongzhen. *Liuchao kaogu* (Six Dynasties Archaeology). Nanjing: Nanjing daxue chubanshe, 1994.

Ma Changshou. *Wuhuan yu Xianbei* (The Wuhuan and Xianbei [Peoples]). Shanghai: Shanghai renmin chubanshe, 1962.

Ma Chi. *Tang-dai fan jiang* (Foreign Generals of the Tang Dynasty). Xi'an: San Qin chubanshe, 1990.

Mabbett, Ian, and Chandler, David. *The Khmers.* Oxford: Blackwell Publishers, 1995.

McCormack, Gavan. "*Kokusaika:* Impediments in Japan's Deep Structure." *Multicultural Japan: Palaeolithic to Postmodern.* Ed. by Donald Denoon et al. Cambridge: Cambridge University Press, 1996.

McCullough, Helen Craig. *Brocade by Night: "Kokin Wakashū" and the Court Style in Japanese Classical Poetry.* Stanford, Calif.: Stanford University Press, 1985.

McCullough, William H. "The Capital and Its Society." *The Cambridge History of Japan. Vol. 2: Heian Japan.* Ed. by Donald H. Shively and William H. McCullough. Cambridge: Cambridge University Press, 1999.

———. "The Heian Court, 794–1070." *The Cambridge History of Japan. Vol. 2: Heian Japan.* Ed. by Donald H. Shively and William H. McCullough. Cambridge: Cambridge University Press, 1999.

———. "Japanese Marriage Institutions in the Heian Period." *Harvard Journal of Asiatic Studies,* 27 (1967).

Mackerras, Colin. *The Uighur Empire according to the T'ang Dynastic Histories: A Study in Sino-Uighur Relations, 744–840.* Columbia: University of South Carolina Press, 1972.

McMullen, David. *State and Scholars in T'ang China.* Cambridge: Cambridge University Press, 1988.

McNeill, William H. *Plagues and Peoples.* Garden City, N.Y.: Anchor Press, 1976.

———. *The Rise of the West: A History of the Human Community.* Chicago: University of Chicago Press, 1963.

Maddison, Angus. *Chinese Economic Performance in the Long Run.* Paris: Organization for Economic Cooperation and Development, Development Center, 1998.

Madsen, Richard. *China and the American Dream: A Moral Inquiry.* Berkeley and Los Angeles: University of California Press, 1995.

Maeda Naonori. "Higashi Ajia ni okeru kodai no shūmatsu" (The End of Antiquity in East Asia). *Chūgoku shi no jidai kubun.* Ed. by Suzuki Shun and Nishijima Sadao. 1948; Tokyo: Tōkyō daigaku shuppankai, 1957.

Maher, John C. "North Kyushu Creole: A Language-Contact Model for the Origins of Japanese." *Multicultural Japan: Palaeolithic to Postmodern.* Ed. by Donald Denoon et al. Cambridge: Cambridge University Press, 1996.

Mair, Victor H. "Buddhism and the Rise of the Written Vernacular in East

Asia: The Making of National Languages." *Journal of Asian Studies,* 53.3 (1994).

———, and Tsu-lin Mei. "The Sanskrit Origins of Recent Style Prosody." *Harvard Journal of Asiatic Studies,* 51.2 (1991).

Mannheim, Karl. *Ideology and Utopia: An Introduction to the Sociology of Knowledge.* Trans. by Louis Wirth and Edward Shils. New York: Harcourt, Brace and Company, 1946.

Mao Hanguang. *Liang-Jin nanbeichao shizu zhengzhi zhi yanjiu* (Studies of Literati Politics in the Two Jin, Northern and Southern Dynasties). Taibei: Taiwan shangwu yinshuguan, 1966.

———. "San guo zhengquan de shehui jichu" (The Social Foundation of Political Authority in the Three Kingdoms). *Zhongyang yanjiuyuan, Lishi yuyan yanjiusuo jikan,* 46.1 (1974).

———. "Wu-chao junquan zhuanyi ji qi dui zhengju zhi yingxiang" (The Transfer of Military Authority during the Five [Southern] Dynasties and Its Influence on the Political Situation). *Qinghua xuebao,* new series, 8.1–2 (1970).

———. *Zhongguo zhonggu shehui shilun* (Essays on Medieval Chinese Social History). Taibei: Lianjing chuban, 1988.

March, Andrew L. *The Idea of China: Myth and Theory in Geographical Thought.* New York: Praeger Publishers, 1974.

Maspero, Henri. "Etudes d'histoire d'Annam, V: L'expédition de Ma Yuan." *Bulletin de l'ecole Francaise d'extreme orient,* 18 (1918).

———. "Etudes d'histoire d'Annam IV: Le royaume de Van-lang." *Bulletin de l'ecole Francaise d'extreme orient,* 18 (1918).

Mass, Jeffrey P. "The Emergence of the Kamakura *Bakufu.*" *Medieval Japan: Essays in Institutional History.* Ed. by John W. Hall and Jeffrey P. Mass. Stanford, Calif.: Stanford University Press, 1974.

Mather, Richard B. "The Conflict of Buddhism with Native Chinese Ideologies." *Review of Religion,* 20.1–2 (1955).

———. "K'ou Ch'ien-chih and the Taoist Theocracy at the Northern Wei Court, 425–451." *Facets of Taoism: Essays in Chinese Religion.* Ed. by Holmes Welch and Anna Seidel. New Haven, Conn.: Yale University Press, 1979.

———. "A Note on the Dialects of Lo-Yang and Nanking during the Six Dynasties." *Wen-lin: Studies in the Chinese Humanities.* Ed. by Chow Tse-tsung. Madison: University of Wisconsin Press, 1968.

———. *The Poet Shen Yüeh (441–513): The Reticent Marquis.* Princeton, N.J.: Princeton University Press, 1988.

———, trans. *Shih-shuo Hsin-yü: A New Account of Tales of the World.* Minneapolis: University of Minnesota Press, 1976.

———. "Vimalakīrti and Gentry Buddhism." *History of Religions,* 8.1 (1968).

Matsunaga, Alicia. *The Buddhist Philosophy of Assimilation: The Historical Development of the Honji-Suijaku Theory.* Tokyo: Sophia University, 1969.

Matsuura Tomohisa. "Kanshibun no sekai" (The World of Chinese Poetry and Literature). *Nihon shisō shi kōza, 1*. Ed. by Furukawa Tetsushi and Ishida Ichirō. Tokyo: Yūzankaku shuppan, 1978.

Maverick, Lewis A. *China a Model for Europe*. San Antonio, Tex.: Paul Anderson Company, 1946.

Meacham, William. "Origins and Development of the Yüeh Coastal Neolithic: A Microcosm of Culture Change on the Mainland of East Asia." *The Origins of Chinese Civilization*. Ed. by David N. Keightley. Berkeley and Los Angeles: University of California Press, 1983.

Meng Siming. "Liuchao shizu xingcheng de jingguo" (The Process of Formation of the Six Dynasties Great Families). *Wenshi zazhi*, 1.9 (1941).

Meng Wentong. *Yue shi congkao* (Collected Studies of Yue History). Beijing: Renmin chubanshe, 1983.

Michihata Ryōshū. "Chūgoku Bukkyō no Chūgokuteki tenkai" (The Chinese Evolution of Chinese Buddhism). *Chūgoku Bukkyō shakai-keizai shi no kenkyū*. Kyoto: Heirakuji shoten, 1983.

———. "Dengyō Daishi nit-Tō ji no Chūgoku Bukkyō: tokuni shomin Bukkyōto no seikatsu ni tsuite" (Chinese Buddhism at the Time When Saichō Went to Tang: Especially concerning the Lives of Ordinary Buddhist Adherents). *Chūgoku Bukkyō shakai-keizai shi no kenkyū*. Kyoto: Heirakuji shoten, 1983.

Miller, Richard J. *Japan's First Bureaucracy: A Study of Eighth-Century Government*. Ithaca, N.Y.: Cornell University East Asia Papers no. 19, 1979.

Miller, Roy Andrew, trans. *Accounts of Western Nations in the History of the Northern Chou Dynasty*. 636; Berkeley and Los Angeles: University of California Press, 1959.

———. *The Japanese Language*. Chicago: University of Chicago Press, 1967.

———. *Japanese and the Other Altaic Languages*. Chicago: University of Chicago Press, 1971.

———. "Linguistic Evidence and Japanese Prehistory." *Windows on the Japanese Past: Studies in Archaeology and Prehistory*. Ed. by Richard J. Pearson et al. Ann Arbor: Center for Japanese Studies, University of Michigan, 1986.

———. "Yamato and Paekche." *Asian Pacific Quarterly*, 26.3 (1994).

Mitchell, Richard H. *Censorship in Imperial Japan*. Princeton, N.J.: Princeton University Press, 1983.

Miyakawa Hisayuki. "The Confucianization of South China." *The Confucian Persuasion*. Ed. by Arthur F. Wright. Stanford, Calif.: Stanford University Press, 1960.

———. "Tō-Shin jidai no kizoku to Bukkyō" (The Aristocracy and Buddhism of the Eastern Jin Period). *Shina Bukkyō shigaku*, 4.1–2 (1940).

Miyazaki Ichisada. "Chūgoku ni okeru sonsei no seiritsu: kodai teikoku hōkai no ichimen" (The Formation of the Village System in China: One Aspect of the Collapse of the Ancient Empire). *Tōyōshi-kenkyū*, 18.4 (1960).

————. "Chūgoku shijō no shōen" (Estates in Chinese History). *Ajia shi kenkyū*, vol. 4. Kyoto: Tōyōshi kenkyūkai, 1964.

————. *Kyūhin kanjinhō no kenkyū: kakyo zenshi* (Studies of the Nine Ranks of Officials Law: A Prehistory of the Examination System). Kyoto: Tōyōshi kenkyūkai, 1956.

Mizoguchi Yūzō. "Chūgoku ni okeru kō, shi gainen no tenkai" (The Development of Concepts of Public and Private in China). *Shisō*, 669 (1980).

Momigliano, Arnaldo. "The Fault of the Greeks." *Essays in Ancient and Modern Historiography*. Middletown, Conn.: Wesleyan University Press, 1975.

Mōri Hisashi. "Sangoku chōkoku to Asuka chōkoku" (Three Kingdom's [Korean] Sculpture and Asuka [Period, 552–645, Japanese] Sculpture). *Kudara bunka to Asuka bunka*. Ed. by Tamura Enchō and Hwang Suyŏng. Tokyo: Yoshikawa kōbunkan, 1978.

Mori Mikisaburō. "Chūgoku chishikijin no Bukkyō juyō" (The Receptivity of Chinese Intellectuals to Buddhism). *Rō-Sō to Bukkyō*. Kyoto: Hōzōkan, 1986.

————. *Rikuchō shidaifu no seishin* (The Spirit of the Six Dynasties Literati). Kyoto: Dōbōsha, 1986.

Morris, Ivan. *The World of the Shining Prince: Court Life in Ancient Japan*. Harmondsworth: Penguin Books, 1964.

————, trans. *The Pillow Book of Sei Shōnagon*. Baltimore, Md.: Penguin Books, 1967.

Morris-Suzuki, Tessa. "A Descent into the Past: The Frontier in the Construction of Japanese Identity." *Multicultural Japan: Palaeolithic to Postmodern*. Ed. by Donald Denoon et al. Cambridge: Cambridge University Press, 1996.

————. "The Invention and Reinvention of 'Japanese Culture.'" *Journal of Asian Studies*, 54.3 (1995).

Mungello, D. E. *The Great Encounter of China and the West, 1500–1800*. Lanham, Md.: Rowman and Littlefield, 1999.

Munro, Donald J. *The Concept of Man in Early China*. Stanford, Calif.: Stanford University Press, 1969.

Munsterberg, Hugo. *The Arts of Japan: An Illustrated History*. Rutland: Charles E. Tuttle Company, 1957.

Murakami Yoshimi. "Kizoku shakai no bunka" (The Culture of Aristocratic Society). *Kizoku shakai*. Ed. by Kyōdai tōyōshi kankōkai. Osaka: Sōgensha, 1981.

Musset, Lucien. *The Germanic Invasions: The Making of Europe* A.D. *400–600*. Trans. by Edward and Columba James. 1965; London: Paul Elek, 1975.

Naba Toshisada. "Oshu kō" (A Study of Fortress-Masters). *Tōa jinbungaku hō*, 2.4 (1943).

Nakamura Jihee. "Tōdai no fu" (Tang Dynasty Shamanism). *Shien*, 105–106 (1971).

Nakamura Keiji. "'Shi-sho kubetsu' shōron: Nanchō kizokusei e no ichi shiten" (A Brief Discussion of the "Distinction between Shi and Commoners": One Viewpoint on the Southern Dynasty Aristocratic System). *Shigaku-zashi*, 88.2 (1979).

Nakamura, Kyoko Motomochi, trans. *Miraculous Stories from the Japanese Buddhist Tradition: The Nihon Ryoiki of the Monk Kyōkai.* Cambridge, Mass.: Harvard University Press, 1973.

Naobayashi Futai. "Torai kei shizoku Bukkyō no ichi kōsatsu" (An Inquiry into the Buddhism of Immigrant Families). *Indogaku Bukkyōgaku kenkyū*, 43.1 (1994).

Naoki Kōjirō. "The Nara State." *The Cambridge History of Japan. Vol. 1: Ancient Japan.* Ed. by Delmer M. Brown. Cambridge: Cambridge University Press, 1993.

Navari, Cornelia. "The Origins of the Nation-State." *The Nation-State: The Formation of Modern Politics.* Ed. by Leonard Tivey. New York: St. Martin's Press, 1981.

Nelson, Sarah Milledge. *The Archaeology of Korea.* Cambridge: Cambridge University Press, 1993.

———. "The Politics of Ethnicity in Prehistoric Korea." *Nationalism, Politics, and the Practice of Archaeology.* Ed. by Philip L. Kohl and Clare Fawcett. Cambridge: Cambridge University Press, 1995.

Ng-Quinn, Michael. "National Identity in Premodern China: Formation and Role Enactment." *China's Quest for National Identity.* Ed. by Lowell Dittmer and Samuel S. Kim. Ithaca, N.Y.: Cornell University Press, 1993.

Ni Jinsheng. "Wu-Hu luan Hua mingri de Zhongguo jingji" (The Chinese Economy in the Aftermath of the Barbarian Invasions). *Shihuo banyuekan*, 1.8 (1935).

———. "Wu-Hu luan Hua qianye de Zhongguo jingji" (The Chinese Economy on the Eve of the Barbarian Invasions). *Shihuo banyuekan*, 1.7 (1935).

Nichols, Johanna. *Linguistic Diversity in Space and Time.* Chicago: University of Chicago Press, 1992.

Nippon Gakujutsu Shinkōkai, trans. *The Manyōshū.* 1940; New York: Columbia University Press, 1965.

Nishibeppu Ganjitsu. "Kōeiden seisaku no haikei: Kōnin makki no Dazaifu to Saikaidō shokoku" (The Background for the Policy of Public Land Management: Dazaifu [Kyūshū] and the Provinces of the Western Seas at the End of the Kōnin Reign Period [810–824]). *Higashi Ajia to Nihon: rekishi hen.* Ed. by Tamura Enchō sensei koki-kinenkai. Tokyo: Yoshikawa kōbunkan, 1987.

Nishijima Sadao. *Nihon rekishi no kokusai kankyō* (The International Environment of Japanese History). 1985; Tokyo: Tōkyō daigaku shuppankai, 1997.

———. "Roku-hasseiki no higashi Ajia" (Sixth through Eighth Century East Asia). *Iwanami Kōza, Nihon rekishi II, kodai 2.* Tokyo: Iwanami shoten, 1962.

Nomura Shigeo. "'Su' o tsūjite mita, Shindai no Jusha" (Jin Dynasty Confucians as Observed through the Term "Simplicity"). *Tōhōgaku*, 61 (1981).

Norman, Jerry, and Mei, Tsu-lin. "The Austroasiatics in Ancient South China: Some Lexical Evidence." *Monumenta Serica*, 32 (1976).

Ōba Osamu. *Kodai, chūsei ni okeru Nit-Chū kankeishi no kenkyū* (Studies in the History of Sino-Japanese Relations in Antiquity and the Middle Ages). Kyoto: Dōhōsha shuppan, 1996.

———. "Nihon no kenkyūsha kara mita Nit-Chū bunka kōryūshi" (The History of Sino-Japanese Cultural Exchange as Viewed by Japanese Scholars). *Nitchū bunka kōryūshi sōsho, 1: rekishi*. Ed. by Ōba Osamu and Wang Xiaoqiu. Tokyo: Taishūkan shoten, 1995.

———. *Qin-Han fazhi shi yanjiu* (Studies in the History of Qin-Han Legal Systems). Trans. by Lin Jianming et al. Shanghai: Shanghai renmin chubanshe, 1991.

Ochi Shigeaki. "Hoku-Gi no kindensei o megutte" (Concerning the Northern Wei Equitable Fields System). *Shien*, 108 (1972).

———. "Nanchō no kizoku to gōzoku" (Southern Dynasty Aristocrats and Magnates). *Shien*, 69 (1956).

———. "Tō-Shin no kizokusei to nanboku no 'chien' sei" (The Aristocratic System of the Eastern Jin and the Quality of Northern and Southern "Regional Affinity"). *Shigaku-zashi*, 67.8 (1958).

———. "Tō-Shin nanchō no mura to gōzoku" (Villages and Magnates of the Eastern Jin and Southern Dynasties). *Shigaku-zasshi*, 79.10 (1970).

Ōkawa Fujio. "Rikuchō zenki no Gokō gun no gōzoku: tokuni Bukō no Shin shi o megutte" (The Magnates of Wuxing Commandery in the First Part of the Six Dynasties: Especially concerning the Shen Family of Wukang). *Shūkyō shakai shi kenkyū*. Ed. by Risshō daigaku shigakukai. Tokyo: Yūzankaku, 1977.

Okazaki Fumio. *Gi-Shin Nanbokuchō tsūshi* (A Comprehensive History of the Wei, Jin, Northern and Southern Dynasties). 1932; Tokyo: Kōbundō shobō, 1943.

Oksenberg, Michel. "Taiwan, Tibet, and Hong Kong in Sino-American Relations." *Living with China: U.S.-China Relations in the Twenty-First Century*. Ed. by Ezra F. Vogel. New York: W. W. Norton, 1997.

Ōmachi Ken. "Higashi Ajia no naka no Nihon ritsuryō kokka" (The Japanese Ritsuryō State in East Asia). *Ajia kara mita kodai Nihon*. Ed. by Tamura Kōichi and Suzuki Yasutami. Tokyo: Sumigawa shoten, 1992.

Ōsumi Kiyoharu. "Tō no reisei to Nihon" (The Tang Ritual System and Japan). *Kodai o kangaeru: Tō to Nihon*. Ed. by Ikeda On. Tokyo: Yoshikawa kōbunkan, 1992.

Palais, James B. "A Search for Korean Uniqueness." *Harvard Journal of Asiatic Studies*, 55.2 (1995).

Pan Guojian (Poon Kwok Kin). *Bei-Wei yu Ruanruan guanxi yanjiu* (A Study of the Relationship between the Northern Wei [Dynasty] and the Ruanruan [Steppe Empire]). Taibei: Taiwan shangwu yinshuguan, 1988.

Pan Wusu. "Xi-Jin taishi ban lü de lishi yiyi" (The Historical Significance of the Laws Promulgated during the Taishi Reign Period of the Western Jin Dynasty). *Xianggang zhongwen daxue, Zhongguo wenhua yanjiusuo xuebao*, 22 (1991).

Pan, Yihong. "Early Chinese Settlement Policies towards the Nomads." *Asia Major*, 3rd series, 5.2 (1992).

———. *Son of Heaven and Heavenly Qaghan: Sui-Tang China and Its Neighbors.* Bellingham: Western Washington University, 1997.

Paper, Jordan D., trans. *The Fu-Tzu: A Post-Han Confucian Text.* 3rd century; Leiden: E. J. Brill, 1987.

Pearson, Richard. *Ancient Japan.* New York: George Braziller, 1992.

———. "Dong-Son and Its Origins." *Zhongyang yanjiuyuan, Minzuxue yanjiusuo jikan*, 13 (1962).

Pelliot, Paul. *Oeuvres posthumes IV: Les débuts de l'imprimerie en chine.* Paris: Imprimerie nationale, 1953.

Peters, Heather A. "Tattooed Faces and Stilt Houses: Who Were the Ancient Yue?" *Sino-Platonic Papers*, 17. Philadelphia: University of Pennsylvania, Department of Oriental Studies, 1990.

———. "Towns and Trade: Cultural Diversity and Chu Daily Life." *Defining Chu: Image and Reality in Ancient China.* Ed. by Constance A. Cook and John S. Major. Honolulu: University of Hawai'i Press, 1999.

Peterson, Charles A. "The Restoration Completed: Emperor Hsien-tsung and the Provinces." *Perspectives on the T'ang.* Ed. by Arthur F. Wright and Denis Twitchett. New Haven, Conn.: Yale University Press, 1973.

Piggott, Joan R. *The Emergence of Japanese Kingship.* Stanford, Calif.: Stanford University Press, 1997.

———. "Mokkan: Wooden Documents from the Nara Period." *Monumenta Nipponica*, 45.4 (1990).

Pirenne, Henri. *Mohammed and Charlemagne.* Trans. by Bernard Miall. London: George Allen and Unwin, 1939.

Pollack, David. *The Fracture of Meaning: Japan's Synthesis of China from the Eighth through the Eighteenth Centuries.* Princeton, N.J.: Princeton University Press, 1986.

Pollock, Sheldon. "The Cosmopolitan Vernacular." *Journal of Asian Studies*, 57.1 (1998).

Powers, Martin J. *Art and Political Expression in Early China.* New Haven, Conn.: Yale University Press, 1991.

Pritchard, Earl H. "Thoughts on the Historical Development of the Population of China." *Journal of Asian Studies*, 23.1 (1963).

Psarras, Sophia-Karin. "Exploring the North: Non-Chinese Cultures of the Late Warring States and Han." *Monumenta Serica*, 42 (1994).

Pu Jian. *Zhongguo gudai xingzheng lifa* (Ancient Chinese Administration and Legislation). Beijing: Beijing daxue chubanshe, 1990.

Pulleyblank, Edwin G. "The An Lu-shan Rebellion and the Origins of Chronic Militarism in Late T'ang China." *Essays on T'ang Society: The In-*

terplay of Social, Political and Economic Forces. Ed. by John Curtis Perry and Bardwell L. Smith. Leiden: E. J. Brill, 1976.

———. *The Background of the Rebellion of An Lu-shan.* London: Oxford University Press, 1955.

———. "The Chinese and Their Neighbors in Prehistoric and Early Historic Times." *The Origins of Chinese Civilization.* Ed. by David N. Keightley. Berkeley and Los Angeles: University of California Press, 1983.

———. *Middle Chinese: A Study in Historical Phonology.* Vancouver: University of British Columbia Press, 1984.

———. "Registration of Population in China in the Sui and T'ang Periods." *Journal of the Economic and Social History of the Orient,* 4.3 (1961).

———. "Zou and Lu and the Sinification of Shandong." *Chinese Language, Thought, and Culture: Nivison and His Critics.* Ed. by Philip J. Ivanhoe. Chicago: Open Court, 1996.

Qian Mu. "Lüe lun Wei-Jin nanbeichao xueshu wenhua yu dangshi mendi zhi guanxi" (A Brief Discussion of Wei, Jin, Northern and Southern Dynasty Scholarly Culture and Its Relation to Social Position at That Time). *Zhongguo xueshu sixiang shi luncong, 3.* 1963; Taibei: Dongda tushu, 1985.

———. "Zhonguo lishi shang de zhengzhi zhidu" (Political Systems of Chinese History). *Shixue huikan,* 11 (1981).

Qin-Han jingji sixiang shi (A History of Qin-Han Economic Thought). Shanghai shehui kexueyuan, jingji yanjiusuo, jingji sixiang shi, yanjiushi. Beijing: Zhonghua shuju, 1989.

Qiu Tiansheng. *Tang-Song biangeqi de zheng-jing yu shehui* (The Political Economy and Society of the Tang-Song Transitional Era). Taibei: Wen jin chubanshe, 1999.

Qu Xiaoqiang. *Bai ma dong lai: Fojiao dongchuan jiemi* (The White Horse Comes East: Uncovering the Secret of Buddhism's Eastward Dissemination). Chengdu: Sichuan renmin chubanshe, 1995.

Queen, Sarah A. *From Chronicle to Canon: The Hermeneutics of the Spring and Autumn, according to Tung Chung-shu.* Cambridge: Cambridge University Press, 1996.

Ramsey, S. Robert. *The Languages of China.* Princeton, N.J.: Princeton University Press, 1987.

Rao Zongyi. "Wu-Yue wenhua" (Wu and Yue Culture). *Zhongyang yanjiuyuan: Lishi yuyan yanjiusuo jikan,* 41.4 (1969).

Rawski, Evelyn S. *The Last Emperors: A Social History of Qing Imperial Institutions.* Berkeley and Los Angeles: University of California Press, 1998.

Ray, Himanshu P. *The Winds of Change: Buddhism and the Maritime Links of Early South Asia.* Delhi: Oxford University Press, 1994.

Reischauer, Edwin O., trans. *Ennin's Diary: The Record of a Pilgrimage to China in Search of the Law.* New York: The Ronald Press, 1955.

———. *Ennin's Travels in T'ang China.* New York: The Ronald Press, 1955.

Ren Jiyu. *Han-Tang Fojiao sixiang lunji* (Collected Essays on Han-Tang Buddhist Thought). 1963; Beijing: Renmin chubanshe, 1973.

Ren Yiming. "Feng Taihou linchao yu gaige" (The Regency [476–490] and Reforms of Empress Dowager Feng). *Bei Wei shi*. Ed. by Du Shiduo. Taiyuan: Shanxi gaoxiao lianhe chubanshe, 1992.

Renondéau, G. "La date de l'introduction du bouddhisme au Japon." *T'oung Pao*, 47 (1959).

Rhie, Marylin Martin. *Early Buddhist Art of China and Central Asia. Vol. 1: Later Han, Three Kingdoms and Western Chin in China and Bactria to Shan-shan in Central Asia*. Leiden: E. J. Brill, 1999.

Robertson, Jennifer. "It Takes a Village: Internationalization and Nostalgia in Postwar Japan." *Mirror of Modernity: Invented Traditions of Modern Japan*. Ed. by Stephen Vlastos. Berkeley and Los Angeles: University of California Press, 1998.

Robinet, Isabelle. *Taoism: Growth of a Religion*. Trans. by Phyllis Brooks. 1992; Stanford, Calif.: Stanford University Press, 1997.

Robinson, Michael Edson. *Cultural Nationalism in Colonial Korea, 1920–1925*. Seattle: University of Washington Press, 1988.

Rogers, Michael C. *The Chronicle of Fu Chien: A Case of Exemplar History*. Berkeley, Calif.: University of California Press, 1968.

———. "The Myth of the Battle of the Fei River (A.D. 383)." *T'oung Pao*, 54.1–3 (1968).

———. "National Consciousness in Medieval Korea: The Impact of Liao and Chin on Koryŏ. *China among Equals: The Middle Kingdom and Its Neighbors, 10th–14th Centuries*. Ed. by Morris Rossabi. Berkeley and Los Angeles: University of California Press, 1983.

Sa Mengwu. "Nanbeichao Fojiao liuxing de yuanyin" (Reasons for the Popularity of Buddhism in the Northern and Southern Dynasties). *Dalu zazhi*, 2.10 (1951).

Sa Shijiong. "Wei-Jin nanbeichao shidai de difang zhidu" (The Local Systems of the Wei-Jin, Northern and Southern Dynasties). *Dongfang zazhi*, 41.17 (1945).

Saeki Arikiyo. "Tō to Nihon no Bukkyō kōryū: nit-Tō junreisō to rai-Nichi dembōsō" (Buddhist Exchanges between Tang and Japan: Pilgrim Monks Who Went to Tang, and Missionary Monks Who Came to Japan). *Kodai o kangaeru: Tō to Nihon*. Ed. by Ikeda On. Tokyo: Yoshikawa kōbunkan, 1992.

Sage, Steven F. *Ancient Sichuan and the Unification of China*. Albany: State University of New York Press, 1992.

Saitō Tadashi. *Chōsen kodai bunka no kenkyū* (Studies in Ancient Korean Culture). Tokyo: Chijin shokan, 1943.

Sakamoto Tarō. *The Six National Histories of Japan*. Trans. by John S. Brownlee. Tokyo: University of Tokyo Press, 1991.

Salway, Peter. *A History of Roman Britain*. 1993; Oxford: Oxford University Press, 1997.

Samuels, Richard J. *"Rich Nation Strong Army": National Security and the Techno-logical Transformation of Japan.* Ithaca, N.Y.: Cornell University Press, 1994.

Sansom, G. B. *Japan: A Short Cultural History.* 1931; Stanford, Calif.: Stanford University Press, 1978.

SarDesai, D. R. *Vietnam: The Struggle for National Identity.* 1988; Boulder, Colo.: Westview Press, 1992.

Sato, Elizabeth. "The Early Development of the Shōen." *Medieval Japan: Essays in Institutional History.* Ed. by John W. Hall and Jeffrey P. Mass. Stanford, Calif.: Stanford University Press, 1974.

Satō Hiroo. "Bukkyō kyōdan to shūkyō seikatsu" (Buddhist Orders and the Religious Life). *Kōza: Bukkyō no juyō to henyō, 6: Nihon hen.* Ed. by Yamaori Tetsuo. Tokyo: Kōsei shuppansha, 1991.

Schafer, Edward H. *The Empire of Min.* Rutland: Charles E. Tuttle Company, 1954.

———. *The Golden Peaches of Samarkand: A Study of T'ang Exotics.* Berkeley and Los Angeles: University of California Press, 1963.

———. *The Vermilion Bird: T'ang Images of the South.* Berkeley and Los Angeles: University of California Press, 1967.

Schirokauer, Conrad, and Hymes, Robert. "Introduction." *Ordering the World: Approaches to State and Society in Sung Dynasty China.* Berkeley and Los Angeles: University of California Press, 1993.

Schmid, Andre. "Rediscovering Manchuria: Sin Ch'aeho and the Politics of Territorial History in Korea." *Journal of Asian Studies,* 56.1 (1997).

Schmidt-Glintzer, Helwig. "Der Literatenbeamte und seine Gemeinde: Oder der Charakter der Aristokratie im chinesischen Mittelalter." *Zeitschrift der Deutschen Morgenländischen Gesellschaft,* 139.2 (1989).

Schopen, Gregory. "Filial Piety and the Monk in the Practice of Indian Buddhism: A Question of 'Sinicization' Viewed from the Other Side." *T'oung Pao,* 70.1–3 (1984).

Schreiber, Gerhard. "The History of the Former Yen Dynasty." *Monumenta Serica,* 14 (1949–1955) and 15.1 (1956).

Seeley, Christopher. *A History of Writing in Japan.* Leiden: E. J. Brill, 1991.

Seidensticker, Edward G., trans. *The Tale of Genji.* By Murasaki Shikibu. New York: Vintage Books, 1976.

Seki Akira. "Ritsuryō kokka no seiji rinen" (The Political Ideology of the Ritsuryō State). *Nihon shisō shi kōza; 1, kodai no shisō.* Ed. by Furukawa Tetsushi and Ishida Ichirō. Tokyo: Yūzankaku shuppan, 1978.

Shaffer, Lynda Norene. *Maritime Southeast Asia to 1500.* Armonk, N.Y.: M. E. Sharpe, 1996.

Shao Taixin. *Han-dai Hexi si jun de tuozhan* (The Expansion and Development of the Four Commanderies West of the [Yellow] River in the Han Dynasty). Taibei: Taiwan shangwu yinshuguan, 1988.

Shi Dongchu. "San guo liang-Jin shidai de Fojiao" (The Buddhism of the

Three Kingdoms and Two Jin Dynasties Era). *Wei-Jin nanbeichao Fojiao xiaoshi.* Ed. by Huang Chanhua et al. Taibei: Dacheng wenhua chubanshe, 1979.

———. *Zhong-Ri Fojiao jiaotong shi* (A History of Sino-Japanese Buddhist Communications). *Dongchu laoren quanji,* vol. 2. 1970; Taibei: Dongchu chubanshe, 1985.

Shi Jiaming. "Riben gudai guojia de fazhan" (The Development of the Ancient Japanese State). *Zhongguo yu Riben,* 141 (1972).

Shi Lihua. "Riben bantian ling yu Tang dai juntian ling de bijiao" (A Comparison of the Japanese Handen Code with the Tang Dynasty Equitable Fields Code). *Riben shi lunwenji.* Ed. by Zhongguo Riben shixuehui. Shenyang: Liaoning renmin chubanshe, 1985.

Shi Nianhai. "Qin-Han shidai de minzu jingshen" (The National Spirit of Qin-Han Times). *Wen shi zazhi,* 4.1–2 (1944).

Shigechika Keiju. "Shin-Kan ni okeru yōyaku no sho keitai" (Various Forms of Compulsory Labor in Qin and Han). *Tōyōshi-kenkyū,* 49.3 (1990).

Shigezawa Toshirō. "Bunken mokuroku o tōshite mita Rikuchō no rekishi ishiki" (The Historical Consciousness of the Six Dynasties as Seen through Literary Catalogs). *Tōyōshi-kenkyū,* 18.1 (1959).

Shryock, John K. *The Origin and Development of the State Cult of Confucius.* New York: The Century Company, 1932.

Sinor, Denis. "The Establishment and Dissolution of the Türk Empire." *The Cambridge History of Early Inner Asia.* Ed. by Denis Sinor. Cambridge: Cambridge University Press, 1990.

———. "The Inner Asian Warriors." *Journal of the American Oriental Society,* 101 (1981).

———. "Languages and Cultural Interchange along the Silk Roads." *Diogenes,* 171.43 (1995).

———. "Some Components of the Civilization of the Türks (6th to 8th century A.D.)." *Altaistic Studies: Papers Presented at the 25th Meeting of the Permanent International Altaistic Conference at Uppsala, June 7–11 1982.* Ed. by G. Jarring and S. Rosén. Stockholm, 1985.

Siu, Helen F. "Cultural Identity and the Politics of Difference in South China." *China in Transformation.* Ed. by Tu Wei-ming. Cambridge, Mass.: Harvard University Press, 1994.

Snellen, J. B., trans. "Shoku Nihongi (Chronicles of Japan)." *Transactions of the Asiatic Society of Japan,* 2nd series, 11 (1934) and 14 (1937).

Snellgrove, David. *Indo-Tibetan Buddhism: Indian Buddhists and Their Tibetan Successors.* Boston: Shambhala, 1987.

So, Jenny F., and Bunker, Emma C. *Traders and Raiders on China's Northern Frontier.* Seattle: Smithsonian Institution, 1995.

Sŏ Yŏngsu. "Si zhi qi shiji Han-Zhong chaogong guanxi kao" (A Study of Tribute Relations between Korea and China in the Fourth through Seventh Centuries). *Gudai Zhong-Han-Ri guanxi yanjiu.* Ed. by Lin

Tianwei and Huang Yuese. Hong Kong: Centre of Asian Studies, University of Hong Kong, 1987.

Sogabe Shizuo. "Kinden hō to handen shūju hō no zeiyaku no hitokusa: chō no seikaku ni tsuite" (One Kind of Obligation in Equitable Fields Law and Handen Distribution Law: Concerning the Nature of the Diao [Craft and Produce Tax]). *Yamazaki Sensei taikan kinen tōyōshigaku ronshū*. Ed. by Yamazaki Sensei taikan kinenkai. Tokyo: Tōkyō kyōiku daigaku bungakubu tōyōshigaku kenkyū shitsunai, 1967.

Somers, Robert M. "The End of the T'ang." *The Cambridge History of China. Vol. 3: Sui and T'ang China, 589–906, Part 1*. Ed. by Denis Twitchett. Cambridge: Cambridge University Press, 1979.

——. "Time, Space, and Structure in the Consolidation of the T'ang Dynasty (A.D. 617–700)." *Journal of Asian Studies*, 45.5 (1986).

Song Jiayu. "Tang-Ri minhu shoutian zhidu xiangyi wenti shishi: juntianzhi yu bantianzhi bijiao yanjiu zhi yi" (Exploring the Question of Differences between Systems of Land Allocation to Subject Households in Tang and Japan: A Comparative Study of the Equitable Fields System with the Handen System). *Jinyang xuekan* (1988.6).

Song Qi. "Fojiao dong chuan ji qi dui Riben wenhua de yingxiang" (The Eastward Transmission of Buddhism and Its Influence on Japanese Culture). *Zhong-Ri Fojiao guanxi yanjiu*. Ed. by Zhang Mantao. Taibei: Dacheng wenhua chubanshe, 1978.

Song Qianggang. "Shilun Tang-dai wenhua fanrong de yuanyin ji Tang-dai Zhong-wai wenhua jiaoliu de tedian" (An Examination of the Reasons for Tang Dynasty Cultural Prosperity and the Special Characteristics of Sino-Foreign Cultural Exchange in the Tang Dynasty). *Sichuan jiaoyu xueyuan xuebao* (1994.4).

Song Yan. "Wei-Jin nanbeichao shizu dizhu zhengquan de yanbian" (The Evolution of the Political Authority of Wei-Jin, Northern and Southern Dynasty Great Family Landlords). *Lishi jiaoxue wenti*, 6 (1957).

Sonoda Kōyū. "Early Buddha Worship." *The Cambridge History of Japan. Vol. 1: Ancient Japan*. Ed. by John Whitney Hall. Cambridge: Cambridge University Press, 1993.

Soothill, William Edward. *The Hall of Light: A Study of Early Chinese Kingship*. London: Lutterworth Press, 1951.

Sotoyama Gunji. "Seiji" (Politics). *Kizoku shakai*. Ed. by Kyōdai tōyōshi kankōkai. Osaka: Sōgensha, 1981.

Stanlaw, James. "'For Beautiful Human Life': The Use of English in Japan." *Re-Made in Japan: Everyday Life and Consumer Taste in a Changing Society*. Ed. by Joseph J. Tobin. New Haven, Conn.: Yale University Press, 1992.

Stein, Rolf A. "Religious Taoism and Popular Religion from the Second to Seventh Centuries." *Facets of Taoism: Essays in Chinese Religion*. Ed. by Holmes Welch and Anna Seidel. New Haven, Conn.: Yale University Press, 1979.

————. *Tibetan Civilization*. Trans. by J. E. Stapleton Driver. 1962; Stanford, Calif.: Stanford University Press, 1972.

Strickmann, Michel. "India in the Chinese Looking Glass." *The Silk Route and the Diamond Path: Esoteric Buddhist Art on the Trans-Himalayan Trade Routes*. Ed. by Deborah E. Klimburg-Salter. Los Angeles: UCLA Art Council, 1982.

Su Shaoxing. "Qianlun liang-Jin nanchao shizu zhi zhengzhi diwei yu qi jingji liliang zhi guanxi" (A Superficial Discussion of the Relationship between the Political Status of Literati Families in the Two Jin and Southern Dynasties and Their Economic Strength). *Dalu zazhi*, 58.5 (1979).

Su Bingqi. *Zhongguo wenming qiyuan xintan* (A New Search for the Origins of Chinese Civilization). Hong Kong: Shangwu yinshuguan, 1997.

Sugimoto Naojirō. "The Life of Abe no Nakamaro (Ch'ao Heng) as Commented on by Waley: A Critical Study." *Acta Asiatica*, 17 (1969).

Sun Changwu. *Zhongguo Fojiao wenhua xushuo* (Introduction to Chinese Buddhist Culture). Tianjin: Nankai daxue chubanshe, 1990.

Sun Shuqi. *Liuchao sixiang shi* (A History of Six Dynasties Thought). Nanjing: Nanjing chubanshe, 1992.

Suwa Haruo. "Kodai Chūgoku Etsu-jin no Bakyō bunka to Nihon" (The Maqiao Culture of the Ancient Chinese Yue People and Japan). *Wazoku to kodai Nihon*. Ed. by Suwa Haruo. Tokyo: Yūzankaku shuppan, 1993.

Suzuki Hideo. *Kodai no Wakoku to Chōsen shokoku* (The Ancient Japanese State and the Various Countries of Korea). Tokyo: Aoki shoten, 1996.

Suzuki Shun. "Tōdai kindenhō shikō no igi ni tsuite" (Concerning the Significance of the Implementation of the Tang Dynasty Equitable Fields Law). *Shien*, 50 (1951).

Suzuki Yasutami. "Higashi Ajia shominzoku no kokka keisei to Yamato ōken" (The Formation of the Various National States in East Asia and Yamato Royal Authority). *Kōza: Nihon rekishi. Vol. 1: genshi-kodai, Part 1*. Ed. by Rekishigaku Kenkyūkai and Nihonshi Kenkyūkai. Tokyo: Tōkyō daigaku shuppankai, 1984.

Swanson, Paul L. *The Foundations of T'ien-T'ai Philosophy: The Flowering of the Two Truths Theory in Chinese Buddhism*. Berkeley, Calif.: Asian Humanities Press, 1989.

Takahashi Tetsu. "Rikuchō-ki Kōnan no shō-nōmin" (The Small Farmers of Jiangnan in the Six Dynasties Period). *Shichō*, 107 (1969).

Takaki, Ronald. *Strangers from a Different Shore: A History of Asian Americans*. 1989; Boston: Little, Brown and Company, 1998.

Takatori Yuji. "Kandai sanrō no henka to kyōka" (The Transformation and Education of Han Dynasty Elders [*San-Lao*]). *Tōyōshi-kenkyū*, 53.2 (1994).

Takeuchi Rizō. "Documents of Local Administration in the Nara Period: the Household Registers and the Tax Registers." *Tang China and Beyond: Studies on East Asia from the Seventh to the Tenth Century*. Ed. by Antonino

Forte. Kyoto: Istituto Italiano di cultura, Scuola di Studi sull'Asia Orientale, 1988.

Takikawa Masajirō. *Ritsuryō no kenkyū* (Studies of the Ritsuryō). Tokyo: Tōkō shoin, 1931.

Tamura Enchō. "Japan and the Eastward Permeation of Buddhism." *Acta Asiatica*, 47 (1985).

————. "Kudara Bukkyōshi josetsu" (An Introduction to the History of Buddhism in Paekche). *Kudara bunka to Asuka bunka*. Ed. by Tamura Enchō and Huang Su-yŏng. Tokyo: Yoshikawa kōbunkan, 1978.

Tan Qixiang. "Lun liang-Han xi-Jin hukou" (On the Population of the Two Han and Western Jin). *Yugong banyuekan*, 1.7 (1934).

Tanaka, Stefan. *Japan's Orient: Rendering Pasts into History*. Berkeley and Los Angeles: University of California Press, 1993.

Tang Changru. "Jin-dai beijing gezu 'bianluan' de xingzhi ji wu-Hu zhengquan zai Zhongguo de tongzhi" (The "Rebellious" Temperament of the Various Peoples on the Northern Frontier during the Jin Dynasty and the Rule of the Five Hu in China). *Wei-Jin nanbeichao shi luncong*. 1955; Shenghuo, dushu, xinzhi sanlian shudian, 1978.

————. *San zhi liu shiji Jiangnan da tudi suoyouzhi de fazhan* (The Development of a Large Landholding System in Third through Sixth-Century Jiangnan). 1957; Taibei: Baishu chubanshe, n.d.

Tang Renwu. "Tang-dai 'yi gong-shang' guoce yu 'zhong-shang' shehui guannian de duili" (The Opposition between the Tang Dynasty Government Policy of Repressing Artisans and Merchants and the Social Concept of Valuing Commerce). *Hebei shifan daxue xuebao: she ke ban* (1995.3).

Tang Yongtong. *Han-Wei liang-Jin nanbeichao Fojiao shi* (A History of Buddhism during the Han, Wei, Two Jin, Northern and Southern Dynasties). 1938; Beijing: Zhonghua shuju, 1983.

Tanigawa Michio. "Hokuchō kizoku no seikatsu rinri" (The Northern Dynasty Aristocracy's Ethics of Living). *Chūgoku chūseishi kenkyū: Rikuchō, Zui, Tō no shakai to bunka*. Ed. by Utsunomiya Kiyoyoshi. Tokyo: Tōkai daigaku shuppankai, 1970.

————. *Chūgoku chūsei no tankyū: rekishi to ningen* (The Search for a Chinese Middle Ages: History and Humanity). Tokyo: Nihon edeitā-sukūru shuppanbu, 1987.

————. "Higashi Ajia sekai keiseiki no shiteki kōzō: sakuhō taisei o chūshin toshite" (The Historical Framework for the Period of the Formation of the East Asian World: Centering on the Investment System). *Zui-Tō teikoku to higashi Ajia sekai*. Ed. by Tōdaishi kenkyūkai. Tokyo: Kūko shoin, 1979.

————. "Kindensei no rinen to dai-tochi shoyū" (The Ideal of the Equitable Fields System and Large Landownership). *Tōyōshi-kenkyū*, 25.4 (1967).

————. *Medieval Chinese Society and the Local "Community."* Trans. by Joshua A. Fogel. Berkeley and Los Angeles: University of California Press, 1985.

———. "Ziying nongmin yu guojia zhi jian de gongtongti-xing guanxi: cong bei-Wei de nongye zhengce tan qi" (The Communal Quality of Relations between Independent Farmers and the State: A Discussion Beginning with Northern Wei Agricultural Policy). Trans. by Yang Qingshun. *Shihuo yuekan,* new series, 11.5 (1981).

Tao Xisheng. *Zhongguo shehui zhi shi de fenxi* (An Analysis of the History of Chinese Society). Shanghai: Xin shengming shuju, 1929.

———, and Shen Juchen. *Qin-Han zhengzhi zhidu* (Qin-Han Political Institutions). Shanghai: Shangwu yinshuguan, 1936.

———, and Wu Xianqing. *Nanbeichao jingji shi* (An Economic History of the Northern and Southern Dynasties). 1937; Taibei: Shihuo chubanshe, 1979.

Taylor, Keith Weller. *The Birth of Vietnam.* Berkeley and Los Angeles: University of California Press, 1983.

———. "Surface Orientations in Vietnam: Beyond Histories of Nation and Region." *Journal of Asian Studies,* 57.4 (1998).

Teng, Ssu-yü, trans. *Family Instructions for the Yen Clan: Yen-shih Chia-hsün.* Leiden: E. J. Brill, 1968.

Thompson, E. A. *Romans and Barbarians: The Decline of the Western Empire.* Madison: University of Wisconsin Press, 1982.

Tian Yuqing. *Dong-Jin menfa zhengzhi* (Eastern Jin Great Family Politics). Beijing: Beijing daxue chubanshe, 1989.

———. "Helan buluo lisan wenti: Bei-Wei 'lisan buluo' ge'an kaocha zhi yi" (The Problem of the Dispersal of the Helan Tribe: A Case Study of the Northern Wei "Dispersal of Tribes"). *Lishi yanjiu* (1997.2).

Tilakaratne, Asanga. "The Development of 'Sacred Language' in the Buddhist Tradition." *Premier colloque Étienne Lamotte* (Bruxelles et Liège 24–27 septembre 1989). Louvain-la-Neuve: Université Catholique de Louvain, Institut Orientaliste, 1993.

Todd, Malcolm. *The Northern Barbarians, 100 B.C.–A.D. 300.* London: Hutchinson and Co., 1975.

Tokuno, Kyoko. "The Evaluation of Indigenous Scriptures in Chinese Buddhist Bibliographical Catalogues." *Chinese Buddhist Apocrypha.* Ed. by Robert E. Buswell, Jr. Honolulu: University of Hawai'i Press, 1990.

Tonami Mamoru and Takeda Yukio. *Zui-Tō teikoku to kodai Chōsen* (The Sui-Tang Empire and Ancient Korea). *Sekai no rekishi,* vol. 6. Tokyo: Chuokoron-sha, 1997.

Torao Toshiya. "Nara Economic and Social Institutions." *The Cambridge History of Japan.* Vol. 1: *Ancient Japan.* Ed. by Delmer M. Brown. Cambridge: Cambridge University Press, 1993.

Tsien, Tsuen-Hsuin. *Written on Bamboo and Silk: The Beginnings of Chinese Books and Inscriptions.* Chicago: University of Chicago Press, 1962.

Tsuda Sōkichi. *Bungaku ni arawaretaru waga kokumin shisō no kenkyū: (1) kizoku bungaku no jidai* (Studies in Our National Thought as Revealed by Literature: 1, The Age of Aristocratic Literature). Tokyo: Rakuyōdō, 1916.

Tsuji Zennosuke. *Nihon Bukkyōshi kenkyū, 6* (Studies in Japanese Buddhist History). Tokyo: Iwanami shoten, 1984.

————. *Nihon bunka shi, 1; jōko-Nara jidai* (A History of Japanese Culture, 1; High Antiquity and the Nara Period). Reprint; Tokyo: Shunjū sha, 1969.

Tsukamoto, Zenryū. "The Early Stages in the Introduction of Buddhism into China (Up to the Fifth Century A.D.)." *Cahiers d'histoire mondiale,* 5.3 (1960).

————. *A History of Early Chinese Buddhism: From Its Introduction to the Death of Hui-Yüan.* Trans. by Leon Hurvitz. 1979; Tokyo: Kodansha, 1985.

————. *Shina Bukkyōshi kenkyū, Hoku-Gi hen* (Studies in Chinese Buddhist History, the Northern Wei Part). Tokyo: Kōbuntō shobō, 1942.

Tsuzuki Akiko. "Nanjin kanmon, kanjin, no shūkyōteki sōzōryoku ni tsuite: Shinkō o megutte" (On the Religious Imagination of Southern Non-Aristocratic Families and Individuals: Regarding the Zhengao [Declarations of the Perfected]). *Tōyōshi-kenkyū,* 47.2 (1988).

Twitchett, Denis. "The Composition of the T'ang Ruling Class: New Evidence from Tunhuang." *Perspectives on the T'ang.* Ed. by Arthur F. Wright and Denis Twitchett. New Haven, Conn.: Yale University Press, 1973.

————. *Financial Administration under the T'ang Dynasty.* Cambridge: Cambridge University Press, 1963.

————. "Introduction." *The Cambridge History of China.* Vol. 3: Sui and T'ang China, 589–906, Part 1. Cambridge: Cambridge University Press, 1979.

————. "Local Financial Administration in Early T'ang Times." *Asia Major,* new series, 15.1 (1969).

————. "Population and Pestilence in T'ang China." *Studia Sino-Mongolica: Festschrift für Herbert Franke.* Ed. by Wolfgang Bauer. Wiesbaden: Franz Steiner, 1979.

————. *Printing and Publishing in Medieval China.* New York: Frederic C. Beil, 1983.

————. "The T'ang Market System." *Asia Major,* new series, 12.2 (1966).

Uchida Gifu. "Kizoku shakai no kōzō" (The Structure of Aristocratic Society). *Kizoku shakai.* Ed. by Kyōdai tōyōshi kankōkai. Osaka: Sōgensha, 1981.

Ueda Masaaki. *Kikajin: kodai kokka no seiritsu o megutte* (Naturalized Persons: Concerning the Formation of the Ancient State). Tokyo: Chūō kōron-sha, 1965.

————. *Ronkyū: kodaishi to higashi Ajia* (Discussion: Ancient History and East Asia). Tokyo: Iwanami shoten, 1998.

Ueda Sanae. "Kizokuteki kansei no seiritsu: shōkan no yūrai to sono seikaku" (The Formation of an Aristocratic Civil Service System: The Origin of Pure Offices and Their Character). *Chūgoku chūsei shi kenkyū: Rikuchō Zui-Tō no shakai to bunka.* Ed. by Utsunomiya Kiyoyoshi. 1970; Tokyo: Tōkai daigaku shuppansha, 1980.

Ury, Marian. "Chinese Learning and Intellectual Life." *The Cambridge History of Japan. Vol. 2: Heian Japan.* Ed. by Donald H. Shively and William H. McCullough. Cambridge: Cambridge University Press, 1999.

Usami Kazuhiro. "Tō Chūjo: Jukyō kokkyōka no suishinsha" (Dong Zhongshu: Promoter of Confucianism as State Orthodoxy). *Chūgoku shisō shi.* Ed. by Hihara Toshikuni. Tokyo: Perikansha, 1987.

Van Dam, R. "The Pirenne Thesis and Fifth-century Gaul." *Fifth-Century Gaul: A Crisis of Identity?* Ed. by John Drinkwater and Hugh Elton. Cambridge: Cambridge University Press, 1992.

Varley, H. Paul. *Warriors of Japan as Portrayed in the War Tales.* Honolulu: University of Hawai'i Press, 1994.

———, trans. *A Chronicle of Gods and Sovereigns: Jinnō Shōtōki of Kitabatake Chikafusa.* 1343; New York: Columbia University Press, 1980.

Vuong Loc. "Glimpses of the Evolution of the Vietnamese Language." *Vietnamese Studies,* 40 (1975).

Wailes, Bernard, and Zoll, Amy L. "Civilization, Barbarism, and Nationalism in European Archaeology." *Nationalism, Politics, and the Practice of Archaeology.* Ed. by Philip L. Kohl and Clare Fawcett. Cambridge: Cambridge University Press, 1995.

Wakae Kenzō. "Shin-Kan ritsu ni okeru 'fukō' tsumi" (The Crime of "Unfilial" [Conduct] in Qin and Han Law). *Tōyōshi-kenkyū,* 55.2 (1996).

Waldron, Arthur. *The Great Wall of China: From History to Myth.* Cambridge: Cambridge University Press, 1990.

Waley, Arthur. "The Fall of Lo-Yang." *History Today* (1951).

Wallacker, Benjamin E. "Chang Fei's Preface to the Chin Code of Law." *T'oung Pao,* 72.4–5 (1986).

———. "Han Confucianism and Confucius in Han." *Ancient China: Studies in Early Civilization.* Ed. by David T. Roy and Tsuen-hsuin Tsien. Hong Kong: The Chinese University Press, 1978.

Walton, Linda. *Academies and Society in Southern Sung China.* Honolulu: University of Hawai'i Press, 1999.

Wan Shengnan. *Wei-Jin nanbeichao shi lungao* (Draft Essays on Wei-Jin, Northern and Southern Dynasty History). Hefei: Anhui jiaoyu chubanshe, 1983.

Wang Chengwen. "Liu zu Hui Neng zaonian yu Tang chu Lingnan wenhua kaolun" (A Study of the Sixth [Zen] Patriarch Hui Neng's Early Years and the Lingnan Culture of Early Tang). *Zhongshan daxue xuebao: she ke ban* (1998.3).

———. "Tang-dai 'nan xuan' yu Lingnan xidong haozu" (Tang Dynasty "Southern Selection" and the Powerful Families of the Streams and Grottoes in Lingnan). *Zhongguo shi yanjiu* (1998.1).

Wang Chuan. "Nan-Yue guo shi yanjiu gaishu" (A General Description of Research into the History of the Southern Yue Kingdom). *Zhongguo shi yanjiu dongtai* (1995.11).

Wang Gungwu. "The Chinese Urge to Civilize: Reflections on Change." *Journal of Asian History*, 18.1 (1984).

———. "The Nanhai Trade: A Study of the Early History of Chinese Trade in the South China Sea." *Journal of the Malayan Branch of the Royal Asiatic Society*, 31.2 (1958).

Wang Jiahua. *Nitchū Jugaku no hikaku* (A Comparison of Japanese and Chinese Confucianism). Tokyo: Rokkō shuppan, 1988.

———. *Rujia sixiang yu Riben wenhua* (Confucian Thought and Japanese Culture). Taibei: Shuxin chubanshe, 1994.

Wang Jianqun. *Hao-tai-wang bei yanjiu* (Studies of the Hot'aewang [King Kwanggaet'o, r. 391–413] Stele). Changchun: Jilin renmin chubanshe, 1984.

Wang Jinlin. *Han-Tang wenhua yu gudai Riben wenhua* (Han-Tang Culture and Ancient Japanese Culture). Tianjin: Tianjin renmin chubanshe, 1996.

———. *Nara bunka to Tō bunka* (Nara Culture and Tang Culture). Tokyo: Rokkō shuppan, 1988.

———. "Tō dai Bukkyō to Nara Bukkyō to no hikaku: kokka Bukkyō no tokushitsu o chūshin toshite" (A Comparison between Tang Buddhism and Nara Buddhism: Centering upon the Special Characteristics of State Buddhism). *Higashi Ajia to Nihon: kōko, bijutsu hen*. Ed. by Tamura Enchō sensei koki kinenkai. Tokyo: Yoshikawa kōbunkan, 1987.

Wang Liping. "Sui-chao de bianjiang jinglüe" (Sui Dynasty Frontier Operations). *Zhongguo bianjiang shi, di, yanjiu* (1999.1).

Wang Sanbei, and Zhao Hongbo. "Sui Yangdi minzu zhengce xinlun" (A New Appraisal of Emperor Yang of Sui's Ethnic Policies). *Xibei shida xuebao: she ke ban* (1996.5).

Wang Shaopu. "Zhong-Ri liang-guo fengjian zhengzhi tizhi de qubie" (Distinctions between the Feudal Political Systems of the Two Countries of China and Japan). *Xueshu yuekan* (1995.2).

Wang Xiaopu. *Tang, Tufan, Dashi zhengzhi guanxi shi* (A History of Tang, Tibetan, and Arab Political Relations). Beijing: Beijing daxue chubanshe, 1992.

Wang Xiaoyan. "Xiaowen di qian Luo yu weixin" (Emperor Xiaowen's Move to Luoyang and Reforms). *Bei-Wei shi*. Ed. by Du Shiduo. Taiyuan: Shanxi gaoxiao lianhe chubanshe, 1992.

Wang Yanwu. "Xuanze de guocheng: Wei-Jin nanbeichao shidai tezheng" (The Process of Selection: A Special Feature of the Wei-Jin, Northern and Southern Dynasty Era). *Zhong-nan minzu xueyuan xuebao: zhe she ban* (1989.4).

Wang Yi. *Sui-Tang yu Hou-San-Han guanxi ji Riben qian Sui shi, qian Tang shi, yundong* (Sui and Tang Relations with the Later Three-Han [of Korea] and the Japanese Movement to Send Embassies to Sui and Tang). Taibei: Taiwan Zhonghua shuju, 1972.

Wang Yitong (Wang Yi-t'ung). *Wuchao mendi,* vol. 1 (Social Position in the Five [i.e., Six] Dynasties). Reprint; Hong Kong: Zhongwen daxue chubanshe, 1978.

Wang Yi-t'ung (Wang Yitong). "Slaves and Other Comparable Social Groups during the Northern Dynasties (386–618)." *Harvard Journal of Asiatic Studies,* 16.3–4 (1953).

Wang Yü-ch'üan. "The Central Government of the Former Han Dynasty." *The Making of China: Main Themes in Premodern Chinese History.* Ed. by Chang Chun-shu. Englewood Cliffs, N.J.: Prentice Hall, 1975.

Wang Yunwu. *Jin-Tang zhengzhi sixiang* (Political Thought from Jin to Tang). Taibei: Taiwan shangwu yinshuguan, 1969.

Wang Zhenping. "Chinese Titles as a Means of Diplomatic Communication between China and Japan during the Han-Tang Period." *Studies in Chinese History,* 2 (1992).

———. *Han-Tang Zhong-Ri guanxi lun* (On Sino-Japanese Relations from the Han through the Tang Dynasties). Taibei: Wenjin chubanshe, 1997.

———. "Speaking with a Forked Tongue: Diplomatic Correspondence between China and Japan, 238–608 A.D." *Journal of the American Oriental Society,* 114.1 (1994).

Wang Zhongluo. "Wei-Jin fengjian lun" (On Wei-Jin Feudalism). *Zehua shan guan conggao.* Reprint; Taibei: Taiwan shangwu yinshuguan, 1990.

———. *Wei-Jin nanbeichao shi* (A History of the Wei, Jin, Northern and Southern Dynasties). Shanghai: Shanghai renmin chubanshe, 1980.

Wang Zhoukun. "Tang dai Xinluo liuxuesheng zai Zhong-Chao wenhua jiaoliu zhong de zuoyong" (The Function of Tang Dynasty Sillan Overseas Students in Sino-Korean Cultural Exchange). *Xibei daxue xuebao: zhe she ban* (1994.2).

Ware, James R. "Wei Shou on Buddhism." *T'oung Pao,* 30 (1933).

Watanabe Shinichirō. "*Kōkyō* no kokka ron: *Kōkyō* to Kan ōchō" (The *Classic of Filial Piety* on the State: The *Classic of Filial Piety* and the Han Dynasty). *Chūgoku kizokusei shakai no kenkyū.* Ed. by Kawakatsu Yoshio and Tonami Mamoru. Kyoto: Kyōto daigaku jinbun kagaku kenkyū sho, 1987.

———. "Shō—aruiwa ni-nana seiki Chūgoku ni okeru ichi ideorogi: keitai to kokka" (Purity—A Possible Ideology in Second- to Seventh-Century China: Form and Nation). *Kyōto furitsu daigaku gakujutsu hōkoku, "jinbun,"* 31 (1979).

Watanabe Yoshihiro. "Kan-Gi kōtaiki no shakai" (Society in the Period of Transition from Han to Wei). *Rekishigaku kenkyū,* 626 (1991).

———. "Sangoku jidai ni okeru 'bungaku' no seijiteki senyō: Rikuchō kizokusei keiseishi no shiten kara" (The Political Promotion of "Literature" in the Three Kingdoms Period: From the Point of View of the History of the Formation of the Six Dynasties Aristocratic System). *Tōyōshi-kenkyū,* 54.3 (1995).

Waters, Geoffrey R. *Three Elegies of Ch'u: An Introduction to the Traditional Inter-pretation of the Ch'u Tz'u.* Madison: University of Wisconsin Press, 1985.

Watson, Burton, trans. *Hsün Tzu: Basic Writings.* New York: Columbia University Press, 1963.

———. *Records of the Grand Historian of China: Translated from the Shih Chi of Ssu-ma Ch'ien.* New York: Columbia University Press, 1961.

Watson, James L. "Rites or Beliefs? The Construction of a Unified Culture in Late Imperial China." *China's Quest for National Identity.* Ed. by Lowell Dittmer and Samuel S. Kim. Ithaca, N.Y.: Cornell University Press, 1993.

Watson, William. *Cultural Frontiers in Ancient East Asia.* Edinburgh: Edinburgh University Press, 1971.

Wechsler, Howard J. *Offerings of Jade and Silk: Ritual and Symbol in the Legitimization of the T'ang Dynasty.* New Haven, Conn.: Yale University Press, 1985.

Weinstein, Stanley. "The Beginnings of Esoteric Buddhism in Japan: The Neglected Tendai Tradition." *Journal of Asian Studies,* 34.1 (1974).

———. "Imperial Patronage in the Formation of T'ang Buddhism." *Perspectives on the T'ang.* Ed. by Arthur F. Wright and Denis Twitchett. New Haven, Conn.: Yale University Press, 1973.

Wells, Peter S. *The Barbarians Speak: How the Conquered Peoples Shaped Roman Europe.* Princeton, N.J.: Princeton University Press, 1999.

Wheatley, Paul. *The Pivot of the Four Quarters: A Preliminary Inquiry into the Origins and Character of the Ancient Chinese City.* Chicago: Aldine Publishing Company, 1971.

———, and See, Thomas. *From Court to Capital: A Tentative Interpretation of the Origins of the Japanese Urban Tradition.* Chicago: University of Chicago Press, 1978.

Wiens, Herold J. *China's March to the Tropics: A Study of the Cultural and Historical Geography of South China.* Washington, D.C.: Office of Naval Research, 1952.

Woodside, Alexander Barton. *Vietnam and the Chinese Model: A Comparative Study of Nguyen and Ch'ing Civil Government in the First Half of the Nineteenth Century.* Cambridge, Mass.: Harvard University Press, 1971.

Wright, Arthur F. "Biography and Hagiography: Hui-chiao's *Lives of Eminent Monks.*" *Zinbun-kagaku-kenkyusyo,* Silver Jubilee Volume (1954).

———. "Buddhism and Chinese Culture: Phases of Interaction." *Journal of Asian Studies,* 17.1 (1957).

———. *Buddhism in Chinese History.* Stanford, Calif.: Stanford University Press, 1959.

———. "The Formation of Sui Ideology, 581–604." *Chinese Thought and Institutions.* Ed. by John K. Fairbank. Chicago: University of Chicago Press, 1957.

———. "Fu I and the Rejection of Buddhism." *Journal of the History of Ideas,*

12.1 (1951).

———. "The Sui Dynasty (581–617)." *The Cambridge History of China. Vol. 3: Sui and T'ang China, 589–906, Part 1.* Ed. by Denis Twitchett. London: Cambridge University Press, 1979.

———. *The Sui Dynasty.* New York: Alfred A. Knopf, 1978.

———. "T'ang T'ai-tsung and Buddhism." *Perspectives on the T'ang.* Ed. by Arthur F. Wright and Denis Twitchett. New Haven, Conn.: Yale University Press, 1973.

———. "T'ang T'ai-tsung: The Man and the Persona." *Essays on T'ang Society: The Interplay of Social, Political and Economic Forces.* Ed. by John Curtis Perry and Bardwell L. Smith. Leiden: E. J. Brill, 1976.

Wu Bolun and Zhang Wenli. *Qin shi huangdi ling* (The Tomb of the First Emperor of Qin). Shanghai: Shanghai renmin chubanshe, 1990.

Wu Chengxue. "Lun wenxue shang de nanbeipai yu nanbeizong" (On Northern and Southern Schools and Northern and Southern Sects in Literature). *Zhongshan daxue xuebao (shehui kexue ban)* (1991.4).

Wu, David Yen-ho. "The Construction of Chinese and Non-Chinese Identities." *The Living Tree: The Changing Meaning of Being Chinese Today.* Ed. by Tu Wei-ming. Stanford, Calif.: Stanford University Press, 1994.

Wu Fuzhu. *Shuihudi Qin jian lun kao* (Studies of the Qin Documents from Shuihudi [Hubei]). Taibei: Wenjin chubanshe, 1994.

Wu Hui. *Zhongguo gudai shangye* (Ancient Chinese Commerce). Taibei: Taiwan shangwu yinshuguan, 1994.

Wu Jianguo. "Lun Tang-chao tudi zhengce de bianhua ji qi yingxiang" (On Changes in Tang Dynasty Land Policy and Their Effects). *Shehui kexue zhanxian* (1992.1).

Wu Shuping. "Yunmeng Qin jian suo fanying de Qin-dai shehui jieji zhuangkuang" (The Class Situation in Qin Dynasty Society as Reflected in the Yunmeng Qin Documents). *Yunmeng Qin jian yanjiu.* Beijing: Zhonghua shuju, 1981.

Wu Tingqiu and Zheng Pengnian. "Fojiao hai shang chuanru Zhongguo zhi yanjiu" (Studies in the Transmission of Buddhism to China by Sea). *Lishi yanjiu* (1995.2).

Wu Xianqing. "Nanchao dazu de dingsheng yu shuailuo" (The Prosperity and Decline of the Southern Dynasty Great Families). *Shihuo banyue kan,* 1.10 (1935).

———. "Wei-Jin shiqi shehui jingji de zhuanbian" (Social and Economic Changes in the Wei-Jin Period). *Shihuo banyuekan,* 1.2 (1934).

———. "Xi-Jin mo de liumin baodong" (Refugee Riots at the End of the Western Jin). *Shihuo banyuekan,* 1.6 (1935).

Wu Xize. "Zhongguo gudai de guojia guan" (The Concept of State in Ancient China). *Wen shi zazhi,* 1.12 (1941).

Wu Ze. "Liuchao shehui jingji zhengzhi de fazhan guilü he tedian" (The Laws of Development, and Special Characteristics, of Society, Economics, and Politics in the Six Dynasties). *Suzhou daxue xuebao: zhe she ban* (1990.3).

Wu Zhuzhu. "Haomen zhengzhi zai nanfang de yizhi: Wang Dao de 'kui-kui zhi zheng'" (The Transplantation of Magnate Politics to the South: The "Confused Government" of Wang Dao). *Fujian shifan daxue xuebao: zhe she ban* (1992.2).

Wyatt, David K. *Thailand: A Short History.* New Haven, Conn.: Yale University Press, 1982.

Xia Yingyuan. "Shin-Kan kara Zui-Tō jidai no Chū-Nichi bunka kōryū" (Sino-Japanese Cultural Exchange from the Qin-Han to the Sui-Tang Periods). *Nitchū bunka kōryūshi sōsho, 1: rekishi.* Ed. by Ōba Osamu and Wang Xiaoqiu. Tokyo: Taishūkan shoten, 1995.

Xiao Qiqing. "Bei-Ya youmu minzu nanqin ge zhong yuanyin de jiantao" (A Review of Various Reasons for the Southward Incursions of the North Asian Nomadic Peoples). *Shihuo yuekan,* 1.12 (1972).

Xie Haiping. *Tang-dai liu Hua waiguoren shenghuo kaoshu* (A Study of the Lives of Foreigners Who Lived in China during the Tang Dynasty). Taibei: Taiwan shangwu yinshuguan, 1978.

Xing Tie. "Liang-Jin nanbeichao shiqi de hudeng zhidu" (The Household Ranking System of the Two Jin, Northern and Southern Dynasties Period). *Hebei shiyuan xuebao: she ke ban* (1991.4).

Xiong Deji. "Wei-Jin nanbeichao shiqi jieji jiegou yanjiu zhong de jige wenti" (Several Problems in the Study of Class Structure in the Wei-Jin, Northern and Southern Dynasties Period). *Wei-Jin Sui-Tang shi lunji, 1.* Ed. by Huang Lie. Beijing: Zhongguo shehui kexue chubanshe, 1981.

Xiong Tieji and Wang Ruiming. "Qin-dai de fengjian tudi suoyouzhi" (The Feudal Landholding System of the Qin Dynasty). *Yunmeng Qin jian yanjiu.* Beijing: Zhonghua shuju, 1981.

Xiong, Victor Cunrui. "The Land-Tenure System of Tang China—A Study of the Equal-Field System and the Turfan Documents." *T'oung pao,* 85 (1999).

Xu Lianda and Lou Jing. "Han-Tang keju yitong lun" (On the Similarities and Differences between the Examination Systems of Han and Tang). *Lishi yanjiu* (1990.5).

Xu Shaohua. "Chu Culture: An Archaeological Overview." *Defining Chu: Image and Reality in Ancient China.* Ed. by Constance A. Cook and John S. Major. Honolulu: University of Hawai'i Press, 1999.

Xu Xianyao. "Dongya wenxian zhong de shanggu Riben Guojia," pts. 1–3 (The Japanese State of High Antiquity in East Asian Literature). *Zhongguo yu Riben,* 79–81 (1966).

———. "Sui-Wo bangjiao xinkao: Wo shi chao Sui bingfei suowei duideng waijiao" (A New Study of Sui-Japanese Interstate Relations: The Japanese Embassies to Sui Were Really Not What Are Called Equal Foreign Relations). *Tang-dai yanjiu lunji,* vol. 1. Ed. by Zhongguo Tang-dai xuehui. 1964; Taibei: Xin wenfeng chuban gongsi, 1992.

Xue Zongzheng. "Lun Gao Xianzhi fa Shi-guo yu Daluosi zhi zhan" (On [Military Commissioner] Gao Xianzhi's Subjugation of Tashkent and the Battle of Talas [751]). *Xinjiang daxue xuebao: zhe she ban* (1999.3).

Yamada Munemutsu. *Gishi Wajinden no sekai* (The World of the "Account of the [Japanese] Wa People" in the "Wei Chronicle" [of the *San guo zhi*]). Tokyo: Kyōikusha, 1983.

Yamamoto Yukihiko. "Kokkateki tochi shihai no tokushitsu to tenkai" (The Characteristics and Development of State Land Management). *Rekishigaku kenkyū*, 573 (1987).

Yamao Yukihisa. "Kodai kokka to shomin no shūzoku" (The Ancient State and the Customs of the Common People). *Kodai no Nihon to Higashi Ajia*. Ed. by Ueda Masaaki. Tokyo: Shōgakkan, 1991.

———. *Kodai no Ni-Chō kankei* (Ancient Japanese-Korean Relations). 1989; Tokyo: Hanawa shobō, 1995.

Yan Gengwang. "Lüelun Tang *Liudian* zhi xingzhi yu shixing wenti" (A Brief Discussion of the Nature of the Tang *Six Statutes* and the Problem of Their Implementation). *Yan Gengwang shixue lunwen xuanji*. 1952; Taibei: Lianjing chuban, 1991.

———. "Tang-dai xingzheng zhidu lunlüe" (A Rough Discussion of Tang Dynasty Administrative Systems). *Yan Gengwang shixue lunwen xuanji*. 1969; Taibei: Lianjing chuban, 1991.

———. "Yang Xiong suo ji xian-Qin fangyan diliqu" (The Pre-Qin Dialectical Regions Recorded by Yang Xiong). *Yan Gengwang shixue lunwen xuanji*. 1975; Taibei: Lianjing chuban, 1991.

———. "Zhanguo shidai lie guo minfeng yu shengji: jian lun Qin tongyi tianxia zhi yi beijing" (The Popular Style and Livelihood of Each State during the Warring States Period: With a Theory as to One Background for Qin's Unification of All-under-Heaven). *Shihuo yuekan*, new series, 14.9–10 (1985).

Yan Shaodang. *Zhong-Ri gudai wenxue guanxi shi gao* (A Draft History of Ancient Sino-Japanese Literary Relations). Hong Kong: Zhonghua shuju, 1987.

Yan Tao. *Kongzi yu Rujia* (Confucius and Confucians). Taibei: Taiwan shangwu yinshuguan, 1994.

Yan, Yunxiang. "McDonald's in Beijing: The Localization of Americana." *Golden Arches East: McDonald's in East Asia*. Ed. by James L. Watson. Stanford, Calif.: Stanford University Press, 1997.

Yang Cuiwei. "Lun Yu Wentai jianli fubing zhi: Xianbei buluo zhi yu Han-hua ji junquan de chubu zhongyang jiquan-hua de jiehe" (On Yu Wentai's Establishment of the Garrison Militia System: A Combination of the Xianbei Tribal System and Sinification, Resulting in the Initial Centralization of Military Power). *Zhongguo wenhua yanjiu* (1998.1).

Yang Debing. "Xi-Jin de bengkui yu menfa de fenhua" (The Collapse of Western Jin and the Dissolution of the Great Families). *Wuhan daxue xuebao: zhe she ban* (1995.3).

Yang Guanghui. "Guanpin, fengjue, yu menfa shizu" (Official Rank, Appointment to the Nobility, and Hereditary Great Families). *Hangzhou daxue xuebao: zhe she ban* (1990.4).

Yang Kuan. "Cong 'Shaofu' zhizhang kan Qin-Han fengjian tongzhizhe de jingji tequan" (The Economic Privileges of the Qin-Han Feudal Rulers as Viewed from the Management of the "Chamberlain for the Palace Revenues"). *Qin-Han shi luncong*, vol. 1. Xi'an: Shaanxi renmin chubanshe, 1981.

———. "Lun Qin shi huang" (On the First Emperor of Qin). *Zhongguo lishi renwu lunji*. Ed. by Li Guangbi and Qian Junhua. Beijing: Shenghuo, dushu, xinzhi sanlian shudian, 1957.

———. *Zhanguo shi* (History of the Warring States). 1957; Shanghai: Shanghai renmin chubanshe, 1980.

Yang Lien-sheng. "Buddhist Monasteries and Four Money-Raising Institutions in Chinese History." *Studies in Chinese Institutional History*. By Yang Lien-sheng. Cambridge, Mass.: Harvard University Press, 1961.

———. "Great Families of Eastern Han." *The Making of China: Main Themes in Premodern Chinese History*. Ed. by Chun-shu Chang. Englewood Cliffs, N.J.: Prentice Hall, 1975.

———. "Notes on the Economic History of the Chin Dynasty." *Studies in Chinese Institutional History*. By Yang Lien-sheng. Cambridge, Mass.: Harvard University Press, 1961.

Yang Tingfu. *Tang lü chu tan* (A Preliminary Investigation into Tang Law). Tianjin: Tianjin renmin chubanshe, 1982.

Yang Tingxian. "Nanbeichao zhi shizu" (Literati Families of the Northern and Southern Dynasties). *Dongfang zazhi*, 36.7 (1939).

Yang Yuan. "Tang-dai de renkou" (The Population of the Tang Dynasty). *Xianggang zhongwen daxue, Zhongguo wenhua yanjiusuo xuebao*, 10.2 (1979).

Yang Zengwen. *Riben Fojiao shi* (A History of Japanese Buddhism). Hangzhou: Zhejiang renmin chubanshe, 1995.

Yao Dazhong. *Nanfang de fenqi* (The Rise of the South). Taibei: Sanmin shuju, 1981.

Yao Weiyuan. *Beichao hu xing kao* (An Examination of Foreign Surnames under the Northern Dynasties). Beijing: Zhonghua shuju, 1962.

Yasuda Jirō. "'Shinan Ō Shikun no hanran' ni tsuite: Nanchō mombatsu kizoku taisei to gōzoku dogō" (Concerning the "Rebellion of Prince Zixun of Jin'an": The Southern Dynasty Great Family-Aristocratic Establishment and Local Magnates). *Tōyōshi-kenkyū*, 25.4 (1967).

Yin Xieli. "Sui-Tang Rujia zhexue de bianhua qushi" (The Tendency of Changes in Sui-Tang Confucian Philosophy). *Zhexue yanjiu* (1985.5).

Yokota Ken'ichi. "Taika kaishin to Fujiwara Kamatari" (The Taika Reform and Fujiwara Kamatari). *Hakuhō tenpyō no sekai*. 1959; Ōsaka: Sōgensha, 1973.

Yoshida Fudōmaro. "Shin dai ni okeru tochi shoyū keitai to nōgyō mondai" (Forms of Land Ownership in the Jin Dynasty and Agricultural Problems). *Shigaku-zasshi*, 43.2 (1932).

Yoshida Takashi. *Ritsuryō kokka to kodai no shakai* (The Ritsuryō State and Ancient Society). Tokyo: Iwanami shoten, 1983.

Yoshikawa Tadao. *Rikuchō seishin shi kenkyū* (Studies in the Intellectual History of the Six Dynasties). Kyoto: Dōhōsha, 1984.

Yoshimori Kensuke. "Shin-Sō kakumei to Kōnan shakai" (The Jin-Song Revolution and Jiangnan Society). *Shirin*, 63.2 (1980).

Yoshimura Rei. "Asuka yōshiki Nanchō kigen ron" (On the Southern Dynasty Origins of the Asuka-style). *Higashi Ajia to Nihon: kōko, bijutsu hen*. Ed. by Tamura Enchō sensei koki-kinenkai. Tokyo: Yoshikawa kōbunkan, 1987.

Yu Taishan, ed. *Xiyu tongshi* (A General History of the Western Regions). Zhengzhou: Zhongzhou guji chubanshe, 1996.

Yü Ying-shih (Yu Yingshi). "Han Foreign Relations." *The Cambridge History of China. Vol. 1: The Ch'in and Han Empires, 221 B.C.–A.D. 220.* Ed. by Denis Twitchett and Michael Loewe. Cambridge: Cambridge University Press, 1986.

———. "Minzu yishi yu guojia guannian" (Ethnic Consciousness and the Concept of the State). *Mingbao yuekan*, 18.12 (1983).

———. *Trade and Expansion in Han China: A Study in the Structure of Sino-Barbarian Economic Relations*. Berkeley and Los Angeles: University of California Press, 1967.

———. *Zhongguo zhishi jieceng shilun (gudai pian)* (Essays in the History of the Chinese Intellectual Class [Antiquity]). Taibei: Lianjing chuban, 1980.

Yu Zongfa. *Yunmeng Qin jian zhong sixiang yu zhidu gouzhi* (Auditing the Thought and Institutions of the Qin Yunmeng Documents). Taibei: Wenjin chubanshe, 1992.

Yuan Zhongyi. "Cong kaogu ziliao kan Qin wenhua de fazhan he zhuyao chengjiu" (The Development of Qin Culture and Its Principal Achievements as Viewed from the Archaeological Data). *Wenbo*, 38 (1990.5).

———. "Cong Qin Shihuang ling de kaogu ziliao kan Qin wangchao de yaoyi" (Qin Dynasty Forced Labor as Viewed through Archaeological Evidence from the First Emperor of Qin's Tomb). *Qin Shihuang ling bingmayong bowuguan lunwen xuan*. Ed. by Yuan Zhongyi. 1983; Xi'an: Xibei daxue chubanshe, 1989.

Zang Zhifei. "Xian-Qin shi-wu xiangli zhidu shitan" (An Exploration of the Pre-Qin System of Village [Administration] by Groups of Five and Ten). *Renwen zazhi* (1994.1).

Zhang Binglin. "Qin zheng ji" (A Record of Qin Government). *Lun Qin shihuang*. 1914; Shanghai: Shanghai renmin chubanshe, 1974.

Zhang Binsheng. *Wei-Jin nanbeichao zhengzhi shi* (A History of Wei-Jin, Northern and Southern Dynasty Politics). Taibei: Zhongguo wenhua daxue, 1983.

Zhang Boquan. *Xianbei xin lun* (A New Evaluation of the Xianbei). Jilin: Jilin wenshi chubanshe, 1993.

———. "'Zhonghua yiti' lun" (On "The Unity of China"). *Jilin daxue shehui kexue xuebao* (1986.5).

Zhang Guangda. "Gu dai Ou-Ya de neilu jiaotong: jianlun shanmo, shamo, lüzhou dui dong-xi wenhua jiaoliu de yingxiang" (Ancient Eurasian Inland Communication: With a Study of the Influence of Mountains, Deserts and Oases on East-West Cultural Exchange). *Xiyu shi, di, conggao chubian.* Shanghai: Shanghai guji chubanshe, 1995.

———. "Lun Sui-Tang shiqi Zhongyuan yu Xiyu wenhua jiaoliu de jige tedian" (On Several Special Features of Cultural Exchange between the Central Plain and the Western Regions in the Sui-Tang Period). *Xiyu shi, di, conggao chubian.* Shanghai: Shanghai guji chubanshe, 1995.

Zhang Junmai. *Zhongguo zhuanzhi junzhu zhengzhi zhi pingyi* (A Critical Evaluation of China's System of Government by Autocratic Monarchs). Taibei: Hongwenguan chubanshe, 1986.

Zhang Qizhi. "Kōshi no bunka to Nihon no bunka" (The Culture of Confucius and the Culture of Japan). Trans. by Wang Weikun. *Kodai no Nihon to higashi Ajia.* Ed. by Ueda Masaaki. Tokyo: Shōgakkan, 1991.

Zhang Renqing. "Liuchao ren de aimei xinli" (The Aesthetic Inclinations of People in the Six Dynasties). *Dongfang zazhi,* reprint, 17.1 (1983).

Zhang Xiong. "Wei-Jin shiliu guo yilai Ba ren de qianxi yu Han-hua qushi" (The Movement and Tendency toward Sinification of the Ba People since the Wei-Jin [Dynasties] and Sixteen Kingdoms). *Zhong-nan minzu xueyuan xuebao: zhe she ban* (1998.4).

Zhang Yonglu. *Tang du Chang'an* (The Tang Capital Chang'an). Xi'an: Xibei daxue chubanshe, 1987.

Zhang Yufa. *Xian-Qin de chuanbo huodong ji qi yingxiang* (Pre-Qin Communicative Activities and Their Effects). 1966; Taibei: Taiwan shangwu yinshuguan, 1993.

Zhao Gang (Chao Kang) and Chen Zhongyi. *Zhongkuo tudi zhidu shi* (A History of Chinese Land Systems). Taibei: Lianjing chuban, 1982.

Zhao Shichao. *Zhou dai guo-ye zhidu yanjiu* (Studies of State and Rural Institutions in the Zhou Dynasty). Xi'an: Shaanxi renmin chubanshe, 1991.

Zhao Yunqi. "Lun Sui-dai juntian ling de zhu wenti" (On Several Questions concerning the Sui Dynasty Equitable Fields Law). *Zhongguo shi yanjiu* (1993.4).

Zheng Dekun. *Zhonghua minzu wenhua shilun* (On the History of Chinese National Culture). Revised ed. Hong Kong: Sanlian shudian, 1987.

Zhong Qijie. "Nanbeichao shiqi xingcheng bei qiang nan ruo jumian zhi zaixi" (A Reanalysis of the Formation of Conditions of Northern Strength and Southern Weakness in the Northern and Southern Dynasties Period). *Beifang luncong* (1992.3).

Zhou Lin. "Qin-Han Jiangnan renkou liuxiang chutan" (A Preliminary Investigation of Population Flow into Jiangnan in the Qin-Han [Dynasties]). *Jiangxi shifan daxue xuebao: zhe she ban* (1997.3).

Zhou Yiliang. "Nanchao jingnei zhi ge zhong ren ji zhengfu duidai zhi zhengce" (The Various Kinds of People within the Borders of the Southern Dynasties and the Government's Policies for the Treatment of Them). *Wei-Jin nanbeichao shi lunji*. Beijing: Zhonghua shuju, 1963.

Zhou Zhenhe. "Cong 'jiu zhou yi su' dao 'liu he tong feng': Liang-Han fengsu quhua de bianqian" (From "Nine Regions Having Different Customs" to "Six Directions with a Common Style": The Evolution of Cultural Divisions in the Two Han [Dynasties]). *Zhongguo wenhua yanjiu* (1997.4).

Zhu Dawei. "Nan chao shaoshu minzu gaikuang ji qi yu Hanzu de ronghe" (The General Situation of Minority Peoples in the Southern Dynasties and Their Blending with the Han People). *Zhongguo shi yanjiu* (1980.1).

Zhu Yiyun. *Wei-Jin fengqi yu Liuchao wenxue* (The Wei-Jin Style and Six Dynasties Literature). Taibei: Wen shi zhe chubansuo, 1980.

Zhu Yongjia. "Lun Cao Cao de yizhi haoqiang ji qi Fajia sixiang" (On Cao Cao's Restraint of Magnates and His Legalist Thought). *Cao Cao lun ji*. Ed. by Guo Moruo et al. Hong Kong: Shenghuo dushu xinzhi sanlian shudian, 1979.

Zhu Yunying. *Zhongguo wenhua dui Ri, Han, Yue de yingxiang* (The Influence of Chinese Culture on Japan, Korea, and Vietnam). Taibei: Liming wenhua, 1981.

Zhu Zongbin. "Lüelun Jin lü zhi 'Rujiahua'" (A Brief Discussion of the "Confucianization" of Jin Law). *Zhongguo shi yanjiu* (1985.2).

Zürcher, Erik. *The Buddhist Conquest of China: The Spread and Adaptation of Buddhism in Early Medieval China*. Leiden: E. J. Brill, 1959.

———. "Buddhist Influence on Early Taoism: A Survey of Scriptural Evidence." *T'oung Pao*, 66.1–3 (1980).

———. "'Prince Moonlight': Messianism and Eschatology in Early Medieval Chinese Buddhism." *T'oung Pao*, 68.1–3 (1982).